EXPEDITION CANOEING

A Guide to Canoeing Wild Rivers in North America
20th Anniversary Edition

CLIFF JACOBSON

FALCON GUIDE®

GUILFORD, CONNECTICUT
HELENA, MONTANA
AN IMPRINT OF THE GLOBE PEQUOT PRESS

Text design: Lisa Reneson
Illustrated by Cliff Moen
Photo credits: The photos accompanying the biographies and testimonials in this book appear courtesy of the individuals. Unless otherwise indicated, all photos are by the author. Pages 39, 218: Bob Dannert; page 43, Pakboats; page 57: Antoni Harting; page 88: Staffan Svedberg; page 105: Ostrom Outdoors; page 147 and color fig. 1-1: Sue Harings; page 205 (top): Mike Wevrick; pages 205 (bottom), 206, 207 (top): Bob O'Hara; page 213 (top): Brian Knauck; page 213 (bottom): Mark Schmeider; pages 228, 229: Doug McKown; pages 235, 236: Hap Wilson; pages 237, 238, 239: Michael Peake; page 264 (left): George Drought; pages 264 (right), 265: Outdoor Solutions.

Library of Congress Cataloging-in-Publication Data
Jacobson, Cliff.
　　Expedition canoeing: a guide to canoeing wild rivers in North America / Cliff
Jacobson.—4th ed.
　　　　p. cm. — (A Falcon guide)
　　Includes index.
　　ISBN 0-7627-3809-X
　　　1. White-water canoeing. 2. Canoes and canoeing—Equipment and supplies. 3. Canoes
and canoeing—United States. 4. Canoes and canoeing—Canada. I. Title. II. Series.

GV788.J33 2005
797.122—dc22　　　　　　　　　　　　　　　　　　　　　　　　　　2004060885

Manufactured in the United States of America
Fourth Edition/First Printing

To buy books in quantity for corporate use
or incentives, call **(800) 962–0973, ext. 4551,**
or e-mail **premiums@GlobePequot.com.**

The author and The Globe Pequot Press assume no liability for accidents happening to,
or injuries sustained by, readers who engage in the activities described in this book.

EXPEDITION CANOEING

20th Anniversary Edition

Praise for a previous edition of *Expedition Canoeing*

"Impressively comprehensive, whether you already are—or want
to be—a 'supercanoeist' with a yearning for the wild."

—Jerry Zgoda, *Minneapolis Star Tribune*

"Jacobson, augmented by a cadre of fellow experts, has produced an authoritative,
practical, and highly visual guide for enthusiasts of all experience levels. Preparation is
everything when expedition canoeing, so before navigating the waters of Canada or
America, consult this classic book, now completely updated. Far more than just a great gear
guide, *Expedition Canoeing* offers firsthand advice for all stages and aspects of the journey.
Interlaced with illustrative essays, Jacobson's magnificent [book] is a user-friendly
reference for better understanding and exploring nature's bounty."

—Andrew C. Hubsch, "Sports & Adventure" Editor, Barnes & Noble.com

"If you want a good book outlining the basics of canoeing and canoe camping
from Acquisition to Zing, this will do it."

—*The Reel News*

Help Us Keep This Guide Up to Date

Every effort has been made by the author and editors to make this guide as accurate and useful as possible. However, many things can change after a guide is published—establishments close, phone numbers change, facilities come under new management, etc.

We would love to hear from you concerning your experiences with this guide and how you feel it could be improved and kept up to date. While we may not be able to respond to all comments and suggestions, we'll take them to heart and we'll also make certain to share them with the author. Please send your comments and suggestions to the following address:

The Globe Pequot Press
Reader Response/Editorial Department
P.O. Box 480
Guilford, CT 06437

Or you may e-mail us at:

editorial@GlobePequot.com

Thanks for your input, and happy travels!

To my father, Henry Jacobson, who taught me to love and respect the wilderness.

CONTENTS

PREFACE TO THE TWENTIETH ANNIVERSARY EDITION

When my friends and I canoed the Hood River to the Arctic Ocean in 1983, we had no detailed trip guide or global positioning system. There was some sketchy information in Sir John Franklin's journal (he ascended the Hood in 1821), but it was too old to be very useful. The large-scale (1:250,000) maps we used for navigation were fraught with errors—we were never quite sure what was around the bend.

It took nearly a year to research a river in those days. Isolated northern communities relied largely on radio telephones (which were very expensive to operate) for communication, so we wrote letters and waited weeks for answers. Most float-plane companies didn't accept credit cards or personal checks, so we had to carry large sums of money—sometimes for hundreds of miles in our canoe.

Now, nearly everything—from researching old journals to paying your bush pilot—can be accomplished on the Internet. Pinpointing your position on a sprawling lake is as simple as turning on a GPS. Satellite phones, which were frightfully expensive when this book was last revised, are finally affordable—or at least affordable to rent. Most canoe parties that go in harm's way now carry one.

When I wrote the first edition of *Expedition Canoeing* (originally titled *Canoeing Wild Rivers*) in 1984, I had canoed just two challenging routes—to James Bay via the Groundhog, Mattagami, and Moose Rivers, and the then, very remote Hood River in Nunavut (formerly the Northwest Territories). In 2003 I ran the Snake River, which flows through the spectacular Bonnet Plume Mountains in the Yukon Territories. It was my forty-second Canadian river trip, and it was quite a rush. I've learned a wealth of tricks in forty-two trips, and they are all detailed in this spanking-new edition.

Canoes and camping equipment will continue to evolve over the years, and there will always be hot new items to try. But the procedures for making a safe, enjoyable canoe voyage are written in stone. So all the wisdom and solid information that made previous versions of this book popular remain. This edition, like the three that came before it, continues to emphasize that skills are, and always will be, more important than things.

People sometimes ask what draws me to wild rivers, when danger and discomfort lurk around every bend. The first time you see a seal surface by your canoe or watch ten thousand caribou do a thunder dance across the tundra, you'll know. Then, all the risky rapids and bad bugs you battled will fade away. If you know what you're doing, driving to the jump-off point is more dangerous than any river you'll ever paddle!

Readers of earlier editions of this book will discover that some of my views have changed over the years. This is inevitable as I continue to gain experience and explore new products and places. Recent examples include my new respect for folding and inflatable canoes; a change in philosophy regarding rain gear and footwear; a love and hate relationship with electronic equipment; and a more patient approach to dealing with dangers. In all, there are more than 100 changes in this new revision—each one targeted to make your canoe trips safer and more enjoyable.

Kayakers and rafters will benefit too: Kayaks and inflatable rafts have become immensely popular in recent years and are now probing waters that were once monopolized by canoes. These boats differ from canoes in how they are paddled, packed with gear, and portaged over land. But the mechanics of wilderness travel—trip research and navigation, camping and cooking methods, transportation and safety concerns, etc.— are the same. This book is aimed squarely at what one needs to know to travel remote rivers with confidence. To that end, it makes no difference what kind of boat you paddle.

Expedition Canoeing is not just for super-serious paddlers who will canoe the unforgiving waters of the far north.

Beginners will find plenty of great ideas to keep the pages turning. It's simple: What works in wind, rain, and thrashing rapids works even better when all is calm.

I am proud of this new twentieth anniversary edition. It contains everything you need to know to canoe in a region where help is an airplane ride away. And every ounce of information has been thoroughly massaged to reflect modern methods, the wisdom of tradition, and my own ornery ways, which I cling to because they work so well for me.

May your life flow as smoothly as the wild Canadian rivers I love to canoe. And may your skill and good judgment keep you safe from harm.

I'd love to hear your questions or concerns. You may contact me by writing or e-mailing my publisher, The Globe Pequot Press.

ACKNOWLEDGMENTS

Expedition Canoeing reflects the views of the international wilderness canoeing community. It is not a work of just one writer-paddler. The following people, publications, and organizations contributed ideas and advice and they should receive a heartfelt thanks:

Annie Aggens, Sharon Chatterton, Bob Dannert, George Drought and Barbara Burton, Dave Bober, Don Mitchell, Kent Ford, Dr. Bill Forgey, Olya Gailish, Fred Gaskin, Laurie Gullion, Gordon Haggert, Alex Hall, Toni Harting, Sue Harings, Bob Henderson, Kay Henry, Bev and Joel Hollis, Mike Jones, Alan Kesselheim, Biff Kummer, Verlen Kruger, Bob O'Hara, Gary and Joanie McGuffin, Dick Person, Inga Schafer, Michael Peake, Sara Seager and Mike Wevrick, Bill Hosford, Doug McKown, Bill Simpson, Buck Tilton, Hap Wilson, and Stephanie Akroyd.

Audubon magazine, for allowing me to reprint a paragraph from Eric Sevareid's September 1982 article, "Return to God's Country."

Alfred A. Knopf, Inc., for its permission to use the quote from Sigurd Olson's book *The Lonely Land*, which appears in chapter 14.

INTRODUCTION: WHY THIS BOOK?

This book began as a dream in 1974 after I had completed my first substantial canoe trip into the Canadian wilderness. To my chagrin I discovered that a decade of predictable paddling on local streams and midsized lakes was only marginal preparation for the harsh realities of northern rivers. And the canoeing literature wasn't much help, either: Even the best books parroted the obvious and avoided the things I really wanted to know.

Sure, they all contained the expected chapters on paddling, lake travel, reading the white water, using a compass and so forth, but there were no specifics on how to research a dangerous river, where to get large-scale monochrome maps and white prints or procedures for keeping warm and dry in the teeth of weeklong rain and snow! Missing also was information on how to cope with persistent bears (I learned that hanging food from a tree is *not* the answer) and bugs; methods for packing equipment that are *really* waterproof; ways to prepare freeze-dried foods so they always taste good; techniques for baking on a trail stove without a commercial oven; mechanics for shipping your outfit by plane, train, and barge . . . and more. That's why I wrote this book: to answer these questions for myself and for others who would tackle the wild rivers of the Far North. It's for paddlers everywhere who love wilderness waterways and want to learn some fresh new ideas as well as the nuts and bolts of canoeing remote waters.

A major failing of most canoe books is that they're the work of a single author. Input is limited to the ideas, methods, and biases of one person. There's no room for debate, for philosophy, for individual differences. In writing this book I thus sought to overcome this shortcoming by enlisting the help of many of the best wilderness canoeists in the United States and Canada (see the credits section).

To make room for the obscure but important things you really need to now, I've necessarily cut some basics—namely, the art of paddling and reading white water. This information is readily available in every elementary canoeing text and would require far too much space to do justice here. Instead I've begun the subject of canoeing wilderness rivers at the far edge of square one—assuming you have some familiarity with the most elementary canoe procedures.

For a more streamlined discussion of wilderness canoeing, see my book *Canoeing & Camping: Beyond the Basics*, published by The Globe Pequot Press.

CHAPTER 1
A TIME FOR REFLECTION

I discovered the canoe at the age of twelve at a rustic scout camp nestled deep in the cedar swamps of northern Michigan. It was 1951—too early to mourn the passing of wood-canvas canoes and solid-ash paddles. I'd heard of aluminum canoes, of course, but I'd never seen one. Pack frames, lugged hiking boots, and lightweight down sleeping bags were novelties.

The outdoor life was simpler then. We had no tubes of fire ribbon or hurricane-resistant nylon tents. No bulletproof canoes, unbreakable paddles, or freeze-dried filet mignon. Canoe camping was a rough-and-ready endeavor, though not nearly so demanding as some modern writers suggest.

In those days my outfit consisted of a military-surplus wool sleeping bag and poncho, a canvas pup tent, an aluminum cook kit, a scout hand ax, and a ragtag assortment of secondhand woolens. Even if sophisticated equipment had been readily available, my friends and I had no money for it. So instead of buying gear, we practiced camping skills. Skills for rigging a snug camp in the teeth of icy April rains; skills for making a fire with a *single* match! We had to cope with what we had. So we read every woodscraft book in print, listened intensely to the advice of those more experienced than ourselves. Ultimately we learned woodsmanship.

Things are different today. Now the emphasis is on equipment, not know-how. (I recently checked the contents of a popular backpacking book: More than 90 percent of its pages were devoted to camping gear and its use.) Polyester sleeping bags and garments have become a substitute for the ability to keep down gear dry in a rain or canoe upset. Fire-starting chemicals are the alternative to correct fire making. And sledge-tough canoes take the place of proper paddling technique. Somehow I think we've lost something of value in our search for better ways.

Four decades ago places like the Quetico-Superior and Allagash Waterway were still very wild—their waters unpol-

luted by acid rain, their campsites untarnished by litter and free of forest service conveniences like fire grates and wooden box latrines. Only canoeists well experienced in the ways of the wilderness dared venture far from popular routes without guides. How I yearned to go there—to canoe those haunting lakes, camp amid the fragrant balsam and pine, hear the lonely yodel of the loon.

But Maine and Minnesota were a long way from my boyhood home in Chicago, Illinois. Besides, I was too young to make the trip, too poor, and inexperienced.

The years passed—college, a job with the Bureau of Land Management, the army, and marriage. But my desire to see America's finest canoe country did not wane. So in 1967 a friend and I loaded my then-new Sawyer Cruiser atop his station wagon and headed north to Grand Marais, Minnesota—the gateway to the famed Boundary Waters Canoe Area.

Our trip lasted ten days and traversed 100 miles—fairly substantial for first-timers. We began at Seagull Lake, swung west almost to Ely, then dashed back to the border, occasionally dropping down into lakes that looked interesting on the map. I was naturally overwhelmed by everything—the sheer grandeur of it all, the endless procession of dazzling beauty, the proud, fearless attitude of the wildlife, the awesome quiet.

But even before the trip's end a measure of disappointment set in. There were simply too many people around to suit me (not a day went by when we didn't see at least one passing canoeist). There were other annoyances, too. Navigating the big lakes was too easy—if we misread the map there was always a sign at every portage to guide the way. Finding campsites was no challenge either; their locations were all neatly marked with little red dots on the Fisher Company maps we carried.

The fishing was only mediocre. Not at all like the vivid description given by the old Quetico-Superior guide who entertained us one evening when we were boys at that camp

in Michigan. He told us that fish were so easy to catch here that commercial lures weren't necessary. Laughing, he described how he'd bet his client five bucks that he could catch a fish *without* a hook. His method was to tear a strip of cloth from his bright-colored bandanna and tie it directly to the fishing line. Then he'd cast out his "lure," jiggling it as he slowly reeled it in. "A northern's [northern pike] teeth slant inward," he explained. "They catch on the cloth and I get 'em every time."

Then he warned us not to wear any shiny rings on our fingers when we were up in "that country." "You jiggle your ring finger in the water and a northern'll hit it for sure!" he said. It all seemed too incredible to believe.

Perhaps we just weren't fishermen; our catch for that ten-day trip consisted of two smallmouth bass, three northern pike, and one walleye. And the biggest of the lot couldn't have weighed more than three pounds. (Many years later I would discover that "fishing that good" does indeed exist in the waterways of the Far North. The old-timer hadn't lied.)

I returned home from my first Boundary Waters trip with mixed emotions. Certainly the area was beautiful beyond words, its waters still unspoiled. But there was no challenge to it, what with portage signs, marked campsites, fire grates, box latrines, cleaned portage trails, canoe rests, picnic tables, and lots of other people to depend on if our own resourcefulness failed. It just wasn't wild enough, isolated enough for my tastes.

My thoughts turned to the waterways of the Far North. Rivers like the Albany and Hays, Missinaibi, Moose, and Fond du Lac. Places like James and Hudson Bay, Athabasca, Fort Chipewan, Yellowknife. Were they real or just a figment of passing fancy? (See color figure 1-1.)

I read all the wonderful old canoeing books I could find. Sevareid's *Canoeing with the Cree,* all the works of Calvin Rutstrum, John Malo, Sigurd Olson. The journals of Thompson, Simpson, Tyrrell, and Alexander.

But I knew I was not yet ready to tackle the unforgiving waters of the Far North. I needed much more knowledge, more experience. So I joined the Minnesota Canoe Association and took lessons on how to paddle. For a while I became interested in covered slalom canoes (C-1s and C-2s), but found these craft too specialized for the type of touring I had in mind. Still, the skittish slalom boats taught me valuable lessons about paddling white water—lessons that helped me better negotiate turbulent wilderness waters in years to come.

I attended seminars by the outstanding wilderness canoeists of the day: Bob O'Hara, Dr. Robert Dannert, Christie Buetow and Katie Knopke, Verlen Kruger and Clint Waddell. Each contact was another notch on my pistol. My thirst for canoeing knowledge was boundless.

I soon discovered that every "supercanoeist" had his or her own definite ideas about how things should be done, though there was general agreement on the basics that affected comfort and safety. For example, canoes should be much bigger and stronger than those used for recreational paddling. Clothing should be wool, fleece, or nylon—never cotton. I listened and questioned, and kept an open mind. Ultimately I developed my own tripping style.

I made seven more trips into the BWCA before I felt ready to tackle a remote Canadian river. Then I proceeded cautiously, armed to the teeth with research. I had little money to spend so I selected a route that featured a road at the start and a railroad at the end. A combination of rivers—the trip began on the Groundhog River near Foleyet, Ontario; traversed the Mattagami and Moose; and finished at Moosonee on Arctic tidewater some 300 miles away.

The weather was bad, the blackflies were worse. And the river was in flood, which made the run extremely dangerous.

Only two other parties attempted the river that year, and neither completed it. One group totaled out in the $\frac{1}{4}$-mile-wide Grand Rapids of the Matagami and walked 40 miles through blackfly-infested spruce bogs to reach the safety of the railhead. The other team experienced a drowning when they upset while attempting to run a falls that we portaged.

But we had no adventures or serious difficulties. Even our close calls were predictable. We had done our homework well. We were prepared—in equipment, skills, and positive mental attitude. Our detailed research, training, and respect for the river brought us home safely with hundreds of memories and pictures to share.

Canadian rivers are addictive. Once you've done one you'll be back for more. Each year I try a new river—some distant and challenging (the two don't necessarily go together), others close to home and less intimidating. In either case I choose my routes carefully and so experience all the wonderful qualities for which Canadian rivers are best known: isolation, freedom to camp and build fires when and where I please, excellent fishing, and the relative absence of improvements—signs, picnic tables, fire grates, and the like.

I still make an annual pilgrimage to the Boundary Waters Canoe Area to guide at-risk teenagers as part of the middle school program where I teach. And sometimes I return again with my solo canoe in late autumn when the air is crisp and the people and bugs are gone. But my first love is the rivers of the Far North, and that's what this book is all about.

CHAPTER 2
RESEARCHING A RIVER

English River. Motel, gas station, small cafe. That's about it. Nothing spectacular, just a jumping-off place for a delightful canoe trip down a picturesque river that bears its name.

Some pretty lakes with creative names and varying personalities, a few interesting rapids, an awesome falls, generally good fishing, and lots of wildlife. Campsites? Great! Not at all what you'd expect from northern Ontario. Plenty of space—level space—for the biggest tent you'd want to carry. In all, a nice predictable run, just right for sharpening your backcountry skills or introducing your family to the wonders of those magnificent Canadian waterways.

That, in essence, is what I told the man who called to ask about canoeing the English River with his wife and two teenage boys.

I laid out the details as best as I could recall (it had been four years since I'd done the river) and suggested he write the MNR (Ministry of Natural Resources) for a trip guide. I also added that the shuttle was *expensive!*

"How expensive?" he asked.

"Eighty bucks for 60 miles. Plus two bucks a day to store your car. Town's got the business down to an art; One guy does all the driving . . . and he won't negotiate."

"I s'pose a lot of people do the river, huh?"

"I don't know. We didn't see a single canoe. Two fishing boats, that's all."

"Any other way in?"

"Just the train out of Thunder Bay—crosses the river about 20 miles down—but you'd still need a shuttle."

"Mmmm. What about farther north, up around Dryden and Grassy Narrows?"

"Don't know," I replied. "There's lots of routes up there . . . and Dryden's a real town, so you might find a cheaper shuttle. You'll just have to check it out."

"Thanks, Cliff. I'll get on it."

Several months later the fellow called again, bubbling over with the usual enthusiasm that always accompanies a good canoe trip. "Great weather, didn't rain once . . . good campsites . . . no bugs!"

"How was the fishing?" I asked.

A long silence. Then, "Pretty good but we couldn't eat 'em. Mercury poisoning from some paper mill in Dryden."

Further conversation revealed that the man had done a reasonably good job of doing his homework. He had good maps, an MNR trip guide, and a contact person in the Dryden area who would shuttle his car for a whole lot less than $80, but he had omitted one small detail—*he hadn't asked anyone about the water quality!*

Moral? Get *all* the facts before you wet your paddle. All the parts of the same river may not be equally appetizing. Failure to check out everything ahead of time is a sure recipe for running into a hydro dam, logging operation, pulp-choked stream, recent burn, high water, low water, no water, or polluted water. Research should begin at least six months before you make the trip!

First, pick your state or province. Then contact the appropriate government agency (addresses in appendix B). Request a road map, a list of canoeable rivers in the area of your interest, and whatever tourist information is available.

If you can narrow your choice to two or three rivers, your letter may bring exactly what you want—monochrome (black-and-white) printed route maps (not suitable for navigation) and specific trip guides. At the very least you'll get the addresses of government agencies that can tell you more about canoeable routes.

MNR district managers are especially accommodating. If they can't answer a question, they'll forward your letter to someone who can.

Besides canoeing specifics, your tourist packet will contain a wealth of details about local fishing, road conditions, hiking trails, and service stations. So don't discard anything until you've read it all.

Next, obtain an index to the topographic maps that cover the state or province you plan to canoe.

To order U.S. maps: Contact the U.S. Geological Survey in Denver, Colorado. You can call the toll-free number (1–888–ASK–USGS) or you can order off its Web site (www.usgs.gov). Request an *Index to Topographic Maps* for the state you plan to canoe. The index will tell you what's in print and the scales available.

To order Canadian maps: Until 1997 you could order Canadian topographic maps from the Canada Map Office. Now you must buy them through a U.S. or Canadian map dealer. The Canada Map Office (800–465–6277) will send you an index to available maps and a list of map distributors. Three indexes cover all of Canada, so you might as well get them all.

Specifics for ordering U.S. and Canadian maps and aerial photos are found in appendix B. The U.S. has gone high tech by placing everything (maps, photos, and support materials) on its Web site. The Canada Map Office may offer a similar service by the time you read this.

When the indexes arrive, you're ready to order maps. At this point I like to simultaneously research two or three nearby rivers that look promising—this helps dispel disappointment if my first choice turns out to be unacceptable for one reason or another.

So I order a small-scale (1:1,000,000) map of the general locale first. This is really too small for serious navigation but it is good enough to help me discover a wealth of nearby routes not covered in the governmental publications or too distant for inclusion on a large-scale map of limited area.

The Canadian government is working feverishly to expand its offerings for river guides, but frankly, it's an overwhelming job, one that may never be completed—much to the joy of those of us who still like to explore!

Some of the best rivers have no guides—but they do exist on maps, and you'll find them if you look hard enough.

The absence of a river guide does not indicate a route is unacceptable; it only means that government voyageurs haven't yet mapped it for canoe travel.

Similarly, if you're like me, the solitary wilderness type—one who reacts negatively when you see another canoe on "your" water—don't give up just because your prospective route is detailed in a fancy brochure. Some of the most

remote, spectacular rivers I've paddled are described in well-written trip guides.

A good example is the Fond du Lac in northwest Saskatchewan. In his wonderful book *Canoe Canada*, Nick Nichels describes the Fond du Lac as a "remote challenging river for expert whitewater canoeists." The river is all of that and more, but the provincial guide that describes it is so fancy (printed on rag paper, complete with photos) that you'd expect to find the area overrun with canoeists. It isn't. I've canoed the Fond du Lac River four times since 1979 (the latest trip was 1996) and never met another canoe party.

A good guide *may* indicate heavy use. On the other hand, it may be little more than a governmental effort to stimulate the economy of a remote, impoverished community.

When you've decided on a specific river section or sections, consult your index and order the appropriate 1:250,000 scale (1 inch equals about 4 miles) maps. This scale has sufficient detail to permit a reasonably accurate analysis of a river's characteristics.

When your maps arrive, go over the route carefully with a large magnifying glass. Mark with a pencil all potential dangers—rapids, falls, and dams. Next comes the river profile—essential to determine drop per mile.

Begin by drawing a broad line along each side of the river, parallel to your route. The lines should be about an inch apart so they won't obscure important topographical features. I use a felt-tip highlighter pen—the kind college kids prefer for marking important passages in textbooks. This ink is translucent so you can read through it.

Next, consult the map scale and mark the miles along your route. I mark each 4 miles, which, on a 1:250,000 map, works out to a mark every inch. This makes it easy to maintain scale relationships, because the average cruising speed of a loaded wilderness canoe is about 4 miles, or "1 inch," per hour. To avoid confusion on large 1:50,000 scale maps (1¼ inches equals 1 mile), I mark every mile. Some canoeists number their miles backward (0 at the end of the trip) so they can tell at a glance the number of remaining miles. Traditionalists like myself place 0 at the start.

If you keep accurate track of time (bring a watch!), you'll seldom be far off course. For precise positioning, you may want to carry a GPS (Global Positioning System) and learn the UTM (Universal Transverse Mercator) coordinate system. You'll find a discussion of GPS technology in chapters 8 and 13.

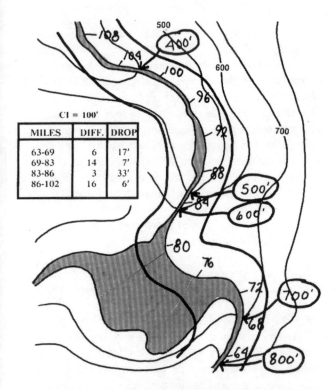

CI = 100'		
MILES	**DIFF.**	**DROP**
63-69	6	17'
69-83	14	7'
83-86	3	33'
86-102	16	6'

Figure 2-1. The map profile illustrates the technique used to determine the drop of a typical river. Handwritten circled numbers indicate contours. Distances (miles) are not circled.

When you've finished marking mileage, stand back and take a hard look. Are you too ambitious? Do you have enough vacation days to cover all those miles? Have you allotted extra time in the event you become windbound (the standard rule is one day in five)? The answers to these and other questions will become clearer as the planning stage proceeds. Nevertheless, you should be able to make some preliminary decisions now.

Figure 2-3. Falls are easy to spot on the contour map. Closely spaced V-points indicate a sudden drop. Notice the difference between the extreme elevation change from 300 to 250 feet and the long decline between 250 and 200 feet.

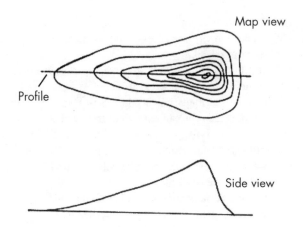

Figure 2-2. Basic contour of a long, sloping hill that gives a rough idea of the interval spacing. Note the significant drop on the right side of the hill and the gentle slope at left.

The next procedure is to draw a small arrow everywhere a contour line crosses the river. Write in the elevation of each contour near the penciled arrow and circle it. Be sure you

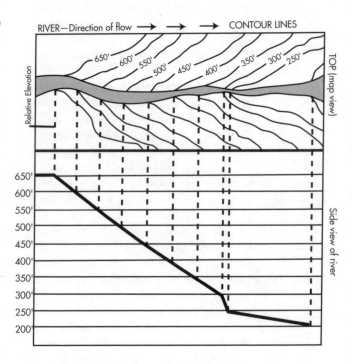

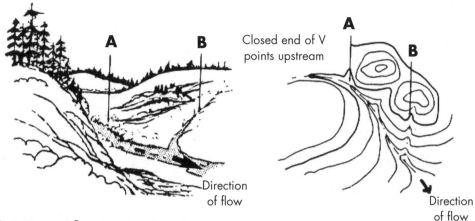

Figure 2-4. Stream B flows into river A.

Closed end of V points upstream

Direction of flow

indicate whether the elevation is in feet(') or meters (M). The contour interval, or vertical distance between contour lines, is given in the lower map margin.

You don't need to be a cartographer to interpret contours. An understanding of these basics will get you through:

■ Contour lines connect points of *equal* elevation. Thus, closely spaced lines indicate lots of elevation change (drop), whereas widely spaced lines show the opposite (figures 2-2, 2-3, 2-4).

■ The closed or V end of a contour line always points *upstream* (figures 2-3, 2-4).

■ Where the contour lines cross or run very close together, you'll find an abrupt drop—a falls or a canyon (figures 2-3, 2-5).

■ The contour interval (CI) is *not* the same for all maps, so look closely! Convert meters (all the new Canadian maps are metric) to feet (10 meters equals 33 feet) if you're confused by the metric system.

■ The larger the contour interval, the less clear are the river's characteristics. In short, a map whose CI is 10 feet gives a clearer picture of the topography than one whose CI is 100 feet.

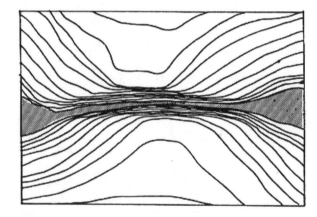

Figure 2-5. Beware the canyon! Contour lines that run very close together and parallel to riverbanks indicate canyons. Be sure to identify the canyon. Once inside, you are committed!

THE DROP

You're now ready to compute drop. Do the computations in a table similar to that in figure 2-1. For example: The 800-foot contour crosses the river at mile 63, while the 700-foot line interacts at mile 69. This is recorded in the table as "63-69." The mileage difference is 6 (69 minus 63). Dividing 6 into 100 (the value of the contour interval) yields a drop of 17 feet per mile.

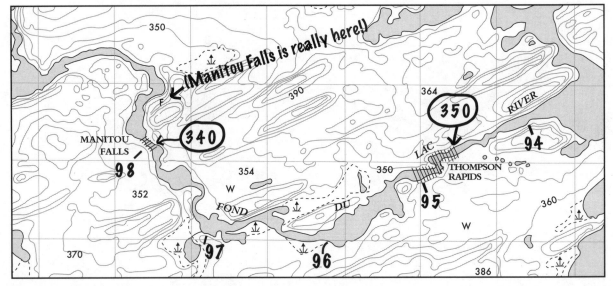

Contour interval = 10 meters

Figure 2-6. This map and the map in figure 2-7 are of sections of the Fond du Lac River in northwest Saskatchewan. Handwritten circled numbers indicate contours. Distances (miles) are not circled. Manitou Falls is incorrectly marked.

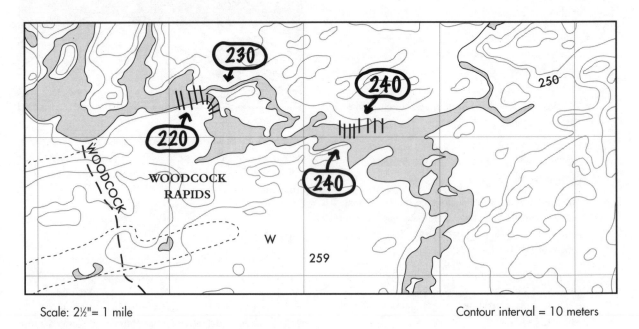

Scale: 2½"= 1 mile   Contour interval = 10 meters

Figure 2-7. The river drops 33 feet per mile between contours 230 and 240, and 120 feet per mile in the Woodcock Rapids section.

EXPEDITION CANOEING

From mile 69 to 83 the river drops less—7 feet per mile. And so on.

To the experienced canoeist drop figures conjure up a vivid picture of a river's personality. Three to 5 feet per mile is nice cruising; better than 10, things get hairy. Fifteen means a probable portage. And 20 or more is about the limit for a loaded open canoe.

Equally important as drop per mile is how the drops occur—whether uniformly or at a falls, dam, or major rapid.

Consider the section shown in figure 2-6. The river drops 10 meters (about 33 feet) from mile 94.5 (the junction of the 350-meter contour) to mile 98 (the 340 contour). Dividing 33 feet by 3.5 (the difference between 98 and 94.5) gives you a drop of 9.4 feet per mile—not too significant.

Runnable? Barely! Look again. Virtually all the drop occurs in two places—the rapid at the 340 contour (a set of formidable sandstone ledges that will swamp you for sure)[1] and Thompson Rapids (runnable at high risk if the water level is right). The midsection, however, is quite placid—easily paddled by inexperienced Boy Scouts.

A more spectacular example is shown in figure 2-7. Here the river drops 33 feet per mile between the 230 and 240 contours, while farther west (Woodcock Rapids section) it spills violently at about 120 feet per mile and creates one of the most awesome pitches of white water imaginable. But again, the quiet water between the two drops is easily canoeable.

Okay, now that you've got the basics, it's test time! Study the river map (figure 2-8) and determine which (if any) sections are runnable.

Answers are at the end of this chapter.

Canyons (figure 2-5)—places where the contour lines run close together—are another hazard you must check out thoroughly before you commit yourself to a river. Maps aren't perfect, so don't depend on drop figures or topographic hash marks (the symbol for rapids) to make your decision of whether to run or portage. Once you enter a canyon you're committed, so it's imperative that you know what's there *before* you proceed. See chapter 17 for a discussion of canyons and their dangers.

Expect also to encounter difficulties (rapids!) at every place the river narrows. Maps occasionally overlook some dandy drops here. Conversely, expect to portage most marked rapids. Most of the rapids I've seen on Canadian topos rate

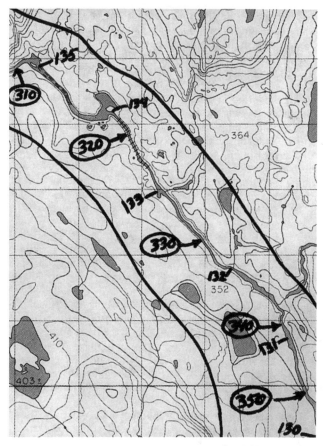

Contour interval = 10 meters

Figure 2-8. Is it runnable? Figure the average drop in *feet per mile* (don't forget to change meters to feet!). Mile marks are indicated in dark black—130, 131, and so on. Values of contours (in meters) are circled.

Class II or better on the international scale—which, if you've forgotten, includes rapids with waves up to 3 feet high.[2] And most of what's marked is much more formidable than that.

Granted, you can always portage the obstacles, but it may not be easy. Contrary to popular belief and the misguided statements of some writers, there's no such thing as a falls or rapids that can't be portaged. The rivers of the Far North are

---

[1]Maps aren't perfect. Manitou Falls—shown at the 98-mile marker in figure 2-6—which will ground you up and spit you out, is actually located ¼ mile downriver at the falls marked F

[2]See appendix E for a description of this rating scale.

littered with the bones of unfortunate canoeists who disagreed. Portage trails along the northern rivers are less used than those farther south and so tend to be overgrown with vegetation. The rule of thumb for negotiating clear trails like those in the BWCA is 20 minutes per mile. But these figures are meaningless where the path is uncertain. It's not uncommon for an anticipated mile-long portage to become a day-long endurance contest.

Some years ago I portaged sixteen hours to get into a remote section of Ontario's Steel River. Thank goodness I was carrying my forty-pound solo canoe and not my eighty-pound Old Town Tripper. Whether that kind of exercise is worth it depends, of course, entirely on your physical condition, mental makeup, and desire for punishment.

You should also realize that maps don't tell the whole story. Imagine how you'd feel if, after completing a 5-mile carry to an isolated lake, you discovered dozens of people who had effortlessly gotten there by driving a logging road that wasn't indicated on your map. Or perhaps after months of planning, you arrive at the headwaters of your river only to discover that the ice hasn't gone out yet—and perhaps won't for another two weeks.[3] This is why you need to contact a local person who has firsthand knowledge of the river.

So back to work. If there's a chamber of commerce in the town, a letter will bring fast results, but for many small villages, the best procedure is to simply address the mayor.

Be sure to ask specific questions and let correspondents know you're an experienced canoeist, not a beginner. You can do this by making a casual statement to the effect or by naming a river you've canoed. Acknowledging your experience is not bragging; it's a subtle way to let your contact know that you have the skills to make a successful trip. Community and government officials receive dozens of canoe trip inquiries each year, mostly from novice canoeists. They don't want to steer a beginner into a route that's too difficult. Your admission of competence will allay concerns and eliminate some of the usual tourist responses.

Many years ago I requested general information about Ontario's Gull River from the Ministry of Natural Resources office in Nipigon. I said nothing about my canoeing background. What I received was a generally useless strip map of the route and a discouraging letter that read:

Dear Sir:

In answer to your request we have forwarded copies of the Gull River Route and in addition a copy of the Master Map for the district which is self explanatory.

If we might suggest, an alternative route to the Gull River should be considered as it is a fairly difficult trip.

We hope we have been of some service.

Very truly yours,

G. O. Koistinen, District Manager
Nipigon District

Some time later I wrote another letter that was much more specific. The detailed response answered all my questions.

If you have a lot of people to contact, you may prefer to send a formal questionnaire instead of a personal letter. But keep the questions short and to a single page. People don't like to answer long forms.

Canadians should enclose a self-addressed stamped envelope when writing private individuals, but Americans had best stick with a simple "thank you." I once requested information about a certain river from Eric Morse—a famed Canadian canoe man. I included a stamped return envelope with my request. Eric was anxious to help and supplied what he could. But he also enclosed a note that read: "Thanks for your thoughtfulness in providing the stamp, Cliff, but it's time you realized that Canada is a separate country with its own postal service and its own stamps!"

A foolproof way to get replies is to address the local Catholic church. Even the smallest village usually has a Catholic church with a priest who is willing to help. Equally important, the local clergyman usually knows who has intimate knowledge of "your river," and for that reason he may be your best contact.

---

[3]Most Canadian rivers within the timberline are ice-free by mid-June, but those above the 65th parallel (tundra rivers) frequently remain frozen well into July.

In all likelihood the Catholic diocese that services your own community can supply names and addresses. Or you can direct your request to the appropriate Canadian archdiocese. You'll find these addresses in the *Official Catholic Directory*—a voluminous publication that's found in the library of every American Catholic church.

You'll also discover that a professional-looking letterhead or rubber stamp will speed up your correspondence. Personalized stationery suggests that you're serious and competent; you're more likely to get a prompt reply.

As the information rolls in, the picture of your river will begin to emerge. Barring unforeseen obstacles such as drought, flood, or a crew that backs out at the last minute, you're nearly ready to commit yourself to a specific route.

But first you must iron out the solutions to the physical difficulties (those canyons, falls, and rapids mentioned earlier) you may encounter. Time to shift gears—or rather map-scales, to 1:50,000 (1¼ inches to the mile). These large-scale maps provide exacting detail—just what you want for locating an obscure portage or a route through the maze of islands on a complex lake.

However, 1:50,000 maps have one serious drawback; they depict so little area that you may need many of them to cover a lengthy route. One answer is to order these maps for specific areas of concern but stick with the larger 1:250,000 maps for less intricate navigation.

Colored maps in 1:50,000 scale are available for almost all the populated parts of Canada, while remote areas may only be mapped in monochrome. The monochrome maps are less expensive, and their high contrast makes them easier to read under typical field conditions. Additionally, monochrome maps reproduce beautifully, so you can make inexpensive copies for everyone in your party.

I used to cut and paste map sections together to form one long strip map that covered my entire route. This saved considerable weight and bulk. But I stopped this practice in 1996 when I bought a GPS and discovered that the coordinate values I had cut off were critical for accurate positioning! You'll find detailed information about GPS navigation in chapter 13.

Still concerned about a particular obstacle? Then order the aerial photographs from which the map was made (see appendix B for ordering information). Aerial photos allow you to observe features as small as 1 meter in size.

Photos are extremely large scale—somewhere between 1:24,000 (1 inch equals 0.4 mile) and 1:60,000 (1 inch equals 1 mile). And since there are *millions* on file, getting what you want requires precise identification of the specific area of interest.

The most satisfactory way to get the right photos is to outline the area on a topographic map and send it along with your check to the USGS or Canadian Air Photo Library. They'll return the map with your order. U.S. photos can also be ordered off the USGS Web site (see appendix B). Or you can order by phone (1–888–ASK–USGS) or fax (303–202–4693) if you know the quadrangle number of your topographic map and the area of concern.

You can also state the *exact* latitude and longitude, to the nearest 5 minutes of arc, of the specific feature—falls, rapids, dam, whatever—about which you are concerned. Photos may be available in color as well as black and white. Usually they are available as stereo pairs. Stereo photos enable you to see topography in three dimensions with the aid of an inexpensive stereoscope, available at forestry and surveying supply houses. Three-D makes it real!

You don't actually need a stereoscope to see in three dimensions, though. As a forester with the Bureau of Land Management many years ago, I learned to adjust my eyes to get a 3-D picture. It takes practice, but the procedure is simple: Set the two photos on a flat surface side by side with the object you want to study about 3 inches apart. Then stare boldly "into" the photos—as if you're looking through them. Each eye should be focused straight ahead, independent of the other eye. Slowly move the two photos around—a few centimeters each way—until the object comes into 3-D focus. The procedure will sting your eyes a bit while you're looking, but the pain will cease instantly when you quit. Foresters commonly leave their stereoscopes at home and use this method in the field.

It would be unfair to leave the subject of maps without mentioning base maps and land-use maps.

In Canada: Base maps—sometimes called white prints, or logging maps, or mining maps—are simply paper prints of forest resources inventory maps. They're drawn from the latest aerial photos, usually on a scale of 20 or 40 chains to the inch. A chain is an old surveying measurement: There are 66 feet or 4 rods to a chain, 80 chains to the mile. Each map sheet commonly covers about 10 to 20 miles.

Many of the Canadian provinces are scarred with networks of logging and mining roads, most of which are not shown on topographic maps but are sometimes visible on the latest base maps. If there are recent base maps available, the

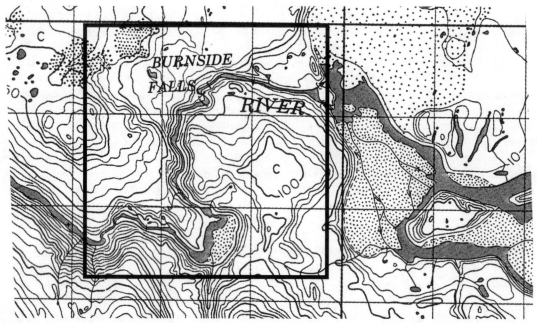

Figure 2-9. Compare this 1:250,000-scale map of Burnside Falls, Nunavut, Canada, with the 1:50,000-scale map and aerial photo.

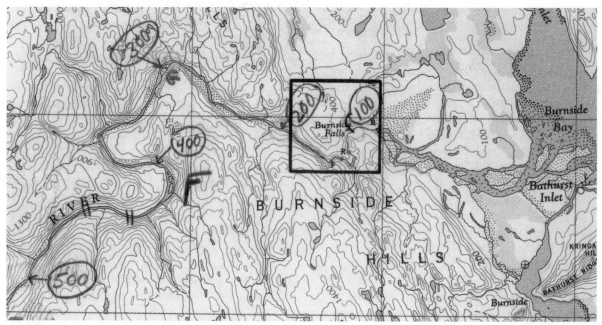

Figure 2-10. 1:50,000-scale map of Burnside Falls, Nunavut, Canada.

Figure 2-11. Shown here is Burnside Falls (Burnside River, Nunavut). This is a small portion of an aerial photograph that can supplement the use of a monochrome map by providing a better idea of the river's terrain.

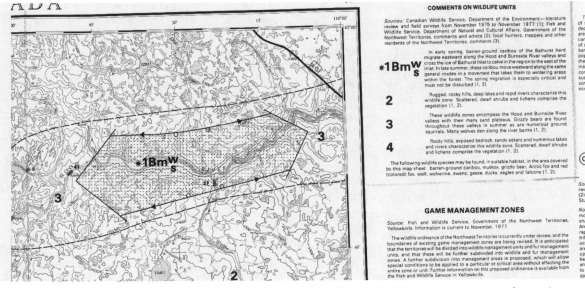

COMMENTS ON WILDLIFE UNITS

Sources: Canadian Wildlife Service, Department of the Environment—literature review and field surveys from November 1975 to November 1977 (1); Fish and Wildlife Service, Department of Natural and Cultural Affairs, Government of the Northwest Territories, comments and advice (2); local hunters, trappers and other residents of the Northwest Territories, comments (3).

*1BmWS In early spring, barren-ground caribou of the Bathurst herd migrate eastward along the Hood and Burnside River valleys and cross the ice of Bathurst Inlet to calve in the region to the east of the inlet. In late summer, these caribou move westward along the same general routes in a movement that takes them to wintering areas within the forest. The spring migration is especially critical and must not be disturbed (1, 2).

2 Rugged, rocky hills, deep lakes and rapid rivers characterize this wildlife zone. Scattered, dwarf shrubs and lichens comprise the vegetation (1, 2).

3 These wildlife zones encompass the Hood and Burnside River valleys with their many sand plateaus. Grizzly bears are found throughout these valleys in summer as are numerous ground squirrels. Many wolves den along the river banks (1, 2).

4 Rocky hills, exposed bedrock, sandy eskers and numerous lakes and rivers characterize this wildlife zone. Scattered, dwarf shrubs and lichens comprise the vegetation (1, 2).

The following wildlife species may be found, in suitable habitat, in the area covered by this map sheet: barren-ground caribou, muskox, grizzly bear, Arctic fox and red (colored) fox, wolf, wolverine, swans, geese, ducks, eagles and falcons (1, 2).

GAME MANAGEMENT ZONES

Source: Fish and Wildlife Service, Government of the Northwest Territories, Yellowknife. Information is current to November, 1977.

The wildlife ordinance of the Northwest Territories is currently under review, and the boundaries of existing game management zones are being revised. It is anticipated that the territories will be divided into wildlife management units and fur management units, and that these will be further subdivided into wildlife and fur management zones. A further subdivision into management areas is proposed, which will allow special conditions to be applied to a particular or critical area without affecting the entire zone or unit. Further information on this proposed ordinance is available from the Fish and Wildlife Service in Yellowknife.

Figure 2-12. Canadian Land Use Information Series maps tell you how the land is used. This portion of Canada map 76L (Burnside River, Nunavut) outlines four major wildlife units. Additional information not shown includes game management zones; information about hunting, trapping, and fishing; hazards to fish and wildlife; recreation and tourism concerns; and more.

Canada Map Office will know where to find them. And where land adjacent to a river is owned by a paper or mining company, some sort of provisional map that shows road access is bound to exist. Occasionally large-scale paper prints that indicate roads and trails are available directly from the company that owns the area.

Land-use maps, which are not available for all parts of Canada, do what their name implies—they tell you how the land is used. Basically, they're standard 1:250,000 topo maps that are overprinted with information about wildlife, vegetation, hunting and fishing, climate, and places of interest. They tend to be pretty cluttered and thus only marginally useful for navigation. But they do provide a wealth of interesting data—reason enough to carry one.

Order these maps from a Canadian map distributor (see appendix B). Be sure to specify "Land Use Information Series."

In the United States: Look for Land Use and Land Cover maps. These American maps are similar to Canadian Land use Information Series maps, with these exceptions: Land Use maps depict the way human activities affect the land (for example, housing and industry). And Land Cover maps describe the vegetation, water, and artificial constructions on the land surface. Scale is 1:100,000 or 1:250,000. Order these maps from the USGS.

Finally, don't overlook tourist maps when planning your trip. These maps—commonly available from local chambers of commerce and area businesses—may be extremely useful. One of the best tourist maps I ever had cost $1.00 at a gas station in Kakabeka Falls, Ontario. The map showed the location of every logging road and horse path, and there were lots of 'em. It even indicated, by lake, the species of fish you might expect to catch. Wish I'd known about that map *before* I canoed the English River. It might have saved a 7-mile portage!

At this point your research is pretty complete. What you've learned should keep you from running into too much of the unexpected. However, if you want to be really thorough, you'll attempt to locate the journals of early explorers—Tyrrell, Raddison, Thompson, Mackenzie, and others—who paddled your route. Here's an example:

Immediately above the portage the channel is very crooked, and there is a stiff rapid with a fall of about twelve feet, which we ascended with a line, above which is a stretch of moderately easy water, up which we paddled with the assistance of a stiff breeze, to the foot of Thompson Rapid, one of the heaviest rapids on the river. The lower part, in which the banks are low, was readily ascended with a line to a short portage thirty-five yards long, across a point on the north side, where we camped for the night of August 12th. Above this short portage, almost to the top of the rapid, the banks are from ten to fifteen feet high and consist of flat-laying sandstone, generally undercut by the water. Past part of this cascade we portaged all our stuff for 300 yards on the north bank, merely tracking up our empty canoes. The total fall in the rapids is about thirty feet.[4]

Though these trip logs are frequently more than a hundred years old, they're still valuable, because most major rapids, falls, and portages have changed little over the course of time.

Certainly it's not necessary to do an exhaustive journal search to ensure a successful canoe trip. On the other hand, the writings of a perceptive explorer might give you just the edge you need to quickly locate a hard-to-find portage or a route through a tricky rapid. If nothing else, the old diaries lend historical perspective that might otherwise be just another canoe trip.

Unfortunately, there's little demand for the old journals, so don't expect to find them sitting boldly on the shelves of your county library. Moreover, many are bound in books that are frequently hundreds of pages long and span many years. Seldom do you need all that. Fortunately, librarians are wonderful people—they'll go the extra mile to help you find exactly what you want. In research, as in other things, patience has its own rewards.

Another place to look for accounts of early explorers is the local historical society that serves the area you'll be exploring. Again, historical librarians are more than willing to help.

Whew! That about does it—river researched, planning

[4]From J. B. Tyrrell, "Report on the country between Athabasca Lake and Churchill River, with notes on two routes travelled between the Churchill and Saskatchewan Rivers, Canada." *Geological Survey Annual Report*. Vol. 8, 1895, 82D–83D.

complete. Right? Not hardly. You've got the river nailed down, all right, but there's much more to do. Like picking a crew—one that likes your route and your tripping style; food to buy and pack; equipment to round up; a time and distance schedule to calculate; and transportation to consider. And don't forget money—the stuff that makes it all happen. How will you carry enough for a four-week trip? Traveler's checks? Cash? Money orders? Credit cards? Can everyone in your party afford your trip? What about fishing licenses, camping permits, wildlife refuge travel permits?

Just the thought of all that's left to do makes you want to abandon the operation and opt for a friendly float down a local stream, doesn't it? No way! Planning is outright fun, almost as much as the trip itself. Besides, planning makes you an active participant in the trip rather than just a tagalong who was picked up at the last moment to fill out the crew. Making a successful expedition is meaningless if you don't take an active part in putting it together. After all, anyone can follow a guide through the wilderness!

Granted, you can be pretty haphazard about planning if your route is well traveled and not dangerous. So what if you get confused for a few hours or run a Class II rapid without first scouting it? Penalties are not severe—a bit of extra paddling, perhaps a dunking. Nothing serious.

But if your dreams take you to the distant north, where rivers run cold and wild and help is an airplane ride away, then you'd better put some effort into rigorous planning!

ANSWERS TO "IS IT RUNNABLE?"
(FIGURE 2-8)

Contour Interval Equals 10 Meters

MILES	DISTANCE (miles)	DROP/MILE (feet)[5]
130.5–131.3	0.8	41
131.3–132.5	1.2	27.5
132.5–133.7	1.2	27.5
133.7–135.4	1.7	19.4
Total miles = 4.9		115.4 feet (total drop)

Total drop = 115.4 feet

Average drop = $115.4 \div 4.9 = 23.6$

Is it runnable? No way! A few isolated sections might be canoeable for short stretches. But this river is *really* moving!

[5] Don't forget to change meters to feet. Remember, there are 3.3 feet in one meter, or 33 feet in 10 meters.

CHAPTER 3
PICKING A CREW

Besides the bush and one's mate, friends are what life is all about.
—Dick Person, Teslin, Yukon

Picking a crew is like buying a used car: What you see outside merely suggests what you get inside. Only miles of driving under a variety of conditions will tell you the true nature of the beast. "You pays your money and you takes your chances," as the saying goes. So it is with canoe teams. A good friend at the office may be incompatible in the wilds, and vice versa; responsible performance under city stress is not a measure of levelheadedness afield. The two variables are quite unrelated.

A canoe crew has an investment in the safety, joy, and well-being of all its members. There's no room for loners or egomaniacs. It takes lots of time, on the river and off, to find enough skilled, responsible, and caring people to fill out a crew—which is why experienced groups are so possessive about keeping their members together on subsequent trips. When a proven individual drops out of a successful team for one reason or another, a semipanic often ensues. After all, filling the void with someone new is like buying boots by mail: Even when you know your size, there's no guarantee of a perfect fit!

Foremost, selecting a crew is compatibility. All other factors—paddling skill, age, physical abilities, woodsmanship, and so on—take a backseat to this requirement. The literature is filled with tales of trips that nearly ended in disaster because canoe partners simply couldn't get along. Intolerance of the views of others spells danger, or at best an unwholesome, acidic experience.

BASIC SKILLS

There are two kinds of skills—those you have and those you think you have! An honest appraisal of your own abilities

is essential to a successful canoe trip, so begin by taking a long, hard look into the mirror. Twenty years of canoeing experience in the Allagash or Minnesota Boundary Waters doesn't qualify you for an Arctic adventure. Neither does equal time spent paddling slalom gates on the national whitewater course. Certainly these experiences are valuable, but what you really need is variety, not years of rote practice in the same environment.

Canoeists new to the wilderness game don't realize that learning when to portage is more important than developing talents for paddling the near-impossible. A backcountry canoeist's greatest skill is good judgment—a quality that takes many years to develop.

Figure 3-1. A canoe crew has an investment in the safety, joy, and well-being of all its members. Lunch break along the Fond du Lac River, Saskatchewan.

High-tech canoeing skills are useful, of course, and the tougher the river, the more essential they become. But more important are the answers to these fundamental questions: Can you thread your way through the maze of islands on a 40-mile-long fog-shrouded lake? Or rig a snug camp in the teeth of an icy rain? Are you able to sniff out a coming storm and locate an unmarked portage in a mess of tangled alders? Have you the mental discipline to keep going in the face of all obstructions—foul weather, grueling portages, persistent insects?

These skills plus you own mature judgment are what will keep you safe and comfortable on a wild and distant river.

Still looking into the mirror? Perhaps you're getting somewhat frightened at your own inadequacy. Good! It's normal. And healthy. Shows that beneath that staunch outward appearance there's a warmly beating heart. *You're not alone!* Virtually every backcountry canoeist I know secretly admits some inner fear (call it profound anticipation, if you will) that his or her own skills are inadequate to meet the challenge.

Mild, controllable fear is nature's way of telling you to slow down and think before you act. At the other extreme is foolhardiness, and every white-water club has some of these people, many of whom are excellent technical paddlers. Follow them down a local river clad in wet suit and helmet if you like, but keep 'em out of the wild. They'll kill you for sure!

Dr. Bill Forgey, a veteran North Country canoeist and author, sums it up:

Somehow on long trips, the uncertainty of the next day's travel, the food supply, the amount of time, all seem to gnaw at me—perhaps in many ways spoiling the trip. . . . Why do I take these things so seriously? Perhaps I'm not cut out for wilderness travel. I asked Sigurd Olson one day about this. He laughed and said that he'd put the same

question past Camsell[1] at the Explorer's Club one day. Camsell replied that he'd spent most of his adult life exploring the bush and had been scared during nine-tenths of it.

The point of the foregoing discussion is elementary: Select your crew members for their maturity and level headedness. Avoid technically competent hot dogs who don't have all their mental faculties. And if the skills of your party suggest that you're not ready for a certain river, don't be disappointed. There's a world of lesser routes out there waiting for you to learn on. And these waterways are often just as beautiful and remote as the awesome bone-chillers of the Far North.

It takes years to develop wilderness canoeing sense. Don't rush it!

It's interesting to note that the best wilderness canoe experts usually don't think of themselves as such. Despite their proven abilities, they know there's still much to learn. Now compare this attitude to that of equipment shop armchair experts who know it all. Humbling, isn't it?

SPECIAL SKILLS

The tougher the river, the better you and your crew had better be! Most of the time you can get by okay if one person per canoe is a skilled paddler. This individual usually takes the stern and trains his or her bow partner during the course of the trip. If the river's not too violent, the procedure works well enough—a few scrapes and dings on the hull during the learning process, but that's all. Most novice bow paddlers become acceptably proficient after the first week of whitewater travel.

Only when the river becomes dangerously demanding does the "train as you go" philosophy fail. It's then that your bow person becomes invaluable—he or she must understand the whys and hows of moving water and react instantly, precisely, without error. Failing this, you'd better portage, and there's no dishonor in that. So again, the bottom line is compatibility.

Another characteristic of a well-matched crew is similar sociological backgrounds. Mix five deep thinkers with one nonintellectual and you've got a recipe for problems—not due to any snobbery or insensitivity of the majority, but because the person who is different may magnify unimportant subtleties. For example, a series of lofty discussions car-

[1]Charles Camsell, a noted Canadian explorer and former commissioner of the Northwest Territories, died in 1958.

ried on for days can make a person who doesn't understand feel genuinely inferior—and outcast. Sensitivity toward each other's feelings can override the difficulties, but it takes conscious and continuous practice.

Ideally, each crew member should contribute some special skill—cooking, white-water technique, map reading, first aid, biology, geology, meteorology, photography, and so on. When the days turn to weeks, you'll discover that there's simply no substitute for good, stimulating conversation. And the more interesting, unique, and diversified are your friends, the more memorable your canoe trip will be.

Other considerations that affect your choice of crew are time, money, and purpose. The more time you have, the less money you'll need to spend on your trip. For example, if you have five weeks to do a river, you may have enough time to start or end your run at a town that has road, rail, or commercial air transportation back to your starting point. Obviously this is much less expensive than a shorter route that requires a flight in or out on a charter floatplane.

Charter flights are incredibly expensive. It's not uncommon for a one-way air shuttle to consume more than half your tripping dollars! Cars, boats, and trains are much cheaper ways to travel. But they're also more time consuming.

The cost-versus-time relationship should be fully explored by all prospective crew members. In general, younger folks—especially college kids—have more time than money. As age increases, with its accompanying responsibilities, the situation reverses, for few jobs allow long periods of time off. Here again, the importance of similar backgrounds comes into play.

Equally important is purpose. Will this be a fishing trip, a canoe adventure, or something in between? You've just got to get this one nailed down right at the start. A lot of canoe trips have been ruined because some people wanted to paddle while others wanted to fish or photograph.

Personally, I don't like to fish. And on the rare occasions when I do fish, I never catch anything. Once on a small tributary of the Moose River, five friends caught more than a hundred northern pike in just ninety minutes (of course we didn't keep them all). I caught three . . . and lost two. One friend felt so sorry for me that he played a tired yard-long fish to shore, handed me the pole, and said, "Here, Cliff, have some fun . . . catch a fish!" Nice buddy, huh?

Nevertheless, I do relish fresh batter-fried fish. So I always like to have someone in my crew who understands the ways of rod and reel. But I make it perfectly clear *before* the

trip that we canoe until we stop for the day. *Then* the fishing begins!

More than once I've paddled out after sunset in search of a friend who lagged behind to fish. For safety's sake it's important that a canoe group stay close together at all times. And you can't do that if one pair is miles behind, casting hopefully into a quiet pool.

Agree on a purpose—a traveling philosophy. Then stick to it. And write the rules in Technicolor so everyone understands.

WHAT SIZE CREW?

The safest and least-expensive way to go is with a crew of six. This gives you two rescue boats in event of an upset, and—more important—there's ample room to get everyone out if you lose a canoe in a rapid.

Six is also the cheapest way to fly. A Twin Otter will carry six passengers, three canoes, and all your packs for little more than it costs to fly four plus gear on two smaller Cessnas. And carrying canoes on board is obviously a safer way to fly than tying them alongside pontoons.

On the negative side, it's not easy to find enough level, open sites to erect three 6- by 8-foot tents. Certainly you can sleep everyone in two tents of this size, but what happens if you lose a tent in a rough-water upset? Is your remaining tent large enough to accommodate the overload? It happens!

It's also more of a hassle to feed six than four—mainly because it takes more time to prepare meals.

But the greatest drawback of six-person crews is getting to and from the river. It's almost impossible to stuff six adults, three canoes, and nine or more bursting Duluth packs into a car or SUV. What you really need is a van and canoe trailer.

What about crews larger than six? Frankly, the farther you get from the standard four-person group, the more difficult things become. I've traveled with many parties of nine over the years and I've had compatibility problems with at least half of them. If you've led many scout or church groups, you know what I mean. Adults are no easier to manage than teenagers—believe me, you'll experience problems. Simple mathematics suggests that the larger the crew, the more and varied the difficulties.

In summary, safety and low cost favor large groups; logistics favor small ones. Except for trips into the remote Arctic, my preference is four.

All this philosophy looks good on paper until you realize

that even small crews invariably emerge solely from the ranks of those who are free to go. Besides, there's always someone who backs out at the last minute and leaves you scrambling for a warm replacement—one who might like to go on a canoe trip. As I think back over the imperfect crews I've had over the years, I wonder why I find it so difficult to follow my own advice. But I'll keep trying!

WHAT ABOUT CHILDREN?

Not everyone enjoys having children along on a canoe trip. The determining factor here seems to be whether everyone's child is involved or just a select few. Thus it's okay if each canoe is manned by a parent and child, but problems will arise when there's just one boy or girl in the company of a crew of adults. Telling a parent his or her child isn't wanted may be the most difficult of all crew problems to solve. But the situation can be worked out to satisfaction if everyone is open and honest about their feelings. Remember, you're "family" on a canoe trip. And no fighting, please!

You should also realize that even the most mature, level-headed youngster has far poorer judgment than the average rational adult. Pick your river with this thought in mind if you're taking children along. Make sure the experience is well within their capabilities.

DUTIES

Okay, you've got yourself a crew! Time to celebrate with a good dinner and fine wine. And afterward you can hit the maps again, assign specific work duties, and get down to serious business of solving the 101 problems that remain.

By and large, canoe trips proceed along democratic lines. What to fix for supper, when to stop for the day, whether to traverse a windy bay or wait it out are all decisions reached via mutual discussion and consent. But often there's disagreement. And the majority is not always right. That's why every group needs an experienced leader who is not afraid to make decisions.

In 1979 I led a *Canoe* magazine–sponsored trip down Saksatchewan's Fond du Lac River. When we arrived at Black Lake near the end of our journey, the wind was howling murder and the lake was kicking up 4-foot whitecaps. We fixed a hasty supper and retired to the shelter of our tents, intent on making the necessary 20-mile crossing later in the subarctic twilight when the wind died down.

When we arose at midnight, the waves were much smaller than before but still running steadily from the west (our direction of travel). Minutes passed. Finally my friend Darrell Foss had had enough. "You're the trip leader, Cliff," he said. "Make a decision!"

"Okay . . . we go!" I replied. And without another word we dropped camp and in thirty minutes we were waterborne.

It was a rough, wet ride but we made it to a protected narrows just minutes before the wind vented its full fury. A delay of even a quarter hour would have seen us caught on open water in a dangerously running sea. Probably we should have stayed the day and waited it out. But the fact that the decision was made quickly saved the day.

Another example: In 1991 I led a twelve-day canoe trip down the remote North Knife River in Manitoba. Fierce headwinds and cold rain slowed our pace, and on the sixth day a gale confined us to our tents for three days. Now just two days remained to paddle 60 miles to Hudson Bay, 6 miles down the bay to Dymond Lake (including a 1-mile portage), where our floatplane would pick us up. We could only canoe at high tide, which occurs just twice a day. Hudson Bay is no place for canoes—a moderate wind could stop us in our tracks.

The timing seemed impossible.

We arrived at Hudson Bay at 9:00 P.M. on day eleven—our last full day. The wind was in our face (as usual) and there were huge whitecaps on the bay. Canoeing the bay was out of the question. We crowded into a decrepit goose-hunters' shack and settled in for the night. There was no talk of paddling to Dymond Lake.

High tide came at 4:30 A.M.—our last window to make the airplane. A friend awoke me at 3:30 with the words, "Cliff, I don't think the wind is that bad." I bolted out of bed and scanned the bay with binoculars for whitecaps; there were just soft riffles. I knew that waves would come with the sun, so I made the decision quickly.

"We go!"

Minutes later we were on roughly riffled salt water, paddling into a deep red sunrise.

The waves picked up when we rounded the point and cleared the protective islands. Now we were riding a gentle but determined tailwind, hell bent for leather. Two polar bears on shore looked curiously our way as we careered downwind. Thankfully, they didn't give chase.

We touched shore at 5:15 A.M. and began the portage to Dymond Lake. The plane set down just as the last pack was carried over. The pilot's first words were: "Let's get goin', boys, the wind is picking up."

THE TRIP LEADER

Biff Kummer

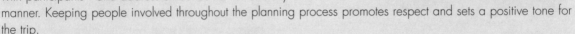

*Biff Kummer is a professor of recreation and parks administra-
tion at Western Kentucky University. He has trekked and climbed in
North America, South America, Africa, and Europe. Since 1989
his summers have been spent paddling the magnificent wild rivers of
the Canadian Arctic and subarctic, many of them with me. Biff was
the best man at my wedding at Wilberforce Falls on the Hood River
in 1992 (see chapter 19). He's a terrific guy and I'm proud to call
him one of my very best friends.*

Good leadership is the key to a quality experience. The leader
starts working long before the event or expedition takes place. The
leader must contact all participants and keep them informed about
all aspects of the planning process. The leader must correspond
with participants—and address all concerns—in a timely and honest
manner. Keeping people involved throughout the planning process promotes respect and sets a positive tone for
the trip.

The leadership process is both direct and indirect. The leader must be able to assign responsibility and
meticulously follow up on his or her assignments. Major concerns include: logistics (getting to and from the river);
food (amount, taste, calories, nutrition, special needs); packing (fair distribution of items); medical and emergency gear; community equipment (tents, tarps, edged tools, and so on); current maps and trip guides; knowledge of compass and GPS; use of journals and other information from past expeditions; personal and group
dynamics (canoe and tent partners); disabilities (physical and mental); weather conditions. And much more.

A good leader is decisive, honest, well organized, and direct, and has empathy and compassion for others. The leader must keep a positive attitude and be able to deal with conflict without creating more conflict.
Good humor may be the most important asset of all!

It's not always easy to get along with everyone on an expedition, especially when times are stressful and
demanding. Wilderness rivers often present unforeseen difficulties that complicate well-laid plans. The leader is
the one who must maintain unity and cohesiveness among everyone when things go bad.

As you can see, serious pressures are associated with
being where you have to be when you have to be. Had we
waited for even thirty minutes, we might have judged the
wind too strong to travel and missed our airplane. Yes, he
would fly back another day—and he'd rightly double our
$2,000 charter fee, too. We would lose our motel accommoda-
tions in Churchill and miss the train that runs to Thompson
every other day. Some people would have to reschedule their
commercial flights home, and everyone would miss some
work. It would be a mess.

That's why every canoe trip needs a leader who is willing
to make decisions.

Generally I go with the majority on matters not directly
concerned with safety and opt for the cautious course, regardless of vote, when the occasion demands. For example, if three
out of four canoeists want to run a questionable rapids, I'll
side with the minority and portage even if I think the drop is
safe. I don't like to cajole someone into doing something he or
she feels is dangerous.

Other crews approach the matter on a partnership rather
than crew basis. Thus one team runs the rapids if they choose
to, while another portages or lines.

Treasurer

It's essential that the expedition have some working capital on hand early in the planning stage. This lets you take advantage of preseason dried food and equipment sales and a fluctuating Canadian exchange rate. Some charter aircraft companies will discount their fees if you send a nonrefundable deposit several months before your trip. Via Rail Canada offers a substantial discount if you purchase tickets well ahead of time (there's more on charter planes and trains in chapter 16). Money down means commitment—it keeps people from backing out at the last minute.

The crew should agree on some sort of graduated payment schedule such as the one shown below:

Total cost of trip (hypothetical) $1,000

Payment Schedule

February 1 .... $200 (nonrefundable deposit)
March 15 .... $400
May 1 .... $400
Trip dates: July 2–26

Note that all money has been collected *two months* in advance of the trip!

Research Technician and Navigator

Someone must take responsibility for making the contacts suggested in chapter 2. Maps must be purchased, studied, and annotated. A realistic time and distance schedule must be computed (see chapter 4). If you bring a Global Positioning System, you may want to preprogram important waypoints (it takes time!) before your trip. Everyone makes mistakes, and the navigator is no exception. For safety's sake everyone should know how to read a map and compass and be able to locate their position with a GPS.

Invariably these organizational and training responsibilities fall on the trip leader, who of necessity must leave no stone unturned.

Transportation Chairperson

This person secures the appropriate road maps and plans the route to and from the river. If special tires or vehicle modifications are required, the cost should be borne in part by the crew. The transportation chairperson is usually the one who owns the vehicle. Owner of the vehicle *does not* pay for gas or oil en route.

Weather Forecaster

You can make this job as easy or complex as you like. Either way, weather forecasting is fun and practical. Instruments range from low-cost thermometers and cloud comparison charts to the sophisticated Sager Weathercaster, which requires an expensive barometer. I might add that the new digital watches that have built-in barometers work great.

Menu Planner

Best handled by two people with dissimilar tastes. The idea is to work up a low-cost, efficient menu for the trip (ideas in chapter 11). My book *Basic Essentials: Cooking in the Outdoors* (appendix B) will get you started right.

Supply Officer

Someone must develop a thorough list of personal and group equipment essentials. Absolutely nothing must be left to chance. Invariably, this is another responsibility for the group leader.[2]

Publications Officer

Essential only if you want to advertise your trip. Local newspapers are always searching for interesting items. Possibly you can get some sponsorship money in return for a short story or trip log and photos.

Now that you have an eager, working crew, the solutions to problems will come much easier. After all, many heads are better than one. But don't let things stagnate until trip time. Keep the pot boiling with a meeting each month.

No one can tell you how much time you'll need to plan a successful canoe trip. That depends on a long list of variables—the general difficulty of the route, remoteness of the area, distance from home, length of stay on the river, and more. Nine months is probably the *minimum* you should allot for planning a major trip; a year or more is not uncommon.

It's *never* too early to plan a canoe trip!

[2]Perhaps you're beginning to discover that most of the burden of organizing a canoe trip ultimately falls on the leader. Effective delegation of responsibility can help lighten the load, but only if those who undertake the duties are sufficiently knowledgeable to rise to the challenge. All too often the leader finds him- or herself in the unfortunate position of doing it all!

CHAPTER 4
LOOSE THREADS

A Compendium of Unrelated Things You Need to Do Before the Wheels Roll North

It was September 14, 1955, on the Dubawnt River in the Northwest Territories, and already there was a crispness in the air. Each day frost grew heavier on the morning ground. The Arctic summer, so intense in early August, was gone, and autumn with its subfreezing temperatures and fierce polar gales had begun. Thirty-six-year-old Arthur Moffatt was leading five young men, ages nineteen to twenty-one, on a traverse of the barren lands. They had begun at Stoney Rapids, Saskatchewan, on June 29 and were bound for Baker Lake.

Trip member Joe Lannouette's diary was published in George Grinnell's book, *A Death on the Barrens*.[1] He wrote:

September 14: This has been the most harrowing day of my life. It started as many others recently: bleak and dismal under a cover of clouds. It was below freezing and the sand was crunchy and hard from its layer of frost and ice. After a fine lunch of fish chowder, we shoved off again at around 2:30. In a few minutes we heard and saw rapids on the horizon. At the top, the rapids looked as though they would be easy going, a few small waves, rocks—nothing serious. We didn't even haul over to shore to have a look, as we usually did. The river was straight and we could see both the top and the foot of the rough water quite clearly, or we thought we could.

Almost immediately it happened: Two canoes swamped, and the third almost did. At one point five men were swimming in the ice-cold water. The rescue dragged on and on.

Ultimately everyone reached shore, bitterly cold. We can only speculate as to why Moffatt died of hypothermia but his friends did not. George Grinnell's account of their ordeal makes it clear that they all could easily have perished that tragic day.

Arthur Moffatt was buried at Baker Lake in the land he loved best. A simple wooden cross in a lonely cemetery marks his grave.

Canoeists were stupefied by the untimely death of this competent outdoorsman. Surely barren-land rivers must be unsafe places, fit only for supermen of incomparable stamina and skill. This myth persisted for a decade after Moffatt's death. Even today few canoeists dare venture north of the 60th parallel.

Nonetheless, Moffatt's crew made many serious errors, all of which are easily avoidable by perceptive men and women with cautionary sense. Most unforgivable was recklessness—failure to carefully check a rapid before running it. Arctic rivers are no place for impulsive decisions. The group also failed to maintain a travel schedule. Indeed, Moffatt's diary, later published in *Sports Illustrated* magazine, gave no indication that he had a trip plan at all. Freeze-up comes early in the barrens. September is no time to be in the middle of a tundra river!

Good maps and common sense are not enough to ensure your safety on a difficult river. You need a realistic travel plan that takes into account the physical characteristics of the route—stoppers like rapids, falls, low water, ice—and the experience and goals of your crew. In every case the bottom

---

[1] This 1996 book tells the complete story of the Moffatt expedition. You can order a copy (some autographed copies are available) from George Luste at Northern Books.

line is the same—be conservative. Don't bite off more than you can swallow!

THE TRAVEL PLAN

How many miles can you expect to average in a ten-hour day on a typical northern river?

Average fast river with few portages ....30–50 miles
Average fast river with frequent portages ....15–20 miles
Lakes, no wind ....30–40 miles
Upstream with occasional rapids...............less than 10 miles

Of course these are averages and they're affected by so many variables that they're probably meaningless.

For example, you'll make much better time if you paddle a fast cruising canoe than a slow white-water boat, even if you have to carry around most rapids. It usually takes more time to check a rapid than to portage it, so you're almost always ahead in the faster canoe.

A good plan is to cover 15 miles a day. This gives you a day off now and then, an opportunity to explore all that beautiful backcountry you've come to see, and a chance to fish and photograph. And it allows for the unexpected—storms, high winds, navigational blunders, difficult portages, injuries. These are the realities of wilderness tripping—realities that should be taken seriously and planned for.

Let's look at some sample plans. Table 4-1 shows the daily mileage of the Keith Thompson[2] party on its 1971 canoe

TABLE 4-1 SCHEDULE

Day (on water)	Day's run (miles)	Distance to Date (miles)	Time (% of total)	Distance (% of total)	Comments
1 (July 19)	4.4	4.4	5.3	1.4	3 hours on water only
2	8.8	13.2	10.5	4.3	
3	4.8	18.0	15.8	5.9	
4	18.0	36.0	21.1	11.8	
5	12.8	48.8	26.3	16.0	behind schedule
6	19.6	68.4	31.6	22.3	
7	13.2	81.6	36.9	26.7	
8	25.6	107.2	42.1	35.1	
9	16.4	123.6	47.3	40.4	
10	35.6	159.2	52.6	52.1	on schedule
11	22.4	181.6	57.9	59.3	
12	20.4	202.0	63.2	66.0	
13	26.4	228.4	68.4	74.6	
14	19.6	248.0	73.7	81.1	
15	19.6	267.6	79.0	87.5	ahead of schedule
16	11.6	279.2	84.3	91.2	
17	8.8	288.0	89.4	94.2	
18	8.8	296.8	94.8	97.0	
19 (August 6)	8.8	305.6	100.0	100.0	
TOTALS	305.6	305.6	100.0	100.0	Mean 16.1

[2]Keith Thompson is an experienced Arctic Canoeist who lives in Yellowknife, Northwest Territories. His average of 16.1 miles per day is fairly typical for a canoe trip of this length.

trip from Rawalpindi Lake via the Coppermine River to the Arctic Ocean.

Table 4-2 is another time and distance schedule, this one put together nearly one year before the trip. It may seem a bit ambitious, but it was right for Verlen Kruger and Clint Waddell—seasoned racers who made the voyage from Montreal to Alaska in a 21-foot epoxy/fiberglass wood-strip canoe of Verlen's design.[3] On some days the pair covered more than 60 miles, as you can see for yourself.

Note that they arrived at the Bering Sea on the precise date they predicted. Exceptional planning!

The schedule includes a layover for filming (a full-length movie was made) and recreation. The original starting date was moved back because of the late winter and persistent ice. Clint and Verlen also made two side trips—a 250-mile race at Flin Flon (six days) and a diversion from Peel River to the

TABLE 4-2 CROSS-CONTINENT CANOE SAFARI TIME AND DISTANCE SCHEDULE

Place	Projected date 1971	Miles between points	Total miles	Travel time	Actual dates
Montreal	4 April	0	0	—	17 April
Ottawa		110	110	4 days	23 April
Mattawa		210	320	8 days	
North Bay		45	365	1 day	1 May
Georgian Bay, Lake Huron		110	475	2 days	
Sault Ste. Marie	8 May	195	670	5 days	11 May
Fort William		420	1090	15 days	27 May
Atikokan (route changed)	3 June	180	1270	6 days	
International Falls		100	1370	2 days	4 June
Lake of the Woods		90	1460	2 days	
Kenora		80	1540	2 days	
Lake Winipeg	12 June	160	1700	5 days	14 June
Saskatchewan River, Grand Rapids		315	2015	10 days	
The Pas		140	2155	5 days	
Cumberland House		80	2235	3 days	
Amisk Lake, Flin Flon	1–5 July	60	2295	2 days	30 June
Churchhill River, Frog Portage		116	2411	4 days	
Buffalo Narrows, Peter Pond Lake		369	2780	11 days	
Clearwater River, Methye Portage		125	2905	3 days	27 July
Athabasca River, Fort McMurray		80	2985	1 day	
Lake Athabasca, Fort Chipewan		200	3185	4 days	2 August
Fort Smith		125	3310	3 days	5 August
Great Slave Lake, Fort Resolution		195	3505	3 days	11 August
Mackenzie River, Fort Providence		165	3670	3 days	
Fort Simpson at Liard River		140	3810	3 days	
Fort Norman at Great Bear River		305	4115	6 days	
Fort Good Hope, 25 mi. S. Arctic Circle		175	4290	3 days	
Arctic Red River		215	4505	4 days	29 August
Peel River, Fort McPherson		60	4565	2 days	
McDougal Pass (over the Rockies)	5 Sept.	130	4695	10 days	8 Sept.
Porcupine River by Bell River		115	4810	2 days	
Old Crow		100		1 day	
Alaska Border, Ramparts House		55		1 day	
Fort Yukon jct. Yukon River		225	5190	4 days	18 Sept.
Tanana jct. Tanana River		320	5510	5 days	
Galena		165	5675	3 days	
Koyukuk River		30	5705	1 day	
Kaltag		52		1 day	
Anvik		140		2 days	
Russian Mission		110	6007	2 days	
Mountain Village		130	6137	2 days	
Bering Sea, Norton Sound	10 Oct.	85	6222	2 days	10 Oct.
Akumsuk		23			

[3]Verlen Kruger, now in his seventies, continues to explore new routes. His greatest expedition was in 1980–83, when he and Steve Landick circumnavigated the North American continent (28,000 miles!) in Kruger-built solo canoes. Verlen's time and distance schedule for this "Ultimate Canoe Challenge" was even more massive than the one here—a tribute to his good planning. If you're going into harm's way, you can't do better than a Kruger-built solo or tandem canoe. See appendix B for information about Kruger-built boats.

Arctic Ocean and back (300 miles, eight days).

A time and distance schedule need not be as fancy as Table 4-1 and 4-2, of course, but it should provide the basic information:

- Miles between checkpoints. I like to indicate the exact distance I expect to make each day.

- The date you plan to arrive at each checkpoint or mile marker. The schedule should reflect planned layover days and reserve *at least one day in five* for wind and the unexpected.

Computing a realistic time and distance schedule is just one of the many loose threads you'll need to tie before the wheels roll north. Here are some others that are less obvious.

WHO SUPPLIES THE GEAR?

It would be nice if every crew member contributed an equal share of equipment. You know, John furnishes the tent, rain tarp, and cookset; Tom and Al supply canoes; Jill contributes the pack sacks and stove; and so on. But things never work out that way. There's always one or two people who provide everything. And that's both unfair and expensive. There's a lot of wear and tear on canoes and gear on a major trip; the farther you go from the beaten path, the greater the abuse. It's all part of the game, of course, but everyone should play!

Some expeditions solve the problem by renting items to group members. The fee insures the user against all damage and loss, even if he or she is directly at fault.

Other crews assign damages to those who are directly responsible. Thus ten partners split the cost of repairing a wind-torn tent, canoe teams pay an equal share toward replacement of a demolished canoe, and so forth. But everyone chips in for a lost stove, cookset, camp saw, and the like.

The rental plan has the advantage of paying full compensation for normal wear but doesn't account for the unexpected, such as loss of a canoe while lining.[4] On the other hand, the fair-share method provides for major damage but has no provision for expected wear. As you can see, there's no just solution; the owner of the gear almost always comes out the financial loser.

Whichever plan you choose, make it clear at the start that everyone *must* supply at least *these* personal items:

- All clothing, rain gear, and bedding

- A comfortable foam-filled life jacket

- Two paddles

- Proper foot gear

- Maps and compass

And *demand* that everything be durable enough to last the trip! You may laugh when your friend shows up with a cheap rain suit and hardware-store canoe paddle. But the humor will fade when these things destruct along the route and you have to repair them. A canoe party can travel only as fast as its slowest member. One person's problem—equipment or otherwise—is everyone's!

I can't stress enough the importance of selecting good, rugged equipment. It's easy to let your sentiments fog your better judgment when you hear "I can't afford it." But stand firm. The price for equipment failure along a remote river is high.

SHOULD WE RENT CANOES OR BRING OUR OWN?

It may actually be less expensive to rent canoes on the spot than to haul your own hundreds or thousands of miles on a car or airplane. Of course, many tourist lodges in Canada and Alaska rent canoes, but what they stock may not be what you have in mind for use on an unforgiving river. As mentioned, you need a reliable, seaworthy craft for canoeing the wild rivers of the Far North—and these aren't always available in the heart of Canada or Alaska.

Exceptions are tourist lodges that cater to canoe trippers and those that service routes north of the 60th parallel. Frequently these rent expedition-quality Old Town Trippers and Discoveries, sometimes with full splash covers. As you might expect, prices are not cheap, but then neither is the cost of flying your own canoe hundreds of air miles into and out of remote locations.

You'd better address these concerns before you rent any canoe:

- Does it have a comfortable padded carrying yoke? Outfitters and canoeists don't always agree on what constitutes "comfortable." My advice is to bring your own custom-built yoke. Also, bring a cordless drill and bolts so you can install your yoke in the canoe!

[4]Lining is the art of working a canoe downstream with the aid of a rope attached to the bow and stern. Hauling it upstream is tracking. Both procedures require perfect coordination between those who are controlling the lines. If the stern of the canoe is allowed to get out too far into the current while lining, the canoe may broach and upset and suffer serious damage.

- Is a fabric splash cover included in the rental plan? (See chapter 7 for a discussion of canoe covers.)

    In 1998 I rented Royalex canoes from a Canadian outfitter for a trip in the Northwest Territories. The canoes had one-piece splash covers fastened with laces that had to be threaded through small loops. Tall packs had to be set flat on the floor of the canoe, because the covers did not expand. We had no access to our gear when the covers were laced down.

    Our covers were durable and reliable, but we grew to hate them because they were so much trouble. One crew refused to use them at all, even when life-threatening situations loomed ahead. We yearned for the easy accessibility of the three-piece expandable covers I designed. Fortunately we knew what to expect, so we'd packed everything in packs and wanigans that would fit beneath the tightly tailored covers.

- Rented tripping canoes usually don't have glued-in knee pads. Those that do have generically positioned pads, which don't fit all knees. I suggest you bring your own closed-cell foam pads and glue them into the canoe. Chapter 6 tells you how.

- Your outfitter probably won't provide lining ropes, let alone install proper fittings in the canoe. Your best bet is to bring your own lines. Drill holes near cutwater (that cordless drill again!) and epoxy a watertight fitting through the hull, as suggested in chapter 6.

- Fitting four or five burgeoning Duluth-sized packs into a 17-foot rental canoe is a lot easier if you move the stern thwart back about 6 inches. You'll need a saw and that cordless drill again.

- Bring some 1/4-inch-diameter bungee cord so you can shock-cord the thwarts and decks as suggested in chapter 6. Yes, you will need to drill holes.

MONEY MATTERS

I've always been very apprehensive about carrying large sums of money on canoe trips. What frightens me most is the thought of watching a pack filled with cash disappear down a foamy rapid.

The money belt is much safer than packing money away. In the old days money belts were cumbersome and easy to detect. But now only the invisible zipper compartments in back suggest that they're anything but ordinary wide dress belts. You can carry hundreds of dollars in a money belt without fear of losing it on a river or in town.

Traveler's checks are another alternative. But they're only safer than cash if you don't lose the serial numbers. An obscure place in your car is more secure than the bottom of a wilderness pack sack or your own back pocket.

Nearly everyone from French Canada to the north slope of Alaska recognizes Visa. But again, a credit card is no good if you lose it. One friend punched a hole in a corner of his Visa card and attached a small metal key chain. He wears the card around his neck on a loop of parachute cord!

A real advantage of using a credit card in Canada is that you're billed at the current rate of foreign exchange. There are no special fees for converting American dollars to Canadian.

One question I always ask when I book a Canadian charter flight is, "Will you take Visa?" Not all charter companies do. And some that do pass the processing fee on to you! Others will give you a discount if you pay by Canadian money order, bank draft, or cash.

CAR KEYS

Many years ago when I was a boy, my family spent three weeks touring northern Canada by automobile. One night while we were asleep in an Ontario campground, we were robbed. The thief came right into the tent and stole my father's trousers and my mother's purse. Both sets of car keys were gone. The next day provincial police gathered keys from dozens of similar-make cars in an effort to find a mate. Ultimately they found a key that fit and had a duplicate made. But it would have been much easier if Dad had kept an extra set of keys in a magnet box under the hood!

HOW DO YOU FIND A RELIABLE PERSON TO SHUTTLE YOUR CAR?

A lot of nice rivers don't get paddled simply because canoeists can't find someone to shuttle their car. Actually, getting a shuttle is easy. It just takes persistence.

First, exhaust the standard resources—chambers of commerce, local fishing lodges, the Ministry of Natural Resources, community churches, and so on. Failing this, write the superintendent of schools in the area. The chamber of commerce or mayor can supply the name. A note in the monthly school bulletin will reach almost everyone in the community—you're sure to get a reply from an interested parent.

Your letter should include all essential details—date of shuttle, time, and exactly where you want to go. Be sure to tell what type of vehicle you're driving and whether it has an automatic or stick shift. If you're pulling a trailer, say so. A lot of drivers don't want the responsibility of a trailer. And don't forget to mention that you're willing to pay a reasonable fee for this service.

WATERPROOF YOUR MAPS

Everyone should have a complete set of waterproof maps onto which they've copied all pertinent data—drop figures, portage locations, dangers, and the like. You can waterproof maps with contact paper or chemicals. Contact paper, available at most dime stores, resists abrasion best and is absolutely waterproof. But it's expensive and bulky and you can't write on it.

Chemicals are cheaper and easier to apply. They make maps *water resistant* rather than waterproof. But you can write over them—a real plus if you plan to make notes on the map later.

I've had good results with Thompson's Water Seal—an industrial-strength compound that's used for sealing concrete block. You'll find it on the shelves of most hardware stores in aerosol cans and tins. I buy it by the quart and apply it to maps and journals with a polyurethane foam paintbrush. The product also does a fine job of waterproofing hats and clothing. Just attach a plastic pump spray head to the metal can and you're in business. Thompson's Water Seal is inexpensive and highly effective.

Water-resistant maps should further be protected by sealing them inside a plastic map case that's large enough to accept a full-size (unfolded) topographic map. A zipperlock or Velcro closure is more reliable than a plastic zipperlock. Cooke Custom Sewing and Grade VI (appendix B) make full-size map cases that are patterned after the wonderful ones I used in the army.

SALTWATER CHARTS AND TIDE TABLES

If your route terminates at salt water, such as James Bay, Hudson Bay, or Chantrey Inlet, you should obtain a local tide table and possibly a navigational chart of the estuary.

For example, the mouth of the Albany River is affected every six hours, twelve and a half minutes by tides that range from 2 to 8 feet. Naturally, islands, bays, and channels in that area will look much different as the water level changes, and of course, camping along tidal flats requires special techniques (see chapter 17).

Conversely, tides along the Arctic Sea's coast at the mouth of the Back, Coppermine, and Hood Rivers are much smaller—a foot or two. An up-to-date tide table will give you the specifics.

Contact the Department of Fisheries and Oceans in Ottawa for tide and current tables and nautical charts of Canada. Call the National Oceanic and Atmospheric Administration/National Ocean Survey (NOAA/NOS) in Riverdale, Maryland, for charts and tide tables of U.S. coasts, the Great Lakes, and sections of major rivers, as well as contoured fishing maps. Addresses are in appendix B.

NATIONAL ATLAS OF CANADA

This is the place to look for hard-to-find specifics about everything from climate and exploration to posts of the Canadian fur trade. You can buy the entire Canada atlas or select the individual sheets you need. Request a free table of contents from any Canadian map dealer. The atlas is sold only through authorized Canadian map dealers.

THE MILEPOST

If you're going to Alaska, you'll want to read *The Milepost,* a giant 800-page annual publication (it weighs three pounds!) that contains road maps, attractions, camping and wilderness travel information, tips for driving the Alaska Highway, customs requirements, hotels, charter air and emergency services, and much more. Everything you could possibly want to know about the forty-ninth state is contained here. And it makes enjoyable reading even if you never visit the land of the midnight sun.

THE NUNAVUT HANDBOOK

On April 1, 1999, the map of Canada was officially altered to reflect the formation of Nunavut, a new territory governed by the Inuit people of northwestern Canada. Nunavut includes those lands that lie roughly north and east of Yellowknife and north of Hudson Bay. At nearly 2 million square kilometers (about 780,000 square miles), Nunavut is more than four times the size of Sweden! Classic canoeing rivers like the Back, Thelon, and Kazan, which were once part of the Northwest Territories, are now part of Nunavut.

About one-fifth of Nunavut is now Inuit owned, and though the land isn't marked in any way, certain access restrictions apply in some areas. If you cross Inuit-owned lands, you should contact the appropriate Inuit Land Administration Office (see appendix B) for information about travel restrictions that may apply. Everything you need to know about canoeing in the new province of Nunavut is clearly spelled out in the giant *Nunavut Handbook*, which includes maps, photos, and regulations. The handbook (see appendix B for ordering information), which is really a small encyclopedia, is updated every few years.

REGISTER YOUR ROUTE

Canoeing in a remote part of Canada? Then file a trip plan with the Royal Canadian Mounted Police (RCMP). Registration is a form of life insurance; it guarantees that someone will come looking for you if you're not back within a reasonable time after your predicted date. The more isolated your route, the more seriously you should take registration and the specific date you set as a deadline.

There is no official procedure for registering Alaskan canoe trips. However, you won't get far into Alaska's back-country without a floatplane, so your pilot will invariably know where you are.

If you're meeting a charter floatplane at trip's end, you'd better be at the appointed place on time. If you're not, your pilot will contact the RCMP or Alaskan authorities and file a missing-persons report, which may initiate an air search.

On the other hand, you can be more liberal with your arrival date if your trip terminates at a town or rail line. Being a *few* days off schedule is only serious if you're meeting an airplane.

In the heat of a new trip's excitement it's easy to drive right past the last town and the RCMP office and neglect to register your route. So plan accordingly! And if you forget, use the phone, or relay your plans through the provincial police.

YOU CAN'T FISH WITHOUT A LICENSE!

Some friends and I once drove 500 miles to canoe a certain Ontario river near Lake Nipigon. We left after work on a Friday evening and drove all night. Several times we stopped and tried to buy fishing licenses, but it was too late—all the stores were closed.

At about 3:00 A.M. we arrived at our launch site—a shallow creek by a dirt logging road, 60 miles from the nearest town and source of fishing licenses.

If you want to fish, you'll need a license, and you can't get one in the wee hours of the morning. So schedule a daylight stop at a town or tourist lodge on the drive up. Or if that's impossible, purchase your license by mail (where permissible). The Provincial Bureau of Tourism can supply details. Alaskan anglers should write to the Alaska Department of Fish and Game (See appendix B).

FIREARMS—A PERMIT TO CARRY?

There's really no reason to carry a firearm on any canoe trip, even those in Alaska and the Northwest Territories. The only exception might be in certain parts of the Arctic where grizzly and polar bear encounters are common. Even here, however, it's unlikely you'll ever be attacked. Most bears will take off at a fast run at the first smell of you!

Nevertheless, some canoeists feel more secure in bear country if they are armed. Many authorities prefer a 12-gauge pump-action shotgun loaded with slugs. Slugs have much greater penetration than 00 buckshot and for this reason are the preferred load for big bears at close range. The pump action also allows for a fast second shot.

If you bring a 12-gauge shotgun, you may want to carry a few firecracker shells. They explode with a loud bang on impact and are often enough to scare troublesome bears away. Your state or provincial DNR should know where to get them. *Caution:* Cracker shells can start a forest fire if they impact in a dry grassy area! Plastic stinger shells (available only to law enforcement agencies) are another option. Experiments in the Churchill area show that stinger shells deter bears nearly 100 percent of the time.

The new short-barreled lever-action Marlin and Winchester Guide Guns, which are chambered for the powerful .45-70, .444, and new .450 Marlin cartridges, are another solution. These slim, handy rifles are easy to carry, and they stow well in a canoe. Chapter 9 suggests a convenient way to carry a firearm in a canoe.

Survival-minded paddlers may want to consider the venerable over/under rifle-shotgun made by Savage Arms Company. One version, called the Camper's Companion breaks apart for easy packing and gives you an instant choice between .22 rimfire (top barrel) and 20-gauge below. There's even room in the stock for extra shells. The Camper's

Companion would make a much better survival weapon than a standard shotgun, if the need arose.

Firearms regulations vary from province to province and state to state, so write for specifics before you pack your gun. Ontario, for example, flatly prohibits guns during the summer when no hunting is allowed. The Northwest Territories and Nunavut, on the other hand, have no restrictions. However, pistols of any kind are forbidden to Americans everywhere in Canada.

You must register your rifle or shotgun with Canadian customs at the border. The current fee is $50 Canadian. The "license" is good for one gun for one year. It's also wise to pre-register your gun with U.S. customs just before you enter Canada. This ensures that your gun won't be confiscated by U.S. authorities when you return to the States.

Be sure to check with the Canadian Wildlife Service or Alaska Department of Fish and Game, as the case may be (see appendix B), if you're going armed down a river that passes through a wildlife sanctuary. It's flatly illegal to hunt or bring any unsealed weapon into a wildlife preserve.

MIGRATORY BIRD SANCTUARIES

Contact the Canadian Wildlife Service or Alaska Department of Fish and Game if you intend to canoe through a migratory bird sanctuary. Migratory birds are very fickle during the nesting season and may abandon their nests if disturbed. The danger period runs roughly from mid-May to early July—the heart of the canoeing season. Wildlife authorities can provide particulars on what areas, if any, are closed to canoe traffic if you advise them of your route and travel dates.

CANOEING IN NATIONAL, STATE, AND PROVINCIAL PARKS

You must have a permit to camp and canoe in Alaskan and Canadian parks. Some parks require a substantial fee; others insist only on formal registration. If you plan to fish in a Canadian national park, you'll need a special fishing license. Contact the Bureau of Tourism or specific park for details.

CROWN LAND CAMPING FEES

Nonresidents of Canada need a camping permit to stay overnight on certain portions of Ontario Crown lands (mainly those north of the French and Mattawa Rivers). The daily fee

of $10 per person is similar to the prices charged in provincial parks, though in this case there are no services or conveniences. Certain nonprofit groups are exempted from this charge, which is also waived if you utilize the services of a tourist lodge. Get your camping permit at the same place you buy your fishing license. A map of the regulated areas may be obtained from any MNR district office or fish and wildlife license issuer.

Frankly, I'm less than enthusiastic about this regulation that, I am told, was designed to tame the bad habits of slob anglers. It's not the money I object to, but rather the daily charge that takes the wild out of the wilderness. On the other hand, I'd be more than willing to purchase a reasonably priced seasonal camping license.

COMMERCIAL GUIDE'S LICENSE

If you are guiding a trip into the Northwest Territories or Nunavut, you will need a commercial guide's license—which, I might add, is nearly impossible for the average American or Canadian to obtain. The Northwest Territories' Travel and Tourism Act (RSNWT 1988, c.T-7) defines a *guide* as "a person who for gain or reward accompanies or assists another person in an outdoor recreational activity." *Outfitter* is defined as one "who provides equipment to be used in connection with an outdoor recreational activity or provides guides or guiding services or both."

I discussed the matter with NWT officials and learned that you are considered a guide if you receive remuneration in any way (including a discounted or free trip) or contribute equipment (such as canoes) for use by participants. Essentially, all trips into the NWT and Nunavut are guided and, if the above conditions are met, require a commercial guide's license. You must apply to the government of the Northwest Territories or the appropriate Inuit Land Administration Office (appendix B).

Naturally, there's a processing fee, piles of paperwork, and documentation. I once tried to obtain a license to guide a Science Museum of Minnesota–sponsored canoe trip down the Back River. After months of calls and an inch-thick stack of communications, I was told that I would have to reapply through a different regional land office. I gave up in disgust and canceled the trip. I might add that the floatplane expenses for our trip would have amounted to $21,000—a real boost to the economy of the area.

There are ways to get around the licensing requirement:

You can arrange your trip through a commercially licensed Canadian outfitter who will supply everything, or you can simply rent essential items (like canoes) and thereby qualify under his license. The downsides are the extra expense and equipment whose quality may not meet your standards.

In all, it's a costly, messy, and difficult situation for U.S. and Canadian scout and church groups, museum eco-tours and scientific expeditions, and others who want to canoe the barren lands with an accomplished paddler they know and trust.

GET YOUR OWN ACT TOGETHER!

It's only common sense to be in good physical condition before you embark on a canoe trip. This means regular workouts during the winter months—jogging, swimming, cross-country skiing, jumping rope, and so on. Portaging your outfit over rugged trails—or no trails—is part of the game, and all too often the worst carries come early in the trip.

You should also get a physical exam before you set out on a major trip. A doctor's okay won't guarantee there'll be no problems later, but it is some assurance.

Equally important is a thorough dental exam. Nothing will spoil your run faster than a gnawing toothache.

Some years ago a friend developed a terrible toothache midway down the Kanaaupscow River in Quebec. For days he pleaded with the crew to pull the tooth out. Finally one man agreed. He doped my friend with a cup of Yukon Jack then yanked the tooth with a small parallel-jaw fishing pliers.

The operation was a success; my friend felt much better afterward. Needless to say, a dentist could have done the job *before* the trip.

DAILY JOURNAL

It's almost impossible to keep the facts and sequences of events correct on a long canoe trip if you don't write things down when they occur. A rapids to one person is a major falls to another; a grueling portage early in the trip becomes a cakewalk later. And of course the fish you catch increase in

Figure 4-1. A wild river is not all dangerous rapids and creature discomforts. Often there are long stretches where you can fish or photograph or drift along and let the world float idly by. Drifting along a quiet section of Manitoba's spectacular Seal River.

size logarithmically with each mile north you travel.

This is why you should keep a daily diary. It won't make or break your trip if you don't, but it will keep you honest when the weeks merge into years.

TAPE RECORDER AND VIDEO CAMERA

A small tape recorder may provide a more personalized account of your trip than a pencil-and-paper journal. A mini cassette recorder consumes less space than a notebook.

Video cameras may be more hassle than they're worth. They must be protected in a padded waterproof case, which discourages immediate use. On a long trip you'll need extra batteries or a solar recharging panel. Even practiced filmmakers will want a sturdy tripod. A lot of video cameras have enthusiastically accompanied me on my northern trips but most come out to play only at mealtimes and on setup whitewater runs. Frankly, I don't think the films they produce measure up to full-screen 35-millimeter color slides.

At this point you may be overwhelmed by all the many things you need to do before the wheels roll north. There seems to be an unending array of problems to solve and skills to accumulate. Details, skills, dangers. It is really worth the effort?

The first time you startle a moose that's feeding quietly among the lily pads, silhouette emblazoned against a backdrop of newborn sun and morning mist, or watch a thousand caribou do a thunder dance across the endless tundra, you'll know.

A wild river is not all dangerous rapids and creature discomforts. It is often quiet and beckoning. There is time to swim and fish and photograph; long stretches where you can lay down your paddle, lean against a pack, and let the world and its important thoughts float idly by.

Canoeing the wild rivers of the Far North makes you understand why primitive man felt so close to God.

CHAPTER 5
THE WILD-RIVER CANOE

In the canoes of the savage one can go without restraint, and quickly, everywhere,
in the small as well as large rivers. So that by using canoes as the savages do,
it would be possible to see all there is, good and bad, in a year or two.

—Samuel Champlain, 1603

My first canoe was a disaster. It measured 15 feet long, weighed an honest ninety pounds, and was slopped together from chopper-gun[1] fiberglass. As an added insult it was trimmed in plastic and painted to resemble the honorable birch-bark craft of a bygone era. In all it was a cheap, ugly canoe that excelled at nothing.

I thought it was beautiful—"a canoeist's canoe."

I paddled that canoe in blissful ignorance for two years. Then I joined a canoe club and rubbed shoulders with experts. Suddenly my beautiful, wonderful, do-everything canoe was a "dishpan," a "meat platter" . . . an ugly, boring pig. It was apparent I'd been had!

I put the tub up for sale. It went within a week to an unsuspecting canoeist.

A hundred bucks plus what I got for the old scow bought me a sleek new Sawyer Cruiser—a 17-foot, 9-inch, U.S. Canoe Association competition canoe that tipped the scales at barely sixty-five pounds. The Sawyer was a real canoe. There was absolutely nothing ugly or boring about it. But my dream boat had a single fault: It was so thin at the ends that it cut cleanly through waves rather than climbing confidently over them. Paddling bow on a wind-tossed lake was invigorating; water lept into my lap by the bucketful with each oncoming wave. It was even worse in big white water. Nevertheless, the Sawyer was fun to paddle—reason enough to keep any canoe. And to buy another.

My new canoe was a 17-foot shoe-keeled Grumman—state of the art for white-water boats in the mid-1960s. At last I had all the canoes I'd ever need. Or did I?

Deep within me was the yearning desire to paddle the wild rivers of the Far North. I wondered which of my canoes was best suited to the challenge. The Sawyer was unalloyed joy to paddle flat out along the nonintimidating rivers near my southern Indiana home, but it wouldn't handle big water or carry much of a load. And the tank-tough Grumman, though admittedly doggy on the flats, was king in white water even with a two-week supply of camping gear aboard. Once I sank the Sawyer in a rough-water crossing on Ontario's Northern Lights Lake; I had no desire to repeat that experience. And the Grumman? Well, it would get me there and back, but without precision, grace, or flair, or even speed.

It began to appear that the North Country was a highly diversified place. There was everything I could imagine—lakes of ocean size, tiny beaver streams and ponds, saltwater seas, shallow rocky creeks, deep lazy rivers, mile after mile of heart-pounding rapids, deep mucky portages, and mean rocky ones. And the list went on. Each trip north brought into play new dimensions, new ideas, and a growing dissatisfaction with the canoe I paddled. Slowly a picture of the perfect wild-river canoe began to emerge.

It should be long enough to track well but short enough to fit between the waves; broad and deep enough to carry a

---

[1]Chopped fiberglass and resin is sprayed into a mold and the whole allowed to harden. The canoe that results is heavy, inexpensive, and not very strong.

good load but with low ends so it wouldn't catch the wind. There should be no keel to catch on rocks, and the bottom would be slightly rounded or feature a subtle V to enhance stability in rough water. The ends would be fine enough for good speed below the waterline and deeply flared above to climb the waves. The canoe would be fast on the flats yet turn instantly on command. It would run dry in the wildest white water with the heaviest load of camping gear aboard, weigh less than seventy pounds, and be impossible to puncture.

I've been searching for my ideal canoe for thirty-five years now and still haven't found it. That's because no single canoe can do everything well. Often what's right for one tripping condition is wrong for another—a reason why experienced canoeists often own several canoes. (I have twelve, and they aren't nearly enough!) Those who regularly trip the wild waters of the Far North are very opinionated as to what is best. And these opinions vary widely, as you'll discover later. For this reason I'm reluctant to recommend specific canoe dimensions or even materials. What works perfectly for one person is all too frequently unacceptable to another.

Everyone has a notion of the kinds of wild rivers they want to paddle. Some envision vast open waters with few rapids and portages—rivers like the Mackenzie, Yukon, and Abitibi. Others conjure up dynamic white-water runs—the South Nahanni, Burnside, and Hood. And of course there's the more common middle ground—Missinaibi, Thelon, and Fond du Lac. Each river is different, and so too is the best canoe for paddling it. If you can identify your own tripping style and the specific kinds of waters you plan to paddle, you'll have no trouble finding the right canoe to meet the challenge. But if you want to canoe all of the above, you'll need to be more liberal in your thinking and select a more generalized craft—one you can trust in all types of water.

Amid your confusion you'll ultimately discover that the bottom line is your own safety. The rivers of the Far North can run very cold, even in early August. A capsize may be fatal. Suddenly the reality of it all appears. A wild-river canoe must be trustworthy and forgiving, strong enough to stay intact after you've hung it up on a midstream ledge with a month's worth of gear aboard, big enough to ride the waves of a giant lake or formidable rapid, yet light enough to portage without breaking your back. And it must be bolted together to stay that way after 1,000 miles of river and 100 overland.

A wild-river canoe is a pickup truck, not a sports car. Sports cars are fine for the easy rivers down home, but they're too flighty for use in the rugged and changeable environment of the Far North.

Enough. Let's get down to the basics of wilderness canoe design.

Figure 5-1 wil help you with terms.

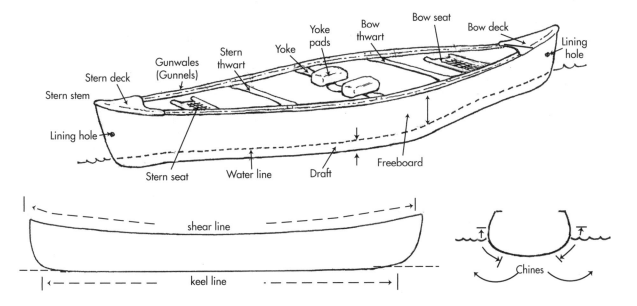

Figure 5-1. Canoe terminology

HOW LONG IS LONG ENOUGH?

Canoes are basically displacement hulls, so their maximum speed is a function of their length. Thus, the longer the canoe, the faster it will run.[2]

You can compute the relationship mathematically by applying this oversimplified formula:

$$S = 1.55 \times \sqrt{WL}$$

That is, speed in miles per hour equals 1.55 times the square root of the waterline length, measured in feet.

Thus, an 18½-footer will peak out at around 6.7 miles per hour while a 16-footer will run about 6.2 miles per hour. The difference is 7.5 percent—significant only at the end of a ten-hour day or when you're pushing hard into a wind.

ASYMMETRY

The displacement formula breaks down in shallow water, however, because a hard-pushed canoe produces a substantial bow wave that's difficult to climb over. Racers refer to this phenomenon as climbing, and they counteract it by paddling canoes that have long, narrow bows (to better cut the water) and fat, buoyant sterns (for better flotation in the wave trough). This asymmetric hull shape (see figure 5-2) produces greater speed *on any water*, especially if it's less than 2 or 3 feet deep.

This said, be aware that severely asymmetric canoes may be unpredictable in tricky currents. Many high-performance canoes built in the 1970s and 1980s featured bizarre asymmetry that caused big problems in bad rapids. But times—and designs—have changed. Now nearly all the best canoes—including beefed-up Royalex models designed for serious white water—are asymmetric.

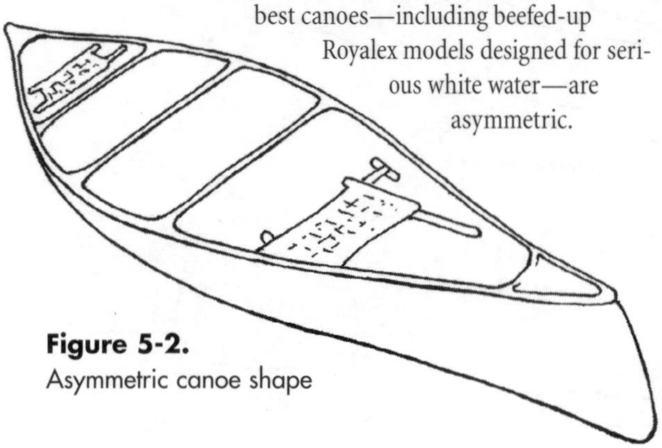

Figure 5-2.
Asymmetric canoe shape

SPEED AND EASE OF PADDLING

Speed and ease of paddling are *not* the same. The formula tells you only the *maximum* hull speed, not the amount of effort required to get it there. It's quite possible for a sophisticated 16-footer to paddle more easily than a workhouse 18-footer. But the longer canoe will always have a higher top speed.

A long canoe will also ride the waves of a wind-tossed lake more smoothly than a short one. A 15-footer is an abomination in a quartering sea—it torques out with each oncoming wave and leaves you fighting to keep on course. Add a foot more length and you gain stability and a better ride. Now you're beginning to feel like you're paddling a canoe rather than a washtub. But increase the length to 18 or 18½ feet and as if by magic the craft becomes completely manageable. It rises and falls gently with the waves like a monster battleship on a rolling ocean.

Okay, long canoes are more manageable than short canoes in a running sea, but they don't always run drier. If the wave phase (the distance between waves) is shorter than the canoe's own length, the canoe may plow and take on water. Under these conditions a shorter canoe—one that fits *between* the waves—would be more seaworthy even though it might make for a rougher ride. Seaworthiness and manageability are not the same. In boats of equal volume, seaworthiness is in fact the *reciprocal* of length.[3] Merely a matter of math: A 15-foot canoe will more easily fit between two waves or clear a low ledge than will an 18½-footer. And it'll be more maneuverable, too—simply because there's less boat to turn. All of which explains why white-water slalom canoes are always less than 16 feet long.

It would seem that you really need two canoes—a 15- or 16-footer for running technical white water and closely spaced waves, and an 18½-footer for everything else. And a magic genie to switch them on command!

The appropriate length is also a function of how you'll get the canoe to and from the river. If you plan to tie it to the outside struts of a Cessna floatplane, you'd better limit your length to 17 feet. (Some Cessna pilots won't carry canoes that are longer than 16 feet!) Of course you can always fly your big 18-footer on the floats of a Beaver or in the belly of a Twin Otter. But these planes aren't always available, and they're much more expensive than the tiny Cessnas.

[2]Lightweight canoes will, over *short* distances, exceed their displacement speed.
[3]Obviously, there's a point of diminishing returns.

Another variable that will affect your choice of canoe length is the amount of gear you'll carry. Sit down now and figure, as best you can, exactly how many number 3 Duluth packs you'll need *per canoe* to outfit a four-week trip. You might get by with four packs, but I'll bet you'll need one more. Really now, just where will you put five packs in a 16-foot canoe? If you remove the forward and aft thwarts, you might be able to stack two packs north of the yoke and three behind it. But it will be tight. Very tight! And what about the camera packs and extra paddles?

Loading a 16-foot canoe for a four-week trip is akin to traveling across America in a Volkswagen Beetle with a family of four. It can be done, but not comfortably. On the other hand, there's *plenty* of room in a good-sized 18-footer!

Ultimately you'll come to realize that for all-around use in the North Country, a high-volume 17- to 18-foot canoe is best. Certainly shorter and longer boats offer advantages, but the craft you may end up paddling is too frequently dictated by conditions beyond your control.

SHIP SHAPE

A canoe's personality is shaped by its ends. A craft with narrow ends will run fast but plunge deep and get you wet when the waves begin to roll. Conversely, a stout-ended boat will do the opposite; It'll be a pig to paddle on the flats but will run dry in the rough. At the far extreme are canoes with ends too wide—most 15- and 17-foot aluminum models— which pitch badly and slap violently into waves.

What you need is a pleasant compromise—plenty of buoyancy above the waterline, substantial fineness below.

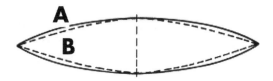

Figure 5-3. Nearly all the carrying capacity of a canoe is borne in the middle two-thirds of the hull. Here canoe A will handle a load much better than canoe B because its buoyant ends will ride up over waves rather than cutting through them. But canoe B is definitely the faster of the two canoes.

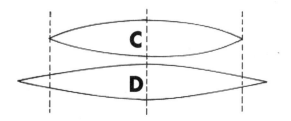

Figure 5-4. Canoes C and D have the same carrying capacity. Canoe D is faster than C, but C will ride the waves and rapids better (run drier).

Such flare permits the craft to fall gently to its deepest, most buoyant point before it rises predictably skyward. Untamed buoyancy had no place in a wild-river canoe—or any other kind. Flared ends are much better and safer.

It's interesting to note that nearly all the carrying capacity of a canoe is borne in the middle two-thirds of its hull. Thus end shape has little real effect on the actual freeboard with a maximum load. Figure 5-3 shows the relationship. Nevertheless, the rough-water characteristics of the two canoes are much different. Load both canoes to capacity and B may sink with the first oncoming wave while A rises confidently above it.

The differences become even more exaggerated when you change the length. For example, hulls C and D in figure 5-4 have the same carrying capacity even though they're not the same length. With an identical load aboard, the longer canoe will be faster, of course, but the shorter one with its more buoyant ends will ride the waves and rapids better. Manufacturers' capacity ratings are only meaningful if you understand these relationships.

WIDE OR NARROW?

Width is commonly measured at four places on a canoe (figure 5-5): at the gunnels or rails, at the widest point (called maximum beam), and at the 3-inch and 4-inch working waterline. It's pointless to talk about width until you understand how these variables are related. A canoe can be wide at the working waterline and narrow at the gunnels or vice versa. Or it can be narrow down low, wider midway up, and narrow again at the rails. Each configuration affects performance differently, and every design is dependent on the shape of the bottom.

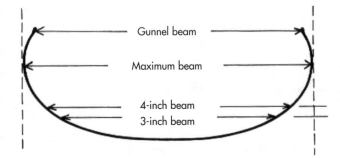

Figure 5-5. Width is measured at four places on a canoe—at the gunnels or rails, at the widest point (called the maximum beam), and at the 3- and 4-inch working waterline.

For example, the typical sportsman's canoe usually follows the outline of canoe E in figure 5-6: It's flat and broad down low and has extreme tumblehome or inward curve higher up. Such a craft feels rock-stable initially but it becomes unpredictable when the waves begin to roll. Lean a highly tumblehomed canoe even slightly in rough water and it'll unhorse you instantly.

Canoe D is a much better design. The bottom is slightly rounded and the sides flare outward. The flare is there for a reason—it directs oncoming waves away from the hull rather than into it. And the more you lean the craft, the more stable it becomes. In canoeing terms it firms up—exactly the opposite of what happens in a canoe with lots of tumblehome.

Okay, flared hulls with gently rounded or V-bottoms have

better sea manners than those with lots of tumblehome and flat bottoms, right? Well, yes . . . other things being equal. Surprisingly, some of the best wild-river canoes flatly defy design logic, or at least so it seems. The 17-foot, 2-inch Old Town Tripper, 18- and 20-foot Grummans, and 18½-foot Alumacraft are a few. That these canoes do so well with heavy loads in big water is due partly to their large size and—for the Old Town and Alumacraft at least—relatively fine V-shaped ends *below* the waterline.

Canoe design is much too complicated to describe fully in a single chapter. So keep an open mind and be aware that there are exceptions.[4]

KEELS—A DANGEROUS AFFECTATION

A keel will make any canoe track (hold its course) better. But it will also catch on rocks and upset you. Many of the canoe accidents in the Far North can be attributed to keeled canoes that hung up on a ledge or rock and dumped their occupants.

Good tracking is achieved by proper canoe design, not by an afterthought tacked lengthwise along the bottom. If keels had value, the Indians and voyageurs would have used them on their canoes. The real reason manufacturers use keels to stiffen a badly designed, flat, floppy canoe bottom. More than anything else, a keel is one feature you should avoid in a serious river canoe. Put your faith in good canoe design and your own paddling skills. Your keel-less canoe will do the rest!

Perhaps the one exception to the no-keels rule is the optional shoe keel offered by the makers of some aluminum

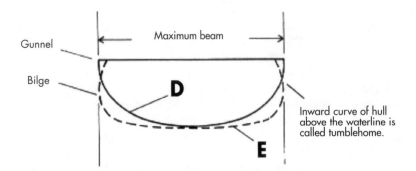

Figure 5-6. The typical sportsman's canoe usually follows the outline of canoe E, which feels rock-stable but becomes unpredictable when the waves begin to roll. Canoe D is much safer. Note that both D and E have the same maximum beam. This maximum occurs at the gunnels on canoe D and at the bilge in canoe E. Manufacturers' specifications are meaningless unless you understand the difference.

[4] Experienced canoeists are fond of judging the performance of a canoe by the shape of its hull. But canoeing is full of surprises. The only way you can be sure of a canoe's real performance is to paddle it!

canoes. Shoe keels are shallow, rounded affairs and so are less likely to catch on underwater obstacles. Nonetheless, they're still more dangerous than no keel at all!

TURNABOUT IS ESSENTIAL PLAY

The upward curve at each end of a canoe is called rocker. The greater the rocker, the more maneuverable the hull, the easier it will rise with waves, and the poorer it will track. A wild-river canoe is usually very heavily loaded, and the weight of all your camping gear presses the hull deep into the water (acts like a keel) and makes it difficult to turn. Consequently you need a fair amount of rocker—$1\frac{1}{2}$ inches at each end is not unreasonable. A canoe that tracks like a mountain lion when empty will turn with impudence when heavily loaded—which is exactly what you *don't* want for all-around wilderness use. Don't let some flat-water racing enthusiast talk you into buying a canoe with near-zero rocker. A wild-river canoe and a racing canoe are not the same. Adequate rocker plus heavily flared ends are essential for good performance in white water and running seas.

ADEQUATE DEPTH

Shallow depth is a real mistake in a wild-river canoe. You need at least $13\frac{1}{2}$ inches of sidewall at the center to keep out big waves. And often this isn't enough. Most of the best tripping boats are built to a maximum depth of around $14\frac{1}{2}$ inches—essential if you want a margin of safety in the rough stuff. Some canoe "experts" recommend a minimum safe freeboard of 6 inches, which is ridiculous: A boat that heavily loaded will drown you in the first big rapid if you don't have a fabric splash cover. Open canoes should maintain *at least* 9 inches of freeboard for safety in turbulent waters.

STRONG OR LIGHT—TAKE YOUR PICK

A wild-river canoe must be light enough to carry long distances but built strong enough to stay intact when you slide it down a ravine, drop it on a boulder, or smash it headlong into a rock with a full outfit aboard.

Unfortunately, weight and strength are closely related. You can have a strong, heavy canoe or a light, fragile one, but you can't have it both ways. Certainly there's a middle ground, but it's much narrower than you think. A canoe that's *big enough* and *strong enough* for running difficult rivers will probably weigh around sixty-five pounds in Kevlar, seventy-five pounds in aluminum or Royalex, and eighty or more in hand-laid reinforced fiberglass.

There are some really nice lightweight, high-performance, high-volume tripping canoes on the market that weigh less than fifty pounds. These are fine for canoeing the Boundary Waters of Minnesota, the outback of the Allagash, and the like. Use 'em in the gentle north of Ontario and Saskatchewan if you like, but watch out if you head into remote country with them. They may not hold up!

I'd flatly reject any deep-hulled 17- to $18\frac{1}{2}$-foot canoe that weighed much less than sixty honest pounds, regardless of claims made for it by the manufacturer. Either the maker is stretching the truth about the weight (a very common practice) or the boat is just too fragile for serious wild-river use.

Remember, northern rivers are not local streams. If your canoe destructs along the route, you may have a long, difficult walk out. And no matter how skilled you are, you'll make mistakes, which is precisely why you need strength and dependability.

Still confused about what to buy? Stay tuned; things will become clearer after I've reviewed the basic canoe building materials and the advice of experts.

ALUMINUM

Still the most abrasion-resistant and weatherproof material available. You can leave an aluminum canoe in a snowbank all winter and it'll come out looking like new in the spring. Aluminum is easy to repair, too. (See color figure 5-7.) Almost every bush pilot carries a rivet kit to fix his plane, and what works for him will mend your canoe. Aluminum doesn't lend itself to the most sophisticated hull shapes (though one defunct manufacturer—Beaver Canoes—has shown it can be done). Aluminum also dents, sticks to rocks, and is noisy and cold to the touch. But it's the longest lived of all canoe building materials.

Aluminum canoes, which a decade ago were the workhorses of the Far North, have now been largely replaced with "abuse 'em as you wish" Old Town Discovery and Coleman polyethylene craft. Polyethylene canoes are heavier but more reliable than aluminum canoes, especially in the rental trade.

If you like metal boats, look for T-6 heat-treated aluminum and flush rivets that won't shear off on rocks. Invariably, 18- and $18\frac{1}{2}$-footers are much better wild-river canoes than the more popular 17-footers. Avoid lightweight construction and standard deep keels.

Tip: Your aluminum canoe will slide off rocks more easily if you apply a thick coat of paste wax to the hull before (and several times during) your canoe trip.

Polyethylene and Royalex were the death knell for aluminum canoes. I don't know any accomplished wilderness canoeist who uses metal canoes anymore.

FIBERGLASS

Some of the best and worst canoes are constructed of fiberglass. There's no such thing as a good, cheap fiberglass canoe. Avoid chopper-gun specials, which are heavy and break easily. Instead look for all-hand layup construction—the telltale sign is the crisp outline of the fabric weave inside the hull.

Sight along the hull for signs of cheek (indents) and examine the inside of the canoe for bubbles, resin-starved (chalky) areas, and resin-flooded areas. Any of these defects indicates careless workmanship.[5]

Check out the stems (ends) of the canoe. They should be slightly rounded and not too square (figure 5-8). Square stems are fine for racing, because they allow the canoe to reach its longest legal length at the waterline. But they catch every thread of seaweed and are prone to break when you hit rocks.

Fiberglass lends itself to the manufacture of the most highly refined hull shapes, so it's natural that enthusiastic manufacturers will try to produce the most efficient paddling canoes possible. However, as I've pointed out repeatedly, the best paddling canoes don't necessarily make the best wild-river canoes. High-performance features have no place on a canoe if they detract from its versatility or ruggedness.

A fiberglass canoe must be carefully constructed to be strong enough for wild-river use. Stick to the most respected manufacturers in the industry and you can't go wrong. And remember that a good, tough fiberglass canoe will be neither ultralight nor inexpensive!

KEVLAR 49

Contrary to popular belief, canoes built of Kevlar 49[6] are not bullet proof. The layup used on a canoe is much less substantial than that of a policeman's flak vest. You *can* put a hole in a Kevlar canoe. All it takes is a really sharp object and a good head of steam!

Unit for unit Kevlar is about 40 percent stronger and half the weight of fiberglass, but the real strength-to-weight difference of a finished canoe is less than you think. That's because much of a canoe's weight is in its resin and trim-seats, decks, and rails. There are also considerable differences between the ways Kevlar and fiberglass are used.

For example, compare an impeccably built eighty-pound

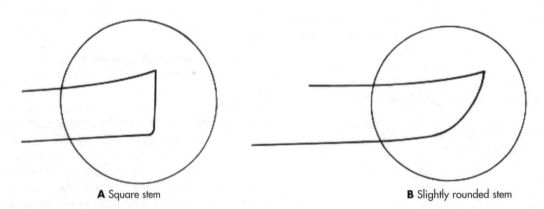

A Square stem   **B** Slightly rounded stem

Figure 5-8. Canoe A has square stems; canoe B has rounded ones. Square stems are fine for racing but they're fragile and they catch seaweed.

[5]Some of the very best canoes exhibit one or more of these defects. An occasional cheek, small resin flood, or the like is permissible, because these defects are cosmetic and don't affect hull strength or performance.
[6]Kevlar is an incredibly strong and very expensive gold-colored fabric that's manufactured by DuPont. It's commonly used in the construction of tires and bullet-proof vests. The product has many industrial applications.

all-fiberglass canoe to an identical canoe of the same weight that's built entirely of Kevlar. The Kevlar version will be much tougher than its glass brother. But manufacturers seldom build them this way; instead you get a fifty-pound canoe that's easy to carry but possibly no stronger than the eighty-pound fiberglass model. There are all sorts of different layups, some strong, others barely adequate. You get exactly what you pay for!

When Kevlar appeared in the early 1970s, canoes built of all Kevlar were the rage. However, manufacturers soon discovered that Kevlar, used alone, wasn't very durable. Indeed, Charlie Walbridge, the guru of American white-water boating, was one of the first to document the problems of all-Kevlar canoes. Charlie states in his *Boatbuilders Manual* that "Kevlar has excellent flexural strength but poor compressive strength." (When you break a stick over your knee, you are elongating it on the top and compressing it on the bottom.) This means that the outer layer of Kevlar frequently breaks, creating soft hinge points in the hull. The point is that an all-Kevlar canoe is less durable than most people think. (See color figure 5-9.)

Today's manufacturers laminate Kevlar with other materials to take advantage of our current knowledge of what works best where. State-of-the-art Kevlar layups utilize E-glass, S-glass (an abrasion-resistant form of common E-type fiberglass), Kevlar, nylon, Dacron, carbon fiber (graphite), closed-cell foams, and other materials in an array of dazzling configurations. Kevlar isn't Kevlar anymore!

When repair time rolls around, be aware that unlike fiberglass, Kevlar can't be sanded. It frizzes up like cotton candy when it's cut. This is why Kevlar canoes are always patched with fiberglass, which can be sanded to a velvet-smooth finish. The bottom of a well-worn Kevlar canoe may look like it needs a haircut! The old frizzy-bottom problem has been largely eliminated by laminating abrasion-resistant materials over the Kevlar.

There's much more to Kevlar-composite construction than can be told in these pages. If you want a good primer, order the We-no-nah Canoe Company catalog (see appendix B). It contains in-depth information about state-of-the-art construction techniques and canoe design.

On a personal note I might add that as much as I love Kevlar-composite canoes (I have three Bell Canoeworks black and gold Kevlar-graphite solo canoes), I would prefer not to take one on a mean wilderness river. Read Final Thoughts About Royalex on the next page and you'll see why.

Figure 5-10. No canoe is indestructible. These remains of what appears to be a 17-foot Grumman canoe were found by Bob Dannert along the remote Back River in Canada's Northwest Territories.

NEW CONSTRUCTION LAY-UPS

Layups continue to evolve as manufacturers blend new composites and wait for time to grade the results. All-Kevlar and ultralight pre-preg (Kevlar cloth is pre-impregnated with resin then cured at high temperatures in special molds) layups loom as past reminders that new ideas aren't always good ideas. But good things like We-no-nah's once revolutionary Tuff-Weave formulation, which combines cross-linked Compet polyester and fiberglass, hang around because they work as promised. Foam-core canoes, which were once bad-mouthed by rough-water trippers, are now rugged enough for demanding trips (though they remain a pain to repair). It is very unusual today to see a foam-core canoe delaminate on impact.

Kevlar remains the preferred building material for strong, lightweight, go-fast canoes. Graphite (carbon-fiber) composites are coming on strong, though, and factory-colored Kevlar (red is the only color available at this writing) commands new buyers. Wood and metal trim options are much neater looking and less obtrusive than those of years past. Check out the Bell Canoeworks, Dagger, and We-no-nah Canoe Company aluminum rails and you'll see how far metal trim has come.

COLOR

When I wrote the first edition of this book, green was the most popular canoe color. Now red appears to be in vogue. Safety-wise, bright colors—red, yellow, almond, and white—are by far the best. Try locating an overturned blue or green canoe in a river and you'll see why!

I once lost my green Old Town Tripper along an undefined—and unrefined—portage in Saskatchewan when I set it down to scout the way. When I returned it took me thirty minutes to find the canoe—its green color blended perfectly with the scrub green vegetation.

My own color preference is white or almond. These colors don't show scratches and (in Kevlar-composite construction) make for a lighter boat. That's because it usually takes less gel-coat pigment to get a white or almond color than a deep red, blue, or green one. Colored Kevlar and fiberglass canoes all scratch white, so it doesn't take long for the bottom of a shiny red canoe to become a mass of white claw marks. White canoes scratch white, too, so the damage doesn't show. It's also easier to get a good color match on a white boat than a colored one when the time comes to refinish small areas.

Admittedly, I have a deep fondness for canary yellow canoes. Yellow canoes are highly visible in the river, on portages, and in photos. Canoe makers tell me that yellow is the most unpopular color. Too bad, because it's the best one for the bush.

ROYALEX

Royalex is an ABS (Acrylonitrile-Butadiene-Styrene) thermoplastic from Uniroyal. The number of thicknesses and laminations used are specified by the canoe maker. Some Royalex layups are quite substantial; others are merely adequate. Again, you get just what you pay for. One popular layup consists of seven layers of material—an expanded ABS foam core, two thicknesses of ABS plastic sandwiched to each side of the core, and an outer sheath of colored cross-linked vinyl to protect the ABS from decomposing in the sun. Royalex is extremely tough and very slippery. It will slide over ledges that stop aluminum canoes in their tracks and break or damage glass or Kevlar craft. A swamped Royalex canoe will often come through the toughest rapids unscathed and pop back into near-perfect shape even after being folded completely around a midstream boulder.

Royalex can withstand severe impact but only limited abrasion. Continued dragging through shallows reduces the smooth vinyl skin to a mass of deep cuts. Nonetheless, the product is incredibly durable, and for this reason is the favorite of many white-water daredevils and Arctic canoe trippers.

Lightweight Royalex

R84 Royalite is a lighter form of Royalex. It's similar to conventional Royalex, but the laminate is usually thinner, and a weatherable plastic skin is used in place of the vinyl outer layer. R84 is stiffer and about 10 percent lighter than conventional Royalex. It's is not as strong as old-fashioned Royalex but it can be formed into tighter curves, which allows the manufacture of more sophisticated hull shapes. For example, my R84 Royalite (Dagger calls its layup R-light 2) Dagger Sojurn solo canoe is 14 feet, 9 inches long and weighs just forty-three pounds complete with American white ash trim. Pound for pound, an R84 Royalite canoe may be no stronger than a good all-fiberglass canoe, but it will probably weigh and cost less.

Are R84 Royalite canoes strong enough for a mean Canadian river? In the hands of a competent paddler, yes! Novices may need more strength, which naturally means more weight.

Final Thoughts About Royalex

Royalex is the choice for remote rivers and mean rapids, simply because no other material takes abuse so well. Here's why Royalex canoes and wild Canadian rivers go together:

- Your canoe is strapped to the struts of a chartered floatplane. The pilot winches the straps so tightly that they permanently dent your canoe.

- You drag your canoe for miles down a shallow rocky river. The bottom is a mass of deep gouges and scratches.

- You slide your canoe down a rock face. The craft bangs along the rocks.

- There's a 3-mile portage through a swamp. You save energy by hauling the canoe on a line, like a dog on a leash (a common practice on the Arctic tundra).

- You load your canoe into the boxcar of a train. Packs are wedged inside the canoe and two more canoes, filled with gear, are stacked on top. The bottom canoe flattens and takes on a tired look.

Would you really want to treat a $2,000 Kevlar canoe this way?

POLYETHYLENE

This is basically the same stuff they make poly bottles out of, only thicker and with added color. Polyethylene is strong stuff, and it's easily molded into the most complex shapes—though manufacturers of open canoes have been less than daring in this respect.

Polyethylene is very floppy, so it must have lots of curves, ribs, keels, struts, and the like to keep it in shape, which defeats the advantages of the material. Polyethylene will give when it strikes a rock, but not if it's held in place with aluminum ribs and struts like those used on the Coleman canoe.

The problem is academic: How do you stiffen a polyethylene hull without resorting to internal supports?

In 1985 the Old Town Canoe Company discovered a practical solution. It sandwiched a polyethylene foam core between two layers of rotationally molded cross-linked polyethylene sheet. The result was the Discovery canoe—a tough, rigid performer whose properties are similar to those of sandwiched Royalex, but at a much lower cost.

Figure 5-11. A Royalex Old Town Tripper gracefully negotiates a rapids along the Hood River, Nunavut, Canada. Caribou antlers, like these, are a common find along rivers of the Far North.

The bad news is that foam-core polyethylene canoes are heavy, and their hull designs are less than daring. Accomplished canoeists refer to these uninspiring canoes as

Figure 5-12. An Old Town 169 Discovery (polyethylene) canoe. Kopka River, Ontario.

pushers, which is an impolite way of saying that they don't paddle efficiently. But press an enthusiast hard and he or she will admit that Discos (Old Town Discoveries) are good, solid canoes that will get you there and back.

There are many models in the Discovery series, but the 169 (16 feet, 9 inches) and 174 (17 feet, 4 inches) canoes are most popular. The 169 model is actually a polyethylene copy of the venerable 17-foot, 4-inch Royalex Old Town Tripper—one of the premier expedition canoes. Due to shrinkage during the molding process, the 169 canoe is slightly smaller than its Royalex cousin, though performance on the water is about the same. Both 169s and 174s have successfully negotiated many of the major rivers in the high Arctic. The 174s have more space for gear than do the smaller 169s-important on a long trip. But the 169s are lighter and livelier, especially in white water. If you want a good strong boat at a very low price, a Disco is the way to go.

FIBERGLASS-COVERED WOOD-STRIP CANOES

Nearly every new canoe begins life as a fiberglass-covered cedar-strip prototype. The finished canoe is polished, and a commercial mold is made from it.

A well-built cedar-strip tandem canoe will weigh well less than sixty pounds and be about as strong as an all-fiberglass canoe of the same weight. It will also be much stiffer and prettier. Practiced paddlers agree that wood-strip canoes are the best paddling canoes of all. (See color figure 5-13.)

Friends and I began building solo strippers in the early 1970s when solo canoes were an industry oddity. We used our wood-strip solos regularly on Class II and III white water (see appendix E), even in the deep Ontario bush. Our boats required occasional patching (with duct tape) but they never let us down. Admittedly, strip canoes aren't strong enough for a major trip down a rocky river, though I'd take one if it were the only canoe I owned.

Strip canoes can, however, be built strong enough for rocky rivers, if you know some tricks. For example, you can use thicker strips on the bottom and cover the inside hull with Kevlar instead of fiberglass; carbon fiber may be used outside the hull below the waterline; S-glass can be substituted for E-glass in abrasion-prone areas. Essentially you're building a modern Kevlar-composite canoe with a wooden core. Join the Minnesota Canoe Association and the expert builders will teach you more tricks.

If you have about a hundred hours of free time (spread out any way you like) and can drive a nail straight, you can build a canoe. Power tools aren't needed. Plans—and the best canoe building book on the planet—are available from the Minnesota Canoe Association. Epoxy resin, precut wood strips, gunnel stock, and more can be mail-ordered from the Northwest Canoe Company in St. Paul, Minnesota. Addresses are in appendix B.

WOOD-CANVAS CANOES

Two decades ago, wood-canvas canoes were a dying breed. Now makers are springing up everywhere, and the boats they build are spectacular! Compare a modern Bourquin, Stewart River, or Loonworks canoe to a turn-of-the-century Chestnut or Old Town and you'll see how far wood-canvas craftsmanship (or craftswomanship, in the case of Jeannie Bourquin) has come. *Canoe and Kayak* magazine's annual buyer's guide lists most of the wooden-canoe builders. If you want to know them all, you'll have to join the Wooden Canoe Heritage Association (see appendix B).

There's a joy to paddling a wood-canvas canoe that no other craft—not even a wood-strip one—can provide. Perhaps it's the smell of varnish and painted canvas, or the lively feel of the wooden ribs and planking. Maybe it's the admiring looks of passersby, or just the knowledge that every part of this canoe is natural and replaceable. Wood-canvas canoes constantly remind you that the first part of wilderness is wild!

Are wood-canvas canoes strong enough for adventurous trips? You bet they are, if you paddle them well and care for them proudly. Would I want to strap one on the floats of a bush plane or drag one through rocky shallows? Absolutely not! These canoes are too beautiful and precious to abuse. Still, they are eminently suitable for use on any river if manned by competent paddlers. I applaud their rebirth.

FOLDING CANOES

Joel and Bev Hollis reported on their 1998 experiences with a PakCanoe on the Kuujjua River in a letter to Alv Elvestad, the chief executive officer of ScanSport:

In retrospect we wish we had our folding PakCanoe rather than our Old Town Tripper, especially since we had such long portages. The Tripper weighs about 95 pounds outfitted, the PakCanoe weighs about 50 pounds.

Figure 5-14. Folding canoes are tough, light, and seaworthy! PakCanoes, like the one shown here, have been proven in the toughest rapids.

Also, the first week of the trip we had low water, and had to drag our boat. Of all the boats on the river, the PakCanoe performed best. The inflatable canoe developed leaks in the bottom and floated very low because of the heavy load of gear. The Tripper did okay, but most of the vinyl outer layer wore off, and the Kevlar bang plates were badly ground down. The PakCanoe developed some minor abrasion on the keel strip, but it was easily patched. Also, the PakCanoe seemed to float higher than the other boats, which made it easier to drag.

I first saw folding canoes in action in 1992, on the Hood River in Canada's Northwest Territories. I was portaging my Royalex canoe around a particularly dicey Class III drop (see appendix E) when I observed three forest green Ally folding canoes heading into the rapids. I just shook my head and said "no way!"

Seconds later a canoe impaled upon a rock and began to fold around it. Suddenly, the hull broke loose and the craft slithered on, bouncing off and twisting around rocks in its path. A second canoe easily negotiated a 3-foot ledge I would have lined. It bent nearly in half as the bow climbed out of the wave trough!

The crew, which was from Norway, put in below the rapid, and we shared some tea and smiles. I learned that they had canoed several Arctic rivers, though this was their first with folding canoes. Our crews continued to play tag down-river for two more days, and I watched the Norwegians run other rapids we chose to line or portage around. I vowed that I would never again thumb my nose at folding canoes.

When I got home I called the manufacturer and asked for information. I learned that many significant canoe trips have been made in folding canoes.

ScanSport is the only manufacturer of folding canoes in North America. It began making boats in 1995. At first its canoes were sold exclusively by Mad River as the Escape Series; then in 1998 the company began its own distribution under the new name Pakboats/PakCanoes.

PakCanoes range in size from 14 to 17 feet and weigh thirty-eight to fifty-three pounds. The 16-footers we saw on the Hood weighed 48 pounds and had an advertised capacity of 760 pounds. Seventeen-footers weigh just 2 pounds more and will carry 910 pounds. Overall, the design is a significant improvement over the Ally folding canoes that are built in Norway. The hulls are formed by a reinforced PVC skin held under tension by an interlocking framework of tubular aluminum. The $\frac{1}{4}$ inch of foam is laminated to the inside bottom for extra strength. Assembly takes about thirty minutes. The seats are adjustable for sitting or kneeling, and rocker can be tuned to suit different paddling conditions. The disassembled canoe stores in a 35- by 17- by 13-inch bag. Prices are similar to what you would pay for a Kevlar canoe.

Figure 5-14A. For big waves and huge holes, SOARs are superior to any hard-shelled or folding canoe.

THE WILD-RIVER CANOE

I discovered inflatable canoes in 2003, when Larry Laba, CEO of SOAR Inflatables, invited me to paddle the Gates-of-Ladore section (big rapids!) of the Green River in Utah. SOAR boats are self-bailing, so water that comes over the side drains right out. You feel invincible after the first rapid. SOARs are much faster and more controllable than rafts but are slower and less responsive than canoes—you have to choreograph long-distance moves. But they literally turn on a dime!

Except for some custom shop products, that's about it for canoe building materials. Read the preferences of the experts that follow. Then sit down and put your thoughts in order.

Bob O'Hara

Bob O'Hara is one of the most widely traveled Arctic canoeists on the planet. Since 1969, he has spent every summer in the Far North. In all, he has canoed twenty-two Arctic rivers, some several times. A partial list includes the Thelon, Coppermine, Back, Dubawnt, Kazan, Elk, Clarke, Meadowbank, Kunwak, Quoich (first descent), Ellice, Horton, Nanook, Lockhart and Hanbury Rivers, plus several historic routes in Quebec and Manitoba. Once he paddled on the ocean from Wager Bay to Repulse Bay.

O'Hara has a keen eye for the unusual and spectacular. His riveting multiscreen slide shows—which detail the flora, fauna, native culture, and nature of a river—are very popular with schools, colleges, conferences, and conventions. He's a member of the Explorers Club of New York.[7]

Bob O'Hara is an extremely competent Arctic traveler. Neither he nor his crew has ever suffered a serious injury, and he has never lost a person to drowning.

My choice of canoes is based more on affordability and function than high performance and good looks.

The first canoes I paddled were made from wood and canvas. They paddled like a dream but they were heavy and easily damaged. So I naturally turned to aluminum canoes, which until fairly recently were the workhorses of the North. From 1969 to 1988 I relied on 17-, 18-, and 20-foot Grummans (the 18-foot shoe-keeled model was my favorite) for most of my travels. Around 1988 I began to use Old Town Discovery (models 169 and 174) poly-ethylene canoes. They were strong and trustworthy, and they slid over rocks (important when lining) more easily than aluminum canoes. They were also very inexpensive. An added benefit is that three 17-foot Old Towns fit into the belly of a Twin Otter floatplane, whereas two 18-foot Grummans are a full load. Adding a third crew to a trip significantly lowers the cost of flying to and from a river.

I frequently store my canoes at a northern village where temperatures can plunge to 60 below. Old Town Discoveries are able to withstand the cold (no cracks) as well as the Grummans.

In 1999 I tried a 17-foot Royalex Dagger Venture. It is a very full-volume boat and it turns on a dime. The Venture has plenty of room for gear (more than a 174 Discovery or Old Town Tripper) and it handles superbly in white water. At barely seventy pounds it is also reasonably light. I really like this boat and plan to use it for more river trips in the North.

Canoes are like cars—there is no one perfect model. What works best for one kind of trip may be awkward for another. That's why I have more than ten different canoes!

Fred Gaskin

Fred Gaskin has paddled many of the major rivers of the Canadian Arctic, retracing the historic tundra and barren-land canoe routes of the eighteenth- and nineteenth-century explorers. In addition to tripping on scores of rivers within the timberline, he was among the first North

---

[7]To reach O'Hara for bookings, write to him at 6001 Goodrich Avenue, St. Louis Park, MN 55416-2424, or call (952) 927–0874.

Americans to canoe in Arctic Siberia using North American (Old Town) open canoes. Fred's stories of his canoeing expeditions have appeared in many Canadian, British, and U.S. publications, including James Raffin's book Wild Waters. *Fred is a fellow of the Explorers Club, the Royal Geographical Society, the Insurance Institute of Canada, as well as president of Bradley Gaskin Marshall Insurance Brokers in Cambridge, Ontario.*

Fred Gaskin has been a part of this book since the first edition appeared in 1984. He told me in 1999 that what he wrote then still stands.

> *Eighteen-foot canoes are the best by far in rough water. Our fraternity has used four types. In the early years we used cedar plank covered with fiberglass, and also fiberglass canoes, and until 1974 we used aluminum canoes. Now we use only Old Town ABS Royalex canoes. No other canoe provides the safety, efficiency, utility, and maneuverability of the Royalex canoe. Our canoes absorbed tremendous punishment on our ascent of the Yellowknife River on our way to the Coppermine River in the Northwest Territories. We dragged them loaded up ledges and rock-filled rapids mile after mile, yet they seemed to shrug off every scrape and impact given them. On one occasion a canoe was dropped several feet onto projecting rocks—it merely bounced and showed no scar. We have used both the 17-foot, 2-inch Old Two Tripper and the 18-foot Voyageur and they are both marvelous canoes, ideally suited to the harsh requirements of the North. The 18-foot Voyageur provides a smoother run through rough water and its lower 13½-inch depths gets you more distance against those inevitable headwinds.*

Alex Hall

Alex Hall is a legend. He spends every summer (the entire summer!) canoeing the rivers in the Northwest Territories and Nunavut. He has canoed more miles in the barren lands than any other person. In the mid-1970s he made two eight-week solo trips in the barren lands without resupply. He once made a seventy-eight day trip without resupply!

"Some summers I paddle more miles than I drive all year," says Alex, who has canoed more than forty different rivers in the NWT (now largely Nunavut). His favorites are

often repeated again and again. For example, he's done the Back River five times and the Thelon fifty!

Alex has a master's degree in wildlife biology and a special affinity for tundra wolves. He helped save the Thelon Game Sanctuary when it was under siege by the mining lobby in the 1980s. In James Raffan's Ph.D. thesis, the final paragraph states: "My hope for the Thelon Game Sanctuary is that it will remain undeveloped in perpetuity and that there will always be an Alex Hall to keep it safe from harm."

Alex Hall was the first professional guide to outfit and lead canoe trips in the Northwest Territories. He began guiding in 1974 and continues to this day. Canoeists who've traveled with him say that he is an encyclopedia of wilderness and biological lore. His guiding service, Canoe Arctic (see appendix B), emphasizes remote wilderness and wildlife, not white-water thrills.

> *In the late 1970s I replaced my aluminum and Kevlar canoes with 17-foot Old Town Royalex Trippers. Today, the Tripper is still the principal canoe I use in my guiding business. The Tripper is a great all-purpose canoe. It can pack a good load, it handles superbly in white water, and it tracks well enough on windy lakes. I've soloed this canoe for hundreds of miles in the barren lands: It may not win any canoe races but it would be difficult to find a better all-around canoe for wilderness tripping.*
>
> *Royalex canoes are still the toughest on the market. They'll slip and slide over almost everything. They're so forgiving that as long as they're pointed downriver, they're likely to get even a pair of novices through the most difficult rock gardens, right-side-up. If you ever put a hole in one, it's easily repaired with fiberglass.*
>
> *I love the classic shape of the Tripper. It rides up on waves instead of knifing through them. If you turn a Tripper over on the ground, there's plenty of room beneath it to store packs and oddities out of the rain. It will also sit squarely on the ground on its side, thereby providing a superb windbreak for your stove. I don't like canoes with V-shaped hulls because they do none of these things.*

For the past dozen years, I've paddled a 20-foot XL Royalex Tripper during the summer. At 105 pounds it's tough to portage, but it handles well with 1,000 pounds aboard, and it's as fast as its 17-foot cousin. An advantage of the 20-foot canoe is that you can nest the smaller 17-foot Tripper inside, and fly them together in one load on a floatplane.[8] This eliminates a second flight.

Bob Dannert

Bob Dannert has paddled the Elk/Thelon, Coppermine, Back, Consul, Simpson, Hood, Ellice, Dubawnt, Kunwak, and Kazan Rivers in Nunavut along with scores of routes in Saskatchewan, Ontario, Alberta, and Manitoba. He has made three solo trips that lasted more than fifty days. In all, Bob has logged more than 6,000 miles on northern rivers. There's hardly a year when Bob Dannert doesn't canoe up North. Bob's favorite river (and mine) is the Hood. Each of us has done it twice.

Bob retired from his job as a foods scientist for General Mills in Minneapolis in 1996. His thoroughness on the job is evident in how he plans his trips. He researches routes much the way he researched his Ph.D. thesis. Bob and I canoed the Hood River together with a crew of six in 1983. He's competent, jovial, and always concerned about the welfare of his crew. Safety is his number one concern.

I have paddled many canoes over the past twenty-five years, beginning with 18-foot Grummans and progressing on to Old Town Trippers and Discoveries—and finally, a Dagger Venture, which is my favorite tandem canoe. But my 15-foot Bell Starfire, which I've named Akaitcho X after the Copper Indian chief who guided Sir John Franklin down the Coppermine River (1819–21), is my favorite solo craft. This tough and beautiful canoe has functioned flawlessly on three solo trips, including two barren-land trips of over fifty days. Akaitcho X (it's my

tenth canoe) cruises easily at around 4 miles per hour with 500 pounds of gear on board. The Starfire is predictable and seaworthy and it maneuvers well in Class II and III rapids. I have confidently paddled my Starfire on lakes with waves large enough to keep my tandem canoes on shore.

My Starfire has withstood the shock of bashing many rocks. It has been dragged over rocks, and the wind has blown it dozens of feet across the tundra. The slight damage that has occurred was easy to repair. The stiff yet forgiving Kevlar/carbon-fiber hull slides over rocks easily (almost as easily as a Royalex canoe). Portaging is a breeze because my Starfire weighs just forty pounds. The Starfire is also strikingly beautiful. When this "Black Beauty" passes by, all eyes on shore turn and look with envy.

Verlen Kruger

Verlen Kruger has paddled more than 90,000 miles—which, according to the Guinness Book of Records, is 20,000 more than anyone else! His first significant trip was in 1971, when he and Clint Waddell paddled from Montreal to the Bering Sea (6,220 miles) in less than six months. Then in 1983 he and Steve Landick completed a 28,043-miles cross-continent

voyage in solo canoes. Soon afterward, Verlen and his fiancée Valerie Fons paddled the length of the Mississippi River in a tandem craft Verlen designed. The speed record they set still stands. Verlen and Valerie later paddled from the Arctic Ocean to the southern tip of South America in Kruger-designed twin solo canoes—a journey of 21,246 miles. In all, Verlen has paddled and portaged the equivalent to nearly three and a half times around the world!

My first time in a canoe was in 1963, at age forty-one. The canoe changed my life completely. It was as

---

[8]Old Town 174 Discoveries can be nested if you remove the trim.

though I had discovered what I was meant to do.

I keep a harem of at least twenty canoes on hand for personal use, but the one I'm presently in love with (my all-time favorite for wilderness travel) is a partially decked solo canoe called the Sea Wind. Best described as part canoe, part kayak, it's number forty-nine of the experimental models I designed and built over the last twenty years, and it is by far the best. It's the canoe I paddle on all my trips.

I prefer a roomy, stable, intensely seaworthy canoe with a fast cruising speed and a hull shape that will handle unexpected turbulence. In the long haul how easily a canoe paddles at cruising speed is more important than its top-end performance at peak racing speed. To me the most important feature is comfort. A canoe must also be tough enough to take a beating without destructing.

My favorite tandem canoe is the Kruger Cruiser (the Mississippi Super Cruiser), which I designed and in which Valerie and I broke the all-time speed record for traversing the length (2,348 miles) of the Mississippi River: twenty-three days, ten hours, and twenty minutes. The Kruger Cruiser is 18½ feet long, 36 inches wide, and 15 inches deep (see color figure 5-15). Like the Sea Wind, it's partially decked and built in an expedition Kevlar layup. I currently build a limited number of Sea Winds and Kruger Cruisers. Inquiries are welcome (see appendix B).

Hap Wilson

Hap Wilson—an artist, author, photographer, wilderness canoe guide, and environmentalist who believes that harmonic bliss is a double shot of single-malt Scotch whiskey in hot chocolate, a dry pair of wool socks, a bouldery Class III rapid, or a wicked tailwind—escapes responsibility by canoeing remote Canadian rivers. Hap's beautifully illustrated  *articles have appeared in* **Explore, Kanawa, Outdoor Canada, Canoe and Kayak** *and* **Canadian Geographic** *magazines. He has written and illustrated six outdoor books, including the best-selling* **Temagami Canoe Routes, Missinaibi,** *and* **Voyages,** *which won the Natural Resources Council of America Award as the best environmental book of 1995. His latest work,* **Wilderness Rivers of Manitoba,** *promises to be a classic resource.*

Hap Wilson is a sincere humanist and dedicated environmentalist—an extremely competent wilderness wild man who relishes remote, physically demanding rivers. I heartily recommend his books, his artistry, and his sage advice.

A favorite canoe should be one that talks to you—lets you know if you are doing all the right things that inspire it to perform. There's an atavistic symbiosis between self and canoe—a legendary respect born of trust and intimacy; a kindred relationship rivaled only by that which you may share with a spouse or best friend.

I find it rather prohibitive trying to strike up warm feelings with my plastic boats. It's much like owning a team of sled dogs that live only for the trail and harness. The harder you push them, the better they seem to like it . . . and they get you where you want to go, but not without coercion, muscle, and mild frustration.

My favorite canoe is a 1930s vintage wood-canvas Peterborough Trapper's Special. It has several broken ribs, leaky canvas pulling away at the gunnels and a partially rotted deck. Some might have retired it long ago, but when I climb into this warm old relic it's like stepping out on the dance floor with a beautiful debutante.

Remote rivers with canoe-eating rapids require a different approach. For short jaunts (pool-and-riffle rivers), I prefer the Swift Dumoine and Old Town Appalachian. Both handle well and are reasonably quick. For extended voyages where additional space is required, cold weather and water a certainty, and running long Class III rapids, the Dagger Venture reigns supreme. I've also relied on the Old Town Tripper, which, like the DeHavilland Beaver aircraft, is the workhorse of the Canadian North. (See color figure 5-16.) Naturally, I use nylon spray covers on rough-water trips.

Cliff asked me to say a word about canoe repair, though he's covered it all in this book. My advice? Avoid *wood-trimmed boats; those with aluminum/vinyl rails are easier to repair in a wrap; bring duct tape, extra bolts, self-tapping screws, a multitool, and a roll of snare wire. The wire's for catching rabbits in case the other stuff fails!*

Bill Simpson

Bill Simpson is a teacher and coach who has been leading wilderness trips for the past thirty years. He started with canoe camps, as have so many other Minnesota wilderness experts. He then branched out to leading trips for schools, the Wilderness Inquiry Association of Minneapolis, the American Lung Association (Adventure Treks), and the Jacob Wetterling Foundation of St. Joseph, Minnesota. He has spent a lifetime canoeing, kayaking, and backpacking throughout the Arctic and other exotic regions of the world. Bill founded the Far North Symposium, an annual event in Minneapolis that attracts hundreds of devoted wilderness paddlers. In 1998 he was recognized for his wilderness leadership by KARE Television as one of the "Eleven Who Care." Bill says that his most memorable wilderness canoe experience was a 1987 descent of the remote Kuujjua River in Canada's Northwest Territories.

Some people tough out obstacles and bull their way through the bush. Bill Simpson travels confidently and comfortably and with a deep respect for his surroundings. He has devoted much of his adult life to helping people of all ages appreciate the wonder of wild places. I'm proud to know Bill Simpson and to have him as a friend.

The We-no-nah Minnesota II is, without any hesitation, my first choice as a canoe for long-distance canoe expeditions. It measures 18½ feet, has a bit of tumblehome, is without rocker, is very light and quick with its Kevlar layup. And it has an interesting history.

Eugene Jensen, who has spent his life designing fast, efficient canoes, originally built the boat in the 1970s for downriver racing. For many years it was in production by We-no-nah Canoes and was called the Whitewater II. I have two of these original canoes from the late 1970s and they still have years of service left in them.

In the 1980s some modifications were made, but We-no-nah still had two very similar models in production. In the 1990s the late Betty Ketter and her son, Karl (Ketter Canoeing, Minneapolis), brought back the original design, again through We-no-nah, and renamed it the Minnesota II. It is now more popular than ever and is the boat of choice for many people in the Boundary Waters Canoe Area, and for groups doing extended travel in the Far North. The Minnesota II has given birth to a stretched version called the Minnesota III. It is 20-feet long and has a seat amidships for a third person. It is very fast, especially when the duffer also paddles. With a boat this long, the bow paddler needs to help initiate even slight turns, and tight, narrow passages (and portages) can be tricky, as its 20-foot length doesn't crank around corners very well. However, I consider these minor disadvantages for a canoe that goes so fast, carries so much, and paddles so efficiently.

Laurie Gullion

Wilderness guide, outdoor program coordinator for Greenfield Community College in Massachusetts, and American Canoe Association instructor trainer Laurie Gullion has paddled 8,000 miles on subarctic and Arctic rivers in Alaska, the Northwest Territories, Norway, and Finland. She teaches canoeing and sea kayaking and has written seven books on canoeing, kayaking, and skiing. In her latest book, Canoeing: A Women's Guide, she interviewed more than one hundred women, including some who have paddled for more than sixty years, and

traced the involvement of women in canoeing since the late 1800s. Laurie is one of a handful of experts who have used folding canoes on remote, rapids-filled Arctic rivers.

Our group of eight American canoeists eyed the choppy waves on the Coppermine River (NWT, Canada) that would test our foldable Pakboat canoes—PVC skins stretched over aluminum frames with stiff, three-chambered air bags that give the boats rigidity. We tightened our spray covers and, for the next three hours, confidently rode waves that may have swamped a hard-shelled canoe. After paddling these folding canoes on the South Nahanni and in Norway and Finland, I was comfortable with the deliberate flex of the hull, which raises the bow and helps deflect water. I smiled at my husband Bruce Lindwall's reaction to his first roller-coaster ride in a Pakboat. Uneasy at first, he came to enjoy the sensation of bucking in the waves. Anyone who has paddled a hard-shelled boat in wind-driven waves would have headed for shore at this point, but we rode high and dry in the Pakboats. Packable in a duffel and much cheaper to transport into wilderness rivers, these canoes are my first choice for remote trips requiring floatplane access.

Michael Peake

Michael Peake spends his free time canoeing Canada's North with his three brothers and friends. In 1985 their group, the Hide-Away Canoe Club, completed a 1,000-mile, fifty-five-day canoe trip from the Saskatchewan-NWT border to the Arctic Ocean to officially name a river for Eric Morse, the dean of Canadian wilderness canoeists. Other trips include retracing George Douglas's Lands Forlorn route from Great Bear Lake to Coppermine, a fifty-day trip from Lake Athabasca to the Back River following the lost route of Dr. King and his search for the Franklin Expedition, three traverses of the Ungava Peninsula (see his

Povungnituk River story in chapter 19), and crossing the Continental Divide via the Rat and Porcupine Rivers. The Hide-Away Canoe Club takes what many people call difficult and remote canoe trips. The Peakes would simply call them pure wilderness journeys. Recent trips dubbed "Onriver. Online" have included daily postings to the Internet (www.canoe.ca/winiskriver and www. canoe.ca/geogreriver).

Michael Peake lives in Toronto and is a staff photographer with the *Toronto Sun*. In 1986 he won Canada's National Newspaper Award for spot news photography. He also publishes *Che-Mun* (appendix B), a journal of Canadian wilderness canoeing.

I love canoes more for where they take me than what they're made of. That said, I suppose I like the Old Town Tripper the best. Trippers were the first canoes we used in the Arctic and we have paddled them thousands of miles. Yes, they are hard to manage and slow on large, windy, lakes, but they handle well in rapids and are incredibly strong. Many of our trips involve upstream travel, which means dragging up, over, and through rocks, so we need canoes that can be badly abused. The pair of Trippers we sold in Kangirsuk after doing three traverses of the Ungava Peninsula were almost devoid of color (vinyl) on the bottom.

I also love my old cedar-canvas Tremblay 17-footer. This working-class canoe, made by a defunct maker in Quebec, is big and beamy. It once saved my life when we were caught out on Lake Superior. Since then, the Tremblay has held a special place in my heart.

Dick Person

Dick Person is one of the great woodsmen of our time. He has degrees in zoology and geology and has worked as a ranger in Glacier National Park and a biologist for the Idaho Department of Fish and Game. He has also been a ski instructor and climbing guide and a member of the Jackson Hole Wyoming Ski Patrol. In 1969 Dick and his family headed to Canada where they lived for seventeen years in a tepee in a remote part of the Yukon. Today he and Sharon Chatterton share a wilderness cabin near Teslin, Yukon. Dick lives largely (and always harmoniously) off the land. "Wild and Woolly" Dick Person is a popu-

lar speaker at U.S. and Canadian outdoor shows. He guides canoe trips and teaches courses on wilderness survival techniques. I consider him a soul mate and am proud to call him my friend. Contact information is in appendix B.

Having grown up with wood-canvas canoes in the 1940s and 1950s, I was shocked by the unaesthetic, noisy practicality of the first Grumman aluminum canoe I paddled. However, during my tepee-living days, I used the 17-foot Grumman like a heavy-duty pickup truck, freighting loads of firewood and supplies, dragging it over river bars loaded with moose meat, and subjecting it to abuse that would seriously damage my more fragile but better-designed fiberglass canoes.

When Royalex canoes were developed, the picture changed radically. I tried some different models and found the 17-foot Mad River Explorer to be an excellent all-around craft for wilderness life and guiding. Later the 17-foot Explorer was replaced by the Revelation, which has greater capacity and is more forgiving in rough water.

Lately, however, I've also been paddling a Dagger

Figure 5-17. Royalex canoes are tough. Kent Swanson pauses for a break as he prepares to "ride" his Old Town Tripper down the hill to the river. Hood River, Nunavut, Canada.

Venture 17 and find it extremely responsive in white water, even when loaded to capacity. At sixty-nine pounds the Venture is also lighter than most other similarly sized Royalex canoes.

Annie Aggens

Annie began paddling with her parents as a youth and fell in love with wilderness canoeing while she was a camper at Camp Manito-wish in Wisconsin. Annie made a twenty-one-day canoe trip in northern Saskatchewan when she was fourteen. Since then she has logged more than 3,000 miles of canoe trails in Saskatchewan and Nunavut and guided three fifty-day trips into the barren lands. Annie is an instructor for the National Outdoor

Leadership School and the director of the Northwest Passage, a Chicago-based adventure travel company. As you read this Annie is probably thinking about her next trip north and hoping that her enthusiasm and respect for the lonely land will rub off on you.

The Old Town Tripper is my favorite canoe for wild northern rivers. The Tripper is stable in big waves and very maneuverable in rapids. This big canoe carries enough gear and food for a month, and it's fun to paddle. The tough Royalex hull holds up well to abuse even when it's lined over jagged rocks and ledges and hauled fully loaded over boulders. In rapids it quietly slides over your mistakes. Some paddlers complain about its eighty-pound weight on portages, but I wouldn't trade its strength for a lighter boat.

Gary and Joanie McGuffin

Joanie and Gary McGuffin live on the shores of Lake Superior in the Algoma Highlands of Ontario, where they pursue a life of adventuring. They are internationally *known for their writing, photography, public speaking, and high-profile conservation efforts. The McGuffins have written five wonderful books:* Where Rivers Run; Journeys on an Inland Sea *(a Great Lakes Book Award winner);* In the Footsteps of Grey Owl, Journey into the Ancient Forest; Great Lakes Journey, Exploring the Heritage Coast; *and* Paddling Your Own Canoe *(see appendix B), which has been described as the most complete (and beautiful!) canoe paddling text of all time. The McGuffins have a Web site, www.GaryAndJoanieMcGuffin.com.*

Gary and I have always loved long-distance wilderness journeys that span weeks or months. The added weight and space required by a larger food supply, an extensive photographic system, our Alaskan malamute, and our daughter requires a long, deep-hulled canoe that's fast and seaworthy, solidly built, and light enough to easily portage long distances. (See color figure 5-18.) On the Great Lakes, Superior especially, a speedy canoe allows you to beat a quick retreat in the face of a rising wind. Our choice is the Kevlar Mad River Lamoille. It is 18 feet, 4 inches long, 33 inches wide, and 14½ inches deep.

Being loners at heart, we have always enjoyed solo paddling, especially on rivers where the margin of safety is increased by paddling two solo canoes instead of one tandem canoe. The Mad River Royalex Guide is our favorite solo canoe for all-around ease of paddling, and portaging, load-carrying capacity, and dryness in waves and rapids. It's 14½ feet long, 29 inches wide, and 14 inches deep.

Cliff Jacobson

For two editions of this book I've remained silent on my choice of canoes, partly because the huge size of this book suggests that I've said enough, and partly because I believe that other viewpoints are as good as mine. But I turned sixty in 2000 and perhaps the wisdom of age qualifies me to speak.

For years I relied on an old reliable Old Town Tripper, an expedition-grade Royalex canoe that still makes me smile. But the Tripper isn't perfect: The flat bottom and not-so-soft chines produce a crisp, catchy feel if you don't lean just right when you cross a strong eddy line. At near-

ly eighty pounds the Tripper is heavy. I weigh 134 and prefer a lighter canoe. And while very capable in big rapids, the Tripper could use more flare to keep out splash. It could also use more speed, but not at the expense of decreased performance in rapids.

In 1989 I posed my concerns to national white-water champion Steve Scarborough, whose Dagger Canoe Company designs are known worldwide. I asked Steve if Dagger could design a whitewater tripping canoe that addressed my needs.

I spelled out the requirements, and Scarborough went to work. The result (in 1991) was the Dagger Venture—which, I think, may be the supreme tripping canoe for big rapids, huge lakes, and large loads. Here's how the Venture compares to the proven 17-foot Old Town Tripper:

■ The Venture has more capacity. It sits about an inch higher in the water with an equal load.

■ It's faster and it runs quieter (no bow gurgle at speed). The downside is that there's a lot of sidewall exposed to the wind: Light loads and headwinds can be a bear.

■ When rocks loom ahead, this canoe turns right now—much faster than a Tripper!

■ It's lighter. My Venture weighs just under seventy pounds, about 10 percent less than a Tripper. Dagger achieves this weight reduction by using strategically thinned and selectively reinforced Royalex sheets, and narrow, lightweight ash gunnels.

■ The hull is asymmetric for speed and boldly flared to deflect waves: Point it downriver and it'll run bone-dry in Class III water. The Venture is drier and quicker than the Tripper. It turns better, too: There is no crisp feel when the boat is leaned as you cross an eddy line. The Venture feels more like a white-water slalom canoe than a big-water tripper.

Unfortunately, Dagger quit making canoes in 2003, and

the Venture is out of production. Now, if I had to choose a big tripping canoe, it would probably be the (new in 2004) 17-foot Bell Canoe Works (Royalex) Alaskan, which was designed by David Yost. I also like the (new in 2004) Kevlar composite, 17-foot We-no-nah Prospector, and for tight Ontario rivers, the 16-foot We-no-nah Prospector.

I'm also madly in love with solo canoes. My favorite wilderness tripper is a thirty-two-pound black and gold (Kevlar-graphite) Bell Wildfire. It pivots on a penny, it cruises effortlessly on lakes, and it's capable in Class III rapids if you paddle well and have a splash cover.

Okay, now that you've read the preferences of the experts, it's obvious there's complete disagreement among everyone. Or is there? Let's take a closer look.

POINTS EVERYONE GENERALLY AGREES ON

- Length. Except for the 16½-foot Mad River Explorer, 17 feet is considered the minimum. Many prefer 18- or 18½-foot canoes even though they can't be carried on the pontoons of small floatplanes.

- The canoe should have substantial depth and high volume. Big canoes provide a margin of safety on rough water. Canoes that are too small are dangerous.

- Keels are dangerous; avoid them! If you paddle an aluminum canoe, it should be equipped with a shoe keel, not a standard fin keel.

- Favored materials are ABS Royalex, Kevlar, and polyethylene.

- The overall weight of the canoe is second to its strength. You need a strong boat . . . period!

- Slipperiness is an important factor: Everyone likes canoes that slide easily over rocks.

- If you plan to overwinter your canoe in a snowbank, get an aluminum model. Canoes built of other materials may not withstand intense cold.

- The canoe must be trustworthy and forgiving on all types of water. If it has unusual quirks you and your partner must be sufficiently skilled to overcome them.

- Almost any canoe of adequate size and strength will get you through if you understand its limitations.

In summary, the major concern is safety. The rivers of the Far North are no place to experiment with specialized canoes that offer a slight technical performance edge at the expense of strength or predictability.

SOLO CANOES ARE DIFFERENT

Recently there's been a revival of interest in canoeing alone. Most paddlers simply solo their big wild-river canoe, but that's not very efficient. Tandem canoes are for tandem crews; they're too big, too heavy, too wind susceptible, and too awkward for one person to handle. If you're serious about going alone, you'll want a true solo canoe!

Compared to the big canoes, a craft that measures only about 15 feet long, 12 inches deep, and 26 to 30 inches wide appears grossly inadequate, even for one person. You'd think a canoe this small would sink in the first big wave. It won't. Hardly ever! That's because you paddle a solo canoe from the center or fulcrum, which leaves its nearly weightless ends free to rise and fall with the rhythm of the waves. Solo canoes are immensely seaworthy—they'll go anywhere bigger canoes will go but with more precision and flair . . . and fun!

Solo canoes are different, so the traditional rules of tandem canoe design don't apply. For example, most variables—speed, tracking, turning, portability, seaworthiness, and general handiness—will be maximized in a canoe of 14 to 16 feet, a width at the gunnel of 26 to 30 inches, and a center depth of 12 to 13 inches. Except in the biggest white water—stuff you should be carrying around anyway—additional depth is unnecessary and unwise. High sides spell crankiness when the wind comes up: Remember, you're your own partner in a solo canoe!

Frankly, there's a limited market for solo canoes, so the majority of what you'll find in the stores parrots inefficient utility designs that paddle poorly but sell well. At the other extreme are some wonderfully designed sport boats, but you'll have to go to canoe specialty shops to find them.

The resurgence of the solo art has brought forth a number of new canoe designs that breed real excitement. Some names to remember are Bell, Dagger, Mad River, Swift, and We-no-nah. Add to this the many small custom builders and your choices widen.

Don't underestimate the performance of these personal-sized canoes. With a fabric cover to shed wind and water, they'll run the biggest waves like a yellow leaf in autumn.

CHAPTER 6

OUTFITTING AND CUSTOMIZING YOUR CANOE

Some people are turned on by beautiful cars. With me it's canoes. So it was natural that I pour on the coal when just downriver I saw what appeared to be a gleaming new wood-canvas canoe. I hailed the paddlers—a middle-aged couple from Nebraska—and slipped quietly alongside. Sure enough, it was wood and canvas—and a 1928 Old Town to boot. It was an 18-foot guide and every inch, from ribs and planking to the polished brass bands on its stems, was like new.

"Restored her myself," said the man proudly. "Took me three years." I glanced along the oiled ash rails of my sophisticated Mad River TW Special, then focused on the ventilated hand-rubbed mahogany gunnels of the Old Town. The TW was pretty to be sure, but the old-timer was *beautiful*. It was no contest.

"Sure would like to try your boat," I said wistfully to the man. "Yeah, and I'd like to paddle that racy boat of yours," he responded. Turned out we were going the same way, so we struck up a bargain: We'd trade canoes until the next portage.

We talked enthusiastically about each other's canoes for maybe twenty minutes. All too soon the portage came into view. "Hey, how's about trading boats on the portage?" I asked. "I've never carried a canvas canoe."

The man smiled knowingly and almost instantly said, "Sure!"

We unloaded our canoes and the man took off down the trail, securely imprisoned beneath the contour padded yoke of my TW. His wife hung behind, still struggling with a pack. I looked down into the Old Town—there was no yoke, only a straight ash thwart. "Where's the yoke?" I called casually to the woman. "Oh that," she responded. "Jim just uses two paddles and that foam pad over there," she said pointed to a rolled trail mattress near her pack. I got the message! That "knowing smile" told everything. Well, it was too late now:

The guy was long gone, probably humming happily beneath my yoke.

It was not a long portage—maybe $1/2$ mile—but it was a tough one. And the old canoe must've weighed at least ninety pounds. Halfway through I developed shortness of breath, felt a severe tightening in my chest. My legs began to wobble, and the pain at the base of my neck became unbearable. I didn't have the strength either to put down the canoe or to continue on. But somehow I managed to struggle forth. Sweating, panting, bleary-eyed, I finally reached the next lake. Ahead was the faint outline of a human at the water's edge. I attempted composure, but it was impossible, "God, this thing is heavy!" I blurted. "Can you . . . please . . . help me?" Instantly the man jumped into action. Together we struggled to unhorse what had now become a loathsome green canvas dinosaur. Finally I was free. Oh glory! I collapsed on a damp cedar log with incredible joy.

It seemed like an eternity before I was able to speak again, and then the words came slowly: "How can you stand to carry that thing?" I asked.

"Ain't easy. You get used to it," replied the man. "Say where can I get a neat yoke like yours?"

Now it was my turn to smile. "You can't," I replied, a bit sarcastically. "There's no such thing as a good store-bought yoke. You'll have to make your own."

The point is, even the best canoe—factory fresh or faithfully restored—is unsuitable for serious use in the backcountry until it's properly rigged. And the first step in proper rigging is to fit a well-designed yoke.

MAKING THE YOKE

If you've never used a wooden yoke, you're in for a pleasant surprise. There's a warmth and springiness to wood that's

Figure 6-1. A contoured canoe yoke is easy to make. Note the water drain holes in the underside of the yoke.

Figure 6-2. Yoke mounted in the author's Dagger Legend canoe. Note the oversized portage pads and parachute-cord security loops tied through the holes in the gunnels.

equaled by no other material. Aluminum yokes are unyielding affairs—much like jogging on cement while wearing ski boots. Wooden yokes, on the other hand, are resilient—they take *some* of the sting out of a nasty portage.

You can make an acceptable yoke out of almost any straight-grained, clear hardwood, but white ash is by far the best. Ash has just the right amount of strength and flexibility. I prefer to use $^7/_8$-inch-thick wood when I can get it, cut to the dimensions shown in figure 6-3. If I can't obtain $^7/_8$-inch

board, I'll use $^3/_4$-inch stock and make the yoke a bit wider—about $2^1/_2$ inches—to ensure adequate strength.

It's doubtful you'll ever break a $2^1/_2$-inch by $^3/_4$-inch solid-ash yoke along its length, but it might split out where it bolts to the gunnels. The yoke should be secured to the rails with *two* $^1/_8$-inch-diameter stainless-steel bolts at each end (figure 6-4), rather than a single $^1/_4$-inch-thick bolt, as is the common practice.

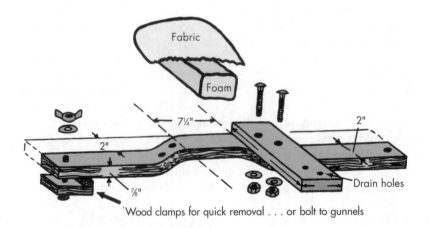

Figure 6-3. The yoke.

Figure 6-4. Bolts work loose as the canoe flexes with each paddle stroke. Two thin bolts set about an inch apart are more secure than one thick bolt.

Install a flat washer and a locking washer on each bolt. Dribble Loc-tite (available at hardware stores and gun shops) on the bolt thread before you tighten the nut. I thread a second (spare) nut over the first nut on one of the bolts just in case a nut works loose and is lost to the great outdoors.

Don't make your yoke wider or thicker than suggested. The idea of using wood in the first place was to gain flexibility—something you'll lose if you increase dimensions substantially.

Your yoke must have a curved neckpiece to enable you to carry the mass of your canoe directly over your shoulders. I've found that a 2-inch inset (see figure 6-3) is ideal. More than this is awkward, while less isn't much better than a straight bar.

Follow this procedure to complete the yoke:

1. Cut two 4-inch by 8-inch by ¾-inch yoke pad blocks from clear pine or Douglas fir (stronger). Don't use plywood: it delaminates with age.

2. Decide on the spacing of the blocks. For most adults 7¼ inches—inside to inside—is about right. Drill ¼-inch bolt holes through the yoke blocks and bar.

3. Drill a few ⅜-inch-diameter drain holes through the face of each yoke block. Commercial yoke blocks don't have drain holes, so the water that accumulates in the foam pads stays there, and the wood blocks eventually rot.

4. Varnish the blocks, especially the inside of the bolt holes.

5. Install large carriage washers on ¼-inch bolts and run them through the holes in the yoke blocks.

6. For each yoke pad cut a 12-inch by 14-inch piece of Naugahyde and set it facedown on the floor. Pile about 8 inches of polyurethane foam pillow padding on the Naugahyde and set the yoke block bolts up on the foam. Compress the foam to a 3-inch thickness and staple the Naugahyde in place. Varnish the staples so they won't rust.

7. Bolt the pads to the yoke bar. Use a standard washer *and* a lock washer under each nut.

8. Secure the finished yoke to the gunnels with ¼-inch-diameter stainless-steel bolts (brass bolts aren't strong enough). Use a carriage washer and a lock washer beneath each nut.

Note that you can either bolt or clamp your yoke to the gunnels, as illustrated in figure 6-3. Bolting is much more secure, and it's essential for a canoe that will be used in white water. However, if you commonly carry a passenger on forgiving waters (no rapids), the clamp-in setup has merit because you can remove it to provide room for a friend.

Portage pads may be bolted or clamped to the yoke bar, as illustrated in figure 6-5. Bolting is best if you usually carry your own canoe. Otherwise, clamp-in pads are more versatile because they can be adjusted to fit the shoulders of your friend in less than a minute. The downsides are that they're a bit bulky and you must (conscientiously) keep the wingnuts tight. However, there is merit in uniformity: If all the canoes in your party have identical clamp-on pads, you can switch them among canoes if you break a pad on a portage.

Bourquin Boats (Jeannie Bourquin) makes the best bolt-on yoke pads I've found; Empire Canvas has the best over-sized clamp types. Gunnel clamps for securing yokes to canoes are available from Bell Canoeworks and Old Town Canoe (addresses in appendix B). You'll find curved ash yoke bars (sans portage pads) for sale at most canoe shops.

The yoke described above has been affectionately dubbed the Minnesota yoke, because the vast majority of canoes that challenge the Boundary Waters (there are *lots* of mean portages in the BWCA!) use this type. There are other yokes, of course. They range in style from dished wood

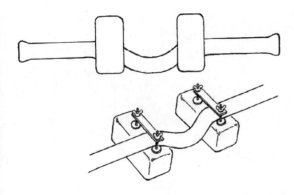

Figure 6-5. Sliding yoke pad setup.

boards (Hansel and Gretel bucket yokes) to form-fitted and padded aluminum shoulder cups. One unusual model has two Y-shaped hangers that protrude from the top of a pack frame. The yoke bar of the canoe (sans pads) rests in the hangers, and the weight of the canoe is borne by the pack's hip belt.

Why no enthusiasm for these other yokes? Because over the toss and tumble of the portage trail, they just don't work very well. Here's why:

- Comfort-curved padded aluminum yoke pads: At first the trail winds tortuously upward, your canoe bow raised 45 degrees; then the trail—and bow—suddenly drop. The harsh curved edges of the metal pads bite deeply into your shoulders as the canoe rises and falls.

- Bucket yoke: Same problem as above but possibly worse because there is no padding to cushion the edges. Or maybe your shoulders just don't fit the generic shape of the dish.

- Yoke on a Y-hanger: You can't roll the canoe onto your shoulders using the standard side lift. Instead you must plant the bow firmly on the ground and roll the canoe over in the dirt (which chews up the end), then walk the Y-hanger up to the yoke bar. You must wear the pack frame, with its Y-hanger, whenever you portage the canoe. Picture going over and under logs

and through thick brush with this setup. Imagine setting the canoe down and picking it up a dozen times as you scout a trail. Remember that you must carry the pack and canoe together, which can be quite a load.

These unique yokes are largely designed for ultralight canoes or controlled situations—level or groomed trails, a handy partner, and so on. If you want to know what works and what doesn't, equip each canoe in your party with a different style of yoke and ask your friends to try them all. Then see which canoe is the last one to be carried over the portage. One tough trip through the bush and you'll see why the Minnesota yoke reigns king.

CANOE TUMPLINE

A tumpline is a wide strap that attaches to a pack, bundle, or your canoe. You place this strap just above your forehead, lean forward, and take off down the trail. The early voyageurs carried hundreds of pounds with tumplines, piling bundles a yard high over their heads.

Like the voyageurs, I swear by my tumpline. But most canoeists I know swear at them—largely because they don't know how to use one properly. Doctors, too, tend to pontificate against tumplines, believing that users will suffer damaged vertebrae and awful pains. Frankly, I've yet to hear of a bona fide problem in anyone who used a tumpline right.

You'll hear more good things about tumplines in chapters 9 and 21. Right now all you need to know is that portaging will go a whole lot easier if you attach a tumpline to your canoe. Canadian paddlers prefer a simple leather strap—which can catch your neck if you trip. I'm sold on the trampoline setup, which is much safer.

You'll need a rectangular piece of canvas (it breathes), two rubber truck straps (not flimsy shock cords), and four steel S-hooks. Snake the truck straps through wide sleeves sewn in the headpiece and secure the S-hooks to loops of parachute cord strung through holes in the gunnels (figure 6-6). The headpiece dimensions aren't critical: My tump measures 12 by 18 inches.

Shortening the loops of 'chute cord tightens the rubber straps and transfers weight from your shoulders to your head; lengthening the cords does the opposite. I adjust the rig to carry about 60 percent of the weight on my head.

If you tire of the tumpline while portaging, just reach across your body to unhook it—and bear all the weight on

Figure 6-6. Portaging with a tumpline.

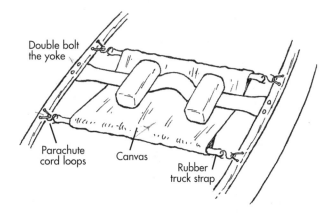

Double bolt the yoke

Parachute cord loops

Canvas

Rubber truck strap

Figure 6-7. Tumpline set up on canoe.

the foam-filled pads of your Minnesota yoke. You'll have to set down the canoe to hook up the tumpline again.

Try a trampoline tumpline on your canoe and see if you don't agree that things go easier when you use your head.

Also check out Bob Henderson's tumpline kudos in chapter 21.

TIE POINTS FOR YOUR GEAR

Opinions vary. Some advise tying in your gear so tightly that the pounding of a rapids on the contents of a swamped canoe can't possibly tear anything loose. Others claim the opposite: "If you capsize and your canoe dives for a deep current or wraps around a rock, you may lose everything—canoe, packs, the works. Better to waterproof your gear so it floats and can be picked up later in the quiet water downstream. Besides . . . your friends will salvage your gear!"

Don't you believe it!

Really now, just what do you suppose are the chances that you'll find packs that float free in a rough-water upset? Maybe they will wind up in a quiet eddy not far from your mishap, but more than likely they'll continue downriver for miles, ultimately to be lost in the gathering flow. And as to "your friends salvaging your gear," perhaps that's true enough on a local stream—but not on a wild river where their first responsibility is to rescue you . . . then your canoe, and last your packs!

However, there is sound support for the never-tie-in-gear theory. Say you're traveling in the company of other canoes on a pool-drop river—that is, one whose rapids are short and feature quiet pools below. If you capsize in the rapids, your packs will float into the pool where your friends can rescue them.

There is no reason to tie in packs if you use a nylon spray cover (see chapter 7) on your canoe. A covered canoe usually turns bottom-up when it capsizes, and the cover and packs remain with the canoe. The twisting motion and susceptibility to abrasion of folding canoes also suggests that packs should not be tied in.

Finally, the Boundary Waters Canoe Area and Quetico Lake country demand a no-tie-in approach. Lakes are small here; often there's a carry every thirty minutes. It's a hassle to tie and untie packs at every portage, even if doing so offers some security afloat.

The time to tie in packs is when you're canoeing a big, brawny river with rapids that run for miles. Capsize here and you'll be lucky to rescue your canoe, let alone packs that float out and are lost in the gathering flow. For example, the lower 150 miles of the Clearwater River in Alberta averages at least 5 miles an hour. Some stretches run twice that speed. In 1996 two canoes in my group, which were running uncovered, capsized in a long rapid. Both teams lost some expensive gear that wasn't tied in. Later we found a lost paddle lodged in some brush 30 miles downstream!

All white-water canoeists know that the higher a capsized canoe floats, the less likely it is to be damaged by rocks. So they fill their boats with closed-cell foam, air bags, inner tubes and other floatation material. Naturally, float bags and foam are out of place in the wilds, but packs that float aren't. Waterproof your packs, lock 'em tight in the canoe, and they'll keep your canoe afloat if you capsize. But they're no help if they dangle out of the canoe in an upset (pack straps may catch between rocks and cause the canoe to hang up!) or bob ominously when you swamp. That's why you need an effective tie-in system that's foolproof and fast to rig.

Over the years I've come to favor the system shown in figure 6-8, which consists of a network of rubber ropes and parachute cords that run from gunnel to gunnel and thwart to thwart. I'll examine the specifics in chapter 9. Right now I'm concerned only with how to rig the canoe with the tie-in points.

If you have an aluminum canoe with broad flat inwales (inside gunnels), drill ¼-inch diameter holes 4 to 6 inches apart along the length of each gunnel. If your gunnels are tubular aluminum, plastic, or wood, drill smaller ⅛-inch-diameter holes through the inwales or just below, then thread short loops of parachute cord through the holes.

Now you've got lots of places to attach your security system and tie in small items.

Accomplished white-water paddlers know that rubber ropes and cords across the gunnels aren't secure enough in a big-water capsize. They glue heavy neoprene patches with nickel-plated steel D-rings onto the floor and sidewalls of the canoe—and they use straps or mountaineering cord to secure their gear to the D-rings. This is a great plan for a day in the rapids but not for a long trip that combines lake and river travel and frequent portages.

SHOCK-CORD YOUR THWARTS AND DECKS

The best way to store maps, wet socks, and oddities in your canoe is to stuff them under hoops of shock cord strung through thwarts (figure 6-10). Shock-corded items will stay put in a wind and on portages. And they'll usually remain with the canoe in an upset.

Shock-cord your decks, too. Bow and stern lines should be coiled and stuffed under the deck cords when they're not in use (figure 6-9). Never leave lines loose in any boat—they could wind around your arms or legs if you over turn in a lively current.

LINING HOLES

Shorelines along rivers within the timberline are usually too brushy to permit much lining, but in the tundra where they're no trees, lining is a way of life. Deck-mounted rings or eyes are generally worthless for lining, because they place the pulling force of the lines too high above the mass of the canoe. If you pull hard on a deck-secured rope while working a canoe through a tricky current, you'll upset it for sure. But get the force closer to the waterline (lower on the mass) and you've got no problem at all.

For this reason some canoe books insist that you abandon deck-mounted rings when lining and instead rig a towing harness around the hull. But a better procedure is to simply install the lining rings where they belong—midway down the stem of the canoe. Aluminum canoe makers have been doing it properly for years, but manufacturers of other canoes somehow haven't caught on.

You can buy fancy brass lining rings or plated steel ones, or simply bore a hole through the stem of the canoe a few inches above cutwater. The latter method is the least expensive and most reliable. Drill the hole large enough to accept a

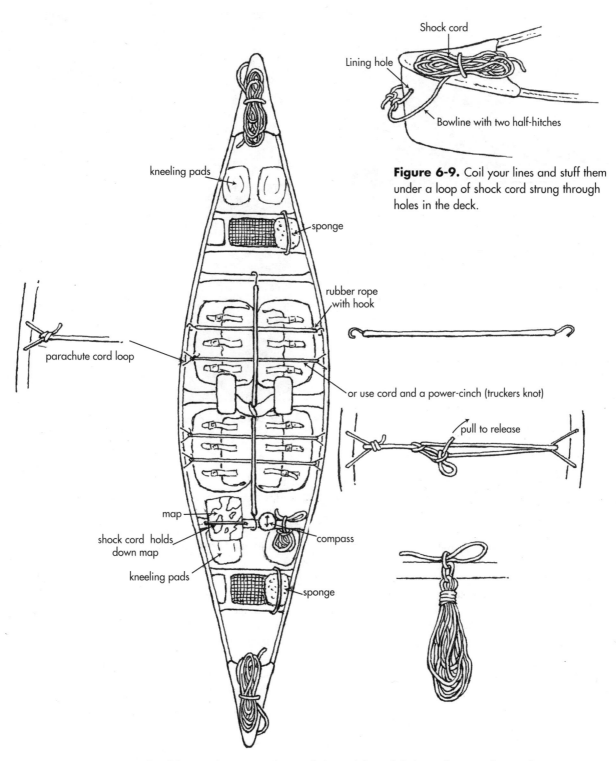

Shock cord

Lining hole

Bowline with two half-hitches

Figure 6-9. Coil your lines and stuff them under a loop of shock cord strung through holes in the deck.

kneeling pads

sponge

rubber rope with hook

parachute cord loop

or use cord and a power-cinch (truckers knot)

pull to release

map

shock cord holds down map

compass

kneeling pads

sponge

Figure 6-8. Canoe outfitted for rough water. Nylon cords looped through holes in the gunnels provide convenient attachment points to tie in gear.

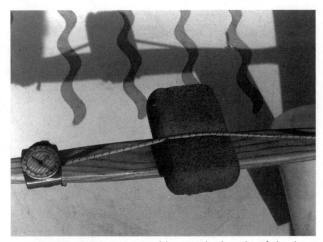

Figure 6-10. Secure oddities under lengths of shock cord strung through holes in the thwarts.

length of ¹/₂-inch-diameter plastic water pipe. Glue the pipe in place with quick-setting epoxy. The pipe will prevent water from leaking into the canoe when the ends plunge deep in rough water.

Granted, it takes some courage to bore a hole through the stems of an expensive canoe, but it only hurts for a second and in the end looks fine.

LINES

To seafaring folks any rope used aboard a ship is a "line." But to canoeists lines are specialized ropes used for hauling a canoe around obstacles (such as rocks, logs, and waterfalls) in the water. In canoe parlance lining implies downstream work, whereas *tracking* indicates the opposite. In either case the ropes used must be strong, nonslippery, snag resistant, and relatively inelastic. And for ease of handling, they should measure *at least* ¹/₄ inch in diameter. Favored materials are bright-colored polypropylene, because it floats, and stiff braided mountaineering rope. The woven nylon utility rope sold in hardware stores is bad news: It snags in its own coils when you throw it and has too much stretch. It makes your canoe feel like it's dangling on the end of a rubber band. The braid-on-braid Dacron sheet line used on sailboats may be the best lining rope of all.

A good lining rope should have a "stiff hand." The stiffer

Figure 6-11. PVC pipe lining hole properly installed. The canoe is a Mad River TW Special.

the rope, the better it will fly when you toss it to a friend on a distant boulder.

My own preference is bright yellow, ³/₈-inch, three-strand braided polypropylene. This is the same stuff they use in some of the best lifesaving throw ropes.

Twenty-five feet of line for each end of the canoe is enough. The longer the line, the less control you'll have of the canoe. Things get pretty hairy when you've got more than 25 feet of rope out. I know some very experienced liners who regularly handle 50-foot lines with only occasional difficulties. But not me—I'll portage before I trust my outfit to that kind of uncertainty.

At any rate, if you need more length, just extend what you have by tying (use a double sheetbend, chapter 12) on some of the extra rope you should always bring along on a wilderness trip.

KNEELING PADS

If you're an avid reader of the canoeing literature, you know that the modern way to run rapids in a open canoe is to sit—not kneel—in the canoe. White-water racing teams never kneel in a open canoe, not even in the toughest drops, so why should you?

You shouldn't if you paddle a skinny high-performance cruiser whose seats are strung 6 or 8 inches off the floor.

You should if you paddle a more forgiving boat with typical high-mounted seats.

It's purely a matter of CG (center of gravity). The lower the CG, the greater your stability on all types of water. And it matters little whether you get that stability by kneeling low or sitting.

Since it's more comfortable to sit in a canoe than kneel, it makes sense to simply lower your seats and always paddle while sitting. Right? Not entirely. Whether you sit or kneel or alternate between the two depends mostly on the type of canoe you have and how it's rigged.

For example, a typical 18½-foot high-performance tripping canoe such as the Mad River Lamoille, Sawyer 222, or We-no-nah Sundowner, with its narrow bows and 9-inch-high seats, feels tippy until you get used to it. And it would be even more tippy if you raised the seats to a comfortable kneeling height of 11 to 13 inches. So it's best to leave the seats where the manufacturer put them and not mess with what works best. Besides, even if you do jack up the seats high enough to fit a pair of size 12s beneath, the bows of these and other fine-lined canoes are too narrow to give your knees good purchase for kneeling. If there's insufficient space in a narrow bow to let you spread you knees wide for a good grip on the hull, then you might as well sit.

On the other hand, you won't gain by lowering the seats on a high-volume Grumman or Old Town Tripper. There's nothing worse than sitting low in a high-sided canoe and paddling with a gunnel in your armpit. And there's no contesting that the higher you sit, the better you feel.

As you can see, whether you sit or kneel is less a matter of philosophy than of canoe design. If you paddle the typical high-seated wild-river canoe in rapids you'll have to kneel.

And that means you must have knee pads of some sort. Some paddlers prefer elasticized or strap-on pads. Others like closed-cell foam kneeling aprons like those used by freestyle paddlers. But loose items that can get lost are unwelcome on any canoe trip. Better to glue knee pads into the canoe. Any

Figure 6-12. An angled seat won't dig into your buttocks when you kneel.

type of waterproof foam, except Ensolite-which crushes badly and crumbles in the sun-will work. My favorite foam is ethyl-vinyl-acetate (EVA): It's expensive, so most camping stores don't carry it.

You can buy pricey closed-cell foam knee pads at canoe shops, or just cut a closed-cell foam sleeping pad into knee-pad-sized pieces and glue them into the canoe. Weldwood waterproof contact cement is the best glue I've found for securing pads to slippery Royalex and polyethylene hulls. Once set, Weldwood never lets go!

A properly tuned kneeling position has your rear planted solidly on the seat and your knees firmly embedded in the foam knee pads that are glued to the hull. If your seat is too high, you lose control; if it's too low, you risk foot entrapment. You can comfort-tune your position with thicker or thinner knee pads. You can also adjust the rake of your canoe seat as suggested in the next section.

Bow pads should have a raised ridge on the inside (closest to the keel line); stern pads should have a raised ridge on each side. The ridges prevent your knees from slipping sideways off the pads when the canoe rolls. If this sounds like finicky fiddling, remember that some northern rivers have rapids that continue for miles. You're often on your knees for hours!

Knee pads are absolutely essential in slippery Royalex and polyethylene canoes, and in aluminum and fiberglass canoes with nonslip floors. Try kneeling for very long in the bottom of a metal boat in the bone-chilling waters of the Far North and you'll see why.

ADJUST THE RAKE OF YOUR SEATS

A dead-level seat is best if you always sit in your canoe. Kneelers will want a seat whose leading edge is dropped about ¾-inch down. The angled attitude prevents the edge of the seat from digging into your buttocks when you kneel.

I commonly alternate between sitting and kneeling, so I prefer a less ambitious ¼-inch to ⅜-inch drop. You'll have to experiment to learn what angle is best for you.

THIGH STRAPS

Thigh straps anchor to the inside bilge and bottom of the canoe. They lock your legs into place and keep you from being tossed around when the canoe heels and bucks in rapids. The new installation systems allow fast exits if you capsize. Thigh straps are essential if you paddle a canoe aggressively in rapids. They can be awkward or dangerous in a wilderness tripping canoe, however, because they hang up on boots and clutter standing space. Packs, camera bags, spare paddles, splash cover, and the like create enough obsta-

cles for you to crawl around. For most wilderness travel thigh straps are simply more trouble than they're worth.

Rigging a white-water canoe can be confusing if you're unfamiliar with the process. Figure 6-13 summarizes the most popular options. You can order thigh straps, knee pads, and more from Mike Yee Outfitting (appendix B) or Dagger Canoe Company. Mike Yee outfits some of Dagger's hottest white-water canoes.

FOOT BRACES

Foot braces are useful in any canoe, but they're downright essential in a high-performance wilderness cruiser that you can't kneel in. The only way to lock yourself firmly into a low-slung seat is to jam your feet against an immovable object.

A foot brace need not be exotic. For the stern, a heavy pack placed strategically will work fine. But a more permanent solution is a telescoping aluminum tube, crushed at the ends and bolted to a pair of aluminum-shod wooden rails that are glassed into the canoe (figure 6-14). Don't pop-rivet aluminum rails to the canoe (as is done on flat-water racing canoes); you might shear off an exposed rivet in rapids or when the canoe smacks a boulder while lining.

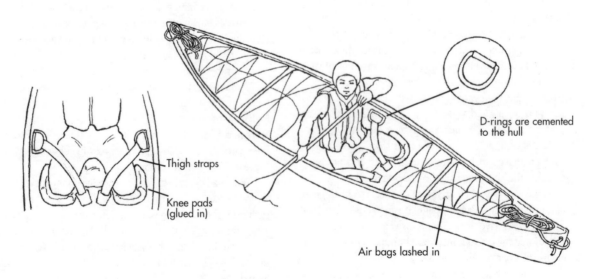

Thigh straps

Knee pads (glued in)

D-rings are cemented to the hull

Air bags lashed in

Figure 6-13. A completely outfitted white-water canoe.

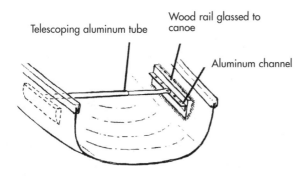

Telescoping aluminum tube

Wood rail glassed to canoe

Aluminum channel

Figure 6-14. There are dozens of ways to construct a suitable foot brace. This method provides a wide latitude of forward and aft adjustment and does not weaken the hull. The foot brace is easily removable.

Make the bow foot brace as suggested or, if your canoe has a sliding seat, simply move it forward until you can jam your feet against the bow flotation tank.

EXTRA THWARTS IF YOU NEED THEM

A rough-water canoe should have a thwart fore and aft of the yoke to brace the hull and tie in gear. But many of the best tripping canoes don't—possibly because the manufacturers want to save a few ounces or a few dollars. The rubber-rope 'chute-cord security system mentioned in chapter 9 depends on three crossbars to work properly.

But it's no big deal—you can always add thwarts if you need them. Bolt the front thwart directly behind the bow seat and the rear thwart 23 inches in front of the forward edge of the stern seat. This spacing should give you barely enough room to squeeze two Duluth packs in front of the yoke and three behind it in a typical 17- to 18-foot canoe.

No sense making the thwarts stronger than necessary. A piece of 1-by-2 ash or oak cut to a modified hourglass shape is adequate. I'd rather have thwarts break out than my canoe break up if it pins against a boulder in a rough-water upset.

DOUBLE-BOLT YOKES AND THWARTS

The yokes and thwarts of most canoes have just one bolt at each end. This isn't strong enough for a hardworking canoe. I replace the thick single bolt with two widely spaced thinner ones. I seal the old bolt holes with epoxy before I drill new holes.

TIGHTEN SCREWS AND BOLTS BEFORE EVERY CANOE TRIP

Canoes twist and vibrate as they are paddled and portaged. Screws and bolts work loose, which can cause woodwork to crack and break. Tighten all screws and bolts before *every* canoe trip and you'll eliminate most problems.

APPLY ULTRAVIOLET PROTECTANT BEFORE EVERY CANOE TRIP

Some years ago I examined a Royalex canoe that had been stored for years in direct sunlight. The plastic rails had a spiderweb of cracks!

It's a good idea to apply an ultraviolet inhibitor such as 303 Protectant or Armorall to your canoe several times a season. The chemical hides scratches—giving a slick new look!—and prevents sun damage. Important: Apply protectant to the inside of your canoe too—especially to unpigmented (gold-colored) Kevlar, which discolors quickly in sunlight. Many canoe companies now recommend 303 Protectant instead of wax.

SITTING PAD

When the temperature drops into the 40s and the rains come, you'll wish you had some insulation between yourself and your canoe seat. Aluminum seats get impossibly cold, cane ones are only a little better, and every seat becomes uncomfortable after many hours afloat. The solution is to line seats with waterproof foam. You can buy commercial sitting pads or simply duct-tape rectangles of foam to the seats. I prefer to make my own pads—it's less expensive, it's lighter, and I get a custom fit.

It's easy to make a seat pad. Just cut a piece of polyethylene or EVA foam (don't use Ensolite; it deforms badly) to the shape of the seat. Sew a canvas[1] cover and attach nylon straps with Velcro tabs. Now you can quickly remove the pad from

---

[1] Canvas provides a better nonslip surface than nylon and is more pleasant to sit on.

the seat and use it around camp.

Everything on a canoe trip should be multifunctional, and the seat pad is no exception. My seat pad becomes part of my sleeping system at night—it extends my foam pad.

CANOE POCKETS

Where to store small items such as eyeglasses, suntan lotion, and mosquito repellent is always a problem on a canoe trip. Of course you can keep these small items in pack sacks, but getting in and out of a waterproof pack every time you want to daub on some bug dope is a hassle. So why not install pockets in your canoe?

An early pioneer of canoe pockets was Verlen Kruger, whose 7,000-mile canoe trip from Montreal to the Bering Sea made canoeing history in 1971. Verlen simply attached plastic bicycle baskets to his canoe thwarts. The baskets provided a convenient—though not lossproof—place to store small articles of equipment.

An alternative to bicycle pockets is the thwart bag, which secures to a canoe thwart or seat frame. A variety of styles is available. I prefer a model that can be opened and closed with one hand. Regrettably, my favorite thwart bag, the Rimizak Pak, is no longer manufactured. It has protective foam padding and can be attached under the canoe seat or clipped to a thwart. Shoulder straps quickly convert it to a small backpack.

You can convert any fabric briefcase into a thwart bag by sewing on Velcro or ties.

The best place to install thwart bags is on the rear thwart and the back of the rear seat. Don't put one on the front thwart—it will hang down and obscure your view when you portage.

THWART- OR SEAT-MOUNTED COMPASS

Like it or not, canoeing northern rivers requires frequent travel on large, sprawling lakes. With the possible exception of Minnesota's Rainy Lake and Lake of the Woods, there is no American waterway that compares in complexity with the bigger lakes you'll find in Canada. For example, Great Slave Lake in the Northwest Territories is more than 250 miles long, while Reindeer Lake in Saskatchewan is half that length. But

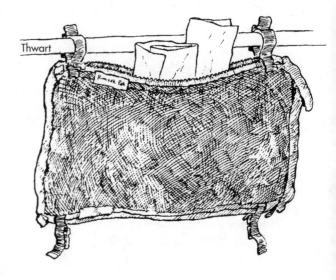

Figure 6-15. Rimizak Pak.

that's only part of the story: I once tried to count the islands on Reindeer Lake. I quit at 200—which was perhaps one-third of the total number!

You need more than good maps to thread your way through the maze of islands on a giant lake. You must also have two (always carry a spare) reliable compasses. But it's a hassle to stop paddling and fetch your compass from a pocket every time you want to take a bearing. Better to install a running compass in the canoe. That way you'll always have accurate directions instantly.

I carry three compasses—a Silva Ranger,[2] which I keep in my shirt pocket; a Silva wrist (diving) compass; and a tiny Silva Huntsman. I mount the wrist compass on the aft thwart when I paddle stern and strap it to a front seat brace when I'm in the bow. The Huntsman, with its hinged base, is permanently attached to the bottom front edge of the stern seat. It folds out from under the seat with a flip of the finger.

[2]The Brunton Company was recently purchased by Silva Production AB of Sweden. Original Silva design compasses are now sold by Brunton under the Nexus name. U.S. compasses that bear the Silva name are made by Suunto of Finland and sold by Johnson Camping (Johnson Worldwide Associates). Confusing, isn't it? All these companies make excellent orienteering-style compasses. However, if you want an original Silva, you'll have to buy a Brunton/Nexus.

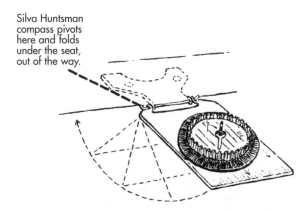

Silva Huntsman compass pivots here and folds under the seat, out of the way.

Figure 6-16. A Silva Huntsman compass mounted beneath the front edge of a canoe seat provides instant directions. The folding mechanism on the compass must be altered (reversed) so the instrument will fold downward.

Two running compasses may seem like overkill, but I've found them quite useful. Once I set a pack with a folding saw inside against the back thwart. The wrist compass needle went crazy! A quick glance at the seat-mounted Huntsman solved the mystery.

You can make a nice fold-out compass to fit beneath your seat by attaching a brass hinge to any flat-base orienteering compass.

All orienteering compasses are liquid filled so their needles will come to rest quickly (within three seconds!) for a fast reading. Early damped compasses would leak fluid if they were left in the sun for long periods, but new models are better sealed, so this is no longer a problem.

GPS MOUNT

Most paddlers mount their GPS on top of the rear thwart so it's handy for the stern paddler. Units vary in size so it's pointless to recommend a specific style of mount. Still, there are some common concerns:

- Your mount must be sturdy. Aluminum or laminated wood is better than plastic. The GPS must be easy to remove so you can tuck it away on portages.
- Design the mount so that you can place your GPS unit

inside a waterproof plastic bag before you secure it to the mount. The special waterproof bags that are designed for GPS units and cell phones are very reliable in rain. I can't speak for their reliability in a capsize.

- Keep spare batteries where you can get to them immediately. Most GPS units use AAs, which fit into a small poly bottle. Keep a flashlight handy if you'll be paddling at night—you'll go through batteries fast if you rely on the screen light that's built into your GPS.

You'll find ideas for packing your GPS in chapter 9.

SPONGE

You'll use a sponge for bailing and cleaning your canoe, for soaking up water that has invaded a leaky tent, and for dozens of other camp chores. But not all sponges are good. The inexpensive plastic ones sold in discount stores don't absorb much water and aren't tough enough to withstand the rigors of a long canoe trip.

The early voyageurs carried sponges that were large enough to absorb more than a quart of water with a single swoop! If you want a sponge like this, you'll have to buy the real thing from an industrial cleaning supplier.

Natural sponges are classified by their texture: A wool sponge is stronger and rougher than a grass sponge and so will best take the abuse of cleaning canoes. A good natural

Figure 6-17. Tools for navigation. Note how the GPS, map, and compass are secured to the thwart.

wood sponge will absorb much more water than a similarly sized plastic sponge and last *many* times longer. But be prepared to pay a substantial sum—big natural sponges are very expensive.

You'll find some small natural sponges at wallpaper stores. Bigger and better ones are available from McMaster-Carr Supply (appendix B).

Store you sponge in your thwart bag or under a shock-corded thwart when you're not using it.

BAILER

When there's too much water sloshing in your canoe to sponge out, use a bailer! White-water folks make bailers from cutoff bleach bottles, but that's not versatile enough for use in a wilderness canoe. A graduated plastic two-quart pitcher works as well. You'll find many uses for the pitcher in camp—measuring water for freeze-dried meals, mixing powdered drinks and instant pudding, and so on. Keep the pitcher tied to a canoe thwart until you need it.

TOYS

You need some diversion when bad weather, mean rapids, or tough portages try your nerves. The internationally known paddler Robert Perkins brings a friendly plastic pink flamingo on his canoe trips. You've probably seen the bird in Bob's videos. When Sue Harings and I were married along Canada's Hood River in 1992, we discovered a mint green inflatable octopus and goodwill note at the wedding site. It

Figure 6-18. Bear Bear goes on all our trips.

was left for us by a party that had canoed the river a few weeks earlier. (See the full story in chapter 19.)

Our toy of choice is Bear Bear—an always happy camouflaged teddy who goes everywhere. Bear Bear has a knitted sweater and a bright yellow fitted rain suit. He rides up front with Susie so he can help make command decisions. Bear Bear has capsized, been rained upon, and been squashed under pack sacks. Once he fell out of a floatplane and floated around the dock for several minutes. But he never complains. He always makes us smile which, after all, is what toys are for.

CHAPTER 7

COVERS AREN'T JUST FOR WHITE WATER

Spray covers are helpful in both wind and white water. They allow you to run some white water that you'd otherwise have to walk around. They also permit you to venture into bigger waves when the wind is up. I heartily recommend them!

— Jill Bubier[1]

A cover would smother the children! I'll put a cover on my canoe about the same time I feel impelled to add a roll bar to my car.

—Carl Shepardson[2]

Splash covers aren't just for running rapids; they keep you dry and warm in icy rain and they cut wind resistance by half or more, which is wonderful if you have a high-sided canoe that reacts to every breeze. A well-designed nylon spray cover weighs barely two pounds and will compress to football size when it's packed away. You can install a cover in a minute and remove it in half that time. I wouldn't dream of canoeing a wild Canadian river without my splash cover.

SAFETY FIRST

When I wrote the first edition of this book in 1984, I questioned scores of canoeists and canoe makers about the safety of fabric spray covers. Larry Jamfeson of Easy Rider Canoe Company had deep concerns. He said:

Fabric covers are dangerous—some because they will not release paddlers easily, and others because they either do or do not come off canoes. Over the last eight years, I've rescued six paddlers who were entrapped in fabric canoe covers. In each case their canoes were turned over, and in two cases the covers remained attached to the canoes but paddlers were unable to get out. In one case the paddlers were still in a full cover that had come off their canoe— they and the cover became entangled in rocks. Tragedy was avoided in each case only because someone was immediately available to rescue them. All the covers were commercially produced and recommended by the canoe manufacturer!

This criticism was valid two decades ago when splash covers were primitive one-piece affairs that attached to canoes with widely spaced snaps or a tight line beneath the gunnels. Today's covers are much safer. In 1980 I designed a three-piece cover with an expandable center (belly). The skirts have a unique quick-release gusset that enable you to exit a capsized canoe quickly: You just pull a rip cord and bail

---

[1] Jill Bubier has paddled the Hanbury/Thelon and Kazan Rivers in the Northwest Territories as well as many ambitious routes within the timberline.

[2] Carl Shepardson has paddled more than 10,000 miles with his family since 1966. Routes have included Kenora to Fort Smith (1,800 miles), Marlborough to Kenora (2,000 miles), Moise River to Labrador, The Pas to York Factory, and more.

Figure 7-1. Three-piece canoe cover. The cockpit sleeve of the forward section is rolled and reefed; the belly is snapped down tight. The rear cover is rolled and tied on the stern deck.

out. The cover sections remain firmly attached to the canoe. Figure 7-2 shows the setup.

This quick-release skirt is very reliable: On two occa-

Figure 7-2. Three-piece cover. Tail section is rolled and reefed.

sions—once on a remote river in the high Arctic—my wife, Susie and I capsized in big rapids. We were out in a flash and our cover stayed on the canoe, which tossed and turned in the maelstrom. Other canoeists who have used Jacobson-style covers in mean water report similar results. I don't know of a single failure.

This said, be aware that *not one* commercially produced spray cover carries a safety warranty. That's because the dangers of entrapment increase when you paddle a decked boat—any decked boat. Still, the advantages of a splash cover in bad weather and big rapids are simply too important to ignore. Indeed, most marathon racing canoes occasionally wear covers, as do nearly all wilderness boats that challenge the wild waters of the Far North. Performance-minded paddlers, too, are discovering that low-sided recreational cruisers and small solo canoes can be safely used on rough water if they're covered. Canoe covers are catching on everywhere!

A VERSATILE DESIGN

Your load height changes as a trip progresses, so a three-piece cover that has an expandable belly is best. Use the belly section alone when wind comes up; add the bow piece in rapids, and close the stern when it rains. When you portage, roll and tie the end caps and leave them on the canoe.

Figure 7-3. Cliff Jacobson and Cliff Welch run a dicey rapids in their splash-covered canoe. Burnside River, Nunavut, Canada.

Figure 7-4. Traveling in wind with just the belly section. North Knife River, Manitoba.

Remove the belly section, stuff it under a pack flap, and you're on your way! It takes less than a minute to snap down the belly when you're back on the water and ready to paddle again.

A three-piece cover is much safer than a one-piece style. Suppose you capsize in a punchy rapids and the current tears your cover off the canoe—and for some reason you are unable to free yourself from the quick-release skirt. This situation could be deadly serious if you had a one-piece cover and became entangled in 17 feet (a canoe length) of fabric. However, the Velcro strips that secure the end caps to the belly of the three-piece model are likely to release. The belly will float away and a 5-foot-long end cap (not the entire cover) will remain on you.

I stress again that I don't know of a single case of entrapment that has resulted from use of the three-piece cover I designed.

Another idea worth repeating is that everything on a canoe trip—including your splash cover—should be multi-functional. You can use the center section (belly) to cover food or firewood in camp and as a ground cloth or light blanket for river naps. Or scroll the belly section around two paddles and set sail when the wind comes up (figure 7-5).

Try this if it rains during your shore lunch. First, unsnap one side (all three sections) of your splash cover from the canoe, then invert the boat and prop it overhead, shoving the bow over a low tree limb. Push the draped cover outward with your paddles to create a narrow fabric umbrella. Now use your pack for a backrest and fire up your stove. Some hot soup will rewarm your spirit until the rain subsides.

ANOTHER COVER OPTION

For long trips and supersized loads—or when you commonly carry a passenger—you may want to consider the split-center, dogsled canoe cover designed by Arctic canoeist

Figure 7-5. Using the belly cover as a sail.

Bob O'Hara. This design allows easy access to gear without unsnapping the sides. To close the belly, simply clip the end pieces together (Fastex buckles), then overlap the two sides and buckle the long straps that run across the fabric. Early covers would not maintain their shape without a high load, but this problem has been solved.

The downside is that this belly section is more difficult to make. And it's bulkier and heavier than the one-piece expandable model. However, O'Hara designed it expressly for traveling tundra rivers that have few portages. If you don't mind a little extra weight and bulk, you'll prefer this style to mine.

BUY IT OR MAKE IT?

Jacobson- and O'Hara-style covers (plus two solo styles) are both available from Cooke Custom Sewing (appendix B). Still, if you can run a sewing machine, you can make a canoe cover in a weekend. You'll be sewing relatively lightweight material and you won't be doing anything fancy, so a simple

Figure 7-6. A Bob O'Hara split-center, dogsled-style cover works well for big loads and long trips.

Figure 7-7. Jacobson style; three piece spray covers on Old Town Tripper canoes. Note where the lining ropes are installed on the canoe.

EXPEDITION CANOEING

straight-stitch machine (I use a 1955 Singer) with a ballpoint needle is all you need. I buy all my splash-cover materials from Thrifty Outfitters (appendix B). They know your needs and will supply the right stuff. Thrifty also has solid brass snaps, webbing, reinforcing tape—everything you'll need to complete the project. The materials will cost about $150 for a tandem canoe, slightly less for a solo.

If you buy, Dan Cooke supplies a no-shrink Mylar template that ensures a perfect canoe-cover fit on any canoe. You install mating snaps in the sides of your craft (a two-hour job). Cooke supplies precise measurements so you won't mess up.

MAKING THE JACOBSON THREE-PIECE COVER

1. Pattern: None. The canoe is your pattern.

2. Snaps: About seventy-five brass snaps for a 17-foot tandem canoe. Check 'em with a magnet to be sure they're not plated steel. Snaps are much cheaper if you buy a box of a hundred. There's no need to purchase an expensive tong-type snap setting kit; a simple hammer-punch tool works fine.

3. Pop rivets and backup washers: You'll need one aluminum pop rivet and one aluminum backup washer for every snap you install. Pop rivets must be long enough to go through the snap, canoe hull, and backup washer, while still providing room to seal.

4. Pop-riveting tool: Get a tong-type tool with a tapered *conical* nose that will fit inside the male portion of the snap that's pop-riveted to the canoe. The snap won't seal tightly against the hull if the nosepiece doesn't fit inside the snap.

5. Waterproof nylon: Fabric that weighs 2.5 ounces per square yard is strong enough for friendly waterways; 4- to 6-ounce stuff is best for big rapids. Not all fabrics are truly waterproof. You'll want to perform these tests before you buy:

- Hold the fabric to a strong light. If you see pinholes, keep shopping!

- Roll the material over a sharp table edge. Don't buy it If the coating flakes off.

- Gather a piece of scrap fabric into a loose sack and pour water into it. Reject the material if it leaks.

You can't improve the waterproof quality of a fabric, but you can line wear-prone areas with more rugged material to resist abrasion.

Here are my fabric choices: For trips into the Arctic where the premium is on durability, I prefer four-ounce-per-square-yard Oxford cloth (Eureka Timberline tent floor material), or six-ounce nylon pack cloth with a Super K-Kote finish.

6. One-inch-wide seam tape or lightweight nylon webbing: You'll need about 40 feet.

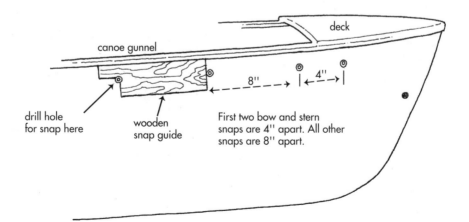

Figure 7-8. A wooden or cardboard snap guide will help you accurately position the snaps for your splash cover.

7. Extras: Long-bladed scissors, tailor's chalk, measuring tape. About 12 feet of 2-inch-wide Velcro; 2 feet of 1-inch-wide Velcro; 12 feet of 1-inch-wide pajama elastic, and 12 feet of $\frac{1}{8}$-inch-diameter shock cord. Small roll of duct tape, four large plastic cord locks, straight pins.

Install Snaps in the Canoe

Pop-rivet snaps through the hull, 2 inches below the rails. Set the first two bow snaps close about 4 inches apart. This close spacing is to prevent the cover from being torn loose when the bow plunges in waves. Position the remaining snaps 8 inches apart all along the hull. Use an aluminum backup washer behind each rivet. A wooden snap guide like the one shown in figure 7-8 will help you position snaps accurately.

Make the Belly Section

1. Cut a 60-inch-wide piece of fabric that reaches from the front edge of the bow seat to just behind the rear thwart. Hem the front and sides then sew nylon seam tape to the inside hem. Next, sew the water deflector channels illustrated in figure 7-9. When the canoe is loaded with packs that reach above the gunnels, the belly will rise up like a camel's hump and direct rain and

splash toward the ends of the canoe. The elasticized channels will contain the runoff and deflect it sideways into the river rather than into your skirts.

2. Set snaps through the side hems to match those on the canoe. Nylon stretches about 5 percent when wet and shrinks when dry, so don't pull the material too tight when you install the snaps!

3. Hem the back of the cover but don't back this hem with seam tape.

4. Sew the four strips of 2-inch-wide Velcro on to the front and back top of the cover, as illustrated.

5. Thread pajama elastic through the water deflector channels and back hem. Tighten the elastic slightly, then sew down the ends. If you want to vary the tightness of the elastic, you can install a buttonhole on the center top of each channel and thread the exposed elastic through a cord lock.

This belly section is generic—it will fit any canoe of roughly similar length if the snap positions on the canoes are identically placed. For example, the belly piece on my 17-foot Dagger Venture also fits my 16-foot Dagger Legend and my 17-foot Old Town Tripper. You can also modify this belly to accept a passenger by installing a quick-release skirt.

Figure 7-9. Midsection (belly) cover. Note the water deflector channels.

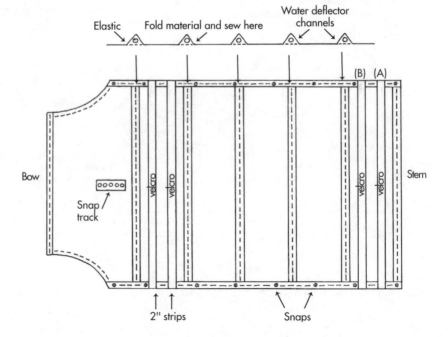

Making the Bow Covers

1. Cut a length of fabric that reaches from the tip of the bow to 12 inches forward of the center thwart. Loosely duct tape the material to the boat and mark the location of each snap with tailor's chalk.

2. Trim the fabric below the snap line, then hem the material along the marked points and sew seam tape to the inside hem. Set snaps through the hem to match those on the canoe.

3. Set the bow piece aside and repeat steps 1 and 2 to make the stern section. The stern piece should reach from the center of the stern deck to 12 inches forward of the stern thwart.

4. Snap the three cover sections on the canoe. The back end of the bow piece should overlap the belly by 2 feet. The front end of the stern cap should overlap the belly by at least 12 inches. Use 2-inch-wide Velcro to join the three pieces. Note that the twin Velcro tracks on the belly piece will provide a wide range of adjustment for loads of various heights. The hems of the bow and stern caps should mate with Velcro strip (B) when the canoe is unloaded or lightly loaded, and with strip (A) when there is a high load in the canoe. You'll have to experiment.

Making the Skirt

1. Snap the bow cover on the canoe, then draw the cockpit's location on the material with tailor's chalk. Next, cut the porthole; you'll find that a sharp jackknife works better for this than scissors. When sizing the cockpit, remember that you need room to both sit and kneel. Be sure to provide for the range of adjustment of a sliding seat.

2. Measure the circumference of the cockpit and add 3 inches. This is the length of material you'll need to make the sleeve. Next, decide how tall you want the sleeve to be. A piece of fabric 80 inches by 26 inches is a good starting size.

3. Make the quick-release skirt illustrated in figure 7-10 and 7-11. The skirt should release with your right hand (right-hand release) if you commonly paddle on the left

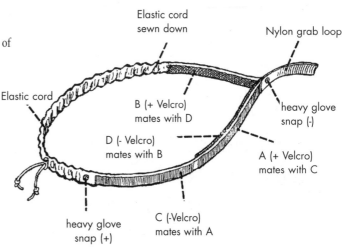

Figure 7-10. Sleeve—top view.

side of the canoe; it should release with your left hand (left-hand release) if you paddle on the right. Practice releasing the skirt so you'll be able to exit quickly if you capsize. Keep hold of your paddle as you bail out.

Final Touches

1. Install a snap (use a small flat-head brass screw) in the top center of the bow and stern thwart. Set the mating part of the snap into the back hem of the belly. A snap track like the one illustrated provides some adjustment. Snap the belly to the thwarts when you're running, white water (no tail cap)—or when you use the belly alone and want a taut cover that won't pool water.

2. Sew ties around each cockpit so you can roll and reef the sleeves in fair weather or when conditions require quick exit and entry. Also, install ties for the end caps so you can roll and tie them near the extreme ends of the canoe when portaging.

3. Sew Velcro tabs to the extreme forward end of each fabric deck to store your coiled tracking lines.

4. You won't have to fumble for a map if you sew mating Velcro strips on your map case and the canoe cover.

5. You may want to sew a spare paddle pocket on the belly section of the cover.

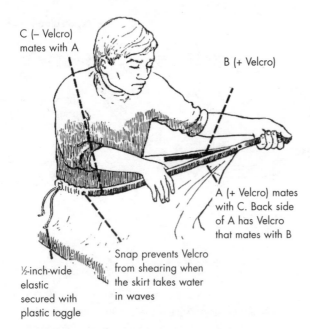

C (– Velcro)
mates with A

B (+ Velcro)

A (+ Velcro) mates
with C. Back side
of A has Velcro
that mates with B

½-inch-wide
elastic
secured with
plastic toggle

Snap prevents Velcro
from shearing when
the skirt takes water
in waves

Figure 7-11. Quick-release gusset. To seal the gusset, fold the sleeve to the right (left hand over right hand) until Velcro strip A mates with Velcro strip C. The Velcro at B will automatically mate with the Velcro on the back side of A. The sleeve can be tightened or loosened by adjusting the elastic hem cord.

6. Use the midsection of your cover as a squaw sail, as a tablecloth, or to cover packs or wood in camp.

Last-Minute Tips

■ You'll save substantial weight and bulk by constructing both skirts and the stern section from lightweight (two-ounce) coated nylon. The stern cap is used more for rain protection than for rapids, so it doesn't need to be as rugged as the other cover parts.

■ Use *two* nylon cord locks back to back on the elastic skirt cords that go around your waist. There's a lot of pressure on the skirt when waves pour into your lap. Twin cord locks keep things tight!

SOLO CANOE COVERS

Solo covers aren't just for white water. Try paddling an open solo canoe across a wind-lashed lake and you'll work much harder than your tandem friends. Now attach the cover. You've cut your wind resistance by half!

A cover will keep your solo canoe drier in calm seas, too. When you hut! (change paddle sides), paddle drips will spill harmlessly onto the cover rather than into the canoe. You can build a two-piece solo cover, like the one pictured in figure 7-12, in about a day.

A two-piece cover with a tail section that terminates just behind the seat and a forward section that overlaps and snaps to the rear section works best. The trim, flat covers won't catch wind, and the versatile two-piece design allows you to get at packs and loose gear without removing the whole cover.

Distribute your gear between two packs. Camping and cooking items go into a large-capacity pack placed in the forward end of the canoe, while frequently used essentials (rain and wind gear, a sweater, and the like) are kept in a medium-sized day pack behind the seat. To get at the small pack, just reach behind the seat and pull open the bow cover. In fair weather reef the front cover just in front of the cockpit; this produces a spacious opening with plenty of room to move about, yet it effectively catches paddle drips.

To portage, roll the front cover all the way to the bow and tie it in place so the fabric deck won't restrict visibility under the yoke. This eliminates the time-consuming practice of removing the entire cover, which is essential with a one-piece

Figure 7-12. A two-piece cover for a solo canoe. The front section overlaps and Velcros or snaps to the rear cover. Note the way the cockpit is rolled and reefed for a fast exit.

design. You'll find more information about covers and solo canoes in chapter 15.

Cooke Custom Sewing and Granite Gear (appendix B) both offer three-piece solo covers. They're similar to my three-piece tandem cover except the belly doesn't expand. I see no advantage in this design. The belly section must be removed to portage (it can be lost), and the Velcro strips that secure it to the end caps add weight and bulk. Installing and removing the center piece is just one more thing to do. I think you'll like the two-piece design best.

MAKING A TWO-PIECE SOLO CANOE COVER

Making a two-piece solo cover is similar to constructing a three-piece model. The only difference is that you want a tight fit along the length of the canoe with no expandable belly. (See color figure 7-13.) Taping the fabric to the canoe,

marking the snap line, sewing the nylon reinforcing tape along the inside hem—all these procedures are the same as outlined above. Also note:

- The bow section of a two-piece solo cover should overlap the stern piece by about 8 inches to allow for shrinkage.
- The covers mate on two Velcro tracks—same as in the three-piece tandem design.
- Two-inch-wide Velcro is overkill and too bulky for a lightweight solo cover: One-inch-wide Velcro holds just fine.

Covers are wonderful! They keep you warm and dry in rain and rapids, and they cut wind by half or more. If you can run rapids, you can run a sewing machine. If you can run a sewing machine, you can make a canoe cover!

CHAPTER 8
GEARING UP

Figure 8-1. Sue Harings, the author's wife, models some important items.

It was 10:00 P.M. and the sky was gentle gray—about as dark as it gets near timberline in mid-July. Not too late to fry another round of fish and make some popcorn.

I pumped some air into the cold brass tank of the Optimus 111B. A flick of my butane lighter brought the stove to life. Momentarily I sat mesmerized by the flickering yellow-blue flame and stunned by the piercing jet roar of its tiny engine.

I picked up the stove and moved it within arm's reach of the falls—close enough so I could feel the penetrating mist rising from the dancing waters below. Overhead a barely visible streak of luminous green flashed high across the sky. Northern lights?

I felt vibrantly alive, part of a vast greatness that was far beyond my comprehension. Here we were, the four of us—all good friends—to share the majesty of it all ... privately.

Then I heard the clanking of someone else's canoes, the voices. Damn! The spell had been broken.

My anger subsided and I regained composure. Less than enthusiastically I welcomed them as one by one they filed into the light and warmth of our small fire.

My God, they're soaking wet! I thought as I stretched out my hand in reluctant friendship. One man took the gesture and shivering, asked politely, "May we use your fire?" Suddenly I understood, and my crew leapt into action. We piled the fire high, prepared tea and honey, and served them course after course of fresh fried fish, biscuits with jam, and goodwill.

We learned they'd run a drop that we had portaged. Both canoes had swamped—one capsized, the other pinned against a rock. It had taken them the better part of the day to free it. Otherwise they'd have made the falls in daylight. They were government men, mapping the river for canoe travel. All were experienced canoeists, though from their looks you'd never guess it.

Later we helped the four of them unpack their gear and set up camp. Everything from the leather boots on their feet to their sleeping bags and food was wet. Their tent—a candy-striped canvas affair with a hard wax finish—oozed water and weighed at least ninety pounds.

They had no canvas Duluth packs or waterproof liners—only discount-store aluminum-frame packs that leaked like sieves. A less-than-watertight hand-built wanigan box contained some canned goods, eggs, and margarine. There was no stove or rainfly.

They were amiable fellows but we were not impressed by their gear or professed expertise.

Next morning they had the opportunity to see our equipment and methods. They stood in awe as we dropped and stuffed our tent in less than ninety seconds, prepared a gourmet breakfast of freeze-dried eggs and pancakes on our two gasoline stoves, filled thermos bottles with coffee and soup, and packed and loaded our canoes—all in barely sixty minutes.

For the most part they couldn't comprehend our equipment or our ways. We were warm, dry, and well organized. They were not. They poked fun at our Royalex canoes—"Tupperware tubs," they called them. But secretly we knew they were impressed. They were ordinary Fords and Chevys: we were the sports cars that just blew past.

In retrospect it's tempting to say, "They couldn't afford better." But I question that, because of their choice of gear. There is, for example, no excuse for wearing leather boots on any northern river, or for using packs better suited to the alpine trail than to the way of the canoe. And to omit waterproof liners for packs and sleeping bags is unthinkable. And about those canned goods …

If your skills are very good and you're very careful, you can get by quite well with pretty shoddy equipment. But if you're the least bit careless of have a run of bad luck, bad weather, bad rapids, or just bad judgment, watch out! You may find yourself in the same boat as the mapmakers you just read about.

Professing your expertise won't keep you warm and dry. Good equipment and the knowledge of how to use it will. Here's what you need.

PERSONAL GEAR

Life Jacket

Always wear your personal floatation device (PFD) when you're canoeing or working around water. This is especially important on Arctic rivers, where water temperatures are very low and a dunking may bring on rapid immobilization and hypothermia.

Paddling isn't the only time when accidents happen. I know of two near-drownings that resulted when canoeists slipped and fell into bad rapids while they were lining their canoes around it. Fortunately, both men were wearing life vests and had good hold of the lines.

Life jackets are getting better. The orange horse collars of the past are largely museum pieces now; most canoe liveries don't even use them anymore. Now you can choose from an array of high-tech models. Some styles are more comfortable (on some people) than others, so you'll have to try them all to know what's best for you.

Panel types feel great when you're canoeing, but they ride up over your head when you have to swim. Outfitters and families like them because one size fits all adults. (See color figure 8-2.) Bib-style white-water vests such as the Kokotat Outfit and Lotus Designs Rio Grande, which are sized like suits, are the exception. These trim PFDs feel good in the water and out, though they can be hot to wear. High-flotation white-water vests, which boast up to twenty-one pounds of buoyancy,[1] are wonderful for keeping you above the foamy white, but they're very bulky and hot.

You'll wear your life jacket from sunrise till sunset, so you want a model that's as comfortable as an old shoe. The only time I take off my PFD is for lunch stops along the river. My greatest fear on a canoe trip is that I will lose my life jacket. I take this fear seriously and instill it in all who paddle with me. When I remove my PFD at a riverside stop, I stuff the vest under the seat of my canoe so it won't be forgotten and an errant breeze won't blow it away. I keep my vest in my tent while we're camped.

Paranoid? Perhaps. But Arctic canoeists have a saying: "Wear your life jackets; it makes the bodies easier to find!"

Melodrama aside, rest assured that experienced canoeists seldom capsize in the wilds. A dunking on a cold northern river is deadly serious, so every effort is made to avoid it. The rule in the North is, "If in doubt, portage!" Your life jacket is a last-ditch safety precaution you shouldn't need. Still, my PFD has saved my life on three occasions: when I fell into a huge rapid that I was lining on an Ontario River; when my canoe capsized along the Hood River in Canada; and when my sailboat upset on a large lake and blew away before I could catch it. I swam for an hour to reach shore!

[1]The minimum flotation for Type III Coast Guard-approved PFDs is 15.5 pounds.

Figure 8-3. Author (left) wears a long-style ribbed white-water vest; his partner wears a kayak shorty. Kopka River, Ontario.

I prefer a standard-buoyancy (15.5 pounds) ribbed PFD like those made by Extrasport and Stearns. This type is comfortable in and out of water and provides good protection against hypothermia. It's also cooler than most other types—a plus when you paddle all day in the broiling sun. Shorty (kayak-style) models, which end a few inches above your waist, are the most comfortable, especially for short-waisted people (most women). However, a vest that covers your kidneys is nice when an icy wind comes from behind.

A good vest is more than just a buoyancy aid: It's a warm garment and an extension for a short-length sleeping mat.

Fitting Your Life Vest

Proper fit is *everything*. How the vest feels on your body is every bit as important as its performance in water. For this reason it's best not to buy a PFD by mail. Sizing, cut, flexibility, and utility vary widely from manufacturer to manufacturer. To test the fit of a PFD that catches your fancy, begin by trying it on over the bulkiest clothing you plan to wear canoeing. Then perform these tests:

- **Ride-up:** Grasp the jacket by the shoulders and lift it upward until the fabric jams under your armpits. This simulates performance in water. Now turn your head right and left. You should be looking over your shoulder, not at fabric-encased foam. Does the V-neck of the vest crunch against your chin? If so, keep shopping. PFDs that force the chin up may have a more positive righting moment that those that don't but they hinder maneuverability in water—exactly what you don't want when you have to swim a rapid.

- **Buoyancy:** Standard procedure for floating rapids is to get on your back with your feet held high to prevent somersaulting in the current. Use your feet and paddle to ward off rocks. In this attitude the flotation foam on your chest is worthless. So reject any PFD that has a skimpy or skeon foam back.

- **Arm function:** Take a seat. This test won't work while standing or kneeling. Now work your arms vigorously in a paddling motion. Reject any vest that chafes

Figure 8-4. Check the fit of your PFD by lifting it upward until the fabric jams under your armpits. Turn your head: You should be able to see clearly. The ribbed vest (left) is a good fit; the panel vest (right) is too sloppy.

ness trip than on a casual float. Remember this when you size your PFD. When my wife and I canoed the Lewis River (altitude 8,000 feet) in Yellowstone National Park, we relearned an interesting eighth-grade science fact—that closed-cell foam expands as altitude increases, and shrinks as altitude decreases. Our trusty foam-filled PFDs, which fit fine back home in Wisconsin (altitude 790 feet) and on scores of Canadian rivers, were suddenly too small! You may want to remember this when you suit up for a mountain river.

I can't stress enough the importance of choosing a well-ventilated life vest that's roomy and cool to wear. Performance in the water doesn't mean much if you can't stand to wear the vest while you paddle.

Tuning Your PFD

Any PFD that has been altered is no longer Coast Guard approved. It's a reasonable law, and for the most part a good one. But some paddlers—especially short-waisted ones—have a hard time finding vests that don't chafe under the armpits. You could try to live with the vest, cussing it at every opportunity, or you could throw it into the bottom of the canoe to be worn only when necessary. A more reasonable alternative is to cut out a small sliver of the obtrusive foam and resew the jacket. Doing so will both negate the CG approval and increase ride-up in water. The trade-off is increased comfort—a jacket you can live with.

If trimming a sliver of foam from a delicate place means you'll wear the PFD *all* the time, then do it, rules or no rules. In any case do try the vest in water under controlled conditions. Don't save the experimentation for the river!

Paddles

Each person needs two paddles—a 12- to 14-degree bent-shaft model for fast cruising, and a beefy straight stick for rapids.

The Right Length

Any prescription for paddle length must take into account the kind of canoe (white-water tripper, flat-water cruiser, racer) you're paddling, the height of the seats, the length of your torso, and how you prefer to paddle-dynamic racing-switch style, moderate-paced North Woods J-stroke, or whatever.

Height of your canoe seat: The higher you sit, the longer your paddle must be to reach the water. Seats on the typical high-volume Royalex tripping canoe are set relatively

under your armpits. You'll find it intolerable to wear over the long haul.

- **Flexibility:** Hold your arms chest high and draw them smartly inward as far as possible. Does the vest bunch up in front and cramp arm motion? If so, keep shopping!

Don't be surprised if you can't find a PFD that passes all four tests. Unless you have a book-perfect built, none will.

Subtle Concerns

You'll wear more clothing under a life vest on a wilder-

high (11 to 13 inches off the floor) for comfort, while those on modern fine-lined cruisers are strung low (7 to 9 inches) for stability. What's best in one canoe may be awkward in another.

Length of your arms and torso: Long-armed folks who sit tall in the saddle can wield long paddles; short-armed people like me need stubbier sticks. To determine the appropriate length for your body, set your canoe in the water and climb aboard. Then measure the distance from your nose (height of the grip) to the water. That's the *shaft* length. To this add the length of the blade (20 to 25 inches, depending on paddle style). That's the correct paddle length for you.

Or try this formula, which addresses the change in freeboard (and seat height) that results when you place a heavy load of camping gear into your canoe. Set your canoe on soft ground and sit on the seat. Measure from your nose to the floor. Subtract 3 inches. That's your shaft length. Add the length of the blade to this figure and you'll be close to your ideal measurement. Bent-shaft paddles may be a bit shorter, straight paddles slightly longer. Generally your bent paddle should be about 2 inches shorter than your favorite straight paddle.

Experienced canoeists will note that this second formula gives an overall paddle length somewhat longer than what's commonly recommended. Good. A heavily loaded tripping canoe needs the leverage of a longer paddle. A 56- to 58-inch straight paddle or a 54- to 56-inch bent paddle is about right for the high-volume tripping canoes I'm talking about.

Straight, Bent, or Both?

If you want to go fast and maximize your energy flow, get a bent-shaft paddle. There's hardly an accomplished canoeist today who doesn't own at least one.

Straight paddles waste energy because they lift water at the end of the stroke and slow the canoe. Bent paddles push water almost straight back and convert nearly all the thrust to energy. Bent blades are easier on your body, too: Users often report that they no longer get "paddler's elbow" (tennis elbow) and "sleeping hand" (tingling fingers) after long hours afloat once they switch to bent blades.

Fourteen-degree bends were popular a decade ago; now the trend is 12-degree bends. The shallower angle encourages a higher, more relaxed position. Bends of less than 12 degrees don't offer much advantage over a straight shaft.

When rapids loom ahead it's time to put aside your bent-shaft and grab your straight one. Sure, you can do hot tricks in rapids with a bent-shaft, but you must reverse the angled blade to brace across an eddy line, and blending strokes requires you to think. Only the best canoeists will have the cool forethought to do both in really mean water. I love my bent-shaft, but I won't use it in rapids. I suggest you don't either.

Features to Look For

Durable edging: Old-time paddles were tipped with metal or fiberglass. Today's best blades are protected by a tough resin tip, which was pioneered by the Bending Branches Canoe Company in Wisconsin. Nonreinforced wooden tips should be fiberglassed. One layer of six-ounce-per-square-yard fiberglass cloth is adequate and doesn't add too much weight. See chapter 20 for procedures; you'll find some suggested epoxies in appendix B.

Solid wood or laminate? Laminated paddles are lighter, stiffer, and stronger than some solid woods. But if you like the traditional look of a solid-wood paddle, go for it. American white ash will stand up to any rapids.

Ultralight Paddles

The lighter the paddle, the better. Even an ounce or two makes a big difference over the long haul. Good wooden paddles weigh eighteen to twenty-four ounces—half a pound lighter than most hardware-store sticks. If you think that's light, check out the ultralight graphite blades that weigh eight to fourteen ounces. My favorite touring paddle is a carbon black Zaveral, a 12-degree bent-shaft that weighs just ten ounces. (Zaveral also makes a six-ounce paddle!) My wife prefers a composite version that's more flexible but weighs three ounces more. Our Zavs have accompanied us on many wild Canadian rivers but show little wear. You're in for a real surprise if you haven't tried a modern graphite paddle.

When rapids loom ahead, I tuck away my beloved Zaveral and switch to an iron-tough white-water paddle manufactured by the Grey Owl company in Canada.

Blade Shape

Blade shape is largely a matter of preference, though there are some rules:

- Stiff paddles are best for bracing in rapids; you'll want some flex for cruising.

- Short, wide blades are for shallow water; long, narrow blades are for deep water. Narrow blades are quieter and easier to control than wide blades, and they produce less torque steer. Eight inches is a good all-

Figure 8-5. The author with his Zaveral paddle. Early June, Shoshone Lake, Yellowstone National Park, Wyoming.

around width for a cruising paddle.

- Avoid paddles that have harsh corners. Square-tipped paddles aren't very durable, and they tend to twist in your hands if you don't set them into the water vertically.

- Both sides of a paddle blade should look the same. Blades that have an asymmetrical face (one side flat, one side cambered)or reinforcing spine often gurgle noisily when pulled sideways through the water.

- If you want a quiet running blade, select one with

ruler-thin edges all around. Naturally, white-water paddles need some beef for durability.

Sleeping Bag

No mystery here: If it packs small and keeps you warm, it's good enough. No need to buy an Arctic bag. Canoe-country temperatures even near the Arctic Circle seldom go much below 25 degrees, and for that any three-season sleeping bag is adequate.

Bulk is much more critical on a canoe trip than weight, so get a bag that packs as compactly as possible. If it won't compress into a 9-inch by 18-inch round-bottomed stuff sack, shop elsewhere. And don't believe that down bags are unsuitable for canoeing because "they won't keep you warm if they get wet." Really, now, have you ever slept in a wet polyester bag? Or tried to dry one under typical field conditions? I doubt that you'll find either experience to your liking.

If you get your down sleeping bag—or anything else— wet on a canoe trip, you need to learn some basic packing and camping skills! I've never gotten my sleeping bag wet. If you pack as I suggest in the next chapter, you won't either.

In case you're wondering, I prefer down sleeping bags. They're warmer, lighter, more compact, more luxurious, and longer lived than any of the synthetics.

Trail Mattress

Look for comfort, reliability and reasonable size when rolled. I prefer a 60-inch-long self-inflating air-foam pad like those made by Therma-Rest and Artiach. For many years I preferred a shorty (48-inch) Therma-Rest and used my life jacket to extend its length. But the longer pad is much more luxurious.

I've owned three Therma-Rest pads since 1974, two of which failed after a season's use. I traced the problem to microscopic punctures in the nylon-vinyl shell. Repair was impossible. Solution? Cover the pad with sturdy fabric. I sewed up a simple envelope of six-ounce-per-square-yard cotton and slid the Therma-Rest inside.

The easily removable cover resists abrasion and punctures, feels comfortable against bare skin, and clings tenaciously to the tent floor. My covered Therma-Rest is fifteen years old now, and it has never developed a leak.

Some thoughts on cover materials: Cotton flannel feels cool and luxurious in hot, steamy weather, but it can become clammy on cold, wet nights. Wool is wonderful when the weather's cold and damp, but it can be scratchy against bare skin. It follows that the ideal pad cover has cool cotton on one side and warm wool on the other. Perhaps a commercial pad cover like this will be available some day. Right now, you'll have to make your own.

Air mattresses are largely a thing of the past. They're slow to inflate and cold to sleep on when temperatures drop below freezing. (Of course, you can team one with a thin closed-cell foam pad; put the pad on top, next to your body.) And even the best-cared-for air product won't last forever. So if cost or extreme reliability is a concern, stick with old-fashioned closed-cell foam or fabric-covered open-cell (polyurethane) foam.

CLOTHING

Hats

You need a hat for sun, a hat for rain, and a hat for cold. It's doubtful you'll find a single chapeau that does it all well.

One solution is to carry a wool-felt crusher hat and a knitted wool stocking cap. The former works marginally well for sun and rain, while the latter keeps your head warm when temperatures plunge.

Though it may seem extravagant, I carry three hats—a lightweight Tilley canvas hat with a wide brim and a grommeted crown for hot, sunny days; a wool stocking cap for cold; and a comical-looking but highly effective neoprene-coated sou'wester for rain. I dislike hoods on rain gear: They restrict visibility, snap around my neck in the wind, and don't protect my eyeglasses from rain. The sou'wester is the logical choice. It folds compactly and weighs almost nothing. When it's really wet and cold, I wear my stocking cap under my sou'wester!

Note: If your hat has a wide brim that can be snapped to the crown cowboy style, be sure it secures with snaps rather than Velcro. Wind will cause the brim to flutter and catch on the Velcro. This can be quite annoying in a storm.

Windbreaker

A good windbreaker is a versatile canoeing garment. Wear it over a wool sweater or jac-shirt to cut the fierce wind, or alone on a hot day to keep the bugs from biting through your wool shirt.

Some authorities dismiss wind gear as superfluous and suggest that a rainjacket will suffice to lock both wind and rain. It won't, for two good reasons:

- You'll broil in your own juices if you wear a nonporous garment and work hard.

- Rain gear won't stay waterproof for very long if you wear it every day for wind protection.

This last point is extremely important. Every time you lean against a rock, you slightly abrade the material of the rain coat; whenever you turn your head or move your arms, you scrape off a microscopic amount of chemical waterproofing from the inside of the fabric. And don't forget the spark holes you'll accumulate when you get too near the fire. In no time pinholes will develop and the garment will be useless for its intended purpose. And it doesn't make much difference whether your jacket is make form polyurethane-coated nylon or nylon-laminated Gore-Tex. Gore-Tex may be waterproof and breathable when it's spanking new, but wear it day in and day out for a month on a wilderness canoe trip and see how well it keeps you dry. If you use Gore-Tex, *decide when you purchase it* which function—wind or rain resistance—you want it to perform, then treat it accordingly!

Some canoeists wear a lightweight Gore-Tex jacket for wind and light rain and add a polyurethane-coated nylon rain shell over it when the occasion demands. This was the combination preferred by Verlen Kruger and Steve Landick on their 28,000-mile cross-continent canoe trip.

It makes no difference whether your windbreaker is constructed of nylon, cotton, or a Dacron blend. What's important

Figure 8-6. Cliff Jacobson (left) and David VanLandshoot model their nylon wind shells. Thlewiaza River, Northwest Territories.

is that it is lightweight and sized large enough to fit over several layers of shirts and sweaters. Some expensive "mountain parkas" have stylishly cut sleeves and waists that won't accommodate layered clothing. The U.S. Army field jacket, available at most surplus stores, is a true mountain parka. It's rugged and quite inexpensive.

Invariably you'll wear your life vest over your wind shell most of the time, so there's little sense paying extra for sophisticated pockets you'll seldom use.

Shirts

Two medium-weight nearly pure-wood shirts are enough for the longest canoe trip. Cotton shirts have no place on a northern river—they provide little insulation and are clammy when wet.

Best buy in wool shirts is the Marine Corps Officers Model shirt, which can be purchased at many surplus stores. This shirt is woven from 100 percent fine wool and has extra-long tails and button-down breast pockets. The last Officers wool shirt I bought in 1986 cost $10—a veritable steal. The sewing and tailoring on these shirts are equivalent to those found on shirts that cost four times as much.

Bugproof your shirt sleeves by sewing Velcro to the wrist openings just behind the cuffs (figure 8-7). This will allow you to seal the shirt cuffs completely.

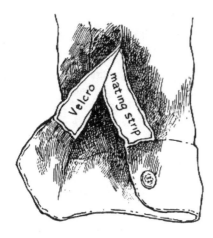

Figure 8-7. Bugproof your shirt cuffs by sewing mating Velcro strips to them.

Fleece Shirts and Jackets

The latest rage in outerwear is polyester fleece. And for good reason: It's soft, nonallergenic, luxuriously warm, and it absorbs very little water. Simply wring it out after a dousing and you're set for the river.

There are some drawbacks. Greatest is bulk: The typical fleece shirt consumes as much pack space as two or three wool shirts. And fleece is neither windproof nor water repellent. A good wool shirt will ward off a light shower; fleece will soak through instantly.

Then there's the matter of tailoring. The generously cut body and balloon sleeves of fleece garments allow unrestricted movement—a plus while paddling or lounging. But extra bulk here is a handicap when layering additional clothing on top. An exception is the paddling jacket—a short-waisted sweater with three-quarter-length sleeves. This garment is designed to be worn under a waterproof nylon shell with tight-fitting cuffs.

Criticisms aside, polyester fleece is marvelously adapted to canoeing. I highly recommend it!

Paddling Shirt/Wet Suit/Dry Suit

A paddling shirt is a lightweight waterproof jacket (most are Gore-Tex) that fits tightly at the neck, cuffs, and waist. White-water paddlers wear one over a wet-suit top or fleece sweater to trap body heat and keep out water. A paddling shirt will provide a measure of protection against hypothermia if you capsize in cold water. It's worth bringing one along if you're going in harm's way.

Wear a wet suit on a wilderness river and you'll sweat when it's hot, freeze when it's cold, and learn about heat exhaustion when you portage. For these reasons, most wilderness canoeists avoid neoprene and take their chances if they capsize. Still, a wet suit (even just one per party) can be useful—not for daily wear, mind you, but in case you need to go into icy water to rescue a wrapped canoe.

Dry suits are more comfortable and less bulky than wet suits. They're worth considering if you're canoeing a cold mountain river where hypothermia is a certainty if you capsize.

Sweater or Jacket

A heavyweight pure wool or jac-shirt or knitted wool or fleece sweater will round out your cold-weather wardrobe. Team long johns, wool shirt and pants, sweater, and windbreaker and you're set for near-0 temperatures. If you're still cold with all this on, put on your foam-filled life vest. And if that doesn't do the trick, you'd best hang up your paddle and wax your skis!

Long Trousers

Wool trousers are warm when wet but are not very mosquito proof. Cotton-canvas pants are the opposite. In the end your choice should depend on how cold it is, how buggy it is, and whether or not you plan to wear long johns.

I usually wear strong nylon hiking pants or army-surplus chinos and pack a pair of medium-weight surplus wool trousers as a spare and for cold weather. But I wear wool or polyester long underwear in all but the warmest weather.

Another solution is to team lightweight long-john bottoms with fast-drying nylon river pants. The disadvantage is that river pants usually don't have belt loops, so you'll need an auxiliary belt to carry your sheath knife, multitool, and so on.

If you can find a pair of U.S. Army tropical (pure) wool trousers, buy them! They're light and cool and they don't take up much pack space: Tropical wool trousers also resist chilling better than nylon river pants, and they dry nearly as fast. Wear them alone on hot days or over long johns when it's cool.

Tuck your pant legs inside your boots or seal them around the boot tops with military blousing bands or Velcro tabs sewn to the bottom of each leg. If you wear your pants outside your boots, the bottoms will get wet whenever you step into shallow water. The open legs also provide an avenue for blackflies.

If you're canoeing above the tree line, you may want to bring lightweight nylon wind pants. Some barren-land paddlers also include fleece trousers for camp. Mix near-freezing temperature with a 50-mile-per-hour wind and you'll be glad you brought some extra-warm clothes!

Long Johns

Long underwear isn't absolutely essential, but it will add greatly to your comfort on cold, rainy days. It's the insulation right next to your skin that does the trick.

For years the fabric of choice was wool—and only wool! No other material kept you as warm and dry in damp, cold weather. Then man-made fibers—polypropylene, polyester, and proprietary blends—came onto the scene, accompanied by reams of research that suggested wool was old hat.

I've tried most of the synthetics under very chilling conditions on long canoe trips in the Far North, but frankly, I keep coming back to wool. The synthetics dry quickly but they don't wear as well as the natural product. They also pill badly and tend to retain body odors. After a week in the bush, some brands reek so badly that they become intolerable. And unlike the case of wool, field washing in cold water without detergent fails to get the smell out.

Once a bottle of bug dope ruptured in a friend's pant pocket and dissolved a swatch of his polypropylene underwear. Wool, on the other hand, is immune to most solvents, and it can be washed or dry-cleaned as you prefer. It also insulates well when loaded with oils and dirt. Exposure to sun and wind tames most odors.

Nonetheless, synthetics remain part of my canoeing wardrobe. I like their light weight and soft, silky feel. But high-grade wool seems to resist chilling better. Hype aside, good wool won't let you down in any weather.

Here are my preferences:

■ Swedish-made Ullfrotté underwear—made from 60 percent wool, 25 percent polyester, and 15 percent polyamide—tops my list. After extensive testing, the Norwegian military recently switched from other synthetics to Ullfrotté. The soft no-itch merino wool defies chilling, and the synthetic components hasten drying and eliminate perspiration. Odors don't accumulate after long days afield. Most people who are allergic to wool can comfortably wear this underwear, which is available from several dealers, including Duluth Pack (appendix B). You can also try the Ullfrotté Web site (www.ulfrotte.com).

Features include a long zippered throat that opens wide for ventilation and converts to a high turtleneck. The heavy-weight jac-shirt model has a full-length zipper and finger-length cuffs (wristlets) that include a thumb hole. Ingenious!

■ DuPont Thermax. My wife, Susie, turned me on to this fabric years ago. She likes it because it's one of the few synthetics that don't absorb odors. Thermax feels silky against the skin; it dries fast and washes up nicely in cold water.

■ On rare occasions I wear old-fashioned polypropylene, which weighs almost nothing and dries instantly. But it smells really foul after a few days afield.

Buy what you like and can afford, but remember that the advantage of one state-of-the-art synthetic over another (or wool) is usually less pronounced under typical field conditions than the manufacturer would have you believe.

Only cotton underwear, in any blend, is unsuitable for use in the wilds. If you wear cotton next to your skin on a damp, chilly day, you'll be colder than if you hadn't worn the garment at all!

You'll discover that long johns of any type reduce black-fly bites and their accompanying welts. Blackflies can't gnaw through clothing of any kind, which means they must get under your underwear to bite. And that's not easy if you seal your lower pant legs and shirt cuffs as I've recommended.

Low-Cost Outerwear

Try a wardrobe of 100 percent Orlon acrylic. Verlen Kruger and Steve Landick chose acrylics for their 28,000-mile canoe trip. Almost every article of clothing they wore was made from this material. Both men claim that acrylics dry faster than wool, insulate about as well, are soft and comfortable to wear, and are nonallergenic.

You'll find all sorts of acrylic shirts and sweaters at local stores, but you won't find acrylic field pants. Steve and Verlen made their own.

Canoeing with children? Inexpensive acrylic garments are ideal for youngsters who grow into a new size each year.

Footwear

Want to start an argument? Just declare your choices of footwear to a group of experienced canoeists. Everyone has his or her own idea of what's best, and debates will range far into the night. When the smoke clears, however, all will agree that you need *two* pairs of boots—one for use in the canoe and on the portage trail, and another for general camp use.

For trips in the barren lands, where frequent lining and therefore wading in bitter-cold water is the rule, *good-quality* rubber boots with steel shanks and 16-inch-high tops can't be beat. Rubber boots are the only foot gear that will keep your feet perfectly dry when you stand in water for long periods of time.

"Tingleys over tennies" are also popular on northern rivers. Tingley rubber overshoes roll to fist size and their soft soles won't slip on wet rocks. Indeed, they're better for rock-hopping (lining) than most wet shoes that are built for the purpose. Wear wool socks and sneakers inside Tingleys and

you're set for both summer sun and an Arctic adventure. Tingleys look fragile but wear like iron—I've used the same pair on three Arctic canoe trips. Most big hardware chains carry Tingley boots. They are very inexpensive.

Another solution is the L. L. Bean (appendix B) shoe-pac, which teams a fully waterproof rubber bottom with a water-resistant leather top. Bean boots aren't as waterproof as rubber boots (a real minus in the bone-chilling waters of the Far North) but they're more comfortable for hiking. They can also be resoled (most copies can't) when the bottoms wear out. And they come in sizes to fit women and children.

Bean boots are best worn with sheepskin-lined leather insoles—available from L. L. Bean. I prefer 12-inch tops for all-around use.

River sandals are fine for wading warm streams as long as there are no pebbles that can catch underfoot and no mosquitoes or blackflies to nip your toes. Sandals work if you're rafting, but they're an abomination on a northern river.

Reef runners are flexible nylon moccasins that secure with Velcro or elastic—neither of which is secure in rapids. Designed for surfboarding and sailing, they work well for warm-water canoeing where there are no portages or pebbles. However, reef runners do protect your feet from sharp rocks while swimming, and for this reason alone they're worth bringing along on a canoe trip.

Figure 8-8. The perfect footwear for canoeing hasn't been invented. Cliff's friends model some ideas on a canoe trip down Manitoba's North Knife River. Left to right: Tingleys, tennies, neoprene booties, Bean boots, neoprene booties, Tingleys, Gore-Tex hiking boots, high-top canvas sneakers.

Wet-suit booties are great for spring white-water runs but not on the portage trail. Whether or not they have a place on a wild river depends on your willingness to change into more rugged boots when you need to carry your stuff overland.

Wearing wet-suit socks inside oversized sneakers is an inexpensive way to keep your feet dry when running a wild river. Get 'em at any dive shop.

On the surface it would seem that neoprene socks with sneakers are ideal for cold-water wilderness canoeing. Not so. They're comfortable to wear for a few hours but not all day long, day in and day out. Sheathing your feet in waterproof rubber for long periods of time is never a good idea, even when conditions seem to warrant it.

Some canoeists who like cold feet wear nylon sneakers or canvas Vietnam boots. This footwear is wonderful for paddling warm waterways, but it's not practical for use on a cold northern river. If you wear sneakers, combine them with wet-suit socks or wear them inside Tingley rubber boots or five-buckle galoshes. Galoshes and sneakers were the footwear Clint Waddell chose for his 7,000-mile canoe trip with Verlen Kruger to the Bering Sea.

Chota Outdoor Gear (appendix B) recently released a line of neoprene boots and accessories designed especially for canoeists. The notable items are the Quetico Trekker and the Nunavut Mukluk. The Trekker is an ultralight, ultratough, ankle-high wading shoe that can be worn with wool socks or a fitted knee-high, fleece-lined wading sock. The Nunavut Mukluk can best be described as a knee-high rubber boot with a fleece-lined neoprene top that retards flooding.

Nylon or leather boots with integral Gore-Tex sock liners are lightweight, incredibly comfortable, reasonably sweat-free and require no break-in period. They also keep your feet dry—a real plus for canoeists who continually step into and out of water.

Nonetheless, Gore-Tex footwear is not popular with canoeists. High cost is one reason, as is the fact that most boots can't be easily resoled (new models are much better in this respect). It's also hard to find summer-weight Gore-Tex boots with tops much higher than 8 inches.

Gore-Tex socks are a reasonably inexpensive way to convert leaky leather boots into fully waterproof ones. To prevent abrasive damage (and possible failure), Gore-Tex socks must be worn over regular hiking socks or sandwiched between a lightweight sock liner and a heavier outer sock (you may need a larger-sized boot to eliminate a too-tight fit).

Over the short haul Gore-Tex socks work great. On a long expedition you may have to contend with abrasion and punctures—which will spell failure. Nonetheless, this product is an interesting alternative to sweaty rubber boots, wet-suit socks, and shoe-pacs.

When it comes to camp shoes, just about any comfortable boot—leather, nylon or shoe-pac—is adequate. The important thing is to select footwear that packs small and dries fast—which eliminates foam-lined hiking boots. Unlined leather boots or lightweight shoe-pacs are the sensible choices. Stay away from hard soles that won't bend with your feet when you kneel in rapids, and aggressive Vibram soles that trap mud and track it into the canoe.

My preference? For the past three years, I have relied on Chota Nunavut mukluks, and I am completely won over to them. I also like the Breathable Top Mukluks, which are cooler but less rugged. My camp shoe is the lightweight Chota Quetico Trekker, which can be worn as a wet shoe, dry portage boot, or in combination with Chota's waterproof knee-high wader. If wading cold rivers is in the cards, I bring neoprene booties with felt soles.

Gloves

Gloves are one of the most essential and forgotten items on a canoe trip. Buckskin gloves dry soft and are a logical choice for warm weather. Wool gloves with leather palms (so you can grip the paddle) are better in rain and cold. Acrylic or polypropylene gloves dry quickly but wet through instantly. Gore-Tex gloves—popular with duck hunters for setting out decoys—work great for frigid-water canoeing but are too bulky for casual paddling. Neoprene gloves, like those used by skin divers, provide the best protection of all when freezing rains come to stay. Water-skiing gloves (these have textured fabric palms and thin neoprene backs) are superb when rain and wind (not cold!) are the culprits.

I carry leather-faced wool gloves for trips within the timberline. In the barrens and everywhere in the North Country during spring and fall, I use leather-faced woolens and neoprene wet-suit or Gore-Tex gloves. You can't paddle with your hands in your pockets—reason enough to give gloves serious consideration.

Rain Gear

No item of clothing is more important than *really good* rain gear! Ponchos and below-the-knee rain shirts don't qualify. Ponchos don't provide adequate protection in a wind-blown rain, and neither garment is safe in a capsize.

A two-piece rainsuit is your best bet. Buy your rain jacket a *full size* larger than you think you need—large enough to wear over several layers of warm clothes *and* your life vest. It's very frustrating (and time consuming) to alternately put on and take off a life vest every time an intermittent shower necessitates a change in your wardrobe. [2]

Pay particular attention to the neck and wrist closures and hood design of a rain garment. It's essential that the neck area seal tightly and as high up the throat as possible. Even the smallest gap here will permit wind-blown rain to slither down your neck—a chilling experience!

If you don't plan to wear a sou'wester hat, be sure the hood is roomy enough to accommodate a wool or canvas broad-brimmed hat. Only a fully waterproof hat or nonwaterproof one worn beneath a rain hood will keep you dry in a downpour.

When rains begin you'll put your rain jacket over your life vest. As the weather worsens you'll add your rain pants . . . and reverse the procedure as rains let up. So don't buy rain pants that have integral bibs (suspenders)—you'll have to

Figure 8-9. The crew models rain gear as the author prepares supper. Note that Cliff is wearing two hats—a canvas Tilley and a waterproof sou'wester. North Knife River, Manitoba.

remove your life vest *and* rain jacket every time you want to put on or take off your rain pants.

If your rain trousers have an elastic waist cord, tear it out and substitute parachute cord and two plastic toggles. Elastic stretches when it gets wet, and rain pants keep falling down. The nylon cord and toggles are more secure and comfortable.

Trim rain pants short enough that they won't catch brush when you walk, and don't use the silly snap closures at the ankle—they restrict ventilation.

Your choice of fabrics depends on how light you want to travel and how dry you want to stay. Good-quality ultralight-weight polyurethane-coated nylon will suffice if you carefully waterproof the seams at least once a year, wear the garment only when it rains, are careful to avoid holes and tears, and store the outfit in a nylon sack when you're not wearing it.

Even then, don't expect any lightweight rain suit to keep you dry in a severe all-day rain. Only heavyweight foul-weather sailing gear that's built to military specs will do this. Using foul-weather sailing gear for canoe trips may seem like overkill, but when the chips are down, weight and bulk are secondary to staying warm and dry.

Many paddlers have found that a rain suit made of waterproof, breathable Gore-Tex is the answer to their foul-weather needs. Early Gore-Tex rainwear was a disaster: The stuff leaked unpredictably. Part of the problem was the Gore-Tex substrate itself, which failed when it became soiled. Then there was the matter of bad tailoring—skimpy weather flaps over zippers and pockets, improper seam sealing, and so forth.

Now improvements in substrate chemistry, machine-sealing of seams, and more thoughtful tailoring have produced a reliable class of garments dubbed Rainwear Without Compromise. I've been wearing one of these parkas for the past five years, and it earns high marks. My jacket has weathered a number of heavy, sustained rains (one of which lasted three days), and it remains watertight.

Two years ago I tried an experiment. I purchased two lightweight, Gore-Tex rain jackets. One jacket has a full zipper; the other is an anorak style that goes quickly over my head. When rain begins I put on the full zip model, followed by my PFD. This allows great freedom of movement and adequate protection in moderate rain. If the storm picks up, I put the anorak over my PFD. This second (separated) waterproof

---

[2]It's recommended that you never wear anything over your life jacket when running rapids. In the real wilderness, however, it's occasionally necessary to make a few compromises for the sake of comfort.

layer eliminates leaks and ventilates well. The two jackets are less confining than one heavier coat. I now prefer this system.

Again, let me stress that no waterproof garment will last long if you wear it as an everyday wind garment.

CURING WHAT BUGS YOU

It's said that fully 95 percent of all the protoplasm in the Far North is concentrated in the bodies of blackflies and mosquitoes. I believe it. There've been times when I'd swear the entire mass of them was on me! I've never been on a canoe trip north of the 55th parallel on which I didn't need my head net and repellent on at least one occasion.

I once saw a cow moose crash wildly into a small clearing along a portage trail in northern Ontario. A huge cloud of blackflies hovered around her head. The flies were everywhere—in her nose and ears, around her eyes and mouth. She stood there dappled in the morning sunlight, wild-eyed, snorting in pain, and repeatedly beat her head against the branches of a scrub birch tree nearby. We came within 20 feet of her, yet she never sensed us. She was obviously quite disoriented. I don't know why she didn't jump into the river, which was just a few hundred feet away.

Frankly, surviving bugs is mostly a matter of attitude. If you harden yourself to their presence and cover most exposed skin, you'll stay sane and avoid most bites. Still, there are

Figure 8-10. Blackflies by the thousands coat the leeward side of this tent in the Dubawnt Canyon along the Dubawnt River.

occasions when repellents, head nets, body nets, and screened tarps are godsends.

Repellents

Almost any commercial repellent will deter mosquitoes, but only those that contain deet (N-N diethyl-metatoluamide) work very well in blackfly country. Generally, the more deet a repellent has, the better it works. The Centers for Disease Control and the U.S. Army recommend 30 percent deet for problem bugs. My own experience canoeing in the Arctic suggests that this is enough for all but the meanest blackflies.

There have been some concerns that extensive use of deet may cause health problems. Extensive tests by the U.S. government reveal that it's safe for adults. However, adults with sensitive skin—and all children—should use a mild, cream-based (no deet) repellent or a controlled release formula like the one recently released by the Sawyer Company. The Sawyer formula uses a newly patented technology called Sub-Micron Encapsulation. A patented skin-nourishing protein builds walls around the deet molecules and encapsulates them. The capsules keep the deet away from the skin. The deet is released as the skin metabolizes the protein. The product works great for mosquitoes, but not blackflies. It must be applied to skin; it won't work if you put it on clothes.

The safest plan with all repellents is to first rub sunblock deep into your skin, wait ten minutes, then apply the repellent. The sunblock keeps your body from absorbing too much of the chemical. If possible, select one of the new bonding-base sunblocks, which penetrate deep into your skin. Film-base sunblocks cover just the skin's surface.

Head Nets

I always carry two head nets in case I lose one. Nonmilitary styles that don't have a helmet hoop around the face are best because they roll to fist size and fit in your pocket. You can make a head net by simply sewing up a wide rectangle of mosquito netting. (Don't use tightly woven no-see-um netting, which can be intolerably hot.) Make it large enough to fit over your head and hat, and long enough to drape lazily on your shoulders. You don't need security buttons or an elastic neckband.

Daub repellent on the hem of your head net and blackflies will be confused. Spray the net with repellent and tiny no-see-ums won't come near. Head nets (and tent screens) should be colored black for good visibility. If you can't find a black head net, darken the eye panel of a light-colored one

Figure 8-11. Loss of a head net can be serious. Always carry a spare. Hood River, Nunavut.

Bug Jackets

The wonderful deet-impregnated Shoo-Bug jacket, which I recommended in past editions of this book is no longer manufactured. Now most canoeists rely on the Original Bug Shirt (appendix B), which is made in Canada. It combines fine-mesh netting and ultralight, bleached white cotton. The zippered hood has an integral face net so you don't need a head net. Cord-lock-controlled elastic closures at the wrist and waist provide an impenetrable seal. The sleeves are long enough to be closed while you nap. Ventilation is adequate for all but the hottest days.

Susie Bug Nets

If bugs drive you batty, you'll want a Susie bug net—a personal-sized bug armor designed by my wife, Sue Harings (figure 8-12). You can make your own or buy one from Cooke Custom Sewing (appendix B).

You'll need a piece of dark-colored mosquito netting 12 feet long and 7 feet wide, plus enough ⅛-inch-diameter shock cord to span the hem. No-see-um netting isn't strong enough, and you can't see through it.

Fold the netting in half to produce a rectangular sheet

with black paint, dye, or Magic Marker. Horace Kephart addressed the stupidity of light-colored nets in his classic book *Camping and Woodcraft,* which was published in 1917—netting manufacturers please take note![3]

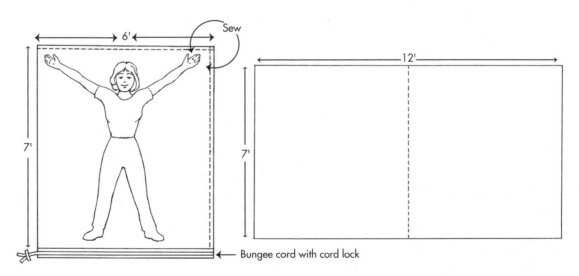

Figure 8-12. The Susie bug net.

[3] Outdoor Research (appendix B) makes a coal black head net with a stainless-steel band that compresses to 4 inches (clever!). If you remove the band (easy), the net will consume almost no space in your pocket.

that measures 6 feet by 7 feet. Sew two adjacent sides and hem the bottom. Thread bungee cord through the hem and install a cord lock. The finished net will weigh less than a pound and compress to football size.

Here are some uses for your Susie bug net:

- Eat inside it; there's room for two.

- Use as a portable outhouse when bugs are bad. This is its finest feature in blackfly country!

- Bathe in it! Wear your life vest and you'll float confidently inside your bug armor. Once ashore, it dries fast.

- Use it as a covering for food to keep bugs away.

- Hang it from a tree branch or rig a tripod inside and you'll have a bugproof teepee to do camp chores.

Stuff your Susie bug net under a pack flap so you can get at it at rest stops.

Cliff and Dan Tundra Tarp

When bugs are bizarre a Cliff and Dan tundra tarp is the way to go. Mine measures 15 feet square and has full bug netting sewn to all four sides. The netting rolls and ties out of the way when it's not needed. There are zippered entries at the four corners. Surprisingly, there's no need to kill or shoo away insects that are trapped inside: The bugs entertain themselves by crawling on the inside netting, away from you!

Figure 8-13. When the bugs are bizarre, you can't beat the Cliff and Dan tundra tarp!

The tundra tarp is expensive—and worth it when you need a bugproof structure that stays up in high winds. I've used mine on the shores of Hudson Bay in winds of 50 miles per hour—with no problems. The outfit weighs about fourteen pounds with three aluminum poles, stakes, lines, and netting. It all fits into a number 2 Duluth pack. Cooke Custom Sewing will build any size of tundra tarp you specify. Twelve feet square is a reasonable size for six. I would not canoe an Arctic river without my tundra tarp. Those who've traveled with me agree.

SIGNALING GEAR

Whistles

Whistles have limited value on a noisy river, where sounds are drowned out by the roar of rapids. If you want to signal the canoe behind you, use the international river safety signals illustrated in appendix E. Everyone should know the basic four—Stop, Help, All Clear, Go Thataway. The real value of a whistle is on land—if you get confused along a portage trail, for example.

The best whistle I've found is the pea-less Fox 40, which produces a loud, shrill sound even when dirty, wet, or blown too hard. The Fox 40 is actually harmonically tuned to produce three different frequencies simultaneously. You'll find it at canoe and sports shops, or you can check the Fox Web site in appendix B.

The best place for your whistle is on the zipper pull of your life jacket.

Shortwave Radio

Before 1992 I never carried any form of communications gear on a canoe trip. Then I had a change of heart (a sign of age, perhaps) and bought a telephone-size CB and an aircraft-band VHF radio. I figured a CB might come in handy because a lot of local residents, and nearly all powerboats, in the northern communities have them.

I bought my aircraft radio—a telephone-size JD-200 VHF aircraft transceiver—from Sporty's Pilot Shop (appendix B). It's the same model used by Japan Airlines ground crews. I reasoned that in an emergency I could use it to contact overhead aircraft. Indeed, airplanes are so common in the north that it's unlikely you *won't* see one sometime during your canoe trip. On some trips I've seen them every day.

I have used my aircraft radio many times to guide my

float plane pilot to my pickup location. It has been especially useful when the pilot can't see my camp because of fog or smoke from forest fires. The JD-200 is powered by eight AA batteries. It has a twenty-channel memory and a full-feature scanner that will find an active frequency. Range is about 15 miles—enough to contact any plane you see. Ask your float plane pilot for his operating frequency before he sets you down—then program it into your radio. If you forget, you can call on the emergency channel (121.5 megahertz), which everyone monitors. Be aware that it is illegal to break in on 121.5 unless there's a problem. Still, with such a short range, the only plane you'll reach will be the one in view. Once you make contact, the pilot may ask you to switch frequencies and continue to talk. Note: A marine band VHF radio cannot be used to contact airplanes.

Emergency Locator Transmitter

Some canoeists carry an Emergency Position Indicating Radio Beacon or EPIRB. When activated these telephone-sized units transmit continuously and simultaneously on the civilian (121.5 megahertz) and military (243.0 megahertz) search and rescue frequencies. They float and are waterproof to 10 yards or more. Multiple lanyards allow you to attach them in a variety of ways. If an emergency strikes, you activate the switch. Then you wait. And hope. The unit will continue to send distress signals for several days. The long-life lithium battery lasts for years.

Be aware that you'd better have a real emergency if you set off an EPIRB—a broken limb doesn't qualify. Most likely you will pay for your own rescue, which may be very costly. You should also know that a lot of EPIRBs are fired off every day, often for relatively minor reasons. You will be rescued, but it may take a while.

Still, miracles do happen. Verlen Kruger and Steve Landick encountered vicious waves and currents while canoeing around Cape Blanco (Oregon coast) on their 28,000-mile cross-continent trip. Suddenly a huge wave struck Verlen's solo canoe and capsized it in the 50 degree water. Verlen reached for the canoe, but the wind whisked it away. Fortunately Landick, who was just yards away, came to Verlen's aid. Verlen crawled up on the tail of Steve's boat and hung on for dear life. Landick immediately activated the EPIRB.

The pair were about 2 miles from the rocky shore and there was no landing place in sight. Verlen had lost his trousers in the capsize (the waves pulled them off) and was down to

his undershorts. He was becoming very hypothermic.

After an hour they were still a long way from shore. Verlen prayed that he would make it. Then out of nowhere a helicopter arrived and fished him out of the sea.

Prices on EPIRBs start at around $400, about the same price as a good VHF aircraft radio. An EPIRB can save your life but can't be used for communication. A radio can. It's your call.

You can order an EPIRB from Sporty's Pilot Shop (appendix B).

Satellite Phone

Satellite phones are finally affordable. At this writing, you can buy a refurbished model for under $400 or rent one for $100 a week. Currently, there are two companies—Globalstar (www.globalstar.com) and Iridum (www.iridum.com); see the Web sites for details. A satellite phone takes some of the *wild* out of the wilderness, which is why I reserve mine for emergencies.

Flares, Smoke, and Mirrors

Search and rescue operations are usually daytime affairs, so flares aren't of much value on a canoe trip. Smoke, however, can be useful. I once used orange smoke to signal an airplane. We had finished our trip and were waiting patiently for our floatplane to pick us up. The plane flew over us several

Figure 8-14. The author uses orange smoke to signal the location of his camp to a floatplane that's circling overhead. Fond du Lac River, Saskatchewan.

times, but the pilot never saw us—and we had plenty of bright colors out there. In desperation I fired an orange smoke signal, which caught his attention.

Orange smoke signals are available at every sailing shop and marina. Smokes, flares, mirrors, and complete signal kits are available by mail from Orion Safety Products (appendix B).

A heliograph mirror (the military model is best) is a must on any canoe trip. I believe mine may have saved a life. A friend and I were canoeing the Boundary Waters in Minnesota for the first time when we met a church group on a portage. They were carrying a teenage girl on a stretcher. She was in deep pain. My friend, John Orr, an experienced Indiana basketball coach, diagnosed her condition as appendicitis and suggested immediate evacuation. Miraculously, a forest service fire (spotter) plane was flying overhead at the time. The pilot saw John's flashing mirror and landed. The girl was flown to Grand Marais hospital, where she had her appendix removed.

MISCELLANEOUS EQUIPMENT

Pocketknife

The rage today is the Swiss Army Knife—a sophisticated version of the old Boy Scout pocketknife. Frankly, I'm not a

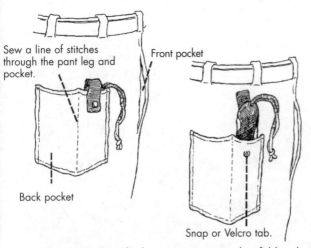

Sew a line of stitches through the pant leg and pocket.

Front pocket

Back pocket

Snap or Velcro tab.

Figure 8-15. The best way to carry a big folding knife is in a sheath sewn into the back pocket of your field trousers.

fan of these red-handled tool shops. If you've got to whittle the center out of a wet birch log to get at the dry wood inside so you can start a fire on a rainy day, a Swiss knife won't cut it. You need something much more substantial-either a thin blade sheath knife or a big single-blade folding knife.

The best way to carry a big folding knife is in a sheath sewn into the back pocket of your field trousers.

Big folding knives are eminently practical on canoe trips. They won't catch in your life jacket or canoe seat. And they're safe, too: There's no way you can accidentally cut yourself with a folded folder.

The best canoe knives have blades that lock into place when they're open. The lock feature isn't to prevent accidental closure of the knife blade but rather to permit effortless-one-handed, if need be-opening. Lock-blade knives don't have pressure springs like conventional jackknives, so they open and close easily. You can pull out the blade on a lock knife while wearing mittens in the dead of winter. Try that with a common pocketknife!

The best way to carry a big folder is in a sheath sewn into the back pocket of your field trousers. Just sew a line of stitches through the pant leg and pocket (see figure 8-15) and attach a snap flap or velcro tab at the top. Equip your knife with a lanyard so you can pull it out with one hand.

Sheath Knife

For years I carried a Puma Plainsman lock blade in a pocket sheath like the one illustrated in figure 8-15. Then I read Bill Mason's wonderful book, *Path of the Paddle*. Bill recommended a sheath knife, so I gave it a try. I purchased a Gerber Shorty (no longer made) and made a custom sheath for it. This combo was faster on the draw than any folder, and the long, thin blade was better for preparing meals. Suddenly my trusty Puma had become a relic.

The primary use of a knife is preparing foods. You'll slice meat and cheese and spread jam and peanut butter. Food gums up the works of a folding blade, but a sheath knife is easy to clean. Also, a fixed blade can be drawn with just one hand—important if you capsize and become entangled in a line or your canoe cover. There are specialized river knives, of course, but they are designed to pierce canoe hulls and cut through thick rope. How do they cut salami and pine? Not very well. Everything should be multipurpose on a canoe trip, knife included.

I prefer a thin, flat-ground (with sides like a butter knife) blade for effortless slicing. Blade length? Four to 5

Figure 8-16. Some great canoe knives. Top to bottom: Gerber Shorty (no longer manufactured), Idaho Knife Works Cliff knife, Grohmann 1 Camper, Grohmann 2 Camper.

Figure 8-17. Four great saws. Top to bottom: Trailblazer, Gerber Exchange-a-Blade, Fast Bucksaw, and Sawvivor. The Trailblazer has a raker-toothed blade; the others have all-toothed blades.

inches is long enough to slice thick cheese and reach deeply into the peanut butter bottle without getting gunked up.

Most outdoor knives have blades that are too thick. *One-eighth* (I prefer less!) inch across the spine is the maximum thickness permissible in a camp knife, no matter how delicate the edge. Slice a tomato with the typical hunting knife and you'll see why.

Your favorite kitchen knife would be perfect for camp use if it had a bit less length, more backbone, and better steel. In fact, the most popular knives on the frontier were the famous Green River models, which were just solidly built kitchen knives.

Figure 8-16 shows some of my favorite canoe knives. I designed the Cliff knife when I couldn't find a replacement for my aging Gerber Shorty (a wonderful blade!). The Cliff is custom-made by Idaho Knife Works (appendix B; I have no financial connection with this company). I encouraged the

flat-ground design of the very practical Grohmann 1 and 2 camp knives.

I prefer high-carbon tool-steel blades because they are (usually) easier to sharpen and take a keener edge than stainless. Yes, tool steel rusts, but so does a fine ax or gun. Simple maintenance—dry your knife after use and occasionally slice oily salami or cheese—will keep steel bright.

Knife Sheaths

The sheaths that come with most factory knives (the Cliff and Grohmann are exceptions) are awful. The leather is too thin, and the snap closure is awkward and unreliable. American Indians knew what they were doing when they designed the molded, case-style sheath, which is safe, handy, and comfortable to wear. My book *Camping's Top Secrets* shows you how to make one.

Figure 8-18. The Fast Bucksaw rips through wood fast. Fond du Lac River, Saskatchewan.

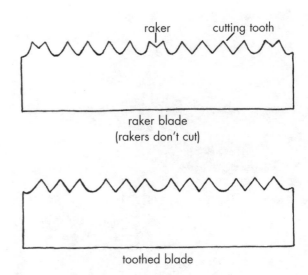

Figure 8-19. Saw blades: raker blade, toothed blade.

Folding Saws

A folding saw is essential for making fires and clearing portages. Avoid the flimsy triangular aluminum models that won't cut thick logs. The best camp saw I've used is a full-stroke rectangular model called the Fast Bucksaw (appendix B). It's constructed of solid hard maple and has an easily replaceable 21-inch blade. The saw locks up rigidly when assembled—and when disassembled! It packs shorter than any folding saw with an equivalent-length blade (it fits well in a Duluth pack). The Fast Bucksaw is fairly expensive and worth it. It will last a lifetime.

The tubular aluminum Trailblazer (appendix B) is another fine canoeing saw. It's a full-stroke rectangular saw in the old bucksaw tradition. It comes with two blades—one for wood, the other for bone or metal. The Trailblazer is harder to assemble than the Fast Buck, however, and its tubular aluminum handle is cold to the touch.

The Sawvivor is the best ultralight saw I've found. Its rectangular aluminum frame assembles in seconds and locks tight, with no play whatsoever. The Sawvivor weighs just 10.5 ounces, complete with its 15-inch blade. Most camping shops have it.

A small jackknife-style saw, like the Gerber Exchange-a-Blade (my preference) is often handy if you need to clear small saplings that block the portage trail. I keep the Gerber strapped to my pack basket, which is the first thing I carry over a portage. This saw opens in a flash and glides through wood up to 3 inches thick.

Lightweight saws feel great when you pick them up, but they lack the heft to run easily through wood. If you have a lot of wood to cut, or a small amount of wood to cut fast, you'll want a fairly heavy saw with a long blade. You'll also want one that goes together fast and takes a standard blade you can buy anywhere.

Rakers are an interesting saw feature. When I was a forestry student at Purdue University in the 1960s, I competed in some cross-cut saw contests. We had saws for hardwood and saws for softwood. The difference is in the number and spacing of the "rakers," which are dull (they don't cut), U-shaped points that rake out the sawdust that can clog the teeth. You need more rakers to cut green softwood than to cut green hardwood, and you need none at all if the wood is dead and dry (for example, a carpenter's saw). Four teeth to one raker is fairly standard for a multipurpose cross-cut blade. Naturally, you lose some cutting efficiency with a rakered blade—20 percent, to be exact, if the ratio of teeth to rakers is four to one.

The good news is that rakers aren't needed on a camp saw, which is primarily used to cut dead dry wood. But raker blades look neat, so makers of folding saws continue to use them. Fortunately, your local hardware store has all-toothed replacement blades.

Keep your disassembled folding saw in a nylon bag. This will keep the parts cleaner and speed assembly time. Strap the saw to the outside of a pack so you can get at it fast. Occasionally spray saw blades with WD-40 (bring a small can on canoe trips) to remove pitch and resist rust.

Ax and Sheath

You need some sort of wood-splitting and hammering tool on a canoe trip. I prefer a quality hand ax. For years I relied on the all-steel Estwing hatchet shown in Figure 8-20. Then in 1998 my friend, Dick Person, who lives in a log cabin in the Yukon, gave me a Gransfors Small Forest Axe, which is far superior to any ax I've ever used. It has a 19-inch hickory handle and a 1.5-pound head. Its hand-forged, razor-sharp (really!) blade is hardened to R57C, which is harder than conventional axes and as hard as most good knives. An excellent sheath is provided.

The Gransfors hatchet is also an impressive tool, and frankly, it's all you need to maintain a campfire. But the Small Forest Axe, which will fit in a large portage pack, is more efficient. Gransfors axes (appendix B) are the best on the planet: Try one and you'll agree. Prices are very reasonable—you won't have to sell the farm. I might add that Gransfors makes a truly exemplary splitting ax (it's better than any maul) that's perfect for splitting stove wood at home.

To use your hatchet, begin by sawing the log you want to split into 12-inch sections. Set one section upright on a flat wood base. Set the blade lightly into its end grain and hold the handle of the hatchet tightly with both hands. Now have a friend pound the head on through with a heavy log chunk. The hatchet functions as an effective splitting wedge rather than a dangerous cutting tool. You won't cut yourself if you use this procedure.

The back side of a hand ax is useful for setting rivets in torn pack straps, straightening bent metal hardware on canoes, and a variety of other tasks. You don't need a long-handled ax as recommended by some authorities. A big ax won't fit into a pack sack, and it's only practical if you need to produce a week's supply of firewood. If you can't start and maintain a campfire with a hatchet, knife, and folding saw, you'd best stay home by your TV and oil furnace!

Make a sturdy sheath for your hatchet by riveting together two pieces of sole leather. Gransfors axes are the only

Figure 8-20. The author's favorite axes, shown in order of preference. Top to bottom: Gransfors Small Forest Axe, Gransfors hatchet, Estwing hatchet. Note the author's heavy riveted sheath on the Estwing hatchet.

ones I've seen that come with good sheaths.

Sharpening Tools

Include a flat mill file, a soft Arkansas or Wachita stone, and some honing oil in your kit. Or if you don't want to mess with oil and stones, carry one of the expensive but efficient diamond hones that you can buy at most camp shops.

Shovel

It's nice to have a tool for digging shallow latrines and burying fish remains. A 12-inch-long length of 1-inch-diameter aluminum tube with one end flattened makes a moderately efficient lightweight shovel and emergency pancake turner.

Rope

Each canoe should carry at least 50 feet of $^3/_8$-inch-diameter nylon rope in addition to its two 25-foot lining ropes. You can never have too much rope on a canoe trip! Coil your ropes so you can use them for throwing lines in an emergency.

Medical Kits

If your trips take you far beyond the last road, you'll need a full medical kit in addition to a standard first-aid kit (the two should be packed in separate canoes).

Two highly recommended medical texts that address the needs of remote country travelers are *Wilderness Medicine,* 5th edition, by William W. Forgey, M.D., and *Medicine for the Backcountry,* 3rd edition, by Buck Tilton and Frank Hubbell. Every canoeist should read Dr. Forgey's book, *Basic Essentials: Hypothermia.*

Appendix D suggests some important things you need in your medical kit. Medical items can be mail-ordered from Chinook Medical Gear. High-tech first-aid kits are available from Atwater-Carey (appendix B).

You should realize that having the right medical gear is meaningless if you don't know how to use it. So read and reread the recommended texts. And take some first-aid courses.

On a positive note, I should say that while I travel with a very extensive medical kit, I've never had to use much more than antibiotics, tape, and Steri-Strips (which are much better than butterflies). It's amazing how careful you are when you know there's no one around to help you!

Camera

If you want good photos, get a good camera, and don't be afraid to keep it handy. I paddle armed to the hilt with camera gear—all sorts of lenses, filters, a tripod . . . the works! Don't worry about getting your camera wet. I'll show you how to pack it in the next chapter.

I bring enough film to shoot eighteen color slides per day. Real photographers don't consider this nearly enough!

If you develop many rolls of film and find you can't remember the order in which you shot the rolls, try this: Write the number of each roll on a slip of paper and photograph it—first picture on each roll. When the slides are developed, one slide in each box will indicate the roll number.

Waterproof Binoculars

Binoculars aren't just for viewing wildlife; they're also essential for navigation and to check rapids. Use them to locate campsite on a distant shore and to find the mouth of an obscure stream portage trail. They'll tell you if a rapids is safe to run and precisely where to run it. A monocular is not an effective substitute for binoculars, because you don't have good depth perception with one eye.

Compass

A compass is essential equipment on every wilderness canoe trip. The orienteering-style instruments by Silva,

Suunto, and Brunton are, in my judgment, the only ones suitable for serious navigation. Orienteering compasses have built-in protractors to enable you to plot courses accurately and quickly, even in a bobbing canoe. My two favorite compasses are the Silva Ranger (because it can be adjusted for magnetic declination) and the Silva Huntsman (because it's so tiny you can carry it comfortably in a shirt pocket). Every canoeist should have his or her own compass!

Global Positioning Unit

Global Positioning System (GPS) receivers are now fairly common, and prices are going down. Basic models—which, frankly, provide all the information you need—cost around $100, or about three times as much as a good compass. With a GPS receiver, you can determine your location to within 100 meters or less and set your watch to the exact time provided by an atomic clock! Expensive GPS units download this information in seconds; cheapies may take more than a minute.

You can also enter the map coordinates of a place you want to go; the GPS receiver will provide a compass bearing and distance, both updated as you paddle. Press a button and you get a speed readout (which is inaccurate at typical canoe speeds) and an estimated time of arrival (ETA).

Or just punch in your starting position and save it as a waypoint. Record other waypoints as you proceed, then, like Hansel and Gretel, follow your electronic "bread crumbs" home.

In the past, the military introduced into the civilian GPS signal what was called Selective Availability (SA)—a random error that varies from 15 to 100 meters. This made locating an obscure portage with a GPS an uncertain thing. Fortunately SA was eliminated in 2000. Position errors now average less than 20 feet.

Most GPS receivers are menu driven, which simplifies operation. Nonetheless, mastery of the instrument requires study and practice, plus a working knowledge of maps and navigational procedures. And all handheld GPS units operate on AA batteries, so you don't want to leave them on for continuous positioning.

The most useful GPS feature is its ability to verify your location on a map—and the least-expensive, most basic GPS units provide this. Older GPS units may not be Y2K compatible; check with the manufacturer if your machine was built before 1996.

Finally, be aware that not all maps have a reference system to which the GPS can relate. I'll deal with the "simple complexities" of GPS navigation in chapter 13.

Judge for yourself if GPS is just another toy. In 1998 I led a Science Museum of Minnesota–sponsored canoe trip down the Tha-anne River in Canada's Northwest Territories. We arranged for a powerboat to meet us on Hudson Bay and take us to Arviat (formerly Eskimo Point), 50 miles up the coast.

The delta at the mouth of the Tha-anne is complex and often too shallow for motorboats. The tide and weather would determine when the boat would come and exactly where it would be. I was asked to call the boat operator on my CB radio before we headed out on the bay.

I called the boat captain shortly after first light on the appointed day. He said, "Get moving fast; I gotta be out of here before the tide."

"I can't see you. Where are you?" I asked.

"Head out east, then go north. You'll see a white boat. I'm about half a mile out after you make the turn."

"Okay."

Thirty minutes passed and there was no boat in sight. Every channel ended in a new channel, which ended in a new channel. I studied the map. My GPS told me exactly where I was, but I didn't have a clue where the boat was!

I radioed the captain and asked for directions. But he was no help because he couldn't see us. However, he was emphatic: "Let's go, boys, we gotta get out of here!"

"What's your position?" I asked. "I've got a GPS."

He read off the numbers and I punched them into the machine. Then I hit the Goto button and followed the little black pointer right to his boat!

The captain said he would have waited another thirty minutes then returned to Arviat. Yes, he would have come at high tide the next day—and doubled our charter fee. My GPS cost $350. The boat ride cost $1,000. Toy? Hardly!

Lighting Units

The farther north you go, the less light you need. At the height of the canoeing season, parts of northern Canada and Alaska have more than twenty-two hours of sunlight a day. Of course, farther south, you'll need a lighting unit of some sort.

A small, LED headlamp is adequate. Bring a more powerful headlamp if you're canoeing with teenagers. I once paddled for hours around a huge lake in the black of night—flashlight in my mouth—in search of two kids who had gone fishing!

In 2004 I had a dicey bear encounter along the Cree River in Saskatchewan. The sky was dark gray when this bad boy came into camp. We tried to shoo him away, but he just kept coming. Ultimately, I fired a shot from my .450 Marlin, a few feet in front of him. He ambled back into the woods and later appeared in a new spot. One man activated his SureFire (www.surefire.com) tactical light (the size of a Magic Marker), which really lit up the bush. I put a bullet in front of the bear's nose. It "barked some brush" and in a flash was gone.

Tactical lights are so bright they will momentarily blind an attacker—perhaps even a bear! I was enough impressed with this light to order one as soon as I got home.

Folding Camp Stool

A folding camp stool is worth its weight and bulk on any wilderness canoe trip. Camp chores—cooking, washing dishes, sharpening edged tools—go easier when you don't sit on the ground. I most appreciate my stool when I must wait out a storm under my rain tarp or endure a long tour of kitchen duty.

Friends scoffed when I first began to bring a camp stool on my trips. Now they've all followed suit. I've tried all manner of stool designs and have ultimately settled on a simple collapsible model like those used at competitive shooting events. Be sure you get a stool that sits on two parallel aluminum rails. Avoid individual pointed legs that can sink into soft ground. My favorite camp stool weighs ten ounces and has a canvas storage pouch beneath the seat. When not in use it folds flat and clips (with bungee cords) to my backpack.

Matches and Fire Starters

I carry three waterproof plastic jars filled with about 150 matches each. The matches are packed with a foam plug on top so the heads won't be damaged. I glue coarse sandpaper inside each jar lid for a striker.

Two butane lighters and a tube of chemical fire ribbon round out my fire-making materials. I consider myself a rabid environmentalist and so am reluctant to recommend disposable butane lighters. But they are much handier than matches and are completely waterproof. My butane lighters are the only concession I make to our throwaway society.

Thermos

I carry a matched pair of one-pint stainless-steel vacuum bottles on all my canoe trips. They ride in thwart bags (one bow, one stern) in the canoe, and in the side pockets of my number 2 Duluth Cruiser on portages.

Figure 8-21. The folding camp stool is secured to a pack basket with a bungee cord and carabiner. Note the handy zippered pocket in the bottom of the stool.

Sometimes I fill the bottles with hot water or tea before I retire so I won't have to start the stove the next morning to prepare a hot drink or meal. Or I fill the vacuum bottle at breakfast so there'll be hot soup or tea for lunch.

Later, in camp, boiling water for tea or dishwater goes into the vacuum bottles, which saves gas because I don't have to restart the stove so often to reheat water.

A pair of trim, pint-sized bottles are handier and easier to pack than one large quart-sized bottle. Twin bottles provide two beverage choices—and if you lose or damage a bottle, you have a spare.

Rain Tarp

Canoeing in foul weather without a rain tarp borders on insanity. Chapter 12 (The Expert's Edge) goes into the specifics of this essential and often underrated item.

Lip Balm, Hand Cream, and Sunscreen

Don't underestimate the importance of these products. Your hands and lips will crack and bleed if you don't treat them frequently with medications. I use hand cream and lip balm almost every day on rigorous canoe trips. Carry plenty! You'll use much more than you think.

Stove and Cooking Gear

See chapter 11 (The Recipe) for a discussion of stoves and cooking gear.

Tent

The tent is so important that I've devoted an entire chapter to it (chapter 10—Canoe Tents Are Different).

Pack Sacks

You'll find everything you want to know about packs and packing in the next chapter.

TOOL KIT

Stuff breaks on canoe trips. Can you mend a busted yoke, torn pack strap or stubborn zipper? Can you patch your leaky rubber boots and maintain your trail stove? Anything can be fixed in the field if you have the right tools.

Going Light

For predictable outings, a Swiss Army Knife and duct tape are all you need. Add a sturdy pliers with a cutting edge and a pounding tool (hand ax), and you're set for emergencies.

For an ultracompact kit, I recommend the original Leatherman multitool or the new Leatherman Wave model. With these tools you can field-strip eyeglasses, fishing reels, and your gasoline stove. The precision long-nose pliers snips fishhooks and wire. There's a file, scissors, an assortment of screwdrivers, and more. The saw blade on the Wave model cuts through hardened aluminum.

Warning: If you have to torque down twisted bolts or straighten metal hardware, you'll want a powerful, full-sized pliers and a crescent or box wrench, plus a one-piece screwdriver with a man-sized handle that won't twist off. Multitools are wonderful when you want to go light, but they can't match full-frame tools that are built for the job.

CONCLUDING SPLASH

The best advice I can give you when choosing equipment for canoe travel is to carefully examine everything before you buy. If a zipper looks weak, it probably is; if there's a knob that can break, it most likely will; if there's an unsecured part that can be lost, bet on it. Go on the assumption that if something can fail, it will, and you'll get real value for your money and be well prepared for the unexpected.

Most important, be aware that some highly touted products that work flawlessly over the short haul fail miserably when the weeks turn to years. So be wary of advertising claims and the testimonials of individuals whose experience is limited to a single expedition. Instead, heed the advice of those who canoe wild rivers year after year. These are the real experts, even though their opinions and methods are seldom seen in print.

Finally, consider the color of every product you buy. Your safety may depend on brightly colored gear. Here are some examples:

Cree River, Saskatchewan: A forest fire prevented us from reaching our take-out spot. We camped instead on an island 5 miles upstream. The sky was smoky yellow, visibility was a bit better than none at all. We had little hope that our bush plane would find us in the morning.

At 7:45 A.M. we heard the roar of an engine, and seconds later a single Otter swooped out of the sky and chugged to our doorstep.

"It was that brightly colored checkerboard tarp that caught my eye," said the pilot.

A tundra tarp saved my marriage! On August 12, 1992, Sue Harings and I were married at Wilberforce Falls along Canada's Hood River. The wedding was nearly aborted ten days earlier, when we discovered that I had left the "wedding pack" (read the full story in chapter 19) at the float plane dock in Yellowknife. When Susie learned the pack was missing, she wanted to postpone the wedding. Really!

But flying out behind us (headed for a different river) was Canada's famed canoe man, Michael Peake. Michael put the pack aboard a Twin Otter bound for Cambridge Bay and asked the pilots to "find Cliff."

They did, and the copilot pushed the pack out the door at an altitude of 300 feet! It fell like a missile (no harm done) and the wedding was on again. Neither pilot saw our five overturned red canoes or our red and yellow tents. It was our checkered rain tarp that saved the day.

Figure 8-22. The author's tool kit.

Quiz: Which of the following is a bush pilot more likely to see? a) Five red canoes placed side-by-side, belly-up in a clearing; b) same arrangement, but three canoes—one blue, one yellow, and one red.

The answer is "b". A small patchwork pattern usually beats one large bright color.

PFDs: You want to be seen if you capsize!

Packs: I tie foot-long streamers of orange, pink, or yellow plastic surveying ribbon to all packs that aren't brightly colored.

Checkerboard tundra tarp: A decade ago I asked Dan Cooke (Cooke Custom Sewing) to make me a high visibility "tundra" tarp that could double as an emergency signal. Dan mixed four flashy colors into an obtrusive pattern that can be seen for miles. Many times, bush pilots have told me that they saw our tarp long before our tents and canoes came into view.

Finally, grass-green gear may be lost in a capsize or left behind on a portage. Bright colors make sense for that reason alone. It bears repeating that "bugs love blue," especially, *navy* blue, so beware this color. Someone tell me why blue is the most popular color for outdoors gear?

CHAPTER 9
THE ART OF PACKING

For close-to-home river floats where there are few portages, you can simply throw your gear into a couple of nested plastic bags. Or you can pack it in a big ice chest or small trash can that has a tightly fitted lid. I once met two youths carrying a galvanized garbage can over a portage trail in Quetico Provincial Park. They'd chained the can lid shut to make a "Bearproof" cache. I couldn't suppress a wry smile when I walked past the contraption, for I knew a big black bear could demolish it with a single pounce.

Plastic bags and garbage cans are all right for local trips where equipment failure isn't critical. But for canoeing a wild river, you need the toughest packs you can get. Surprisingly, canoeing is much harder on packs than backpacking, probably because canoeists carry heavier loads than backpackers. A fifty-pound pack is the rule on a canoe trip; an eighty-pound one is not uncommon. Heavy packs must be built tough enough to withstand the abuse of being tossed into canoes and on rocks.

DULUTH PACKS

If you've ever paddled a fine wood-ribbed canoe, you know the joy of natural materials. So it is with traditional Poirier-designed Duluth packs of sweat-stained canvas and hand-oiled leather. Like a pure wool shirt and a fine-ground ax, Duluth packs "belong."

If you've never used Duluth packs—or used them incorrectly—you may wonder why experienced canoeists often prefer them to modern, more sophisticated packs. After all,

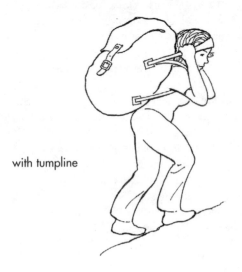

with tumpline

Figure 9-1. Packing uphill with a tumpline.

without tumpline

what could be attractive about a floppy, century-old design that has no padded shoulder straps or hip belt, no sternum strap, zippered pockets, supporting frame, or quick-release plastic buckles? Why on earth would anyone choose a shapeless mass of heavy, rot-prone canvas over a decay-defying, crisply patterned nylon pack built from indestructible modern materials?

To understand the lure of the ageless Duluth pack, I must explode some myths.

Myth: Modern nylon tripping packs are more comfortable to carry than traditional canvas Duluth packs.

This is true only if you place hard items against your back and don't use a tumpline (figures 9-1and 9-2). Most Americans don't like tumplines because they use them wrong. You should place the tump strap about 1 inch above your forehead and lean forward until the pack rises off the small of your back and bears against your shoulders. All the weight is now borne by your strong neck muscles. The shoulder straps aren't needed—and neither are other expensive features, like contoured frames and hip belts.

Loosen the shoulder straps about 3 inches before you try the tumpline. The setup won't work if the straps are too tight.

The key to comfortable packing is *keeping the load tight against your back*—easy enough when you're hiking on the flats or downhill. But ascend a steep grade and gravity will tear at your pack and threaten to bowl you over backward.

Figure 9-2. Packing with a tumpline: Sue Harings, the author's wife, shows how it's done. Hood River, Nunavut, Canada.

Contoured pack frames and padded hip belts help stabilize the load, but only a tumpline anchors it against your back.

You can prove this by carrying a heavy backpack up a staircase using the shoulder straps alone. Now add a makeshift tumpline and try again. Be sure you attach the tumpline below the point where the shoulder straps are sewn to the pack. The stability provided by the tumpstrap will astound you!

Myth: Duluth packs ride too high in a canoe. Modern sidewall packs can be set belly-down in the hull, which lowers the canoe's center of gravity.

The recommended number 3 (24 by 30 inches) Duluth pack is designed to sit upright in a canoe, with its opening out of contact with bilgewater. A properly loaded number 3 pack extends about 6 inches above the rails of a deep-hulled tripping canoe—just high enough to support your fabric splash cover.

Portaging is a way of life in canoe country—you may load and unload your canoe many times a day. Landings can be precarious and the footing unsure. Imagine loading the canoe from a rock face high above. If you have Duluth packs, you'll just grab 'em by the ears and drop 'em down—no bending or stooping is required (figure 9-3).

Now try the procedure with an external-frame or modern box-sided pack. These long packs raise the center of gravity too high if they're placed upright in the canoe. They must be set belly-down or sideways. Rearranging packs in the canoe requires considerable bending and stooping—a scenario that is repeated at every portage.

More important, the mouth of an upright Duluth pack is out of contact with accumulated bilgewater, while that of a belly-down, long-profile pack is submerged. Carelessly waterproof the contents of a horizontally placed pack and you'll know it when the first wave comes over the bow. An upright Duluth pack is more forgiving.

Myth: The zippered pockets on the face of modern packs are great places to store small items. That is, until you discover that they're submerged in bilgewater when the pack is placed facedown in the canoe. If you set the pack belly-up in the hull, its back will lie in bilgewater. *Your* back will know it when you portage.

Myth: Modern nylon packs will outlive traditional canvas Duluth packs.

This is pure baloney. I have canvas Duluth packs that are more than thirty years old and have seen upward of a hundred canoe trips with grueling portages of up to 4 miles.

A

Pack's "right side up." No adjustment needed.

B

Each long pack must be set belly-down on the canoe.

Figure 9-3. Duluth packs are easier to load than packs with frames and box sides. **A.** Grab the Duluth pack by the ears and set it into the canoe—no need for a helper. **B.** For frame packs and box-sided packs, set the pack into the canoe, then turn it belly-down and position it properly. You need a helper.

There are some patches, but they're all still going strong. Quick: What's the first thing to fail on a tripping pack? If you said "straps," you're on target. To replace foam-encased nylon shoulder straps, you must rip out the straps and foam and resew the yoke—a task best reserved for the manufacturer.

On the other hand, leather shoulder straps usually break at a buckle hole. Field first aid simply means riveting on a healthy piece of leather or nylon webbing.

Myth: Padded nylon straps are more comfortable than leather straps.

At first they are, but give the leather time to soften and it's no contest. Bikers will vouch for the comfort of a well-broken-in leather seat.

Myth: Modern tripping packs are more waterproof than Duluth packs.

No pack is 100 percent waterproof over the long haul. Those that are watertight when new are either slow and awkward to use or uncomfortable to portage and difficult to stow in a canoe. All develop holes after a few years of strenuous canoe travel.

Experienced canoeists know that any pack sack advertised as waterproof may fail at a critical time. For this reason they prefer to build a reliable waterproofing system—like the one I'll explain later in this chapter—inside each pack.

Myth: Nylon dries faster than canvas.

It's true that waterproof nylon dries faster than porous canvas. However, the roles are often reversed after a heavy rain or capsize.

Imagine this scenario: A huge wave swamps your canoe, and two packs—one canvas, one nylon—get soaked. Thank goodness you've lined them both with two heavy-duty plastic bags, as discussed later in this chapter.

You paddle ashore and remove the packs from the canoe. Then you momentarily invert them on a rock to drain accumulated water. It's hot and sunny, so you repack the canoe and paddle on. You'll attend to wet gear later, when you camp.

In ten minutes the outside of the nylon pack is dry. An hour passes before the canvas follows suit. Later, at your campsite, you open the Duluth pack and discover that everything—even the space between the outer plastic bag liner and the canvas—is dry. You chuckle at the observation. Canvas is breathable, remember? Trapped water oozed out through the canvas, and the remaining moisture simply evaporated.

Now to the waterproof nylon pack. The outside is dry but the inside is soaking wet. And there's accumulated water between the coated nylon pack fabric and the plastic liner nearest the pack. Of course—water can't escape through a fabric that has no holes. You'll have to remove the pack contents-plastic liners and all—and turn the nylon pack *inside out* to dry. Whoop-dee-doo, another thing to do!

Yes, coated nylon does dry faster than porous canvas, but only if both sides of the material are exposed to the warmth of the sun!

Myth: Plastic Fastex buckles, like those found on modern tripping packs, are faster to use than the nickel-plated steel roller buckles on traditional Duluth packs.

It's a matter of learning some tricks. You can make a quick-release buckle out of any leather Duluth pack strap by leaving a small loop of leather between the steel buckle pin and strap retaining bar on the roller. If you want a faster release, run the buckle pin through the hole in the closing strap, but don't push the strap end through the roller bar. Experienced Boundary Waters and Quetico Park travelers often use this half-locked procedure.

Myth: A hip belt (which Duluth packs don't have) is needed to carry heavy loads comfortably over rough terrain.

The best hiking packs all have padded hip belts, which transfer part of the weight from your shoulders to your hips. Hip belts increase control on the flats and downhill grades, but they have no effect when you climb uphill. Hip belts also interfere with anything (sheath knife, multipliers, and so on) you wear around your waist.

Hip belts are terribly awkward in canoes. They catch on thwarts and seats during loading operations, and they remain submerged in bilgewater and muck for long periods of time. Each time you portage you clip the dirty, foul-smelling strap around your waist. Whenever you set the pack down, abrasion and crud take their toll. Eventually, the nylon shell tears and exposes the foam padding inside.

Hip belts are great for serious hiking, but they're a nuisance on the short portages that characterize most canoe country. I think a tumpline is a better plan.

Myth: Modern packs give you more storage space.

Duluth packs are huge! After a rain or capsize, you'll have some wet, bulky gear that won't fit inside your pack. There's always room to stuff one more thing under the long closing flap of a classic Duluth pack. Most modern packs have closing flaps that are way too short. There is no such thing as a pack flap that's too long!

Myth: Duluth packs are too expensive.

Sophisticated features don't come cheap. A state-of-the-art canoeing pack costs much more than a Duluth pack. A backpacker needs just one pack; a serious wilderness canoeist requires three or four.

HIGH-TECH PORTAGE PACKS

A number of state-of-the-art canoe packs are so comfortable they can double as full-fledged hiking packs. Most notable are those made by Grade VI, Granite Gear, Camp Trails, Cooke Custom Sewing, and Ostrom Outdoors (appendix B). These packs have straight-through construction (no compartments) and a sophisticated shoulder-harness/hip-belt system that is more comfortable than the standard Duluth design. My wife, Susie, loves her huge Granite Gear pack; I like the Cooke Custom Sewing Pioneer, whose closing flap is longer than the pack itself! Dan Cooke will add a tumpline to any pack if you bug him real hard.

WATERPROOF RAFTING PACKS WITH ROLL-DOWN CLOSURES

PVC-coated waterproof pack sacks, like those made by Cascade Designs, appear attractive for canoeing because they are absolutely watertight, even when submerged in a pounding rapid. This makes them ideal for rafting trips, where floating comes before portaging. However, it's tedious to roll and seal the mouths of these waterproof bags every time you need to get at something—and there are no outside pockets, lash points, or pack flaps under which to store the loose items that accumulate on a canoe trip.

Rafting packs are really more like waterproof bags than packs. They aren't very comfortable to carry. Some rafting packs have hip belts; none have tumplines. The long, narrow shape of these packs requires that they be placed facedown in the canoe, which consumes tons of room. Hard granite and sharp thorns take their toll on the PVC coating. *When* holes develop, you'll have to find and patch them—or sandwich-pack your gear as suggested in Waterproofing Your Outfit later in this chapter. If you get the idea that I don't like these packs, you're dead right!

RIGID PACKS

If you have fragile or difficult-to-pack items like vacuum bottles, stoves, or gasoline fuel bottles, you'll want one or more rigid packs. The woven-ash pack basket available from L. L. Bean and Duluth Pack (appendix B) has, for centuries, been the traditional hard pack, and it's still my favorite. I nest my pack basket inside two heavy rubberized army clothes bags and set this combo inside a number 2 Duluth Pack Cruiser Combo pack. A loop of shock cord seals the mouth of each rubberized bag. This very sturdy waterproof unit packs well in the canoe. Order an 18-inch-high basket and a long-flap number 2 Cruiser Combo pack.

Be sure you specify the Combo, which has a longer pack

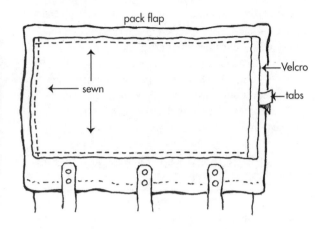

Figure 9-4. Sew a flat pocket to the top of your pack flaps.

flap. Here's how to make this outfit even better:

1. Sew a flat pocket on top of the pack flap. Stitch down the two long sides and use Velcro closures at the ends (see figure 9-4). Now you have a handy place to stuff your gloves, map, or wind shell without opening the pack flap. The Velcro closures allow you to access the pocket from either side. For greater security, you may stitch one end closed as illustrated.

2. Remove the two wooden rails on the bottom of the basket—they concentrate abrasion over a small area and will rapidly wear holes through the canvas bottom. Insert a sheet of closed-cell foam between the back of the pack and basket. Your back will appreciate the soft cushioning. Place another foam sheet under the basket, inside the pack. This floor layer will absorb abrasion that would otherwise be transferred to the fragile ash strips on the basket bottom.

3. Sew up some pockets out of nylon or canvas and tie the pockets to the inside rim of the basket. Place spare glasses, billfold, and sundries in the pockets.

WANIGANS

Trappers and fur traders commonly transported tools and equipment in heavy wooden boxes called wanigans. Wanigans were quite popular in the early part of the twentieth century, though you seldom see them today. A few companies make very nice modern versions of these boxes from sturdy ABS plastic. One model has detachable table legs and

Figure 9-5. The author's customized pack basket.

Figure 9-6. The Stormy Bay wanigan.

converts to a cartop carrier; another has built-in pantry shelves.

Wanigans are great for carrying canned goods and other bulky items, but traditional designs take up a lot of space in the canoe and they don't carry very well. Exceptions include the Stormy Bay Canoe Pack and Pantry, which was formerly the E. M. Wanigan I've recommended for years, and the new CLG Hard Pack (appendix B).

The Stormy Bay wanigan is portable, watertight, and strong enough to stand on. It has padded shoulder straps and fast, foolproof latches. Accessories include a plastic dishpan and shelves. It's easy to attach a tumpline. The box will sit crossways, on edge (suitcase style), or on its back in a narrow tandem canoe. Unfortunately the wanigan is molded from Norel plastic, which tends to crack with hard use. However, you can repair it with epoxy and fiberglass, just like a canoe.

The CLG Hard Pack is a molded polyethylene box that looks like a bulky rectangular trash can. It loads from the top like a pack basket and has an optional carrying harness. A snug-fitting lid (which can double as a food tray) and tough rubber gasket keep out rain and splash. However, the box will take on water if you capsize. CLG is in the process of redesigning the Hard Pack to make it waterproof. The new model may be available by the time you read this.

You can make any wanigan waterproof by simply nesting it inside a Duluth pack that's lined with a waterproof bag—the same setup as for a woven-ash pack basket. All wanigans are unwieldy, especially on uphill grades. A tumpline is a must!

PLASTIC OLIVE JARS AND PICKLE BASKETS

Many years ago a resourceful Canadian, who was on the prowl for a low-cost wanigan, tried an experiment: He packed some hard items that would gouge his back into giant plastic pickle barrels and olive jars. Everything came through the trip bone dry and without a dent or scratch. The word that there was a new round wanigan in town spread like an Ontario bushfire, and soon Canadian paddlers everywhere copied the plan. Then capitalism reared its ugly head, and the smelly plastic jars that were once free for the asking began to sell for big bucks.[1]

Olive jars and pickle barrels are more watertight than

Figure 9-7. A Voyageur Barrel Harness from Ostrom Outdoors.

any wanigan, but they're a pain to pack and portage. A few pack makers (notably Ostrom Outdoors—see appendix B) offer clever foam-padded harnesses, which help.

Some pickle packers place the jars or barrels in conventional pack sacks. Three or four 15-inch-diameter olive jars will fit in a number 3 Duluth pack. Twenty-four-inch-high pickle barrels can be purchased from western rafting companies.

SOME RELIABLE WATERPROOF BAGS

Attaining *reliable* waterproofing isn't as easy as it sounds. Simply stuffing sleeping bags and clothing into packs or bags that are constructed of waterproof material isn't enough. The weakest part of any waterproof bag is its closure, not its stitching or fabric. Stitching may be waterproofed with paint-on chemicals or tape, and fabrics are either waterproof or they aren't. But there's not much you can do with a "waterproof" bag whose mouth won't seal. Still, there are some reliable waterproof bags:

- Roll-and-fold gear bags: A number of small waterproof bags roll and fold, then can be secured around the neck with Fastex clips. My experience with the popular Cascade Designs SealLine models has been positive. Punctures are easily patched in the field with duct tape.

[1] Any relationship between this account and the true story of how this all began is purely coincidental.

I mourn the passing of the amphibious-assault military gas-mask bags, which were truly marvelous. I still have a guarded few, but I'll probably use SealLine bags when these wear out.

■ **Gear bags with sliding tube closures:** Bags with sliding tube closures, such as the proven Voyageur (appendix B) models, are waterproof even when compressed under the weight of a heavy object. However, the tube closures are slow and awkward to seal, especially when your hands are cold. The plastic tubes also tend to cut through the plastic bags after they've been used a lot. And the bags don't fit well in a Duluth pack. This is a good system for white-water runs but not for wilderness canoe trips. The Voyageur bags that roll down and seal with Fastex buckles are better.

■ **U-tie-'em bags and bags with zippers:** Other bags that are easy to use but of questionable reliability are those with pleat-and-tie closures and standard zippers.

The value of bags that pleat and tie depends entirely on how skillful you are in gathering and tying the fabric. Zippers are fast and easy to use but they don't seal completely and eventually they fail. Yes, there are waterproof zippers, but they're expensive and usually found on scuba bags, which aren't practical for wilderness travel. Leaf- and lawn-sized plastic bags with sealing tops are too fragile for canoe tripping.

If you think that the ideal waterproof bag hasn't been invented, you're dead right. Waterproof bags tend to be either reliable and awkward to use or undependable and easy to use. And they almost never come in the sizes you need.

Two good commercial waterproof bags are the super-strong ones designed for trash compactors, and the huge 36-inch by 60-inch, 6-mil-thick plastic pack liners you find in canoe shops. You can mail-order them from CLG Enterprises or Duluth Pack (appendix B).

You can also make a serviceable plastic liner for your pack by taping (use silver duct tape) up bags from 6-mil plastic sheeting, which you can buy at every hardware store. The tape will stick better if you roughen the edges of the plastic with sandpaper beforehand.

Aloksak "hermetically sealed" plastic bags are certified waterproof to 60 meters. They function like ziplock bags but are much stronger. They come in many sizes. Great for cell phones, GPS units, food, maps, etc.

SOME CLOSING THOUGHTS TO PACK AWAY

I am often asked what pack or wanigan or waterproof bag is best. If you stick with canoeing long enough, you'll discover how heavily loaded this question really is. My best advice is to remind you that you're ahead if all your equipment can be fixed with simple tools. A lot of new gear can't. The throwaway syndrome began with shoes and now runs rampant across equipmentland. Natural materials like leather, wood, canvas, and brass remain popular because they're so easy to repair. The trick is to know when to go high tech and when to follow tradition. Experienced trippers usually have a mix of old and new.

For example, I use a mix of canvas Duluth packs and box-sided nylon portage packs, plus a Maine pack-basket combo and Stormy Bay wanigan on my canoe trips. Each has advantages. I prefer upright (top-loading) baskets or dry boxes for fragile items like eggs and optics, and side-loading wanigans for hard gear like stoves and cookware. Why? Things slide around when wanigans are tipped up to portage. Baskets are never tipped.

Take a long, hard look at your equipment and your tripping style, then select the packs and waterproof bags that will meet your needs and make you smile.

WATERPROOFING YOUR OUTFIT

No waterproof bag will remain watertight forever. Eventually it will develop pinholes and abrasions, and you'll have to repair or replace it. So it makes little sense to spend a lot of money for fancy waterproof pack sacks. Instead, use an inexpensive waterproof liner inside conventional packs.

Holes almost always develop from *within* a plastic bag, not without. Every time you stuff a sleeping bag or pair of boots into a pack sack, you stretch or abrade the plastic liner. In no time there's a hole. And it makes no difference whether the bag is a 6-mil-thick plastic Duluth pack liner or the PVC-coated walls of a fully waterproof pack sack!

The answer? Nest a tough abrasion liner inside each waterproof pack liner. The abrasion liner may be standard 6-mil plastic, a woven polypropylene bag (better), or a sack you've sewn from heavy nylon or cotton. It need not be waterproof. (Ostrom Outdoors has an excellent [huge!] waterproof pack liner.)

The abrasion liner will protect the waterproof plastic bag from being punctured by your gear inside, and the pack sack will eliminate tears from the outside.

When you've filled your pack with equipment, roll down the top of the abrasion liner, then twist, fold over, and seal the outer plastic bag with a loop of shock cord or band cut from an inner tube. *Hint:* Be sure that the abrasion liner and waterproof bag liner are long enough so you can roll or twist them to provide a good seal. Bags should be *twice* the length of the pack!

If you have a pack with zippered compartments, you'll have to waterproof each compartment with the double-bag method recommended. This is a major reason why experienced canoeists scorn packs with exterior pockets. Besides, zippers are often the first thing to fail on a rugged canoe trip.

Packing the Sleeping Bag

If there's one thing you must keep absolutely dry, it's your sleeping bag. The recommended procedure for waterproofing a sleeping bag is to stuff it into a nylon sack that has first been lined with a plastic bag. This is foolish advice! If you reread the second principle of waterproofing, you'll see why.

My method: Stuff your sleeping bag into a nylon stuff sack (which need not be waterproof), then put the sack into a 4-mil-thick plastic bag. Seal the plastic bag with a loop of shock cord and set this unit into an oversized waterproof nylon stuff sack. Note that the puncture-prone plastic bag is where it should be—sandwiched between two protective layers of tough nylon.

Note: It's hard to find a strong, correctly sized plastic bag that will fit the sleeping bag. Four-mil-thick Minnow bags (they measure 17 by 33 inches) are ideal. Minnow bags cost about 50 cents apiece at bait shops. Similar-weight trash compactor bags are also good—most supermarkets have them.

How to Pack Cameras, GPS Units, Radios, and Satellite Phones

Most camera buffs use military ammo boxes or plastic Pelican boxes (appendix B), for fragile items like cameras and GPS units.

I've seen a lot of dry boxes fail on canoe trips. And some of them were Pelicans, which I think are by far the best. A blade of grass, a plant seed, dirt or other foreign material may break the seal and cause it to fail. You must meticulously maintain the seals.

Before I close any waterproof box, I carefully eyeball every inch of the seal. I wipe away foreign matter with a clean

bandanna. Every few days I wipe the seal with clear water. When I return home I wash the seal with soapy water and rinse and dry it. Then I spray silicone on the seal and wipe off the excess with a dry cotton cloth.

It's probably not a good plan to leave waterproof boxes tightly sealed for months on end. The compressed seals can take a permanent set. If you've ever stored a car for long periods, you know the problems you can have with rubber seals.

Unfortunately, the rigors of canoe trips demand compromises, and attention to seals is not always a priority. For this reason I can't commit my heart to waterproof boxes.

Here's how I pack my camera, GPS, and telephone-sized VHF radio:

- **Camera:** My waterproof Nikon rides in a thwart bag or around my neck, tucked inside my life jacket: My Cannon reflex, with its telephoto lens, goes inside an old amphibious-assault gas-mask bag. I'll switch to a Cascade Designs SealLine bag when it wears out. The beauty of a bag is that a small amount of foreign matter won't corrupt the roll-down seal.

- **GPS:** I used to keep my GPS in a small foam-lined Tupperware box, which was packed inside a transparent Cascade Designs plastic See Bag. The crush-proof Tupperware box was reasonably waterproof, and the See Bag was completely waterproof. But I recently discovered a lightweight plastic waterproof case called Cell-Safe (appendix B), which is designed for cell telephones. It fits my GPS perfectly and seems to be quite reliable for general canoe travel. I place my Cell-Safe inside a See Bag for extra security when I paddle mean rapids.

- **VHF Radio and Satellite Phone:** I keep my aircraft radio and satellite phone in foam-lined Pelican cases, stored inside my pack basket.

PUTTING IT ALL TOGETHER

You'll need three to five Duluth packs per canoe, and one or more hard packs for the crew, for an extended trip. I usually allow slightly less than one number 3 Duluth pack for each person's clothing and sleeping gear.

Each individual packs personal gear in a separate pack. If a pack sack is lost, as in a capsize, at least there'll be some extra clothing and sleeping bags to share.

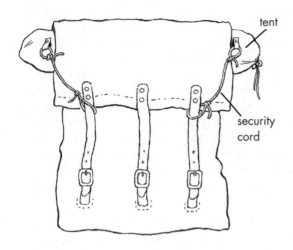

tent

security
cord

Figure 9-8. Pack the tent and poles separately—set the pole and stake bag just under the pack flap and run the closing straps of the pack flap through loops of nylon cord sewn to the ends of the pack bag.

Food is distributed among as many packs as possible, both for the reason above and to equalize weight.

The tent and rain tarp are packed last. They go at the very top of the pack—between the rolled abrasion liner and sealed waterproof pack liner. The system keeps these items—which may be wet from rain—separate from dry pack contents, and protects them from getting soaked if you capsize. The rule is to pack things in the reverse order you'll need them. The tent and tarp are on the top because they're the first things you'll need when you make camp.

I encourage everyone to bring a small nylon day pack for frequently used essentials like rain gear, fleece jacket, gloves, warm hats, and wind shell. Clip the day pack to a thwart with a carabiner so it won't be lost in the gathering flow if you capsize. A day pack is also handy for long hikes—you've come to see the country, remember?

Here's how to pack a tent with obnoxiously long poles:

1. Stuff or roll the tent without the poles or stakes and pack it between the sealed abrasion liner and waterproof liner of your pack, as explained above.

2. Place the poles and pegs in a sturdy nylon bag with a drawstring closure. Sew a loop of nylon webbing to each end of the bag and attach lengths of parachute cord to the loops. Tie a loop (use a bowline: see chapter 12) at the end of each cord.

3. Set the pole bag under the pack flap and snake the closing straps of the pack through the loops in the cord ends. Now your pole bag can't fall out of your pack if you capsize.

Note: The mouth of the pole bag should have a protective security flap (like those on sleeping-bag stuff sacks) so that poles cannot migrate out of the opening. Use a plastic cord lock on the bag drawstrings . . . and for complete security, tie the cords!

CARRYING FIREARMS

As I pointed out in chapter 4, there's no reason to carry a gun on any canoe trip. Nevertheless, grizzlies and polar bears can be unpredictable; they may not respect your "live and let live" philosophy. For this reason many canoe expeditions choose to go armed.[2]

If you decide to go armed, here's a good way to pack your weapon: Load the magazine but not the chamber and place the gun inside an unlined canvas (breathable) case. Insert the canvas case into a GunBoat watertight case, and tie the GunBoat to a gunnel of your canoe (figure 9-9). The GunBoat was developed by Alaskan hunting guides to protect firearms from water. It's made from industrial-grade PVC-coated nylon, which is absolutely waterproof. There are no zippers to leak or padding to absorb water. The butt end of the case rolls and seals with a Fastex buckle—just like a white-water dry bag. Air that's trapped within the case will float the gun. When I capsized on Canada's Hood River in 1992, my .444 Marlin rifle was enclosed in a GunBoat case. Not one drop of water got in!

When it's time to portage, remove your gun from the GunBoat case but not from the canvas case. Set the gun across the top of your pack (between the shoulder straps and pack) or place it under a pack flap and hit the trail. There's no need to remove the GunBoat case when you portage.

You can order a GunBoat case (they're inexpensive) from Recreational Specialties in Anchorage, Alaska. The address is in appendix B.

[2]The new (2001) Canadian Firearms Act requires that all guns must be registered when you enter Canada. Naturally, there's a registration fee.

Figure 9-9. The GunBoat gun case is absolutely watertight. Note how the case is tied under a gunnel so it won't interfere with packs.

Native people who live in the Far North usually set their rifles in the canoe with no security or protection from the elements. That's fine for hunting, but it's a bad way to treat a good gun. Do this on a canoe trip and you'll have a pile of rusty parts when the floatplane arrives.

Many years ago I shot competitively on the U.S. Army's rifle team, where I learned to respect and meticulously care for my guns. When I do go armed on a canoe trip, I usually carry my classic old .444 Marlin. It's a beautiful rifle and I've shot it a lot. It would break my heart if I saw a single rust spot. Here's how I maintain it, and any other guns that go on my canoe trips:

- Condensation will cause a gun to rust if you leave it stored inside a waterproof case for very long. As soon as you're camped, then, remove the rifle from the waterproof GunBoat case but not the breathable canvas case. Put the cased rifle inside your tent, away from the weather and people.

- Once a week wipe down the outside of the rifle with a special gun-care product or WD-40. If the gun is left in the waterproof GunBoat case for several days, run a lightly oiled patch through the barrel at the first opportunity. You'll need to carry a jointed stainless-steel cleaning rod and gun cleaning materials.

God forbid you should ever have to shoot a bear. But if

you do, you'd better not have a misfire—a possibility if your bullets are wet from pouring rain or a capsize. Military ammunition is sealed against the elements, but most factory ammo isn't. I paint a thin layer of lacquer around the cartridge case's neck and the primer of every loaded round. This guarantees ignition even in a torrential rain.

My old Marlin has accompanied me on four canoe trips to Hudson Bay and two trips above the Arctic Circle. It looks like new.

SECURING YOUR GEAR

Everything should be secured so tightly in your canoe that it can't possibly fall out if you capsize. And running a pack strap around a canoe thwart isn't good enough: A pack that bobs out of an overturned or swamped canoe may be sheared off between passing rocks—or worse, snag the canoe and cause it to wrap up.

Small items can be placed under shock-corded thwarts or in the thwart bags mentioned in chapter 6. But pack sacks must be locked tightly into the canoe with rubber ropes and/or nylon cords, as shown in figure 6-8.

I run two heavy rubber ropes with adjustable steel hooks over each pack sack and secure them to loops of parachute cord in the gunnels (see chapter 6, Outfitting and Customizing Your Canoe). As an extra precaution I string one or two lengths of parachute cord fore and aft from the yoke to each thwart. Cords are tied with a quick-release power cinch, explained in chapter 17, Hazards and Rescue. The final touch is to snap the belly section of my nylon splash cover over the load.

This entire procedure takes only a minute and produces a compact, buoyant mass that will function as a giant life preserver if the canoe swamps or overturns.

When it's time to portage, I stuff the belly cover under a pack flap, snap the rubber ropes to the gunnel, and tie the parachute cords to the thwarts. This eliminates loose cords that might snag on brush along the trail.

Note: It bears repeating that in a capsize, gear usually stays with a splash-covered canoe, so there's probably no need to tie things in. A good plan is to use 'chute cords or rubber ropes under your cover in big, powerful rapids when you want to leave nothing to chance.

Figure 9-10. After a month on the trail your canoe may look like this. Note the Caribou racks and author Cliff Jacobson in the stern. Thlewiaza River, Nunavut, Canada.

SOME FINAL SUGGESTIONS FOR PACKING

■ You may need your wind jacket, first-aid kit, or a roll of film sometime during the day, so plan ahead. Pack frequently used essentials near the top of your pack, or carry a small day pack just for these items.

■ You could lose a canoe in a rapid, so don't put all your eggs in one basket. Distribute food, matches, cooking gear, and other necessities among the two or more boats in your party.

■ Equipment may have to be carried over some pretty grueling portages, so don't overload your packs. You may be able to muscle a ninety-pound Duluth pack 2 miles down a groomed trail, but can you carry it 30 feet up the side of a canyon wall?

■ Keep your extra paddle, map, and compass within easy reach. And wear—don't pack—survival items (knife, matches, bug dope).

Packing for an expedition requires careful attention to detail. You can't afford to omit anything. For example, did you test your waterproof bags and hard packs to be sure they're really waterproof? Have you checked the straps and fittings of your packs to be sure that threads are secure, rivets tight? Did you remember of pack the extra compass, insect head net, or canoe repair kit? Use an itemized checklist like the one in appendix C so you won't forget anything.

CHAPTER 10
CANOE TENTS ARE DIFFERENT

Take a midmorning paddle along a popular canoe route after a major storm. You'll see wet clothes, sleeping bags, boots—all strung from a network of lines that seemingly run everywhere. Look closely at the tents in each camp as you paddle by. A thoughtfully designed tent, properly pitched, is the key to storm survival.

Note that some campers have well-designed, badly pitched tents, while others have badly designed, well-pitched ones. In between these extremes are scores of moderately experienced trippers who've weathered the rains with a modicum of comfort, a sprinkling of know-how, and an array of gear.

Let's get one thing straight. You don't *need* a sophisticated tent for canoe camping. A knowledge of basic outdoor skills will do more to ensure your comfort than the most eye-popping supershelter. But the right tent plus the right skills will keep you on the canoe trails in weather that sours all but the most committed paddlers.

The least-satisfactory tents for canoeing are those advertised as canoe or portage tents. Simple A-frames, lean-tos, and open-front Baker tents are the usual bearers of these titles. Though adequate for canoe tripping, the designs of these tents date to the last century B.N.E. (before the nylon era) and are not well suited to the camping style of modern paddlers. Tents good enough for Grandpa still work today, but they're heavier, less wind stable, more time consuming to pitch, and more cumbersome to carry than sophisticated models of modern design.

Good backpacking tents are usually good canoe tents, but not always. The requirements of canoeists are much different from those of backpackers. For example, hikers are free to travel to an ideal camp spot (scrambling up a rock face to reach a flat, grassy area is par for the sport). Canoeists are less mobile, because our sites are limited by the often unforgiving

terrain that lines our waterways. Consequently, canoe tents are frequently pitched on solid rock, loose pebbles, or sand.

It follows that a canoe tent should pitch quickly and easily on any terrain, be small enough to fit on the skimpiest sites, yet be large enough to assure a measure of sanity when bad weather or hordes of insects confine you to its fabric walls. It should also be lightweight, compact when packed, able to withstand a minor hurricane, *absolutely* weatherproof and bugproof, quick to dry after a rain, comfortable in warm and cold weather alike . . . and affordable!

WEIGHT

Most canoe portages are less than 2 miles long, so canoeists can afford to carry more gear (and weight) than backpackers. A *few* extra pounds won't affect how a canoe handles and will hardly be noticed when the outfit is carried overland. An item's bulk is usually much more important than its weight. For example, a ten-pound tent that rolls compactly enough to fit *crossways* in a number 3 Duluth pack is better for canoeing than a seven-pound model that won't fit. The villain is usually the length of the pole sections. Twenty-three inches is about maximum for a good fit in a number 3 Duluth pack. Tents longer than this may have to be stood lengthwise in the pack, which fouls up the whole packing system. Or tent and poles will have toe packed separately, as explained in the last chapter.

Figure on a maximum tent weight *per person* of about six pounds. Good canoe tents are available that weigh much less.

SIZE

A tent 6 or 7 feet wide by about feet long is ideal for two people. Larger tents are awkward to pitch on small wilderness

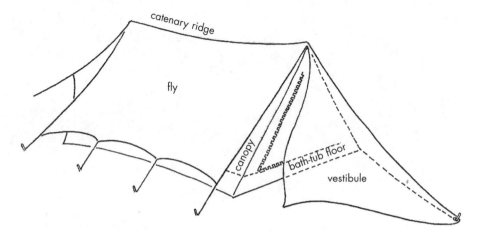

Figure 10-1. Tent nomenclature—A-frame tent.

sites, while smaller ones may be too confining. For ease of dressing, the peak height should be around 5 feet. This is high enough for comfort yet low enough for stability in high winds. In a pinch four people can sleep crossways in a tent this size—important in the event a tent is lost in a capsize or destroyed by wind.

Some tents are put out of commission quite easily. For example, the Eureka Timberline (which is a fine tent) has three critical components—the center ridge-pole sections, and a pair of pole junction tubes. Lose any one of these and the tent won't go up! Some years ago on a canoe trip in Minnesota, some friends lost the ridge pole from their Timberline tent. They had packed the rolled tent (poles inside) just under the flap of their Duluth pack (which I advised you not to do in the last chapter), and the pole slid out of the badly secured tent bag into the lake. Fortunately, there was enough room in my Cannondale Aroostook to sleep the crew. It was crowded, but we survived. (See color figure 10-2.)

SINGLE OR DOUBLE WALLED?

It's interesting to note that Bedouin tribes have used double-walled tents for thousands of years. Bedouin tents traditionally are constructed of two layers of dense wool (usually black colored to reduce the sun's glare) to provide a cool (or at least cooler) respite from the hot desert sun.

My own experience suggests that a single-walled (*any* single-walled) tent—Gore-Tex or otherwise—is a handicap for canoeing. Here's why:

- Double-walled tents are cooler when it's hot and warmer when it's cool.

- The fly wears out long before the tent. You can patch the holes or recoat the damaged fabric, or you can just buy a new fly. If the roof on a single-walled tent goes, you buy a new tent!

- A spark hole in the tent fly of a double-walled tent won't cause the roof to leak in rain. Why? Because water that leaks through the hole will slither down the inside of the fly to the ground. If you hole a single-walled tent, rain drops on you!

- The most carefully sealed seams can eventually fail—that's why a full-length fly that covers every seam and zipper is so important.

The size and method of attachment of the fly is important. To save weight and cost, and to provide good ventilation, many tents have short (cap) flies. A cap fly will protect a tent in a vertical rain but wind-whipped water will blow up under it and if there's enough force, will tear the fly right off the tent. For this reason flies should be generous in size—*long enough to touch the ground on each side of the tent*. The extra length adds a few ounces of weight to the fly, but it makes the tent much more wind stable and watertight.

The space between the fly and tent at ground level can also be used to store muddy boots and damp gear. Boots have no place in a tent. They take up valuable space and dirty sleeping quarters.

A few of the early double-walled tents had their flies

attached at the ridge (the Gerry Fireside and clever Cannondale models)—a design that's badmouthed on the grounds that the tent can't be pitched without the fly (invalid criticism, because you seldom use a tent without a fly). However, knowledgeable campers know that it's a hassle to install a fly on a tent, especially in a high wind. Still, tents with built-in flies have all but disappeared from the American (though not European) camping scene, probably because they're more expensive to produce.

FABRICS

Nylon

Best is a two-layer nylon tent—one that has a waterproof fly suspended over a nonwaterproof inner canopy. Body-produced moisture passes out through the inner tent and condenses on the inside of the cooler fly, where it slithers harmlessly to the ground.

Avoid tents that are constructed of one layer of waterproof nylon (single-walled tents). They drip condensed water from their inner walls and leak through they're many exposed seams, which are almost impossible to waterproof.

To keep condensed water from contacting the inner tent, the fly should rig drum-tight and be separated from the porous canopy by several inches. This construction also provides a dead-air space that maintains the interior of the tent at a fairly uniform temperature—a modified thermos effect.

Single-walled Gore-Tex

Gore-Tex has had its ups and downs. Early Gore-Tex tents were unreliable in rain, and they have always been expensive to produce. Serious rock climbers are all familiar with Bibler tents. A mountaineering friend summed up the Bibler as the only Gore-Tex I've seen that works. Admittedly, I've had no experience with Bibler tents, so I can't comment.

Cotton

Some canoeists still prefer cotton tents. But *good* cotton tents are hard to find—mainly because recent fire-retardant legislation has boosted the weight of cotton fabrics too high. An advantage of cotton over nylon is its greater resistance to abrasion. Nylon fabrics whose waterproof coating has become abraded cannot be easily repaired by home remedies, whereas canvas can easily be rewaterproofed with brush-on chemicals that are available at every hardware store. However, cotton tents are heavy when dry, heavier when wet, and they mildew. For these reasons, nylon tents are better for canoeing.

Dacron

Theoretically, Dacron is used in tent construction because it's more resistant than nylon to the degrading effects of the sun. Why is it, then, that so many Dacron tents have nylon flies?

The truth is that manufacturers use Dacron in tents because it stretches and shrinks much less than nylon. Some tents—notably domes—depend upon uniformly stressed construction to retain their form.

GEOMETRY

There are A-frames, tepees, wedges, boxes, domes, lean-tos, and sophisticated geometric shapes.

As far as space is concerned, domes are the most efficient tent designs. The high, gradually sloping sidewalls of a dome tent provide a pleasant spacious atmosphere, and the polygonal floor permits occupants to sleep in any direction—a real advantage if the tent is pitched wrong or on a sloping site.

Though domes are highly efficient at shedding rain, they're badly ventilated (the fly covers the windows and door), and getting into and out of a dome in driving rain calls for surefooted skill: Whenever you unzip the fly, rain pours into the tent. Good domes have awnings and/or vestibules.

You get just what you pay for when you buy a dome. Spend one night in the rain in a discount-store cheapie and you'll know that the designers never did! Cheap domes blow down when a breeze blows up; expensive (geodesic) domes hardly ruffle in winds of 50 miles an hour.

Tunnels (figure 10-3) combine the best features of A-frame (which consists of two angled poles joined at the ridge) and dome tents. They go up fast and they tolerate wicked winds. But they have less headroom than domes or A-frames, and hence are rather doghousy for long stays. Still, tunnels can be useful. George Drought, who operates a Canadian canoe tripping company called Wilderness Bound, has a giant tunnel tent with screened entrances at both ends. George's community tundra tunnel earns high marks when winds are big and bugs are bad.

Tepee-style nylon tents have disappeared from the outdoor scene, probably because they're a hassle to pitch and

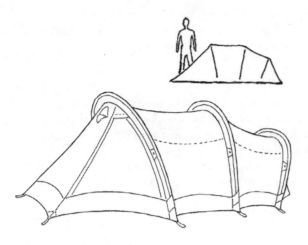

Figure 10-3. Tunnel tent

they don't use space effectively.

If you want a reasonably priced all-around canoe tent for use in all but the most extreme conditions, consider a model that has a modified A-frame and is largely self-supporting. Tents like the Eureka Timberline, its derivatives, and all the Moss models go up fast on any terrain. "U-stake-'em" tents take time, especially if you have to search for rocks or logs to hold stakes in uncooperative ground. A conventional-style tent will usually flatten in a wind if one or more of its stakes pull out, but an unanchored freestanding tent may become

10-4. Dome tent

airborne if it isn't tied down. The real advantage of a completely or semi-self-supporting tent is that it can be anchored securely with four to eight stakes, or about half the number required to pitch a conventionally supported tent.

Besides a relatively freestanding A-frame design, other features distinguish a good canoe tent. First is a bathtub or wrap-up floor. In this construction the waterproof floor is sewn to the porous tent body a few inches above the ground. This eliminates seams at ground level. It's next to impossible to prevent ground—level seams—or indeed *any* exposed seams—from leaking if they're in contact with water for long periods of time, no matter how carefully you've coated them with seam sealant. Be aware that the polygonal floors of dome style tents prohibit bathtub construction—which is why dome tents *must* have a fly that covers every seam and stakes right to the ground!

The door panel should be *inside* the mosquito net so you won't have to unzip the bug screen every time you need to adjust the door for ventilation or to see outside.

The bug screen should be colored (preferably) black or deep olive drab so you can see through it clearly. Light-colored screens reflect and distort light.

I don't like fine-mesh no-see-um netting on a tent: It restricts ventilation, it's hard to see through, and it's not as strong as conventional mosquito netting. If tiny no-see-ums are a problem, simply spray bug dope on the net. Or close the nylon door.

A canoe tent should have a vestibule (an integral or add-on extension that secures to the front of the tent) at one or both ends. Vestibules provide a protected place to store gear, out of the main sleeping compartment. Equally important, they waterproof the door end of the tent by sealing off zippers, eaves, and seams. And they improve the aerodynamics of the tent by presenting a sharp wedge shape to the wind.

Twin doors are worthwhile on any tent, especially one that will be used in buggy country. If a zipper goes bad, you have a spare entrance. You can also use the twin doors to discourage bugs. Here's how: My favorite canoe tent is an old Cannondale Aroostook (no longer manufactured) that has opposing doors and vestibules. When I pitch the tent in buggy country, I leave *both* doors and vestibules wide open while I'm arranging gear. The bugs just fly on through.

When everything is in place, I leave the tent for a while. I return when the last bug is gone. Then I close the bug screens—the upwind one first, then the downwind. I close the vestibules halfway, which allows air to flow through and

Figure 10-5. Cheap domes blow down when the wind blows up! Back River, Nunawt, Canada.

creates a small wind eddy behind each vestibule flap where bugs can hide. They congregate in the protected eddy behind the upwind vestibule. I just have to remember to enter and exit through the *downwind* door.

Some tents have niceties like lantern loops and inside pockets for the storage of small items. These features, which require only a few minutes at a home sewing machine to make and install, add considerable cost to a tent without significantly increasing its utility. Some of the best canoe tents have a minimum of interior niceties.

Construction features are overrated. All the hullabaloo

Figure 10-6. Good geodesic domes, like this North Face VE-25, hardly ruffle in winds that would blow lesser tents down. Porcupine River, Saskatchewan.

about number of stitches per inch and reinforcement of zipper ends and such, proudly touted by tent makers, takes a backseat to good design. I've experienced bent poles and torn stake loops, and I've seen flies ripped loose and carried away by high winds, but I've never seen a *well-designed* tent come apart at its seams or a zipper tear out of its stitching. Zippers jam and break; their seams rarely pull loose. A well-sewn, badly designed tent is more apt to blow apart in a high wind than a badly sewn, well-designed one. Quality of construction is not always an indication of good design!

TENT STAKES

The 6-inch aluminum wire stakes (pins) that come with most tents are adequate for grass, but not much else. Eight-inch-long aluminum skewers are best for hard ground; 12-inch aluminum staples are better for soft ground; 12-inch arrow-shaft stakes and orange plastic twist-in stakes are superb in sand and boggy tundra. Bring a variety of tent stakes (figure 10-7) so you'll be set for any ground.

In summary, the best canoe tents have semi-self-supporting modified A-frames, bathtub floors, fine-mesh mosquito netting, and a vestibule. They weigh less than six

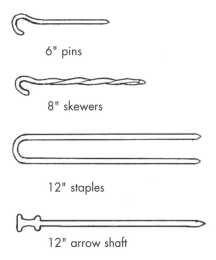

6" pins

8" skewers

12" staples

12" arrow shaft

Figure 10-7. Types of tent stakes: 6-inch pins (general purpose); 8-inch skewers (better general purpose); 12-inch staples (for soft ground—they have double the holding power); 12-inch arrow-shaft stakes and plastic screws (for sand, mud, and spongy tundra).

pounds per person and measure about 6 feet by 8 feet, with a 5-foot ridge. Their flies stake right to the ground, and their longest pole section is no more than 23 inches.

STORMPROOFING AND MAINTENANCE TIPS

River camps are often pitched in low areas where rain can cause flooding. You'll stay dry if you use these tricks to stormproof your tent:

1. A plastic ground cloth inside your tent will prevent groundwater, which gets through worn floor seams and fabric, from wetting your sleeping gear. *Do not* put the plastic sheet under the tent floor: It may trap water, which will be pressure-wicked (by body weight) into the sleeping compartment.

Make your ground cloth large enough to flow 12 inches up each side of the tent. You'll appreciate this bathtub-style protection when your tent is crowded and you're sleeping against the sidewall.

2. The least-stormproof part of a tent is the doorway, where zippers and seams come together. If possible, pitch your tent with its back facing into the wind.

3. Waterproof the seams of a new tent. I prefer Thompson's Water Seal—a common hardware-store chemical used for waterproofing concrete blocks. TWS won't crack or peel. Apply it sparingly with a foam varnish brush and immediately wipe off the excess with paper toweling. One application lasts for years. TWS is also great for waterproofing maps, journals,[1] and cotton hats.

Note: Don't use TWS on plastic or on nylon whose waterproof coating has worn off. TWS will slightly discolor fabrics.

4. Reduce wind stress on guylines. Attach loops of shock cord to guylines. Nylon cords stretch when wet; shock cords keep them tight and absorb the wind stress normally reserved for seams and fittings.

5. Add extra stake loops to the tent perimeter. Most tents have only three or four stake loops per side, which isn't enough in high winds. If the hem of your tent flaps in wind, sew on more stake loops!

6. Sew storm loops to the face of the fly. If wind crushes the waterproof fly against the canopy sidewall, condensation and leakage may result. Storm loops stiffen the fly and help spill wind. Try to position storm loops directly over poles. Back (on the inside fly) each loop with heavy fabric, and sew on mating Velcro.

When a storm blows up, secure the Velcro tabs around the adjacent poles and guy the outside loops. This transfers wind stress from the fabric to the poles.

7. Double-guy the windward end. The two lines should be about 30 degrees apart. Attach cords to the aluminum frame (or to poles or Velcro tabs around poles), not to a D-ring on the tent fly.

8. Reinforce seams. If a seam looks weak, it probably is. Reinforce stress points with carpet thread and nylon webbing.

9. Cover exposed seams with waterproof material. Seam sealant (glue!) *will not* keep out rain that falls on exposed seams. Unfortunately, many (most?) modern tents have stitching that is exposed to the weather. Can you glue a watertight patch over the stitching, or buy a vestibule that will cover the exposed seams? Tip 13 suggests another option.

10. Double-stake windward loops. Two stakes per loop—each through a separate hole, and at a different angle—doubles the surface area and holding power.

11. Use anchors on rocky ground. The method illustrated in figure 10-8 works well on rock.

12. Tie 3-foot lengths of parachute cord to each stake loop before your canoe trip and you won't have to mess with cutting and tying these anchor lines in a storm!

13. Extend the walls of the fly to ground level. Cap flies, which allow wind-driven rain to blow on to the porous canopy, can be disastrous above the tree line. Instead, cut off the bottom of the fly, all around the tent. Make the cut just above the fittings (stake and guy loops) and sew on a band of waterproof nylon. To this sew on the strip you cut off. Now the hem of your fly will touch the ground. Matching material can be obtained from the tent manufacturer and many outdoor stores. Sewing is easily done on a light-duty sewing machine.

[1]Waterproof pens, paper, notebooks, and sketchbooks are available from the J. L. Darling Corporation; see appendix B.

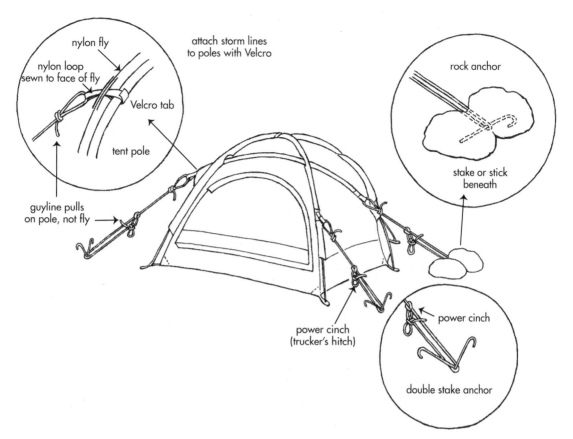

10-8. Stormproof your tent! Whenever possible, attach guylines to poles with Velcro fasteners. Use rock anchors on rocky ground and sand. Double-stake lines on soft ground.

Suitable fabrics are available from Thrifty Outfitters, a division of Midwest Mountaineering (appendix B).

14. Shock-cord all tent poles. Shock-corded poles are more rigid than those whose sections are held together by friction alone. Shock-cording kits are available at most camping shops.

15. If your tent doesn't come with an oversized stuff sack, make one. A snug-fitting sack looks nice in the store but the tent won't fit when it's water soaked and caked with mud.

16. It's faster and easier on the fabric to stuff a tent than to roll it. Stuff in the reverse order you'll pitch the tent—fly first, tent second.

Tents with self-supporting frameworks that depend on brass hooks, pins, and spring clips for attachment to the poles must be rolled. Be careful that hard fittings don't abrade the nylon fabric when you roll these tents. Whenever possible, pull hooks and pins to the edges of the roll, where they won't bear on adjacent material.

17. Sun-dry your tent thoroughly before you store it away. Microorganisms will attack the waterproof coating on a damp tent and cause it to peel. Who says nylon tents won't mildew?

You can pay a fortune for a good tent, especially if you want bomb-shelter design, hurricane stability, a profusion of interior niceties, and extra-light weight. These things are nice, of course, but they're not essential—not even for trips above the timberline.

Fortunately, many of the best canoe tents are relatively inexpensive. To be sure, they will lack refinements: You may need to reinforce seams, shock-cord poles, construct a larger stuff sack, and so on. But the end result will be a tent you can live with on the best of terms in the worst of times.

The Recipe

One high ledge overlooking a misty falls.

A crisp, clear evening.

A sprinkling of sunset.

A small, bright fire.

One or two well-blackened pots, dented with memories.

Generous servings of camp-brewed coffee.

Appetites honed by the passage of a long, tough day.

One full bottle of camaraderie.

Stir well until mixed and simmer with a dash of
inspiring conversation. Serve as needed to experience the
flavor of the North Country.

CHAPTER 11
THE RECIPE

I prefer to keep foods simple. If it takes longer than thirty minutes to prepare, forget it! Sure, I'll occasionally fry fish, make popcorn, or bake blueberry right-side-up cake well into the night. But these are special occasions. It's unrealistic to expect to make time on the water if you spend half your waking hours cooking and washing dishes. I'm generally on the water at dawn, lunched by 11:00 A.M., and camped by 4:00 P.M. This routine enables me to enjoy the early-morning solitude, cover plenty of distance, and select a decent campsite before sunset. To keep this schedule, here's what my meals necessarily look like.

WORKING MENUS
WITHOUT A LOT OF WORK

Breakfast

About half my breakfasts require only boiling water to prepare; one-fourth are cold meals (no cooking whatsoever), and one-fourth can be made on my gasoline stove in less than thirty minutes. The menu for a given morning is determined by what lies ahead that day. For example, if we've just got to make time before the wind blows up, we'll eat our granola bars and jerky and run. But if the weather's cold or we've got more time, we'll crank up the stove and boil water for oatmeal or hot cereal. If the day is short and predictable, we'll lollygag and cook pancakes. Nothing is cut and dried on a canoe trip. We take our cue from nature.

Here are some of my favorite breakfasts.

SLOW-COOK BREAKFASTS

CINNAMON BURRITOS, BROWN-SUGAR STEWED APPLES, AND SMOKED PORK SAUSAGE

Cinnamon tortillas taste like cinnamon rolls. They are big-time favorites! The following recipe makes one burrito, but it's easily multiplied to feed your gang.

1 giant tortilla
3 tablespoons brown sugar, plus more for the fruit
¼ teaspoon cinnamon
Dehydrated apples (every supermarket has 'em)
Liquid margarine
Smoked pork sausage

First, start the stewed fruit and smoked porkies. You'll need one pot to boil the sausage, another to boil the fruit. To the fruit, add brown sugar and cinnamon to taste. The fruit will absorb only so much sugar, so there's no need to measure. When the water boils, give the fruit a stir, then remove the pot from the heat and set it on an insulated pad. Add a cozy cover (see Cooking Tricks later in this chapter) and allow the fruit to stew for ten minutes.

To make the burritos, evenly distribute a generous amount of liquid margarine, then the brown sugar and cinnamon, on the face of each tortilla. Roll to form a burrito. Place the burrito seam-down on a warm pan lightly oiled with liquid margarine. (You can cook six burritos at a time in a 12-inch skillet.) Cover and fry at low heat for twenty seconds, then turn the burritos (use bamboo tongs) and add a dash of water to steam. Cover and cook for thirty more seconds then serve.

Can you taste it? A cinnamon-roll burrito, oozing with melted brown sugar and hot cinnamon-flavored margarine, covered with sweet steaming apple slices, served with a side of smoked sausage. Bush breakfasts don't get much better than this!

STURDIWHEAT PANCAKES WITH CINNAMON SYRUP AND WALNUTS

It's pointless to make pancakes from scratch when good mixes are available. The best commercial mix I've found is Sturdiwheat, which is made in Red Wing, Minnesota (appendix B). It's been around since 1939 but has just recently mushroomed in popularity. Just add water; the batter rises to form a light, bubbly meringue. Sturdiwheat cakes have a light, almost sourdough taste and consistency.

Sturdiwheat pancake mix
Water
Liquid margarine
Cooking oil
Syrup
Cinnamon (optional)
Walnuts

1. Disregard the mixing directions on the Sturdiwheat package. Pour dry mix into your two-quart plastic pitcher and add water, a little at a time, stirring frequently until the consistency is moderately runny. The tendency is toward a too-thick mix, which cooks badly. The batter thickens as it sets; you'll have to thin it again later.

2. Add about 2 tablespoons (the amount isn't critical) of liquid margarine to each 6 cups of liquid batter. The margarine will make the cakes more flexible and less likely to stick to the pan.

3. Allow the batter to set for about five minutes before you start cooking.

4. Use medium heat and just a few drops of oil to fry the first half-dozen cakes. It's par for the course to Frisbee the first cake into the fire to get the skillet heat right.

After the first half-dozen pancakes, you can limit your use of cooking oil to a few drops every few cakes. The margarine in the mix will provide the lubrication you need.

5. Meanwhile, pour your cold syrup into a small covered pot and add half again as much margarine and a dash of cinnamon, if you like. Heat until hot and set aside. To serve, smother the cakes with the hot syrup mix and strew them with walnuts.

You might want to pour stewed (rehydrated) apples over your pancakes before you add the syrup. And have you tried peanut butter on pancakes? Serve these with canned bacon, Canadian bacon, fried salami, or stewed fruit.

HEARTY FIFTEEN-MINUTE BREAKFASTS

- Red River Cereal: This is a nutritious blend of crunchy grains that's served in the best fishing camps in Canada. It cooks to a rich, creamy consistency in just five minutes. Most supermarkets have it.

- Sturdiwheat hot cereal has a rich taste (the outer wheat layers are left on the grain). Get it from the Sturdiwheat company in Red Wing, Minnesota (appendix B).

- Kashi is a breakfast pilaf made from seven whole grains and sesame. It's a pleasant change from traditional hot cereals.

- Old-time, slow-cook oatmeal: Instant oatmeal is traditional for fast moving days when you want to get up and go. But old-fashioned, slow-cooking, Quaker Oats are much better. Really, now, when did you last have the real thing?

- Big Bill's Multigrain Cereal (available from Harvest Foodworks; see appendix B): This wonderful Canadian cereal has a distinct malted milk taste. It's packaged in crew-sized servings.

Add dehydrated fruit bits, dates, and brown sugar to the cold water before cooking any of these hot cereals, if you like, and stir in walnuts just before serving. No cereal is complete without milk, which you'll have to rehydrate from powdered form.

You can serve these cereals with breakfast meats. Sodium-nitrite-rich, vacuum-sealed pork sausage will keep for a week on the typical canoe trip. Bacon will last two weeks if it's thoroughly fried (drain the grease on paper toweling) and then vacuum-sealed. Hard salami makes a great omelette, and it keeps for weeks.

BOILING-WATER-ONLY BREAKFASTS

- Instant oatmeal (maple and brown sugar flavor is most popular).
- Cream-of-Wheat with raisins.
- Granola mix.
- Mixed evaporated fruit.

NO-COOK BREAKFAST

HUDSON BAY BREAD

This is a chewy, granola-style bar. It's the traditional traveling fare in youth camps from Maine to Minnesota. Charles L. Sommers Canoe Base in Ely, Minnesota, has been serving it to Boy Scouts since 1960. Before that it was used by the Minnesota Outward Bound School. This recipe provides a ten-day supply for four hungry trippers.

> *3 cups soft margarine or butter*
> *4 cups sugar*
> *$\frac{1}{3}$ cup light Karo corn syrup*
> *$\frac{2}{3}$ cup honey*
> *2 teaspoons maple flavoring (Mapleine)*
> *$1\frac{1}{2}$ cups sliced almonds*
> *1 cup (or more!) chocolate chips*
> *Shredded coconut and raisins (optional)*
> *19 cups finely ground rolled oats (not instant oats!)*

Cream together the margarine, sugar, corn syrup, honey, and maple flavoring. Gradually stir in the remaining ingredients. Press the mixture into a greased cake pan; it should be $\frac{1}{4}$ to $\frac{1}{2}$ inch thick. Bake at 325 degrees for about twenty minutes, until golden brown. Don't overcook!

Press down on the Hudson Bay Bread with a spatula (to prevent crumbling) before you cut and remove the squares from the pan. "Scout serving size" (twice what most adults

will tolerate) measures $3\frac{1}{2}$ inches square, so as to fit exactly in protective half-gallon milk cartons. I wrap each square in plastic wrap then vacuum-seal each day's lunch supply. The shelf life is a full summer or more. Unused bars freeze well and keep till next year. Serve with beef jerky and mixed evaporated fruit.

TRAVELING SNACKS

On a strenuous canoe trip, you need a continuous supply of calories. Lunch isn't always enough to get you through till supper. So I include individual packets of mixed candy, beef jerky, or nuts (cashews have the greatest energy value) with each day's breakfast. These between-meal snacks become a blessing when the day stretches into night.

Lunch

It's a hassle to stop and cook lunch. Not only do you have to ferret out the pots and stove (or take time to build a fire), but you also have to clean up the mess when you're through eating. For this reason experienced wilderness canoeists prefer a no-cook lunch. The typical hot shore lunch is just too time-consuming to prepare.

You can build only so much variety into a no-cook lunch. After two weeks on the water, any instant lunch gets boring. However, variations on the entrees suggested below will be relished for weeks.

Figure 11-1. Lunch should be a no-cook affair. If you can't unwrap it and slice it or spread it, forget it!

PITA TREATS

Pita (Mediterranean pocket) bread contains preservatives and keeps nearly three weeks. It's my mainstay bread for noon meals. You can also use bagels, which last three days; Pilot biscuits, which last forever and can be used as Frisbees; or Seasoned Rye Krisp. One pita per person is plenty.

Stuff your pocket bread with:

- **Any good hard cheese:** Fresh cheese keeps about a month if it's vacuum-sealed and kept frozen till you begin your trip. Avoid soft and sliced cheeses, which spoil quickly. Processed cheeses (which really aren't cheeses at all) are tasteless and oily. Mold won't grow without air, so a vacuum seal or full wax covering is a must.

- **Hard kosher and Italian salamis** taste great and need no refrigeration. Two ounces per person per day is plenty.

- **Jam or jelly:** Kraft jellies in the rugged, squeezable plastic containers are convenient, but canned Canadian Malkin's jam (there are tons of flavors!) is a class act. You can order this delicious jam from Joynes Department Store in Grand Marais, Minnesota (appendix B).[1]

FRUIT AND NUT CRUNCH

I am indebted to Mary Bell,[2] whom midwesterners affectionately call the "Dehydrator Lady" for this scrumptious recipe, which is practically a complete meal.

2 cups rolled oats
1 14-ounce can fat-free, sweetened condensed milk
1 cup dried grated coconut
1 cup dried banana slices
1 cup dried canned peaches
1 cup beer nuts
½ cup dried pear slices
½ cup dried cranberries
½ cup raw cashew pieces
½ cup slivered almonds

Place the oats in a large bowl and use a knife to cut in a third of the condensed milk. Add the coconut. Separate the banana and canned peach slices so they don't stick together, then add to the mixture. Add the beer nuts and mix. Add the second third of the condensed milk and blend. Separate the pear slices from one another and add, along with the cranberries, cashews, and almonds. Add the final third of the condensed milk. Blend thoroughly. Let sit for one hour.

Lightly oil two fruit-leather sheets on your dehydrator tray. Spread the mixture evenly on each sheet. Splash water on the palms of your hands in order to press this sticky mixture flat on the sheets. Dry for about three hours, or until the texture is like peanut brittle. Cool and break into 2-inch squares. Package in an airtight container.

You can vary the fruits you add, if you like. Try apricots, mandarin oranges, plums, or strawberries, for instance.

OTHER LUNCH IDEAS

- Something salty: The craving for salt intensifies on a long trip. Salted nuts, pretzels, sunflower and pumpkin seeds, and salty snack mixes are lunchtime favorites.

- Something sweet: Chocolate nut and wafer bars and classy (expensive) chocolate and fruit-filled cookies are popular.

- Granola bars.

- Hudson Bay Bread.

- Instant drink mixes (iced tea is most popular).

- Mixed evaporated fruit.

- Fruit breads (banana, pumpkin, date-nut).

- Fruit cakes (they keep forever!).

- GORP.

Supper

After two boring meals, supper is a blessing. You can vary suppers as much as you wish, depending on how much

[1]By the way, Joynes also offers the wonderful Red Rose tea, which is imported from England. No wilderness trip is complete without an evening cup of Red Rose.

[2]Mary Bell has authored three wonderful books about dehydrated foods: *Mary Bell's Complete Dehydration Made Simple*, 1980, Magic Hill Press; *Mary Bell's Complete Dehydrator Cookbook*, 1994, Morrow Books; *Just Jerky*, 1996, The Dry Store. Mary says she started drying food more than twenty-five years ago because she wanted to preserve the great food she grew in her garden. Check out her Web site (www.drystore.com).

time you're willing to slave over a hot stove. If you're new to instant foods, you'll develop your own ideas of what's good or blah quickly enough without my biased suggestions. And if you've boiled and stirred for years, your prejudices are too well rooted for my suggestions to overcome.

Here are two elegant meals that will wow your crew!

PITA PIZZA

This is by far everyone's favorite meal. The recipe serves four.

½ cup dried tomato powder or canned pizza sauce
Oregano
Garlic powder
Salt
Cayenne pepper
Basil
4–8 pieces pita bread
⅓ pound fresh cheese (hard, fresh
  cheese keeps nearly a month if it's vacuum-sealed)

Suggested toppings: pepperoni, summer sausage, hard salami, Canadian bacon, fresh onion, green pepper, black olives, canned mushrooms, anchovies, smoked oysters

1. Prepare your chosen toppings: Slice and fry the meat and drain the grease on paper toweling. Thickly dice the vegetables and mushrooms, fry them in light oil, then drain the

Figure 11-2. Bob Dannert prepares supper along the Dubawnt River, Nunavut. Note how the canoe is being used as a windbreak.

grease and set them aside.

2. To make the pizza sauce, pour the tomato powder[3] into a bowl and add enough water to make a thick paste. Sprinkle on oregano, garlic, salt, cayenne, and basil.

3. Fry an unsliced pita over low heat in a well-oiled, covered skillet. When the bottom of the pita is brown (about twenty seconds), flip it over and thickly spread on tomato sauce, cheese, and toppings to taste. Immediately add a dash of water (to steam-melt the cheese) and cover the pan. Let the pizza cook over very low heat for half a minute or until the cheese has melted. Terrific!

GARLIC-CLAM LINGUINE

I adapted this recipe from an elegant garlic-clam linguine entree that a friend of mine serves in her Italian restaurant. My crews think it's superb! The recipe serves eight.

1 small onion (optional)
4 cloves fresh garlic (or garlic flakes)
Heavy dash of basil
¼ cup olive oil
¼ cup margarine or olive oil
4 4-ounce cans minced clams
1 tablespoon dried parsley
2 pounds linguine
1 pound Monterey Jack cheese
Black pepper

1. Dice the onion, garlic, and basil and sauté in olive oil for about two minutes. Stir in the margarine. Add the minced clams, juice and all. Continue to gently sauté for about five minutes. Add the parsley and continue to cook over low heat in an occasionally covered skillet for about five minutes.

2. Meantime, prepare the linguine in another pot. For the most effective cooking, use the cozy system explained later in this chapter.

3. When the linguine is nearly done (twenty minutes), slice the cheese and add it to the clam skillet. Cook slowly and stir vigorously until all the cheese is melted.

Pour off the water from the linguine and quickly toss the

---

[3]Order tomato powder from your local co-op. Or make your own tomato sauce by dehydrating tomato paste: Line a dehydrator tray with plastic wrap and pour on the tomato paste. Dehydrate at the highest temperature setting for twenty-four hours. Roll up the dried tomato (like a fruit roll-up) and vacuum-seal it or seal it in a zipper-lock bag. The shelf life is at least a month.

cooked clam mixture over the pasta, coating linguine thoroughly. Sprinkle ground black pepper on top and serve immediately. Try serving this with garlic-cheese tortillas as an appetizer.

SUPPER TIPS

- Vacuum-sealing increases pack life substantially. Most large grocery stores will vacuum-seal your purchases if you request. Or you may wish to buy your own machine. I've had excellent results with the Foodsaver by Tilia (appendix B). This machine was developed by a white-water kayaker who was tired of eating damp oatmeal. It will produce enough vacuum to crush a pop can.

- Dried hamburger is the mainstay in chili, spaghetti, and stews. It's easy to make. Simply brown ultralean ground beef and drain the grease. Then pour a full kettle of boiling water through the meat, to strip away the remaining fat. Line your dehydrator tray with a few sheets of paper toweling, then spoon on the well-drained, cooked hamburger. One pound per tray is about right. Dehydrate at *high* temperature (140 degrees) for twenty-four hours. Vacuum-seal the dried hamburger, or store in a zipper-lock bag. Use dehydrated hamburger just like fresh. Cook or soak for twenty minutes to rehydrate.

- Here's a fast, filling meal for two: Add half a pound (uncooked weight) of dried hamburger, a handful of dried shiitake mushrooms, and one beef or chicken bouillon cube to Ramen or instant soup. Add 20 percent more water than is called for in the directions. Stir in a few slivers of cheddar cheese just before serving.

- You may also want to try Cajun cooking. Packets of gumbo and jambalaya come complete with seasoning and rice and are available by mail from Tony Chachere's Creole Foods and Oak Grove Smokehouse (see appendix B). Both cook up in around twenty minutes. This tasty recipe will feed six: one onion (fresh or dried), one green pepper (fresh or dried), two cans of Polar shrimp or crab, dehydrated tomato, and a generous amount of Tony Chachere's famous Creole Seasoning. You can substitute sausage or fish for the shrimp. Don't forget the hot sauce!

- Green peppers, celery, and tomatoes will stay fresh for more than a week if you wash the vegetables, then float them in a sinkful of drinking water that has been treated with about 2 tablespoons (the amount isn't critical) of chlorine bleach. Allow the vegetables to soak for several minutes in the treated water before you dry and pack them away. The bleach will kill the surface bacteria that promote spoilage. A similar procedure is used in some of America's finest restaurants to keep vegetables fresh.

  You may use only a small piece of tomato or pepper at each meal. Cut off, and wash in fresh water, only the portion you need. Do not wash the entire vegetable! Doing so will introduce waterborne bacteria, which may precipitate spoilage.

  Separately wrap each vegetable in clean paper toweling. Pack towel-wrapped veggies in a paper or cotton sack and set the sack inside a teakettle or other crush-proof container. Do not seal vegetables in nonporous plastic! Semiporous Ziploc vegetable bags are the notable exception.

- Red cabbage makes a tasty salad and keeps for weeks without refrigeration. Get ready for raves when you serve shredded red cabbage mixed with carrot and onion slices, topped with green olives and a favorite dressing. Really, now, when did you last have fresh greens on a wilderness canoe trip?

- Ever watch a novice camper make biscuits? His or her hands and clothes are invariably covered with gluey batter. There's a messy pot to clean, and scattered about is enough batter to furnish a feast for several curious animals.

  I always mix batter in a plastic bag. Just pour the correct amounts of mix into the bag, add water, and knead the bag with your hands. When the consistency of the mixture is correct, punch a hole in the bag's bottom and force the gooey mess into your awaiting oven. Burn the plastic bag!

- You can make excellent low-cost main dishes by adding dumplings, rice, or instant mashed potatoes to a heavy-bodied soup mix. Mix dumpling batter in a plastic bag as suggested above. For a gourmet treat, drop chunks of raw fish into boiling soup. It tastes much better than it sounds.

- If you're tired of trying to season popcorn in a pot

that's too small, try this: Carry some large paper grocery sacks on your next trip. As you complete each batch of popcorn, pour the corn into the paper bag (don't use a plastic bag—hot popcorn will melt right through it!). Season the corn and shake the bag to mix it. When the popcorn's gone, burn the bag or fold it and store it in a zipper-lock bag for future use.

COOKING TRICKS

Insulated Cozies Save Time and Stove Fuel

It's a cold, blustery day and you're preparing oatmeal for six. You pour Quaker flakes into the boiling water and stir to mix. Then you cover the pot and adjust the heat to simmer, with hopes the gruel won't burn. Fifteen minutes later you stir and taste. As expected, one bite is raw, the next is burned, and there's a hard black spot glued to the pot bottom. Better eat fast; seconds won't stay hot for long! And thank goodness you don't have to do the dishes.

Try this instead. Make insulated cozies for your cooking pots from quilted cotton material or insulated ironing board fabric. A two-piece cozy—top hat and belly band—is better than a one-piece model, because the wide band insulates the pot sides when you remove the cover to stir. The skirted top hat can also be used (skirt-up) alone on top of a skillet when frying fish or bacon.

Here's how to use your cozy:

1. Velcro the band tightly around the pot before you begin cooking. Position the bottom of the band ½ inch above the bottom of the pot so the band won't scorch when the stove runs full blast.

2. Measure water for the meal into the pot. Then cover the pot and put on the cozy cap. If you're making a freeze-dried or dehydrated entree, add meat, spices, and vegetables to the water. *Don't* add sauce mix, rice, cereal, or pasta yet.

3. Turn the stove to high and do other chores. The cozy will reduce the boiling time and save stove fuel.

4. When the water boils, reduce the heat to a simmer and add the cereal, rice, pasta, or sauce mix. Stir vigorously till the fixin's are blended and the water is boiling again. Then turn off the stove and set the pot on a square of closed-cell foam. Put on the cover and top hat,

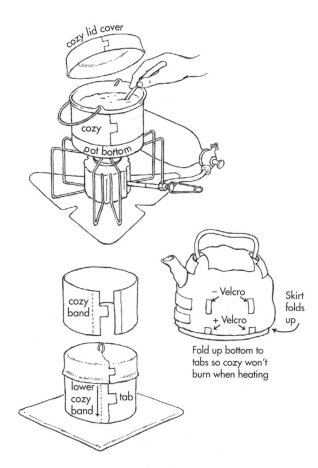

Figure 11-3. Cozies speed cooking time and save stove fuel.

working the belly band down till it covers all the bare metal of the pot. Your food will slow-cook in twenty minutes and stay hot for an hour.

Tip: If it's extremely cold and windy, place a second cozy (or a jacket) over the first cozy when the meal is off the stove. I use a large, one-piece toaster cover for the second insulating layer. Be careful how you use commercial tea cozies and toaster covers: Most are made from acrylics, which melt and shrink when exposed to heat.

In 1982 I canoed the Hood River in Canada's Northwest Territories with five friends. We relied on two Optimus 111B gasoline stoves for all our cooking, using an overturned canoe as a windscreen. Our stoves consumed six gallons of Coleman fuel in thirty-one days, or about a gallon and a half a week.

We did not have pot cozies, so we were very careful to conserve fuel. For example, we boiled fresh-caught fish in soup instead of frying it, and we never baked or heated water for dishes.

I canoed the Hood again in 1992 with a crew of ten and brought double-insulated cozies for all my pots. I even made a special cozy with a spout hole for the 24-cup teapot. Same two stoves as before, but four more people. We fried fish, boiled dishwater, and routinely made popcorn. We used barely a gallon of fuel a week. Naturally, every meal I prepared was perfect![4]

How to Prepare Freeze-Dried Foods So They Always Taste Good

Freeze-dried foods are fickle. Prepare 'em according to directions one day and they're great. Repeat the procedure another time and . . . ugh!

Take heart. Here's a foolproof cooking method that works regardless of the weather, the Zodiac, or a cranky stove.

1. Read the cooking directions, but don't take them too seriously. What works at home on the range often fails on a flat rock in a nor'wester.

2. Separate the component parts of the food. There are usually two parts: a meat portion and a noodle, rice, or vegetable portion. Sometimes there's a third spice packet.

Typical directions say: "Add contents of all packets to X cups of boiling water. Reduce heat, simmer 15–20 minutes or until noodles [or whatever] are tender."

3. Put 20 percent *more* water in your cooking pot than the directions call for, and add the *meat portion only* to the water. Bring the water to a boil and add a healthy dash of All-Spice.[5]

4. When the water is at a rolling boil, add contents of the spice packet (if there is one). Reduce heat to a slow boil and let the spices and meat stew together for a full five minutes. If there is no spice packet, let the meat stew for five minutes before you proceed to step 5.

5. Add the contents of the noodle, rice, or vegetable

packet to the boiling water. Reduce the heat, cover, simmer, and stir occasionally for the amount of time indicated in the directions (fifteen to twenty minutes, for example).

6. Eat and enjoy. All portions of the meal are thoroughly cooked and the taste has been fully developed.

Why Some Meals Fail

■ You haven't cooked the meat long enough. Half-cooked reconstituted meat spoils the whole stew. Except in very warm weather, cook-in-the-bag foods just don't get done. It's best to place the cooking bag in a covered pot of near-boiling water for ten minutes. Add about 10 percent more water to the cooking bag than the directions call for.

■ You burned the pasta. This is easy to do on a one-burner trial stove, especially if you plop the contents of all the food packets into the boiling water simultaneously. If your stove's on high, you may burn your meal quicker than you can say "turn the heat down, Jack!" You'll save grief—and stove fuel—if you use the cozy system explained earlier.

■ Insufficient water. Remember, you can always boil off too much water, but there's not much you can do with a stew that's so thick it's burned and glued to the pot bottom.

■ Not enough spices. Don't underestimate the value of spices when preparing freeze-dried or dehydrated foods. Most quick-cook products are unacceptably bland unless they're well spiced. All Spice (see footnote 5 below) works wonders on everything from spaghetti to shrimp creole.

■ Spoilage. Dehydrated foods usually come packed in plastic and so have a shelf life of about a year. This is because plastic is very slightly permeable to the passage of water molecules. If the food contains bacteria of the right kind, enough moisture may eventually pass through the plastic wrapper to cause spoilage.

---

[4]CLG Enterprises (appendix B) in Minneapolis now produces a commercial version (it's made of wool) of my cozy design. Very nice and reasonably priced. I receive no gratuities from CLG for the use of my design.

[5]To make All-Spice mix approximately equal amounts of oregano, marjoram, and seasoned salt-and-pepper mix (I use a commercial blend) with a dash each of onion powder and thyme. A two-week supply will fit nicely into a 35-millimeter film can.

Freeze-dried foods, however, come packaged in aluminum foil, which is an absolute vapor barrier. Consequently, these products have an unlimited shelf life; they can be used safely even when they're many years old.

This should tell you something about end-of-season food sales. Don't buy dehydrated foods in September if you plan to use them the following July. Your autumn bargain may turn out to be summer indigestion.

It's important to realize that many products contain both freeze-dried and dehydrated components (for example, Spaghetti with Freeze-Dried Meatballs). While the foil-wrapped meatballs won't spoil, the plastic-wrapped spaghetti or spices might. Only foods that are *completely* sealed in aluminum foil are immune to spoilage. Unfortunately, you almost never see these products offered at sale prices.

■ Introduction of bacteria and/or water vapor during repackaging. Don't handle dried foods or expose them to air any longer than necessary when you repackage them. This will reduce the chance of bacteria and water vapor getting into the food.

Slice meat and cheese with a knife that's been dipped in boiling water for a full minute. (The boiling-water treatment does not kill *all* bacteria. If you want to really sterilize the knife, place it in a pressure cooker at fifteen pounds of pressure for fifteen minutes.) And never repackage foil-wrapped products—like instant soups—in plastic.

You'll find more recipes and cooking tricks in my book *Basic Essentials: Cooking in the Outdoors.*

FOOD-PACKING SUGGESTIONS

■ To eliminate confusion and shorten preparation times, package each meal for your crew as a complete unit. Remove all unnecessary cardboard and paper wrappers for foodstuffs to save as much weight and space as possible.

■ Flowable solids, like sugar, baking mixes, Tang, and so on are best premeasured in the amounts required, then placed in small plastic zipper-lock bags encased in sturdy nylon bags.

■ Breakable and crushable items like crackers, cheese,

and candy bars should be packed inside rigid cardboard containers. I use cut-down milk cartons, which also make great fire starters.

■ Liquids are best carried in plastic bottles that have screw-cap lids. I've found that genuine Nalgene bottles (available at most camp stores) are most reliable. Plastic bottles with flip tops and pop-up tops usually leak. I melt these tops shut in the flame of a gas stove or replace them with trustworthy metal screw caps.

■ Hospitals and clinics throw out plastic "sterile water for irrigation" bottles after a single use. These marginally flexible bottles range in size from half a liter to one and a half liters and have raised milliliter graduations on one side. They are incredibly strong, and they won't hold odors like containers made from more porous plastics. Some types have a molded ring (for hanging) on the bottom. Ask your doctor to save some for you. (These bottles are rapidly being replaced by sterile plastic bladders, so best get them while you still can!)

■ Food tubes are okay for packing flowable solids but not liquids for which they were designed). The first

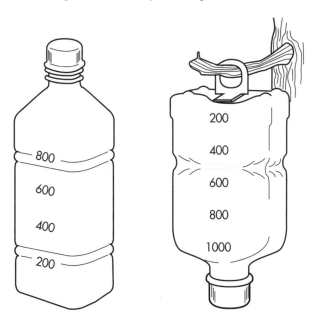

Figure 11-4. Sterile water for irrigation bottles are free for the asking.

time a honey-filled tube ruptures in your pack, you'll understand why. If you use food tubes, pack them inside zipper-lock bags so you'll be well prepared for the inevitable.

■ When packaging each meal, carefully fold over the edges of all foodstuffs that are packed in aluminum foil. The sharp foil edges of breakfast bars and soup packets will cut through plastic bags.

■ Never pack moist items in the same bag as dry products. I once packed beef jerky and Velveeta cheese together in heat-sealed plastic bags. The jerky absorbed moisture from the cheese and mildewed in just four days.

■ For additional protection place each plastic-bagged meal into its own color-coded waterproof nylon sack. I traditionally pack breakfasts in green nylon bags, lunches in yellow or blue, and suppers in red. Since I don't like surprises, I attach cardboard tags to the drawstring of each sack.

If you pack your food as I've suggested, you'll have no trouble finding the specific meals you want even if they're at the bottom of your pack. And you'll never have to eat damp oatmeal!

COOKING PARAPHERNALIA

For a crew of six, you'll need the following:

■ **One relatively straight-sided, 12-inch-diameter, Teflon-lined skillet:** I purchase a high-grade Teflon-lined skillet and replace the plastic handle with a removable one, which I bend from 0.187-inch-diameter spring wire (see figure 11-5). The mounting bracket for the handle is made from hardware-store aluminum flat stock. It secures with two brass bolts that are easily removed when the pan wears out. I also outfit some of my pots with these rigid wire handles.

I recently encouraged Kevin Carr of Chosen Valley Canoe Accessories (appendix B) to make a handle kit like the one illustrated. Installation takes about five minutes.

■ **Eight-cup coffeepot or kettle:** A wide-base kettle heats faster and is less tippy than a coffeepot, and you can pour with one hand.

■ **An oven of some sort:** Specialized trail ovens like the

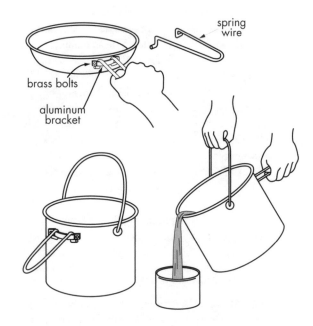

Figure 11-5. The universal spring wire handle fits all pots and pans.

Figure 11-6. You can make a Dutch oven from any pot and lid.

efficient Bakepacker, are nice, but they're excess baggage on a go-light trip. You can make a Dutch oven from any pot and lid, as illustrated in figure 11-6. Or use the gelatin-mold oven illustrated in figure 11-8.

- **Two nesting stainless-steel Sierra cups:** Use these as compact ladles and emergency drinking cups. Steel cups won't warp or melt when you set them on a stove or by the campfire to heat tea.

- **One nesting bowl per person:** Metal bowls are heavy, and they transfer heat to your hands. Plastic bowls are cooler and easier to clean. Why doesn't someone make a stainless-steel bowl with a removable, heat-resistant plastic bottom?

- **Individual items:** One metal spoon per person is enough. Gourmet cooks will add a fork. Everyone carries his or her own knife and insulated mug. Be sure the mug has a fitted cover to keep drinks hot and heat-seeking insects out. Leash the cover to the mug with fishing line.

- **Utensil roll:** After years of scoffing at these, I decided to make one. A fabric roll is more than just a utensil organizer; it simplifies the preparation of rainy-day

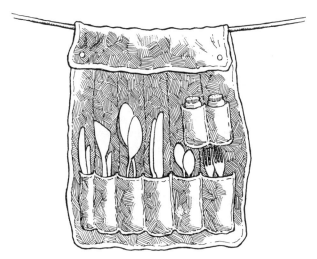

Figure 11-7. Fabric utensil roll.

meals, as you'll see in chapter 12. You can buy one from Duluth Pack (appendix B). Be sure the roll has snaps or ties on top so you can hang it from a clothesline. The next chapter tells why.

- **Cutting board:** You need a flat surface to slice meat and cheese, dice vegetables, and fillet fish. Old-timers used the blade of a canoe paddle—a practice that will definitely damage an oiled or varnished blade and possibly destroy a carbon-fiber one. I carry a lightweight 8- by 12-inch plastic-composite cutting board. I keep the board in a *breathable* cotton-polyester bag, along with two edged sandwich spreaders.

Using an Improvised Dutch Oven

Grease the pot and put your bakestuff inside. Slip on the cover and build a small, hot fire on top. Provide some heat from below with a number of coals. Cooking time depends on the amount of heat your fire provides.

Using a Gelatin-Mold Oven

1. Grease the mold and pour your bakestuff into the outside ring. (Decrease the suggested amount of water by up to one-fourth for faster baking.)

2. Bring the stove to its normal operating temperature, then turn down the heat until you have the lowest possible blue-flame setting. Center the gelatin mold over the burner head, to it with a high cover (to provide sufficient room for the baked good to rise) . . . and relax. Cooking times are nearly identical to those suggested in the baking directions.

3. Cool the mold by setting it in a shallow pan of water for a few moments.

You can also fire your gelatin mold with a *small* ($2^5/_8$-ounce) can of Sterno. Don't use the large-sized can; it puts out too much heat. To ensure ample draft, use a pair of sticks to prop up the ring about $^1/_2$ inch above the Sterno. Vent the lid with a matchstick.

Sterno is useful for those times when you want to use your stove for cooking but don't want to build a fire for baking. However, Sterno is temperamental; the slightest breeze will blow out the flame, so be sure to keep your oven well protected from the wind. Obviously, Sterno isn't suited for use on lengthy expeditions.

Figure 11-8. The gelatin-mold oven allows fast, fuel-efficient baking for those special occasions.

You'll note the conspicuous omission of the reflector oven from this discussion. Reflectors are heavy and awkward to carry, and they require a highly polished surface to work properly. They also have a voracious appetite for wood. Both Dutch ovens and gelatin-mold ovens are much better suited to modern canoe tripping. You'll find other clever baking tricks in my book *Basic Essentials: Cooking in the Outdoors* (appendix B).

THE STOVE

A lot of canoeists, even those who regularly trip above the timberline, travel without a stove. There's usually enough scrub willow or driftwood along tundra rivers to permit making occasional fires. To each his own. As for myself, I wouldn't consider undertaking a canoe trip of much significance without my trusty Optimus 111B. There are just too many times when rough weather and a tight schedule preclude making a fire.

If a stove is essential in the northern wilds, it's even more important on well-traveled routes where all the good wood has been picked clean. And if you've driven many miles

to favorite wilderness and found a fire ban in effect, you'll wish you'd brought a stove!

A Review of Stove Types

There are gasoline, kerosene, alcohol, butane, propane, multifuel, and wood-burning stoves. Only gasoline and mulitfuel stoves make much sense for wilderness canoeing.

Be aware that commercial aircraft will not accept any type of stove fuel on board. If you travel by commercial airline, you'll have to dump your fuel (and burn your stoves dry) before you board, then buy fresh stove fuel at the trailhead. Not all bottled gas cylinders fit all stoves. In remote parts of Canada, you'll be lucky to find white gasoline, let alone a specialized bottled fuel that fits your stove.

Gasoline

Gasoline stoves are the most reliable of all trail stoves, especially in difficult weather. And gasoline has the highest heat output of all stove fuels.

Generally, gasoline stoves accept only white gas or Coleman or Blazo fuel (highly refined forms of naphtha). It's not safe to burn leaded gasoline in them. An important distinction must be made between additive-free white gasoline (which is difficult to obtain in most areas) and additive-packed automotive unleaded gasoline (which is available at every gas station). Unleaded gas is more volatile than white gas and may produce excessive pressures in stoves designed for white gas only.

Kerosene

Kerosene has about the same BTU rating as gasoline but it's less volatile. Where a gasoline stove will explode, a kerosene one will burn. Unfortunately kerosene stoves don't start unless they're first primed with alcohol or gasoline—a hassle. Nonetheless, kerosene stoves are very reliable, and kerosene is available everywhere. White gas isn't! If you can get a good deal on a kerosene stove, buy it.

Butane

Butane stoves are popular because they don't have to be primed, pumped, or filled with gas. You just turn the adjuster knob and light the escaping fumes. Refueling takes seconds and consists merely of replacing the exhausted gas cylinder with a new one. And because butane is so clean burning, there are no clogged fuel jets to clean. Sound great? It isn't!

The efficiency of bottled butane is directly proportional to the temperature outside.

Butane stoves quit working altogether when the temperature drops below freezing (you can burn propane-butane blends for better performance). Few are very windproof or stable enough to support heavy pots. Equally important, thoughtless campers leave the empty gas cylinders in the woods for those of us who care to pack them out.

Propane (Bottled Gas)

Propane stoves burn hot, even in subzero temperatures. Just turn the adjuster knob and light! In seconds you'll have a bright blue flame that can be adjusted high or low. Propane gas containers are refillable, but they're too heavy and bulky for canoeing.

Alcohol

Alcohol stoves, such as the Swiss Trangia, are safe and reliable. Just light the burner and you're ready to cook. However, these stoves are slow to heat. Most require ten or fifteen minutes just to boil a quart of water!

Sterno is a solid form of alcohol that comes in a can. It puts out enough heat to warm food but not cook it.

Dual Fuel and Mulitfuel

Dual-fuel stoves, such as the Coleman Apex II and PEAK 1 Feather 442, burn two types of fuel—white gas and unleaded auto gas. Multifuel stoves, like the MSR Dragonfly and Optimus Explorer, burn kerosene, diesel, jet fuel, white gas (naphtha), and unleaded auto gas. Dual-fuel and multifuel stoves run best (cleanest) on white gas, so why pay extra for the multifuel feature if you don't need it? The table below compares three popular fuels. Diesel and kerosene are most efficient, but they're smelly, they're hard to prime (you must use alcohol or gasoline), and they produce lots of soot, which clogs the stove jet.

Wood

If you like campfires, you'll love wood-burning stoves! Woodstoves are lightweight and powerful, and the twigs they burn are free. But the wood burns fast, so you'll have to keep stoking as you cook.

The Super Sierra stove has a battery-operated fan and damper to control the temperature. It works like a blowtorch and adjusts low enough to simmer.

TABLE 11-1

Fuel	Burn Times* (minutes)	Boil Times* (minutes)
White gas	126	3.5
Kerosene	153	3.9
Diesel fuel	136	3.5

*Tests performed using an MSR Dragonfly multifuel stove with a twenty-two-ounce fuel bottle at twenty psi and a starting water temperature of 70 degrees. Data was supplied by MSR Corporation.

Stove Features

Stability

The stability of a stove is really important if you're cooking for large groups. There's nothing more frustrating than cooking a big pot of spaghetti on a precarious little beast that wobbles with every stir of the spoon. Before you buy a canoe stove, be sure it will comfortably accommodate your largest pot. A gallon of water plus pasta for six weighs about ten pounds, which is enough to crush some stoves!

Figure 11-9. The Sierra Stove runs on an AA battery and burns wood.

Windscreen

The first time you've got to build a rock wall around your stove to keep it perking, you'll understand the value of a good windscreen. Avoid stoves with thin aluminum windscreens that burn up, and detachable ones which can be lost.

Ruggedness

The Optimus 111B, which is no longer manufactured, is the most rugged stove ever built. It's constructed entirely of brass and steel and housed in a strong steel case. I once watched a nylon day pack that contained a 111B bounce 200 feet down a rocky cliff. When we recovered the pack, the metal case was dented but the stove worked fine. This kind of ruggedness should be built into every stove.

Regrettably, it's not. Most trail stoves are sold to hikers who count every ounce. The emphasis is on light weight, not protection against hard knocks. Some stoves, such as the Peak 1 gasoline models, have exposed wires and burner parts that can bend or break. Others, like MSR and Coleman Apex/ Xtreme models, have exposed fuel lines and knobs, and plastic parts that can break or burn. I miss the solid old Optimus and Phoebus expedition stoves. There was nothing on these stoves to lose, break, or burn.

Integral Fuel Tank or Separate Bottle?

The trend is away from stoves that have built-in fuel tanks. The MSR XGK started the revolution years ago; now all the MSR stoves have separate tanks, as do four Coleman Peak 1 models. These stoves are light, powerful, and fuel efficient, but they're a hassle to put together and disassemble. Lose or break a part and the stove is out of commission.

When it comes to equipment, I value reliability, ruggedness, and ease of use above all other features. And that's why I continue to use an ancient Optimus 111B.

This said, I must admit a fondness for the new MSR Dragonfly stove. It starts easily, puts out tremendous heat, and it throttles down to a gentle simmer. But that plastic pump worries me if the stove flares up.

Pump

Pumps are necessary on kerosene stoves and some gasoline models. Some good little backpacking stoves (like the ancient Svea 123) are self-priming, which means they generate their own heat. But pumps increase the efficiency of any gasoline stove and so are highly desirable. An expedition stove should have a pump.

Roarer or Silent Burner?

As the name implies, roarer burners make noise—lots of it! The gas feeds through a single hole in the vaporizer tube and strikes a flat plate on the burner head, where it dissipates. Simple, efficient, and always reliable. If you spill pancake syrup on the burner head, there's a built-in cleaning needle that will clear the jet.

Silent burners are more refined. They have a network of tiny holes around the head and look almost exactly like the burner on a modern gas range. These have two drawbacks: They're not very windproof (you need an exceptional windscreen to keep them humming in a gale) and they're a hassle to clean if you spill food on the burner head (the cleaning needle clears only the generator tube, not the burner holes). I once inadvertently set a plastic bowl on top of a hot Coleman Peak 1 (yeah, I know it was dumb!). The plastic melted all over everything and sealed many of the tiny burner holes. It took me two hours to clean the stove. A roarer burner would have been much easier to clean.

Still, I like silent burners. Noisy stoves drive me nuts.

Recommendations

As I pointed out in chapter 8 (Gearing Up), some highly touted products that work flawlessly over the short haul fail miserably in the long run. The adage couldn't be more true for stoves. Some stoves have steel tanks that rust, plastic knobs that burn off or break, parts to fit together, and wires that bend. Nonetheless, any gasoline, kerosene, or blended-fuel stove can be made to perform reliably if you maintain it rigorously, keep it protected in some sort of rigid container, and learn to cope with its eccentricities.

The important thing is to know the shortcomings of your stove and how to correct them. After you've used a certain stove for a time, you'll develop such efficient ways of dealing with problems that they'll cease to exist. Ask any Svea 123 owner how he or she keeps this cranky little stove running in rain, wind, and snow. It is being done. Efficiently!

When it comes to specific models, I'm frankly not wild about any of the new stoves. None are as rugged and reliable and as easy to use as my old 111B. If I had to choose a new stove, though, it would probably be one of these:

■ **Coleman Peak 1, Feather 400/442 Dual Fuel/Multifuel:** Keeping the leather pump washer oiled is a major inconvenience, as are all the exposed dials and wires that can break or bend. And Peak 1s

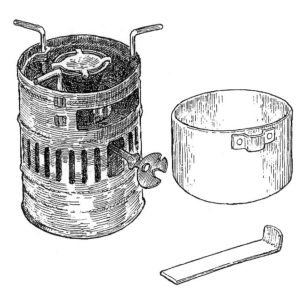

Figure 11-10. Svea 123.

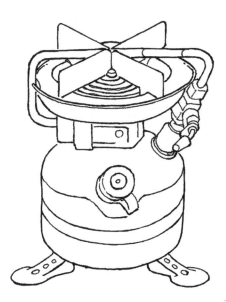

Figure 11-11. Coleman Peak 1 Feather 442, Dual Fuel.

don't perform flawlessly in wind. They run, but not efficiently. One of the four quadrants that are protected by a unique X-shaped windscreen blows out, which increases cooking times. And in cold weather you've got to pump and pump and pump these stoves to make them start. Still, they are good stoves at a very attractive price.

■ **MSR Dragonfly, Primus Omnifuel, Optimus Nova:** These are stable, powerful, and easy to start in cold weather. There are some bugs: The Dragonfly has a complicated plastic pump that can break or melt; the simple all-aluminum pump on the Primus and Optimus may be more reliable. The fuel connector on the Omnifuel and Nova stoves has a ball valve that seats against an O-ring. Dirt can clog the ball valve or score the neoprene washer, which will allow gas to spew out when these stoves are removed from their fuel bottles. A friction-fit cover (easy to make) keeps dirt out of the connector when these stoves are disassembled. A dental tool can be used (carefully!) to depress the ball—and/or reseat the O-ring—to allow pressurized gas to flush out dirt.

■ **Coleman twin burner:** You'll see these stoves wedged among piles of gear in every native watercraft in the North Country. That says enough about the reliability of this venerable warhorse.

■ **Optimus 111B:** If you ever come across one of these ancient stoves, buy it! It remains the premier expedition stove. Old 111s never die; they just accumulate new parts. The 111B is powerful, stable, and windproof; also, it always works. Its only bad habit is minor: You must keep its leather pump washer well oiled, a biweekly chore.

The 111B, with its deafening roarer burner, is no longer available in the United States. In its place is the 111 Hiker, which is identical except for its low-simmering, silent burner, which puts out about 15 percent less heat. Nonetheless, the Hiker is a formidable stove. Like its workhorse cousin, the 111B, it won't let you down. Price, well over $100—if you can find one!

Stove Maintenance

Camp stoves are like cars: New or low-mileage models are pretty reliable, at least at the outset. But run 'em continu-

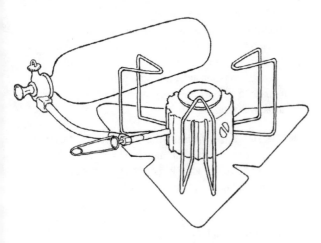

Figure 11-12. MSR Dragonfly, one of the author's favorite stoves.

ally for days on end and gremlins creep into the mechanism and cause all sorts of problems. In fairness to manufacturers, l should say that no stove—not even a well-maintained one—is completely trouble-free when you hammer it over the long haul. Over the years I've blown pressure caps and check

Figure 11-13. Optimus 111B—the author's choice.

valves on just about every gasoline trail stove. Usually I'm able to fix the problem in the field, but not always. That's why I carry two identical units on my trips. Scavenging parts so you can keep on boiling is the rule on expeditions where you can't depend on fire to prepare your meals.

Unfortunately, the directions that accompany most trail stoves aren't very helpful when things go wrong. To replace a varnish-clogged check valve or burned wick isn't easy, even when you have the right tools. These dos and don'ts will help you avoid most problems.

Stove Dos

- **Do** carry fuel only in recommended containers. Gasoline and kerosene are best transported in aluminum liter bottles, the original steel can, or gallon-sized jugs designed for carrying volatile liquids.

- **Do** occasionally check the temperature of the stove tank with your hand. If it's too hot to touch, reduce the pressure and/or pour water on the tank to cool it. If overheating doesn't blow the check valve, it may fry the leathers or rubber gasket in the filler cap!

- **Do** store liquid fuel in containers that are *nearly* full. A significant air interface at the top of a fuel bottle causes fuel oxidation, which may later gum stove parts. A half-full aluminum fuel bottle left to overwinter on the shelf is likely to cause stove problems next summer!

- **Do** clean your stove once a year. A capful (no more) of carburetor or fuel-injector cleaner mixed with half a tank of gas removes most varnish and keeps the burner humming like new.

- **Do** filter white gas (the felt-lined Coleman funnel is ideal) to remove impurities. (This isn't necessary with prefiltered Coleman and Blazo fuels.)

- **Do** empty the fuel in your stove at least once a season. Impurities in fuel left in stoves can cause malfunctions. Burn your stove dry if you will store it for more than a month.

- **Do** replace the rubber gasket inside the pressure cap each season! Stove heat cooks and hardens the rubber seal inside the tank gasket cap. Eventually air leaks out and the stove loses pressure. At first the pressure loss is so slight you may simply attribute the problem to old age. You can check for a pressure leak by squirting liquid detergent around the pressure cap. If bubbles form, the gasket is at fault. A dental tool with a sharp, 90-degree bend will remove the rubber washer without scoring it.

- **Do** keep the leather pump washer *lightly lubricated* with high-grade gun oil or synthetic motor oil. *Don't* use vegetable oils, which gum. *Don't* overoil the leathers. Excess oil may run off and clog the check valve.

- **Do** keep your stove protected in a rigid container when it's not in use.

- **Do** carry extra stove parts and tools. An extra pressure cap and leather pump washer are usually enough.

Stove Don'ts

- **Don't** loosen or remove the filler cap of a gasoline stove when the stove is burning. This could result in an explosion!

- **Don't** refuel a stove that is hot. There may be sufficient heat still available to ignite the gas fumes.

- **Don't** set oversized pots on stoves. Large pots reflect excessive heat back to the fuel tank, which may cause overheating of the stove. Run the stove at three-fourths of maximum heat output if you use oversized pots.

- **Don't** use automotive gasoline (regular or unleaded) in a stove designed to burn white gas.

- **Don't** start a stove inside a tent or confined area; the resulting flare-up can be dangerous.

- **Don't** operate any stove where there is insufficient ventilation. A closed tent is not sufficiently ventilated!

- **Don't** set stoves on sleeping bags, nylon tent floors, or plastic or wooden canoes. There's enough heat generated at the base of some stoves to melt or warp these items.

- **Don't** run stoves at full power for extended periods of time. The tank may overheat and cause the safety valve to blow.

- **Don't** poke wire cleaning tools into burner jets from the outside. This pushes foreign matter into the vaporization barrel and clogs the stove. Always remove jets (most unscrew) and clean them from the inside.

- **Don't** enclose a stove with aluminum foil to increase its heat output. The stove may overheat and explode.

- **Don't** fill gasoline or kerosene stoves more than three-fourths full. Fuel won't vaporize if there's insufficient room for it to expand.

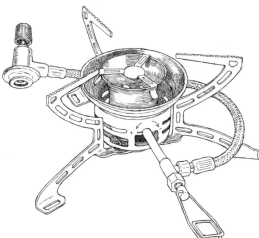

Figure 11-14. Primus Omnifuel stove—a favorite of the author.

CHAPTER 12
THE EXPERT'S EDGE

The great Arctic explorer Vilhjalmur Steffanson, on return from one of his many expeditions, was asked if he had had any adventures. After some thought, Steffanson curtly replied: "Nope . . . no adventures, just experiences!"

There's a notion that exploration—whether by canoe, foot, or dogsled—is fraught with dangers. A major falls at every river bend, a fierce gale each morning, impossible portages, impassable rapids, unending hordes of insects, ravaging wild beasts, and dozens of death-defying encounters.

Nothing could be farther from the truth. If you've done your homework, even the unexpected can be predicted and prepared for. As Steffanson pointed out, experts have "experiences," not adventures. Only incompetent fools suffer the latter!

I know canoeists who've paddled and camped for thirty years and still can't start a fire in the rain or rig a snug camp. They tolerate the misery of being unprepared, mistakenly assuming that their years of experience will provide all the answers. Their thirty years of experience is but a single year of continuous repetition.

Simply paddling and camping a lot won't teach you the right way to do things if you've never capsized, become lost, or encountered long stretches of bad weather, bugs, or determined hungry animals. Groups of inexperienced teenagers, led by only slightly more experienced leaders of college age, are now regularly tripping the most remote northern rivers. That these people survive indicates perseverance, not expertise. The human body is a tough machine; it'll take a lot of abuse before it flatly quits. *Experts are distinguished by the style in which they travel, not by the difficulty of the trips they take, the frequency of those trips, or the number of days out.*

Contrary to popular belief, you don't have to trek to the Arctic to perfect your canoeing skills. You can learn almost all of what you need to know on challenging routes near your home if you go out in all kinds of weather and water conditions, and keep an open mind. (See color figure 12-1.)

I won't pretend the procedures outlined in this chapter are the "best" or "only" way to do things. The wilderness is too varied a place to apply formula solutions. But hopefully you'll get some useful ideas from these pages.

RAIN

Day and night, the drizzle did not cease for so much as an hour. With the rain, the water we shipped over the gunnels in the fast stretches, and the water that seeped through the many cuts in the bottom of the craft, our equipment sloshed about constantly, our clothing and food were soaked through, our blankets were equally soaked. The woods oozed with water, every leaf held a pond, every dead twig and log was rotten with wetness. In order to build a fire at night we would spend two or three hours whittling out chunks of heartwood. Not even birchbark would burn. In our wet clothes we slept, wrapped in wet blankets.[1]

I once asked my friend Bob Dannert to define the word *expert*. Bob thought awhile then replied . . . "details." A perfect answer, for an expert considers the most minute details when planning a trip; a beginner seldom gets down to details at all.

Canoeing in foul weather is largely a matter of details, like putting on your rain gear *before* you get wet; making sure the waterproof liner in your pack is *really* weathertight; gath-

---

[1]From "Return to God's Country," by Eric Sevareid, *Audubon Magazine*, September 1981. Originally from Sevareid's wonderful book *Canoeing with the Cree*, which should be required reading for every wilderness canoeist.

ering dry kindling *in advance* of the coming storm; and knowing *when* the lake is too rough for traveling. (See color figure 12-2.)

Of course, there are other skills, too. Making a fire in the midst of a major downpour is no easy task; threading your way through a maze of islands in a foggy drizzle requires navigation know-how; and keeping your craft upright when a sudden squall turns the lake on edge demands paddling competence.

Even experts don't profess to know everything about foul-weather canoe tripping. They still get plenty scared when they're caught on open water in a lightning storm; very uneasy when they've used two matches and a carefully built, rain-soaked fire won't start; and downright mad when their hat blows out to sea because they didn't have sense enough to tie its chin strap.

It takes practice to become a proficient rough-weather paddler, but it only requires diligent studying to learn its procedural details. The continuing emergence of new equipment and materials suggest that there is no one right or wrong way to camp and canoe. If a method works for you, stick with it, even if an expert says you're wrong! It's not unusual for some casual paddlers to have better tripping habits than many of the big guns in the sport.

Traveling in the Rain

If you dress in wool, polypropylene, Dacron, or fleece from head to toe, then add waterproof rain gear, boots, and

Figure 12-3. Canoeing in rain. The author's wife, Sue Harings, enjoys a rainy day on Ontario's Steel River. Her canoe is a Bell Flashfire. Zaveral carbon-fiber paddle.

gloves, as I've advised, you're off to a good start. To this add a fabric canoe cover, a shock-corded thwart to secure your map in its waterproof case, a thwart or seat-mounted running compass, and a sponge for bailing the canoe (see chapter 6 for the procedures of outfitting your canoe). You're set for the worst rains. The only thing you really need fear is storms!

Storms

The often-quoted advice to "get off the water" when a storm brews up is sound. And when lightning strikes, getting to shore fast is even more important, because a canoe on open water is a perfect lightning rod. Lightning strikes the highest thing on the water—and on a lake that's usually you! Along the shoreline there's a cone of protection that extends about 45 degrees from the top of the trees. If you must paddle in a storm, stay within this cone of protection, but don't get so close to the tree trunks that lightning may jump from them to you. Where possible, follow the same procedure when making camp: Pitch your tent away from the highest points of land, not too close to the trunks of taller trees.

There's a common misconception that canoes built of wood, fiberglass, and Royalex are safer in a lightning storm than those built of aluminum. No way! A bolt of lightning can generate millions of volts—enough to thoroughly fry any canoe (regardless of material) and its paddlers.

The most difficult thing about paddling in a storm is keeping your canoe upright and free of water in big waves. Virtually every canoeing text recommends quartering waves (paddling into them at an angle of about 30 degrees), rather than knifing straight into them. Quartering exposes more of the canoe's hull to the water and gives it more buoyancy, which translates into a drier ride.

Quartering is sound practice provided that you and your partner are sufficiently skilled to prevent the canoe from broaching (turning broadside to the waves), and your canoe has a very straight keel line, is very heavily loaded, or has extremely narrow ends.

Lightly loaded, blunt-nose canoes, unless equipped with deep keels for stability, are very difficult to keep on a quartering course in heavy seas. And the shorter the canoe, the more difficult it is to control. If the wind isn't too strong, a good canoe team can usually maintain a 30-degree angle by simple paddling on the same side (the downwind side) of the canoe. But if the wind is really severe, even the strongest paddlers may not be able to keep the canoe on a tack for very long. Since the penalty for failure in maintaining the proper quartering angle is broaching—and possibly dumping—the best thing to do when conditions get scary is tighten your quartering angle 10 to 20 degrees to lighten the bow by moving the bow paddler closer amidships, then paddle aggressively into the waves. Actually, you should lighten *both* ends, not just the bow. Canoes don't run well with one end dragging! Most novices will be safer in a rough sea if they forget about quartering waves and instead follow the head-on procedure.

Obviously, a canoe cover eliminates all chances of swamping!

You might think that running downwind in a heavy blow is the reverse of running upwind. It isn't. You don't have to lighten the stern (again, if you change the weight distribution, do it equally to both ends) in a following sea if your canoe has good forward speed. As long as you *keep paddling,* you'll maintain directional control and have enough buoyancy at the tail to keep the biggest waves from rolling in.

The only thing you need worry about when running downwind is surfing on big waves. Once you get stuck on a giant roller, it's not always easy to get off without swamping. Fortunately, heavily loaded canoes don't usually remain on waves for very long; if you can go with the flow for a short time, the wave will ordinarily pass harmlessly by. The alternative is to get up enough forward speed to break the surf—a maneuver that requires a very fast canoe and powerful paddlers. Generally, surfing poses a threat only if you're headed toward a rocky shore. Under these conditions you may have to break the surf by broaching the canoe—a procedure that's almost guaranteed to swamp you (unless, of course, you have a canoe cover).

To summarize; Don't quarter into man-eating rollers unless *both* you and your partner are highly skilled in handling the canoe. Instead, lighten the ends (or attach your spray cover) and paddle aggressively into the waves. For downwind travel, maintain your positions on the seats and *keep paddling!*

Snug Camp

Campcraft books are rich with advice on choosing the right campsite. But most commentary is a waste of space since even rank novices know better than to pitch their tents in a depression, on unlevel ground, or in a bog. Since it's unethical (an often illegal) to clear trees and brush to improve a camp spot, you usually have to take what's available and use your ingenuity and wet-weather skills to make your stay comfortable. Shorelines along northern rivers are fre-

quently very unforgiving; most of the time I'm overjoyed just to find a level place to set my tent. After that I worry about other creature comforts like a south-facing slope, proximity to good water, effective drainage, shade, wind protection, and a nice view. Nonetheless, here's one bit of advice worth repeating: Don't camp in a meadow or flat, mossy area. Cold, damp air settles in meadows, and the effect is much like sleeping in a refrigerated greenhouse! Moss also acts as a giant sponge— it traps water for miles around. If it rains while you're camped on moss, you'll be elbow-deep in water by morning. Even the most watertight ground cloth won't save you under those conditions!

A Dry Place to Work and Cook Outside Your Tent

If you've read Bill Mason's book *Song of the Paddle,* you may have chuckled at his review of an earlier edition of this book. Mason wrote:

One of the best on expedition canoeing . . . I was amazed at how often we came to the same conclusions on so may aspects of canoeing and living outdoors. He's "out to lunch," though, on tents!

Too bad I never had the privilege of meeting Bill Mason. He would have discovered that philosophically we are both in the same camp, even though we prefer different tents. Mason liked a large canvas Baker tent for both sleeping and lounging; I prefer a medium-sized nylon tent for sleeping, and a big tarp for loafing. Whereas Bill liked a cozy one-room home with a cot in the corner, I prefer a small bedroom and a huge den. I think Mason would have loved my 15-foot-square Cooke Custom Sewing (appendix B) tundra tarp, which has full bug netting all around!

Bill Mason loved his comfort, and so do I. That's why I wouldn't be without a roomy tarp, under which I can do camp chores on rainy days.

Tarp Styles

There are rectangular tarps and parabolic tarps.

Parabolic tarps (figure 12-4) are cut on a strong catenary curve to eliminate sag. They go up easy: You just tie off the opposing ends and run out the wings and stake them. What could be simpler?

Disadvantages:

■ They are difficult to pitch on a small site. For example,

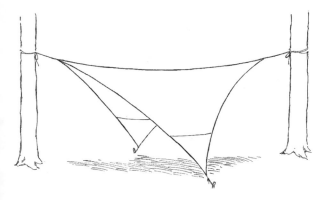

Figure 12-4. Parabolic tarps go up fast but they're breezy and can't be pitched on a short site. Rectangular tarps are much more versatile.

a 12-foot parabolic tarp cannot be pitched in a 10-foot space.

- The opposing ends bear most of the wind load. Guess what happens if a ridge loop tears out?

- The typical parafly has just one stake point on each sidewall. This may not be enough if a big wind blows up.

- The tapered sides produce a rather airy shelter which can be unpleasant in wind-driven rain.

The bottom line: Parabolics go up fast. Two trees and two to six stakes are all you need. However, they're not as versatile as rectangular tarps.

Any rectangular tarp, on the other hand, can be easily pitched on a short site. Simply tie off the usable center and guy down the wings. Two box-shaped tarps can be overlapped and paired to make room for a large group.

The bottom line: If you're tripping on the tundra where icy winds can blow for days, a versatile rectangular tarp whose long edge can be staked to the ground is the way to go.

When it comes to tarp size, an 8- by 10-foot square tarp is about right for two; a 10- by 12-foot is better for four. I like a 15-foot square tarp for eight or more. The difference in weight between a small and large tarp is less than a pound—hardly a concern on a canoe trip.

The bottom line: Bigger is better when it rains all day!

Tarp Fabrics

Clear plastic sheeting tears easily and it lets you broil in the sun. Caring canoeists don't bring plastic tarps on canoe trips. Ever!

Nylon-reinforced plastics (truck tarps) are reasonably light and very strong. But they're stiff, noisy and bulky to pack.

Nylon or polyester is what you want, and take your pick. Polyester keeps its shape better than nylon when exposed to rain and humidity, which is why it's used for parabolic tarps and sails. It's also slightly heavier and less elastic than nylon; a tarp that gives with the wind is less likely to tear than one that doesn't. Nylon, on the other hand, is slightly stronger than polyester, but less resistant to ultraviolet light. All good nylon tarps all have a UV coating.

Tarps usually tear at the hem, not at the face (though badly reinforced face ties can pull out). Ultralight tarps are usually as reliable as heavier tarps in high winds, if they're well reinforced and you rig them right. Abrasion is the main enemy of lightweight tarps, Keep 'em clean and don't drag 'em on the ground when you pack them away, and they'll last almost forever.

The most popular rain tarps are constructed from 1.9-ounce-per-square-yard rip-stop nylon with an approximate 1-ounce polyurethane waterproof coating. This may not be waterproof by government standards, but it's adequate for a tarp, where water doesn't stay pooled on the surface. Heavier coatings are more waterproof—and heavier!

Cooke Custom Sewing recently introduced a line of nylon tarps coated with ultralightweight silicone. They weigh nearly 50 percent less (and cost 50 percent more!) than identical polyurethane-coated tarps. The silicone coating makes the cloth very slippery as well as highly water resistant. Fibers that slip under stress are less likely to tear than those that don't. If a tear begins in a silicone-coated fabric and an identical polyurethane-coated one, the tear will be more than twice as likely to continue in the polyurethane-coated fabric!

The bottom line: Ultralight fabrics will stand up to strong winds about as well as heavier fabrics *if they are well reinforced* and are protected from abrasion.

Construction Features

Here are some features of the best-made tarps:

- Nylon seam tape is sewn all around the hem. There are no grommets (anywhere!) that can cut and pull out.

- Corners are reinforced with extra material.

- Rectangular tarps have at least five storm loops on the face. Storm loops are backed by heavy material.

- The more tie tabs on the hem, the better. Tie tabs should be spaced no more than 20 inches apart.

Tarp Color

Light-colored tarps let in cheery light on cloudy days. Dark colors produce a dreary atmosphere. I like a brightly patterned tarp that my floatplane pilot can see for miles. Navy blue attracts mosquitoes and blackflies.

Customize Your Tarp

Tarps are seldom right as they come from the factory. Figure 12-5 shows some modifications you'll want to make. Well sewn nylon loops (get inch-wide nylon webbing at any camping shop) are much more reliable than grommets. If you're a belt-and-suspenders person, you'll replace critically located corner grommets with nylon webbing. Allow about 12 inches of space between loops or grommets. Be sure to back what you sew with heavy material. And don't forget to waterproof all seams.

Also note the clever pole patch, which secures a center pole in high winds. To make this, sew an 8-inch-square pole patch of heavy material to the inside center (opposite the center guyline) of your fly, then sew on the two butterfly pole loops as illustrated. Thread parachute cord through the loops and secure the cords with a heavy-duty cord lock. This will stabilize a center pole when there are no trees to which you can attach an outside guyline.

To use the butterfly pole loops, center the pole in the socket and tighten the cord lock. The loops will wrap around the pole and hold it in place when the tarp is buffeted by wind. For extra security, wrap the cords around the pole several times and tie them with a simple bow.

Attach loops of parachute cord to each grommet or loop. Loops should be large enough to accept a wire stake. Also attach 'chute cord loops to each of the five webbed loops on the face of the fly. Tie the loops with a single sheetbend (see the knots section later in this chapter). A 20-foot long cord may be permanently tied to the center face loop if you wish. If you sew matching loops inside the tarp opposite those on the outside, you'll have a handy place to hang flashlights, candle lanterns, and the like.

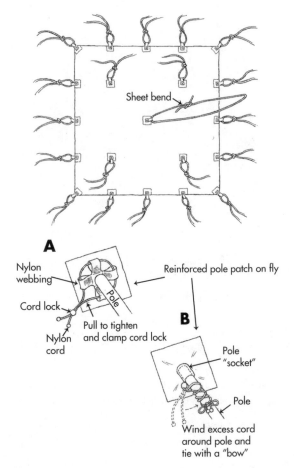

Figure 12-5. Rigging the rainfly for rough weather.

Pack these items in the stuff sack that contains your tarp:

- One hundred feet of $\frac{1}{8}$-inch-diameter parachute cord for each tarp you plan to rig. Cut the cord into 15- to 20-foot lengths and burn the ends so they won't unravel. Then tightly coil each hank and secure it with a quick-release loop (figure 12-6).

- At least a dozen tent stakes. Bring a variety so you can rig the fly securely on any type of ground.

Rigging the Tarp If Trees Are Available

String a tight line about 6 feet high between two trees and tie one edge of the fly to the line. This will distribute the wind load among several points along the fly. Wrap the corner

Figure 12-6. Quick-release loop.

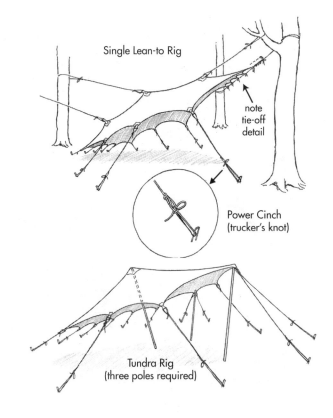

Figure 12-7. The quick-rig lean-to (top) stays up in any storm. Use the three-pole tundra rig when there are no trees to tie to.

ties around the line a few times before you tie them. This will produce sufficient friction to prevent the fly from sliding inward along the line when it's buffeted by wind.

Stake or guy out the back end of the fly. Then guy the center to an overhanging tree limb, or to a rope strung overhead. If this is impossible, prop up the center from the inside with a pole or your longest paddle. Don't try this unless you've sewn a protective pole patch to the fly, as I've recommended. Without one, you'll stretch the fly out of shape or tear it.

Complete all knots and hitches with quick-release loops (discussed later in this chapter) so you can change or drop the outfit at a moment's notice. Except where absolute security is desired (as when lining a canoe), it's always best to complete all knots and hitches with a quick-release loop. The first time you have to pick apart a "gobber" knot to drop a clothesline or change the orientation of a rainfly, you'll understand how important this is. When severe winds threaten, simply lower one or both ends of the ridge rope.

Six people can snuggle comfortably under a 12-foot-square fly that's pitched lean-to fashion, as illustrated in figure 12-7. For large groups, join a second tarp at the ridge (overlap it so rain won't get in) opposite the first. This will create an airy tent that everyone can crowd under. If you build a campfire beneath the tarps, you'll need to "float" tarp 2 over tarp 1 to create a draft hole that will exhaust the smoke. The

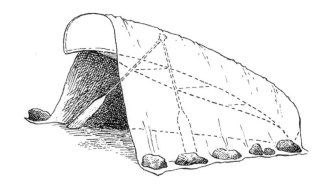

Figure 12-8. Use this method to prop up two canoes side by side. One canoe can provide instant shelter with the use of a tarp.

THE EXPERT'S EDGE

Figure 12-9. The quick-rig lean-to goes up fast and withstands high winds.

details of this rig are found in my book *Camping's Top Secrets.*

If you're canoeing above the tree line, use the three-pole tundra tarp. Important: When high winds develop, run one or more guylines off the ridge, as illustrated. I've used this setup in 50-mile-per-hour winds. It's noisy but solid.

Rigging the Tarp If There Are No Trees

Prop up two canoes on paddles (see figure 12-8). Space the canoes about 6 feet apart, parallel to one another, and cover them with your rain tarp. Stake and guy the fly and push out the center with a pole or paddle so it won't pool water. Don't trust this setup in a strong wind!

If it's perfectly calm, you can prop up the back ends of the canoes as well as the front to produce a nonsloping shelter with more interior space.

I don't like the canoe-prop method. It's hard on paddles and not very secure. But it's useful in light rain and handy when you need protection for a small fire.

Protect Your Food and Gear from Rain and Dampness

You just can't leave things lying around in a rainy-day camp. Everything must be secured under your rain tarp or in your tent. Even then, equipment and food may get wet unless protected by a waterproof covering. I make waterproof nylon bags for everything—clothing, rain tarp, folding saw, trail stove, even my dirty clothes. (*Hint:* Pack a waterproof nylon sack *inside* your waterproof clothes bag to separate damp dirty clothes from clean dry ones.) And don't leave open pack sacks scattered around your camp! If you think this is needless advice, stroll through a typical rainy-day camp sometime: You'll see wide-open packs and tent flaps, everywhere.

If flooding results from a heavy rain, anything placed on the ground beneath your rain tarp will get wet—another reason to store everything in waterproof bags. A convenient solution for keeping things off the wet ground is to simply string one or two lightweight clotheslines just beneath your rain

Figure 12-10. Sometimes there's a cabin.

tarp. Hang everything you want to keep dry from these lines.

I store all my cooking utensils and spices in a fabric roll that has snaps at the top edge. When it rains, I hang the open roll from a protected clothesline. Everything from spoons to spices is then instantly available yet immune from the weather.

A Place to Sit

There's nothing more disconcerting than standing around because you can't find a dry place to sit. If you've outfitted your canoe with removable sitting pads as I've recommended, you've got the problem solved. If not, carry a square of closed-cell foam. It bears repeating that a folding camp stool is worth bringing on any canoe trip.

Cabin Fever

We were about 100 miles into the trip, pushing hard into the face of wind-whipped rain. My head was down, obscured in the hood of my rain parka. Only occasionally did I look up—directly into the icy drizzle—to check the course. This weather system had been with us for eight days now. Not once had the sun shone between the clouds of twisted gray. And the blackflies . . . they seemed inexhaustible!

My partner and I said little. We just plodded methodically ahead, one stroke, then another, and another. Occasionally we squinted toward shore in search of a level clearing to pitch our tents. But there was nothing—only endless tag alders punctuated by an occasional bog.

"Sure wish we'd find a nice cabin," I mused aloud. I'd

barely finished the words when my friends pointed to the right and said, "There!" Sure enough, it was a cabin, incredible as it seemed.

We back-ferried (See chapter 17, Hazards and Rescue, for a discussion of the ferry technique) to shore and eagerly scrambled up the mucky bank to the old cabin. The door was unlocked so we let ourselves in. There was a woodstove, four bunks with rotting mattresses, a kerosene lantern (but no kerosene), some rusty tools, and a profusion of whiskey bottles. A stench of musty rottenness pervaded everything. But it was dry and there were no bugs. For tonight, at least, we'd call it home.

We fired up the old tin stove then flipped a coin to see which four of the six of us would get to sleep on the bunks. I lost and reluctantly unrolled my foam pad on the drafty board floor.

A good supper, fresh coffee, a hit of brandy, and instantly to bed. We'd had it!

It was well into the night when I heard them scratching, cussing, scratching again. Bed bugs? I chuckled to myself . . . the floor wasn't so bad after all! About 4:00 A.M. someone turned on a flashlight and, with much profanity, suggested we "get the hell out of here!" In thirty minutes we were gone, paddling into the teeth of an icy rain.

Over the next three weeks we passed at least a dozen winter trapping cabins like the one that had befriended us that night. But we found only two that were free of bugs, drafts, and intolerable smells.

As you travel the northern rivers you'll come upon many unoccupied cabins, most of which are in bad need of repairs and are inundated by bugs and rodents. In all likelihood you'll find your tent a much more welcome home. However, if you do find a habitable dwelling, it's an unwritten law that you're welcome to use it. Just fill the stove box with wood and leave a note of thanks on the door.

FIRE

The ability to make a fire is one of the most important of all campcraft skills. Yet it is one that few outdoors people have mastered.

"Aw c'mon," you say. "*Anyone* can build a fire; all you need is some birch bark or paper, dry wood, and a match. In fact, fires often start *too* easily—they get out of hand and burn down forests!"

A convincing argument? Not really. Certainly anyone can set a bone-dry forest ablaze on a breezeless summer day. But add a 30-mile-per-hour wind and a weeklong rain and you may discover that where there's smoke, there won't be fire!

Outdoor handbooks define dozens of campfire types: the keyhole, beanpot, tepee, log cabin, lean-to, chimney rock, and more. And along with this information is usually a detailed comparison of the heat efficiency of various wood species. (Evidently the authors think everyone can tell a stick of oak from that of hickory, or a splitting of pine from spruce).

A discussion of fire types and heat production of woods makes interesting reading, but it won't help you get a fire going. What will is a basic understanding of what makes fires burn. (Don't laugh: The U.S. Forest Service Forest Fire Experiment Station at Missoula, Montana, has been studying this question for years and it still doesn't have all the answers.)

An experienced woodsman lights a match only when reasonably certain of success!

If you've ever watched an experienced outdoorsperson make a fire under difficult conditions, you'll find the presence of these variables:

- A cool deliberateness—he or she knows exactly what to do.

- Nonuse of paper or gasoline, even when these materials are available.

- Painstaking, almost scientific placement of each piece of tinder and kindling on the fire base.

- A fire that almost always starts with one match.

- A fire that burns brightly with a nearly smoke-free flame, even if the wood is damp.

Generally a good woodsman can make a cheery fire within five minutes, even on a wet or windy day. But not always. In severe conditions the process may take much longer. However, the extra time is spent in securing and splitting dry wood—not in wasting matches trying to ignite materials that won't burn. Herein lies the difference between the veteran fire maker and the novice. The former lights a match only when reasonably certain of success. The latter strikes away haphazardly, one match after another, until he or she is matchless . . . and frustrated.

The key to a successful one match fire is the tinder, highly flammable material that ignites instantly and produces great heat.

Tinder is, of course, bone-dry. But equally important (and seldom mentioned), it is thin in cross section—the rule being that *it must be no larger in diameter than the thickness of a matchstick*. Attempting to ignite materials thicker than a matchstick is generally a waste of time.

Some favored tinders include birch or cedar bark, very dry leaves and grasses, straw-thin dead twigs taken from the dead lower branches of evergreen trees, abandoned bird or insect nests, and long-dead pine needles and cedar foliage. Or take splittings from a dead evergreen stump. This is called "fatwood," and it contains highly flammable pitch.

You'll note the conspicuous absence of paper from the list of preferred tinders. Paper works fine in dry weather, but in damp conditions it absorbs moisture from the air and burns reluctantly.

Waxed paper is an exception: It burns efficiently in any weather and so makes an excellent fire starter. A flattened waxed milk carton can also help you get a fire going quickly. If you tear the carton into thin strips, it will burn nicely for several minutes. Candles, wax crayons, and cotton balls dipped in Vaseline also make good fire starters.

If you want to make more sophisticated fire starters, simply roll small pieces of newspaper into miniature logs and soak them in melted paraffin. Or buy one of the excellent commercial fire starters (solid or paste) available at every camping shop. One of the best natural fire starters is resin from the balsam fir tree. The outer bark of the balsam fir produces big resin blisters. Just break a few blisters and collect the resin, which is nearly as flammable as kerosene.

The trouble with natural tinder is that it often doesn't work when you need it most. For example, if it has rained for several days, those dry grasses, pine needles, and even birch and cedar bark may be too wet to burn. It's then that the fire starters prove their worth.

Okay, fire starters are great. But what do you do if you don't have them? Where do you get suitable tinder on a wet day?

The answer is to split the driest log you can find—which on the outside may not be very dry at all—and cut wafer-thin shavings (tinder) from the heartwood with your pocket knife. The center of a 4-inch-diameter or larger log is almost always dry enough to burn, even if the log has been exposed to a weeklong rain.

In fact, a demonstration I regularly perform when I teach fire building is to fish a small floating log out of a waterway, split it, and secure tinder-fine shavings from its heart. A single match almost always produces a reliable blaze.

You'll find some of the best fire-starting materials in old beaver lodges and dams along lakeshores. The debarked aspen sticks left by the beaver make excellent kindling and shavings for tinder. The heart of beaver wood is bone-dry, even after it has been exposed to weeks of rain. But for the sake of the beavers, please take only a few sticks.

Dead and downed trees that are not in contact with the ground also provide exceptional firewood. You'll find these blowdowns along lakeshores, along river fronts, and in open areas where constant exposure to sunlight has killed off the bacteria and fungi that would otherwise rot the wood and make it unsuitable to burn. The wood of these trees is frequently wet to the touch after a rain, but, like beaver wood, it is usually dry in the center.

Don't begin to build your fire until you have a good supply of shavings and kindling. A handful of shavings is enough, but you'll need three times that much kindling. Kindling should range in size from pencil-thin to no thicker than your thumb.

Though there are dozens of fire styles, a real expert will usually avoid them all. He or she will simply set a ball of fine shavings or natural tinder on the ground. Light a match to it, then carefully feed, one at a time, shavings or tiny sticks of increasing size into the tiny blaze.

As the flame picks up, the fire maker will add thin kindling, taking care to place each stick a half diameter's width away from the next (for example, two ½ inch-thick sticks should be separated from each other by ¼ inch). Substantial separation of sticks ensures a rich oxygen supply for the young flame. Lack of oxygen is the major reason why most young fires fail. For this reason novice fire makers are routinely taught to be sure they see light between every shaving, stick, or log, placed on a fire.

Let's summarize why fires don't start or burn properly:

- Wood is damp or wet. Even here, wet wood will burn *if you cut it thin enough.*

- Not enough oxygen. Are pieces of wood placed so you can see light between them?

- The tinder is too thick, or is balled up too tightly.

Unfortunately, I can only share with you the techniques of fire making. The mechanical skills you need to implement these techniques must be acquired through diligent practice. So don't wait until the first rainy or windy day of a trip to try these procedures. Get out and practice them now while they're fresh in your mind.

Keep the campfires burning. And don't forget to put them out when you leave!

BEARS

Kay Henry of the Mad River Canoe Company describes an encounter along Alaska's Koyukuk River:

When we saw the grizzly he was walking toward us along the riverbank about 300 yards from where we were standing. He wasn't aware of us; he just ambled along, stopping occasionally to dig for ground squirrels. His silvery coat shimmered with every step. We watched for several minutes, fascinated. Ultimately, we decided he'd come close enough so we naively rang our bear bells to scare him away. He never changed course, never missed a step. In unison we yelled! Nothing. Then I remembered my tiny compressed air horn (the type used to call a yacht club to launch). That did it. He stopped, ran back into the woods, then a moment later returned to identify the problem. Finally he seemed satisfied that we posed no threat, and slowly, on his own terms, he ambled off. We hadn't scared him away; he chose to leave!

I've had many encounters with bears in the years I've been canoeing. On two occasions I've been forced to pack up and leave. Once, along the Hood River in Canada's arctic, I was charged by three grizzlies. Yelling did not alter their course. When they were about 100 feet away, I curled into a tight ball and prayed for Manitou to intervene on my behalf. The bears came within 50 feet, then bolted for the tundra. The adrenaline high that came resulted after being literally scared almost to death was indescribable!

The recommended procedure for scaring off an intruding bruin is the one described by Kay Henry in her anecdote. Sometimes it works, sometimes not. I've clanged pots, blown whistles, and even fired guns with no effect. If you've got a determined bear on your hands, you'll have to make a very loud noise to scare him away. An air horn, cherry bomb, or stick of dynamite might do it. And if that fails, you'd better retreat to the safety of your canoe.

Kinds of Bears

Which bear—black or grizzly—maims and kills more humans? If you said "grizzly," you're dead wrong! Black bear maulings outnumber grizzly maulings by a huge margin.

Does this mean you should fear black bears? No. But it does mean you should take certain precautions when you travel in bear country. What you should do largely depends on the kind of bear you meet. Bear experts classify bears as:

- **Wild:** These bears are curious and unafraid. Many have never seen a human before. They'll gallop in to investigate, and when they're satisfied that you don't present a threat, they'll usually leave of their own accord. What most people interpret as a charge, is often curiosity.

- **Man-wise** bears have learned fear of humans from past experience or Mom. They are usually hunted bears. One glimpse of you and they're usually gone.

- **Habituated:** These are the typical Yellowstone Park and Boundary Waters bears that have learned they're safe around humans.

Which of these bears—wild, man-wise, or habituated—

Figure 12-11. Tundra grizzly.

do you think are most dangerous to people? Surprisingly, the answer is wild bears, probably because unlike the others these animals don't know what to expect.

Bear Attacks

Authorities categorize bear attacks as either defensive-aggressive or predatory. A bear in the defensive-aggressive mode feels you are a threat and will try to bluff you away. This may happen if, for example, you get between a mother and her cub or come upon a bear that's quietly grazing on grass. In a defensive-aggressive encounter the bear will usually rush in, huffing and clacking its teeth. It will make a big show and try to scare you away with the intent of getting back to what it was doing as quickly as possible.

Don't run or throw things at the bear! Play dead until the danger has passed. Roll over on your stomach and clasp your hands behind your neck. Shove your head deep into the duff and spread your legs wide so the bear will have trouble turning you over. Once the bear perceives you're not a threat, it will usually leave. You may get roughed up a bit, but you will probably survive. *Don't* fight back with a defensive-aggressive bear: This may trigger a vicious attack!

Here's the rationale behind this strategy: Imagine you're a bear quietly strolling through the woods with your cub. Suddenly a strange being appears between you and your baby. What to do? You must remove the threat, but you don't want to leave your baby alone for long. So you make a big show and dash in, hoping the intruder will submit so you can get back to Junior as fast as possible. It's what any prudent mother—animal or human—would do.

In predatory attacks, on the other hand, you are food and the bear is stalking you!

In 1987 two canoeists were mauled by a black bear in Minnesota's Boundary Waters Canoe Area. A father and son watched the bear (a small female) peer at them from the edge of the forest for several minutes before she attacked. Convinced that the bear was merely curious, the man sent his son to gather firewood. As soon as the boy was out of sight, the bear ran in. The man leapt into the lake, and the bear followed. Ultimately, the son beat off the bear with a canoe paddle, which saved his dad's life. When Forest Service personnel later killed the bear, they discovered she was starving.

A more serious attack occurred in Algonquin Provincial Park in 1992, when two hikers—a man and a woman—were killed and eaten by a black bear. Authorities found a clean camp and said that the hikers had done nothing wrong.

Figure 1-1. *A time for reflection. Hudson Bay, at the mouth of the Seal River.*

Figure 5-7. *This rented Alumacraft was damaged in Horsetail Rapids on the Granite River, which bisects Minnesota and Canada. The paddlers made repairs with duct tape and finished their trip. The outfitter didn't buy their "It's as good as new" argument and charged the crew for a new canoe!*

Figure 5-9. *The author's Kevlar Mad River Explorer wrapped around a boulder in a dicey rapids along Ontario's Steel River. Surprisingly, the American white ash rails did not break. Says Cliff: "We rescued the canoe, stomped it back into shape, applied duct tape, and finished the trip without incident. Later at home I repaired the canoe to its former strength with Kevlar and fiberglass and paddled it for three more years. I eventually sold the craft for $500."*

Figure 5-13. *A hand-built wood-strip solo canoe. The author has used wood-strip solos on tough Canadian rivers.*

Figure 5-15. *Winter canoeing in a Kruger Cruiser.*

Figure 5-16. *Two top expedition canoes. The Dagger Venture and the Old Town Tripper.*

Figure 5-18. *Gary and Joanie McGuffin surf in a tandem canoe.*

Figure 7-13. *The two-piece spray cover on the author's Bell Wildfire solo canoe is rolled and reefed.*

Figure 8-2. *Panel-style vests are comfortable when you're canoeing, but they may ride up over your head when you have to swim. One size fits all adults. On the shores of Hudson Bay near the mouth of the North Knife River, Manitoba.*

Figure 10-2. *Cannondale Aroostook tents (no longer manufactured) on the tundra. Along the Hood River, Nunavut, Canada.*

Figure 12-1. *The expert's edge. Hood River, Nunavut, Canada.*

Figure 12-2. *Rain. Thelon River, Nunavut, Canada.*

Figure 12-13. *A polar bear on Hudson Bay near the mouth of the Knife River.*

Figure 12-14. *Morning, looking through the tundra tarp. Tha-anne River, Nunavut, Canada.*

Figure 14-4.
Portaging around a huge falls along the Kopka River in Ontario. The author (white hat) is in the foreground.

Figure 14-5. *The final leg of the portage around wedding Cake Falls on the Kopka River.*

Figure 15-6. *Solo canoes set you free to follow your own star in your own way. The author paddles his Bell Wildfire canoe on Shoshone Lake, Yellowstone National Park, Wyoming.*

Figure 16-8. *Unloading a Twin Otter on Point Lake, Nunavut, Canada.*

Figure 17-3 *Canoeing through a burn, Seal River, Manitoba.*

Figure 17-18. *Recovering a wrapped canoe along the Missinaibi River, Ontario.*

Figure 18-4. *Nadlak, an island along the Burnside River, is located about 100 miles southwest of Bathurst Inlet. These unique dwellings, built entirely of caribou antlers, are the remains of structures abandoned by Inuit about 200 years ago. One of the fifteen houses contained an estimated 4,400 antlers! Nadlak was first visited by archaeologists in 1985. They speculated that the Inuit—who traditionally lived in coastal regions and ventured to the interior only to hunt—moved to the island around 500 years ago, when caribou migration patterns changed due to a series of cold winters (there was a mini-ice age that lasted from* A.D. *1400 to 1800). Bones from more than 100,000 caribou have been unearthed on the island.*

Figure 18-9. *Relaxing in the tundra tent, Thlewiaza River, Nunavut, Canada.*

Photo: Doug McKown

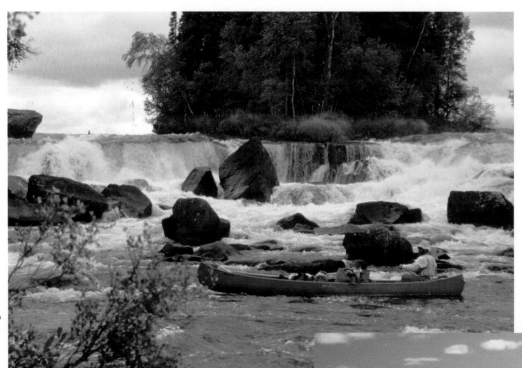

Figure 19-3. *Doug McKown at a waterfall on the upper MacFarlane.*

Photo: Hap Wilson

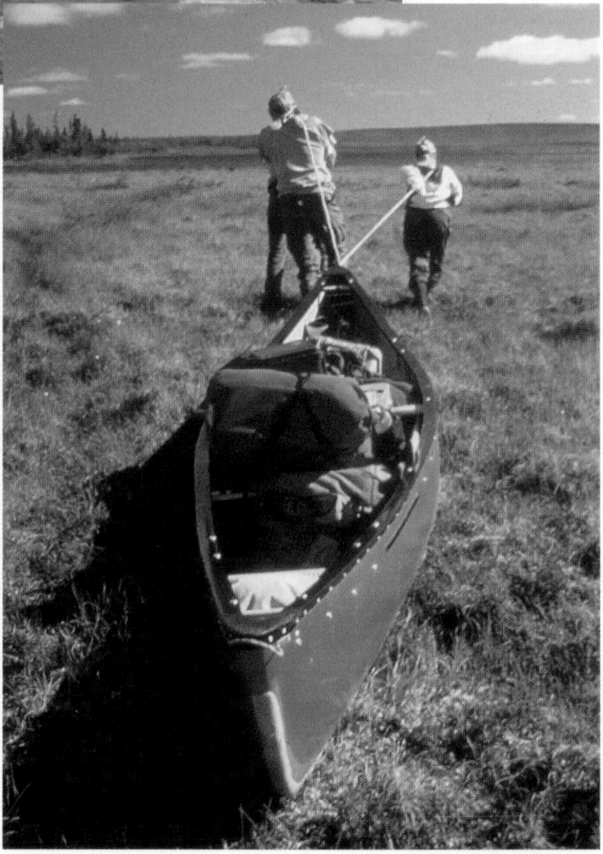

Figure 19-8. *A typical portage on the Roberts River.*

Note that both of these predatory attacks occurred during the day.

Three words—*fight like hell*—describe the recommended course of action. If you have a knife, ax or big rock, use it. If you fight hard enough, you will probably survive. *Do not play dead* with a predatory bear!

If a bear tears through your tent while you're inside at any time it should be treated as a very serious predacious attack. Again, fight with all your might!

Despite what you may have heard or read, black bears are not always timid—or predictable! But they are incredibly intelligent, actually smarter than the smartest dogs. They sense that humans can be dangerous, so they carefully weigh the odds before they attack. Pretend you're a bear again and decide which of these is the easiest meal:

1. Six big men are sitting around camp. You could dash in and attack one.

2. A man is standing alone at the edge of camp.

3. A child is standing alone at the edge of camp.

If you said "number 3," you're right on target. No bear with good sense will attack six men. And it's a lot less risky to pick off a child than a grown man. Bears do size up people before they attack.

It follows that you should *watch your children* when you travel in bear country. A predaceous bear will almost always seek out the smallest person in the crowd. Wouldn't you, if you were a bear?

There are dozens of cases where putting up a good fight saved the day. In a recent incident a twelve-year-old-girl was picking berries outside a cabin in Ontario. A small black bear attacked her, chasing her right into the cabin! The screaming girl threw furniture and pots and pans at the animal. Ultimately, the terrorized bear ran out of the cabin. All of which supports the premise that bears are intelligent and will call off the fight if things get too mean for them.

Bear Encounters

An encounter is not an attack, though it can become one if you do something stupid. Most people view an encounter as the highlight of a canoe trip.

I've had numerous encounters with black bears, grizzlies, and polar bears. Each has ended with a smile and a deeper admiration for these creatures. Here's what to do if you meet a bear in the wild:

Figure 12-12. A curious black bear explores our camp. Porcupine River, Saskatchewan

- **You see the bear but the bear doesn't see you:** Leave quietly! Do not do anything to attract the bear's attention. Doing so could make you a target!

- **A chance meeting:** You're hiking down a portage trail, say, and a bear crosses your path. The bear looks your way.

  Don't look the bear in the eye! Back off slowly; talk quietly to the bear in a tone that indicates you don't want trouble. The bear will probably skedaddle as soon as you reach a safe distance.

- **A bear comes into your camp at night:** The bear has probably been watching you all day. It was too scared to come in broad daylight so it waited till dark. It's doubtful you have much to fear. Under these conditions I usually just roll over and go back to sleep. If you wish, you can step outside your tent and watch the show—Just stay out of the bear's way as it searches for food. The bear knows you're there, and as long as you stay put, you pose no threat. If it's a truly wild bear, blowing whistles, or the like, may scare it away. A practiced camp bear will be oblivious to the noise, snooping around for a while then quietly leaving.

- **A bear comes into your camp during the day:** You've got trouble, right here in River City! This is one bold bear. It could have waited till the safety of night, but it came in the day. It is determined to have its way! You should respond by treating this as a dangerous situation (which it is). Begin with active discouragement: Yell, bang pots, blow whistles. Shoot off cherry bombs. Stand together with friends and spread your arms wide. Make yourselves look huge, put on a big show.

Some authorities suggest that you throw rocks at the bear—and try to hit. This can be a *very* bad idea. I tried it once on an obscure campsite along Saskatchewan's Fond du Lac River. A nasty sow with cubs in tow marched into our camp around suppertime and came within a yard of our bonfire. We yelled and screamed, which did no good. Then we threw rocks at her and hit her several times. She yelped and scampered off, only to return shortly, teeth bared and clacking, head swaying, woofing loudly. (Experts say the situation has begun to "deteriorate" when this happens.)

We beat a hasty retreat to the canoes, where we watched her glare at us from shore for several minutes before wandering off. Ultimately, she allowed us to return to shore just long enough to tear down camp and move on. When we put to sea for the second time, she waddled confidently out on a high rock face to see us off, snapping, woofing, and reaffirming her unfriendliness. I think she would have had us for supper if we had hung around. Right then, I vowed I would never throw rocks at a bear again!

James Gary Shelton, author of *Bear Encounter Survival Guide,* recorded six attacks that came after people yelled at a bear (both black and grizzly) that had already given an aggressive signal (blowing or growling). Shelton suggests that if you are carrying only pepper spray (see the following section) or have no defense system at all, do not yell at any bear that is blowing, growling, or popping its teeth and trying to locate you visually. Stand still and be quiet. The bear will usually leave.

Grizzlies

Most of the above advice applies to grizzlies as well as black bears, with these exceptions:

- Most people who are killed by predatory grizzlies are camping in a park at night, whereas most people who are killed by predaceous black bears are doing things during the day. Children are major targets.

- You are safer sleeping inside a tent than in a sleeping bag on the ground. Evidently, grizzlies mistake the warm, smelly sleeping bag for their natural food! A tent provides a psychological barrier that discourages most bears.

- Black bears develop an immunity to pepper spray (see below). Grizzlies don't. A black bear that has been sprayed several times may continue to be ornery. Once educated, a grizzly will usually run away at the first blast.

Pepper Spray

You need powerful pepper—and lots of it—to stop a determined bear. Authorities suggest that you carry a 230-gram (half-pound) or larger can. It may be a good plan to bring two cans! The pepper formulation should contain at least 1 percent capsaicin—the flaming ingredient in red pepper. Be sure the can has a fogger nozzle, not a stream pattern.

International bear expert Dr. Stephen Herrero says that if properly used, pepper spray will stop aggressive bears about 75 percent of the time. Herrero found that even a dangerous mother with cubs will usually run away from the spray. He has not heard of a single case in which spraying a bear with pepper enraged it and made it more aggressive.

This account, excerpted from the *Bear Encounter Survival Guide,* by James Gary Shelton, illustrates the importance of having the largest can of pepper spray you can find:

On May 16, 1996, an engineer was working by himself in a cut-block north of Prince George, B.C. He was doing GPS locations of the creeks in the area. Earlier that day the belt buckle had come off his belt (his spray was in a holster on his belt) so he had to put his bear spray in the back of his vest.

As he was moving along he saw a large black bear approaching from his left at a fast walk. As he turned to face the bear and started trying to reach the spray, he realized he wouldn't get it in time. The bear was only ten feet away when he threw his hat off to the side of the bear; it immediately pounced on the hat and started ripping it apart.

The bear was occupied with the hat for about ten seconds, then turned and headed toward its intended victim when it received a three-second blast of spray at a distance of about five feet. It immediately backed up about ten feet, coughing and shaking its head. It put its face down into the ground moss and started rubbing the spray off.

The engineer started walking at a fast pace toward

POLAR BEARS

Cliff Jacobson's North Knife River Journal

July 19, 1992: This river is not at all what I expected. Rapids around every bend, and they are all huge ones that require inspection. We get out of the canoes at every drop and study the river. There are no defined portages, only occasional animal trails that peter out after a few dozen yards. No sign of people anywhere—not even a tent site or fireplace. Does anyone ever paddle the North Knife?

The ice went out real late this year so we'll probably see polar bears near the Bay (Hudson Bay). Doug Webber, owner of North Knife Lodge—and just about everything else around Churchill—suggested we bring a gun. We did. Three of 'em! Tom Anderson has a beater 12-gauge Ithaca. Dick Magnuson has a new 760 Remington slug gun, and I'm carrying my old .444 Marlin, with 275-grain Barnes (bullets) hand loads.

God, I hope we don't have to shoot a polar bear!!

We're 50 miles into the trip and no sign of bears anywhere. Actually, we don't figure on seeing any till we reach the bay. Even then it's doubtful we'll luck out and see one up close. For this reason no one but me has bothered to load their gun. I've been taking a lot of razzing about carrying a loaded rifle at this point in the trip, but I think it's stupid to haul around useless metal. If a dangerous condition develops I want to be able to act quickly. After all, I *am* the leader!

July 20: Coming around a bend, my partner Joanie points and says: "Hey, Cliff, look at that mountain goat up there! Seconds later the goat materializes into a full-grown male polar bear, which slides down the bank and swims straight toward our canoe.

"Back-ferry"! I yell. Oh please back-ferry! It's like we're paddling through glue, and the bear keeps coming. Luckily, when he's barely 50 feet away, the powerful current sweeps him around the bend. Will he come ashore and crash back through the bush toward us? Soon as the boat touches land I'm out, rifle in hand and praying I won't have to shoot. Seconds later Dick and Finette arrive, sheet white. Suddenly it's turned into a comedy—everyone massed in a tiny group, scared as hell, me clutching the half-cocked Marlin while Dick drops shotgun slugs into the sand and Tom gropes in his pack for shells. We're 75 miles from Hudson Bay and no one but me is ready to shoot. What a rush! Saw three more bears today—two swimming, one on land. Bear tracks everywhere. We've arranged tents like a fort. Perimeter teams have capsaicin (bear mace). I served everyone double shots of Pusser's rum tonight.

Aftermath: Twenty miles from Hudson Bay we came upon Doug Webber's hunting cabin. The windows were heavily barred and huge spikes protruded from the door—testimony to the destructive power of polar bears. We saw another cabin on Hudson Bay—a decrepit goose hunting shack—which had been invaded by curious bears. Everything—cots, carpeting, you name it—had been torn to shreds. We climbed onto the roof to get a better view of the ocean and promptly saw two more bears. After that no one went out hiking without a gun.

At 3:00 the next morning we paddled into a red rising sun and the misty salt water of Hudson Bay. Around the point we ran into three more bears and saw scores of porpoising beluga whales. Our final bear count for the trip was eleven!

Polar bears are not like other bears. They can swim faster—even through rapids—than I can paddle my canoe. You can't outrun a polar bear, and there no trees on the tundra big enough to climb. If a great white bear wants your hide, he'll get it! (See color figure 12-13.)

It is politically correct (at least in the United States) to suggest that guns have no place in polar bear country. But residents of Churchill, Manitoba, who have had lots of experience with polar bears, always carry a 12-gauge slug gun or high-powered rifle when they go out into the wild. Canoeists are urged to do likewise.

Certainly you should leave guns at home if you are not well practiced with them. A charging polar bear can cover 100 yards in about three seconds, which is faster than most people can fire an accurate shot. That's why bear experts unanimously recommend pepper spray over guns. I carry both when I travel among the great white bears.

his pickup. After he traveled about 200 feet he saw the bear paralleling him off to the side. It disappeared, and then a couple minutes later came out in front of him and, once again, came at him at a fast walk.

The second blast was at about the same distance, and the bear reacted with the same backing up and wiping his face in the moss routine. The young man then semi-circled the determined bear and headed for the road at a fast trot. He kept looking back, and sure enough, after a few minutes, the bear was hot on his trail but stayed back about 100 feet, not wanting a third blast.

Needless to say this was the happiest engineer in British Columbia, for when he arrived at the truck he discovered he had used up all his spray with the second blast!

Shelton and others offer these suggestions when using pepper spray:

■ Carry your spray in a holster on your belt. Can you draw and fire in less than two seconds? You may have to!

■ Everyone in your group should carry pepper spray and be ready to use it simultaneously.

■ When the bear approaches within 30 feet (the range of your pepper spray), give it a warning blast, which places a cloud of spray between you and the bear. Fire a second blast at 20 feet. Aim for the face and hope the bear is breathing in! At 10 feet fire a four- or five-second continuous blast aimed at the face and eyes. Keep shooting until the bear leaves or you're out of spray.

■ If you use up all your spray and the bear attacks, Shelton advises you to "Beat the bear with anything you can find." Bill Schneider, author of *Bear Aware*, recommends playing dead. It's your call.

■ Research reveals that habituated bears usually move off a short distance when sprayed, then return quickly, whereas attacking wild bears usually hightail it for the bush. It follows that pepper spray is more useful in remote wilderness than in a heavily traveled park setting.

■ *Do not* test-fire a can of pepper spray near your camp or keep a test-fired can in your tent. Studies suggest

[2] *Backpacker* magazine, April 1998.

FROM *BACKPACKER* MAGAZINE[2]

Bears in the High Peaks region of New York's Adirondack Mountains . . . have learned to associate white bear-bagging rope with free delivery of a tasty treat; one swipe and a meal drops from the sky. Clever backpackers are now stringing two lines—a white one to fake out the bears, and a black rope to hang food in a separate tree.

that while bears don't like to be sprayed with pepper, they do like the taste of it. When rafters in Alaska sprayed their rafts with pepper to keep bears away, the bears devoured the rafts!

If you test-fire a can of pepper spray, clean the nozzle with alcohol afterward to remove residual pepper that may attract bears.

■ Be aware that pepper spray is illegal in Canada, but animal protection devices are not! Canadian officials will allow cayenne-based products if they are clearly labeled "For Use on Animals" and have a pest control number printed on the label. Not all U.S. pepper sprays meet Canadian requirements, so check with the manufacturer of the product before you cross the border.

■ Also be aware that it is illegal to carry pepper spray on commercial airplanes.

■ Do not trigger pepper spray if the wind is blowing in your face!

Bear mace is available at many outdoor stores and western U.S. national park shops. I rely on a 230-gram can of Counter Assault (there's a bear on the label!). See appendix B for sources.

Protecting Your Food from Bears

In all my years of canoeing, I've never been injured or suffered the slightest damage or loss of equipment to bears. I know many other canoeists who have been less fortunate, mostly because they've taken camping books and government publications too literally. For example, the common advice is to hang your food packs from a tree limb out of reach of a bear. "Even if he smells your food he won't get it," they say. *Don't you believe it!* Survey some campers who've been

CARS NOT SAFE FROM BEARS AT YOSEMITE by Suzanne Charle[3]

It is the second effort at bear-proof locks; the first, using a spring-loaded bolt system, was figured out by the bears in two weeks. A bear would take the top bolt in its mouth and hold the bottom with its paw, apply force and have dinner. New locks require the use of opposable thumbs.

"Bears have elaborate schemes for getting food," Thompson (the park ranger) said. "One time-honored precaution, hanging bags of food from a rope high in a tree, is now seen as useless. Local residents call the food bags bear pinatas.

"The bears chew off the rope that has been attached elsewhere, or chew off the branch that is supporting the bag," Thompson said. "If the limbs are small, they'll send the cubs out. If that doesn't work, they'll just climb above the bags, launch themselves out of the tree and grab the bags on the way down."

robbed by bears, and you'll probably discover that the *vast* majority hung their food in trees. Black bears are excellent climbers. The cubs live in trees. Grizzly cubs climb up easily until their fourth or fifth year; then their hooked claws straighten and they must hook-climb with their limbs, just like humans. Black bears—and grizzlies—can easily out-climb most humans. And bears of all ages are adept at getting food out of sealed containers, locked cars, and trees, no matter how creative your system. Highlights from newspaper articles printed in this section drive home the point.

By the way, bears like to break into some cars more than others. They prefer Hondas and Toyotas by a huge margin!

Clearly, bears are smart and can reason, and they are not easily fooled by simple solutions.

Here's my philosophy: *If a bear can't smell your food, he won't get it!* And if you pack as I've suggested in chapters 9 and 11, and are extremely careful with your food in camp, you'll eliminate almost all odors. Bears are creatures of habit; they're classically conditioned to respond positively to what pleases them. And what pleases them is food. They learn quickly that food comes in bottles, cans, and packs—and in places where there are humans! How else can you explain why

[3]*Milwaukee Sentinel*, 30 Nov. 1997 (reprinted in *New York Times*).

they bite open tin cans or tear up packs that don't have an ounce of food or food smell in them?

Just what does this have to do with hanging food packs in trees? A lot, if you use the same trees as every other camper. Most campsites don't have a lot of good, high bear trees. There's often only one suitable tree—or a jury-rigged horizontal pole setup—that's used by everyone. Once a bear has discovered his special tree, he'll tear apart whatever you hang in it, be it food pack or football!

My system is more logical. I simply place food packs on the ground out of the main camp area. On the barrens, there are no trees. You have to cache your food on the ground. I space the packs *at least 50 feet apart* for safekeeping. And I seal the plastic pack liners tightly. I've never had a problem. On one occasion two hungry black bears walked through my campsite, nosed around a while, and left. They hit another site down the lake, destroying everything, including a new pack basket hung in a "bearproof" tree!

I asked Lynn Rogers (*the* North American black bear authority) about my method. Lynn agreed the system makes sense.

I never put my food packs under my canoe or cover them with pots and pans as suggested by some old-time woodsmen. A powerful bear can break the back of a wooden or fiberglass canoe with one swipe of his paw if he has a mind to. And topping your food pack with pots so you'll hear the bear when he comes suggests you've done something wrong in the first place. Pack your food securely in plastic, get it out of the immediate tent area when you leave camp or retire; clean up your mealtime messes, and you won't have trouble with bears or any other animals.

Final Bear Thoughts

I've been fortunate enough to see a number of grizzly bears on my canoe trips. In each case the behavior was the same: The bear was curious and galloped in. As soon as it discovered humans, it reversed engines and galloped off into the tundra. Frankly, I am much more afraid of a hungry black bear than a tundra grizzly. And I am convinced that a lot of the bear advice that you read in national park publications simply doesn't apply to canoeists. Here's why:

The density of bears in U.S. and Canadian national parks is a lot higher than that in the remote Canadian and Alaskan wilderness. For example, most of the area adjacent to

Yellowstone National Park is fenced private land where troublesome bears aren't tolerated. In some national parks bear populations are already at or above carrying capacity. James Gary Shelton believes that there are just too many bears in some places. I agree. Canoe-country bears have more space to maneuver than park bears—so they're likely less stressed.

Canoeists spend much more time canoeing than hiking, which eliminates most serious bear encounters. If you drift by a bear that is munching berries on shore, he'll probably look your way then run away. On rare occasions the bear will trot down the shore and follow you, out of curiosity. But as soon you're lost in the gathering flow, the bear will be gone, too.

I've never encountered a bear on a portage, probably because I make too much noise. Besides, the sight of a human with a canoe overhead must be terrifying to a wild bear. I've never heard of an attack.

However, confrontations with habituated bears, like those in the Boundary Waters, do occasionally occur on portages. But these encounters almost always end peacefully.

Camp is the major site of most bear encounters. But national park campsites and wilderness canoe camps are not the same. National park sites are usually occupied every night. Bears learn the location of these camps and seek them out: They know that people and food go together. Park authorities respond by providing a safety net for hikers—separate your kitchen from your sleeping area, put food in a tree, and so on. Wilderness managers have a responsibility to protect you, not your food!

River camps, on the other hand, are passing fancies. Remote-area sites may be occupied only a few times each season, which isn't enough to encourage bad habits. Finally, be

[4] *Wall Street Journal*, 1999.

aware that bears are intimidated by large groups of people. The sight and sound of four or more noisy paddlers will discourage most bears.

You'll find more information about bears in the abovementioned books. Complete references are in appendix B.

MORNING

A good morning just doesn't happen; it's the result of good planning the night before! It's no fun fumbling through packs in twilight to locate food, cookware, or stove fuel. And if you've got to search for things in rain, your problems will be compounded. (See color figure 12-14.)

So begin your morning the night before. Get fresh water, filling your largest pot and plastic water jug. Set these together in the middle of your cooking area or under your rain tarp or tent vestibule. Then clean and gas the stove and put it in a convenient place along with your dishes and eating utensils.

Now comes a monumentous decision: "What's for breakfast?" When you've decided that, find the right meal and set it at the top of a food pack so you won't have to search for it when you arise. If you'll need cooking oil, coffee or the like, get these foods and pack them in the nylon breakfast bag. And while you're at it, ferret out the next day's lunch. Take some time now and organize this meal. Invariably lunch will require food, such as jam, peanut butter, or margarine, that have been packed separately in large containers. Combine all your lunch foods into the nylon lunch bag so you'll have one unit to pull out of your pack when it's time to eat. Rotating the peanut butter, jam bottle, and so forth from lunch to lunch is a daily evening routine.

Put your lunch sack in the pack along with breakfast. Then seal the pack and set it under your cooking fly. You did rig a nylon rain tarp, didn't you? You should, even if it doesn't look like rain. A heavy dew will dampen anything that isn't covered—and if it does rain, breakfast can go on as planned.

If you're camped in a popular spot where bears are a concern, hide your food packs in the woods, as suggested in the previous section. Bears walk the shoreline in search of carrion, so don't put food right under their nose. Ditto any spots near trails, streams, and meadows. Setting a well-sealed (no odors!) food pack in deep brush away from traveled areas is enough. I have never had a problem.

Next, fine-tune your rain tarp. Attach one or two *brightly colored* (so you won't trip over them) guylines to the main ridge line and stake these lines to the ground in front of the fly. The lines will keep the tarp from billowing and becoming a kite if a big wind blows up while you sleep. If you sense a storm brewing, drop the ridge line a foot or two and add more guylines. Then turn your attention to the tents. Nylon fabrics and cord stretch when the temperature drops and dampness sets in. You may have to tighten guylines and reset stake points. Better to do it now than at midnight in a driving rain.

While you're tuning tents, take a hard look around the campsite. Is everything under wraps? Half-dry laundry will only get wetter if it's left out, so put damp things under the tarp or in your tent vestibule. You can resume drying them in the morning when the sun comes out. Or run a tight clothesline (parachute cord) under your tarp and hang the clothes from diaper pins. *Tip:* Diaper pins have a multitude of uses on a canoe trip.

Check the canoes. Are they tied to a tree or boulder, bellies facing *upwind*? What—no trees or boulders to tie to? No problem; tie the boats to each other—parallel, gunnel to gunnel. Tilt each paired canoe opposite the other so wind can't turn them into kites.

My last chore before I retire is to pack everything I won't need when I arise—extra clothing, camp shoes, hand ax, saw, first-aid kit, and so on. The more time you can save organizing things now, the less you'll have to do in the morning.

Now that you've got everything under control, you can settle down to the warmth of your sleeping bag and visions of what tomorrow will bring.

Here's the procedure upon awakening: Pack all personal gear—sleeping bag and foam pad, clothing, the works—*before* you exit your tent. When you make your grand entry to the newborn day—a matter of perhaps 10 minutes—take everything with you and set it in a pile under the vestibule or alongside the tent (unless it's raining, of course).

Though you're still bleary-eyed, ferret out the stove and fire it up. Put water on to boil.

That accomplished, stagger down to the river's edge and splash some chilled champagne-clear water on your face, neck, arms. Wow! Now you're ready to embrace the day.

Then to work. Pull the ground cloth out of your tent and fold it neatly. Pack your Duluth pack—sleeping bag and foam pad on the bottom, nylon clothes bag next, then camp shoes and sundries, finally your ground cloth. Next, drop your tent.

Stuff your tent, don't roll it! Rolling takes far too much time. So what if the tent's wet from an all-night rain? It'll dry when you pitch it that evening. If not, you've got a *dry* groundsheet to put inside.

Check the stove. Water boiling? It should be. About twenty minutes have passed since you emerged from your tent—just about the time required to boil a gallon of water on a good stove.

Set out the breakfast bars and oatmeal, beef jerky, tea, and honey. And shut off that mindless stove—the noise is driving everyone crazy! While the water's hot, charge your thermos bottles with tea, soup, or whatever. Use what water is left in the pot for breakfast . . . and don't forget to save some to wash the dishes.

I pack insulated cups and bowls and a metal spoon for each person so there's not much to wash. Everyone washes their own breakfast dishes: They just swish some water in their bowls and cups and dry them with the four sheets of paper toweling I pack with each breakfast and supper meal. Trash goes in a plastic-lined nylon sack to be fished out and burned in the evening.

Bellies full and sun's arisin'—everyone finished packing and readies the canoes. The cook puts away the stove and cook set and places that day's lunch beneath the flap of the pack basket so he or she will know exactly where to find it when the pangs of hunger strike at high noon.

Obviously, more exotic breakfasts take more time, but the general procedure is still the same. Getting out in the morning should never take more than ninety minutes.

Let's summarize the time savers: Stuff sleeping bags, tents, and rainflies—don't roll them.

Use quick-release knots and hitches on all your tent lines and tarp.

Have a method to your madness: Know the exact order you plan to do things. Remember, it takes at least fifteen minutes to produce boiling water for your crew, so fire up your stove first thing, not after you've completed half your packing.

If my procedures seem too military for a good time, consider this: If it takes you sixty minutes to get out in the morning under ideal conditions, it'll take twice that long when the weather is really bad. So unless you want to waste away the day doing camp chores, you'd best develop an efficient, orderly system. An early start means an early camp: time to fish, hike, photograph, and do all the things you planned. And there's no contesting that good morning habits set the tone for the day, if not the voyage. Have a good morning and you'll have a good day!

HYGIENE

Misery sets in fast if you don't keep your body and cookware clean and free of bacteria. Here are some tricks:

- **To sterilize dishes and eating utensils:** It's hard to get dishes squeaky-clean on a canoe trip. You can sterilize them (after washing) by adding a splash of chlorine bleach to the final rinse water. Or add a convenient Effersan (appendix B) tablet. Effersan tablets have 30 percent available chlorine in a handy dry form. Half a tablet in a gallon of lukewarm water kills just about everything.

  I also bring a bottle of Preventx hand sanitizer (appendix B) and ask the cooks to use it before they prepare meals. Preventx is nontoxic and alcohol-free, so you can disinfect the cutting board before you cut the cheese! A new spray bottle simplifies kitchen chores. The product also soothes itching, poison ivy, athlete's foot, and minor cuts and abrasions. Its aloe vera formula is very soothing to the skin.

- **Bathing:** Bathing can be a chore if the weather or water is cold. But you can bathe on shore (even in your tent!) if you use N/R Laboratories' No Rinse Body Bath and Shampoo (appendix B). Just apply the product to your hair or skin (the Body Bath should be diluted with water) and lather up. Then towel—dry—no rinsing needed. No Rinse cleaning products were first used on hospitalized patients who could not bathe normally. Now NASA's astronauts have discovered their merits.

  Sharon Chatterton, who lives with Dick Person in a log cabin in the Yukon, suggests that you bring a small body brush. If you can't bathe, rub the brush briskly over your body and you'll feel like a new person.

- **Personal chafing and itching** can be miserable, especially on long, sweaty days when you're confined to the canoe for hours. I pack antibacterial moist towelettes (Wash'n Dry and Wash-up are two popular products) with my toilet paper. They help prevent problems and they keep underwear clean. You can buy moist towelette's at most grocery and discount stores. They come in handy individual sized packets.

A sprinkle of cornstarch or medicated foot powder soothes chafing and itching. Or try Gyne-Lotrimin—a nonprescription medication that's used to treat women's yeast infections. This soothing cream works great for men too!

- **The call of nature:** A urine bottle is so important it should probably have been listed in chapter 8 as essential equipment. In the middle of the night or when the weather howls bloody murder and you're confined to your tent for hours, a bottle is the only way to go. A *well-labeled* (I use pink surveying ribbon), two-liter rectangular (so it won't roll around in the tent) poly bottle seems to work best. The cap should have a leash. If you put the leash on the bottle upside down, then twist the cap right-side up to seal, the cap will spring away—and stay away—from the bottle when you use it.

  Rinse the bottle with fresh water every day, if you can. Wash it with detergent and hot water when you get home.

  Women may also want to bring a Sani-fem device, which simplifies urination. In typical mixed-gender tripping situations, men just walk a few yards out of camp and turn their backs. Women usually prefer more privacy. A woman can easily go in a tent vestibule or canoe if she has a Sani-fem and urine bottle.

- **Small cuts** on dirty hands can become infected fast. I keep two Band-Aids and two hygienic cleansing pads in a shirt pocket. I clean and bandage cuts immediately.

KNOTS

Most canoeists never learn to use their ropes effectively. As a result, it takes them far longer than necessary to rig (or drop) a snug camp. Sophisticated canoe rescue procedures require a working knowledge of knots and hitches; an overhand knot just won't do for everything!

Superior knowledge of rope-handling techniques is the expert's edge in camp or canoe.

Here are some of the most useful knots and hitches.

QUICK-RELEASE DOUBLE HALF HITCH

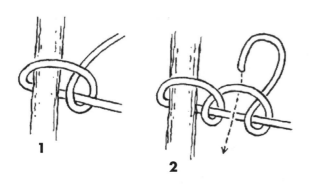

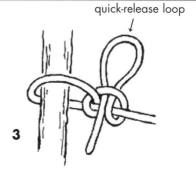

quick-release loop

1

2

3

Figure 12-15. Use the quick-release double half hitch whenever you want to secure a rope to a tree or boulder. It tightens under a load yet releases instantly.

QUICK-RELEASE SHEETBEND

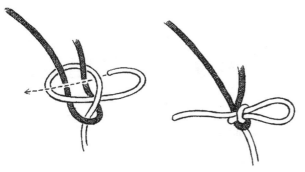

Figure 12-16. The quick-release sheetbend is the best knot to use whenever you want to tie two ropes together. Be sure the free ends of the ropes are on the side illustrated or the knot may slip. This knot is handy for rigging rainflies, extending clothesline and tent guylines and the like.

DOUBLE SHEETBEND

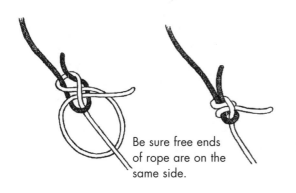

Be sure free ends of rope are on the same side.

Figure 12-17. The double sheetbend is more secure than the single sheetbend shown in figure 12-16. Use it when ropes are very dissimilar in size or will be subjected to a severe load. This is the knot to use when you want to extend the length of a tracking line. It absolutely, positively will not slip!

POWER CINCH OR TRUCKER'S HITCH

Figure 12-18. The power cinch or Trucker's Hitch is a quick-release, single-pulley knot that's useful whenever you need a combination knot and pulley. I use it for tying canoes on cars, tightening clotheslines, rigging rain tarps, and guying tents. Since it's a very powerful hitch, it has many applications in canoe rescue work (see chapter 17, Hazards and Rescue).

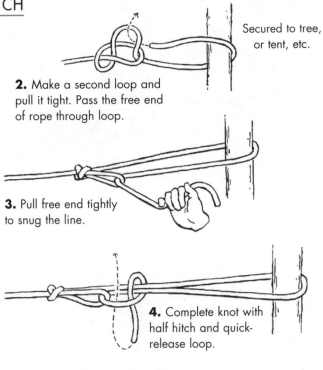

Secured to tree, or tent, etc.

2. Make a second loop and pull it tight. Pass the free end of rope through loop.

3. Pull free end tightly to snug the line.

4. Complete knot with half hitch and quick-release loop.

free end (around tree)

1. Make a loop

5. Snug hitch tightly. (A single pull on the free end releases the hitch instantly.)

BUTTERFLY NOOSE

Twist the loop as indicated, fold it up, pull it down through the center.

Figure 12-19. Climbers use the butterfly noose to attach carabiners or wherever they need a nonslip loop in the middle of a rope. These loops are secure and will accommodate a load in any direction. Butterfly loops can be spaced along a line to provide purchase points for a winch line—essential in canoe rescue work.

PRUSSIK KNOT

Figure 12-20. Use the prussik knot whenever you want an absolutely secure loop that won't slip along a tight line. Mountaineers use this knot to help them climb a vertical rope. I've found it's useful for rigging rainflies and for canoe rescue. Make a loop from a length of parachute cord, tied with a sheetbend or fisherman's knot.

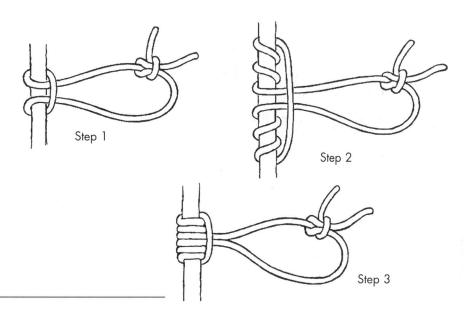

Step 1

Step 2

Step 3

FISHERMAN'S KNOT

Single fisherman's knot

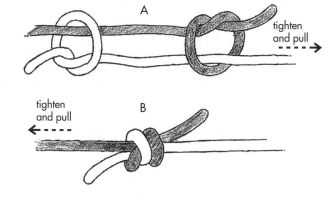

A

tighten and pull

tighten and pull

B

Double fisherman's knot

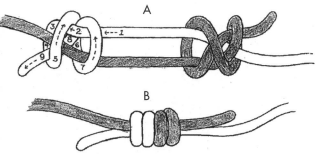

A

B

Figure 12-21. Climbers use the double fisherman's knot for making prussik slings, tying rope to climbing nuts, and joining unequal-sized ropes. (I prefer the sheetbend for this purpose.) The single fisherman's knot is good enough for most canoeing applications, but the double version (coil an extra loop around the main line) is the secure way to go when you can't afford a failure.

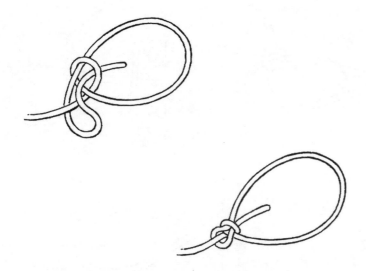

Figure 12-22. Use a bowline whenever you want a nonslip loop. The bowline won't jam under the heaviest load, and it's absolutely secure. The bowline is the mountain climber's most essential knot.

Figure 12-23. Tie your lining ropes to the canoe with a bowline. Finish with two half hitches on the loop for extra security.

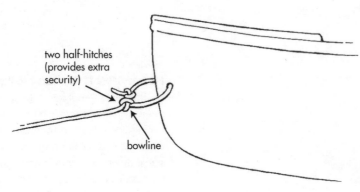

two half-hitches (provides extra security)

bowline

CHAPTER 13

NAVIGATING WITH MAP, COMPASS, AND GPS

The 40-mile lake was dead-calm; not the faintest breeze rippled the water. An hour of aimless paddling failed to bring into perspective a single identifiable ground feature. Sundown and subtle reality. We were lost!

Reluctantly we put ashore at the tip of a peninsula to check things out. I unfolded the map sheet on the ground, went round robin for suggestions—anything that might help unravel the mystery. But it was no use. We could agree on nothing!

I dug out the stove. We were too weary to think straight; perhaps some tea and brandy would clear our minds. Later I walked out to a high rock point and began to shoot compass bearings to distant islands in hopes of triangulating our position.

An hour later we discovered the problem—a simple misinterpretation of the map. Evidently we'd paddled through a narrow opening in what was shown on the map to be a contiguous land mass. Had water levels been a foot lower when the camera shot the aerial photo from which the map was drawn, there'd be no channel—just a pile of boulders. Instead of canoeing around the big island as we supposed we'd gone through it!

Pretty dumb, huh? Not really. Mistakes like this happen among the most experienced canoeists. The important thing is not to panic or keep trucking aimlessly down the lake in the hope that blind luck will see you through. Better to resort to sophisticated compass skills, confidence . . . and patience.

EQUIPMENT FIRST

The map! Enough has been said about the importance of good maps that you're sure to have the best. The compass is another matter. A lot of canoeists still take to the wilds with antiquated dial or hunter-style compasses when they should be carrying liquid-filled orienteering compasses.

Crossing a complex lake often requires precise directions, and therefore an accurate instrument with a built-in protractor to compute them. Orienteering compasses, like those made by Silva, Suunto, and Brunton score A+ in both categories. They permit computation of true directions from a map *without* orienting the map to north—a real advantage when you've got your hands full paddling a canoe. Don't sell the little plastic orienteering compasses short: Even the least-expensive models are capable of consistent accuracy within 2 degrees of an optical transit!

For the greatest accuracy when sighting (orienteering compasses aren't sighted; they're held waist-high and pointed) and for computing map directions, select an instrument with a base plate at least 3 inches

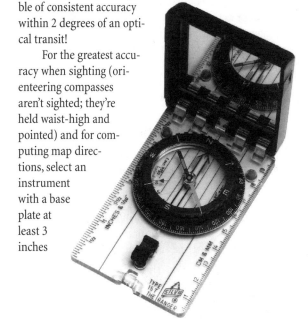

Figure 13-1. The orienteering compass permits computations of true directions from a map *without* orienting the map to north—a real advantage when you've got your hands full paddling a canoe. This is a Silva Ranger.

long. Long-base compasses point more naturally than short-base ones and are more efficient protractors.[1]

DECLINATION

In Alaska and most parts of Canada, there's quite a discrepancy between true (geographic) north and magnetic north (where the compass needle points).[2] This variation between the two norths is called declination and it's something you'll need to consider if you want to avoid serious navigational blunders when you use your compass.

A line of 0 declination—called the Agonic line—runs roughly from the true North Pole through Churchill, Manitoba; south to Thunder Bay, Ontario; and down through Indiana and Florida. If you're east of this line, your compass will point west to compensate for the earth's magnetic field (west declination), and if you're west of the line, it will point east (east declination). Obviously, the farther you get from the Agonic line, the greater the declination. In the eastern and western regions of northern Canada, declinations may reach 40 degrees and more!

Failure to account for declination can lead to serious problems. For example, the declination on the Aylmer map sheet (figure 13-3), as indicated in the rectangle below, is $32\frac{1}{2}$ degrees east. Mathematically, 1 degree of compass error equals 92 feet per mile of ground error. Compound a $32\frac{1}{2}$-degree variation over a 1-mile distance and you'll miss your objective by 2,900 feet (92 x $32\frac{1}{2}$) or more than $\frac{1}{2}$ mile!

Dealing with Declination

The numerical value of the declination is indicated in the margin of all topographic maps. It may be portrayed as a series of curved lines as on the Aylmer map, or in a standard declination diagram like that in figure 13-4. Diagrams are ordinarily used only when the declination holds constant for the entire map sheet, which unfortunately isn't always the case. The declination spread shown on the Aylmer quadrangle is quite typical for maps of this latitude and longitude.

You'll understand declination much better if you learn these definitions:

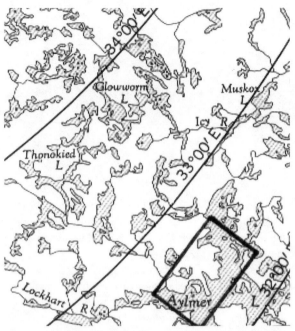

Figure 13-2. Declination diagram for the Aylmer Lake map on the facing page (figure 13-3). The declination of the compass needle from the 1963 Aylmer Lake quadrangle (figure 13-3) is decreasing 7.5 minutes annually.

- **True north:** The actual direction of the geographic North Pole. Lines of longitude—the values of which are indicated in the upper and lower map margins—indicate the direction of true north and south.

- **Magnetic north:** The direction of the north magnetic pole. A compass doesn't actually point to magnetic north; it really lines up with the earth's north–south magnetic field.

- **Grid north:** The direction of the grid lines on the map. Topographic maps *do not* have lines of longitude imprinted on their face, but they do have grid lines. The two are not the same! When you peel the skin off a globe (earth) and lay it flat, you distort the curved meridians. This distortion, or variation from true north, is reported in all declination diagrams (see figure 13-4).

[1]The procedures suggested in this chapter, while quite elementary, assume you've mastered the basics of using a map and orienteering compass. If you need a refresher course, see my books *Canoeing & Camping: Beyond the Basics* (Globe Pequot, 2000), and *Basic Essentials: Map and Compass* (Globe Pequot, 1999). You may also want to read Bjorn Kjellstrom's fine book *Be Expert with Map and Compass* (appendix B).

[2]The north magnetic pole is currently located about 1,000 miles south of the true North Pole—on Bathurst Island (100 degrees west longitude).

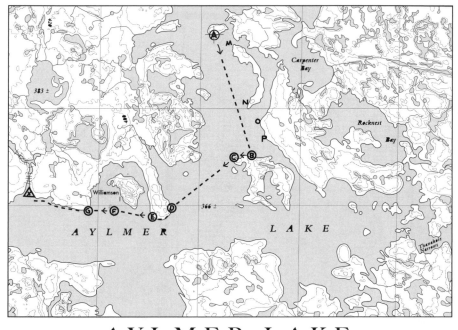

AYLMER LAKE

Scale 1:250,000 Échelle

Miles 5   0   5   10   15   20 Mille

Kilometres 5   0   5   10   15   20   25   30 Kilométres

Figure 13-3. Your true north–south reference line is the 108°00' east map border of longitude (lower right-hand corner). *Do not use the grid lines;* they point to grid north, which in this case is 3 degrees to the east of true north. You must correct the grid lines for declination before you can use them for navigation. The next section shows how. Figure 13-2 gives the declination for this map sheet.

■ **Azimuth:** An azimuth is a direction. More precisely, it's a horizontal clockwise angle measured from north (true, grid, or magnetic) to the direction of travel. If the measurement is taken from true north, it's a true azimuth; if made from magnetic north, it's a magnetic azimuth; and if determined from grid north, a grid azimuth.[3] Diagrammatic comparisons are shown in figure 13-5.

Bearing is a nautical term that relates the degree reading east or west of a north–south reference line. A bearing compass is divided into four quadrants of 90 degrees each. It is *not* numbered from 0 to 360 degrees, as is the standard azimuth compass. The following is a comparison of some azimuths and their equivalent bearings:

An azimuth of	Equals a bearing of
45°	N45°E (north 45 degrees east)
225°	S45°W (south 45 degrees west)
350°	N10°W (north 10 degrees west)

Bearings have an advantage when you compute reciprocal (back) directions. The back azimuth of 45 degrees is 225 degrees. But the back *bearing* of north 45 degrees east is simply south 45 degrees west. Surveyors, foresters, and professional people prefer bearings over azimuths and choose compasses that are calibrated accordingly.

When you use the protractor function (no magnetic needle) of your orienteering compass to compute a direction from one point to another off a map, you'll have to use one of the three norths as a reference.

[3]*Azimuth* and *bearing* are not the same, though the terms are commonly used interchangeably. *Azimuth* always relates to the 360 degrees of the compass dial. A numerical reading of, say, 20 degrees is technically a compass azimuth.

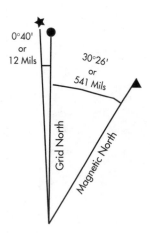

Figure 13-4. Standard declination.
Key:
- ★ The star: direction of true north
- ● The sphere: direction of grid north
- ▸ The flag: direction of magentic north

Magnetic declination indicated in this diagram is 31°06' east (30°26' + 0°40' = 30°66' or 31°06'). Information is also indicated in mils for use by the armed forces. There are 6,400 mils in the 360-degree compass rose (circle).

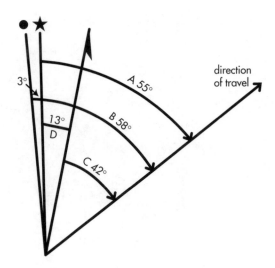

Figure 13-5.

- ★ = true north
- ● = grid north
- ▸ = magnetic north
- A: True azimuth of 55°
- B: Grid azimuth of 58°
- C: Magnetic azimuth of 42°
- D: Magnetic declination of 13° east

Note that azimuths are always measured clockwise!

When working from standard topographic maps, the true north direction is preferred. If your map has uniform UTM (Universal Transverse Mercator) grid lines, you'll want to use grid north. See Using UTM Coordinates and Your GPS later in the chapter. Magnetic north can be used as a map reference *only* when the magnetic north–south meridians are overprinted on the map sheet—which is *never* on standard topographic and military maps.

Establishing a True North–South Reference Line on Your Map

The east west neat lines (lines of longitude at the east and west map borders) are defined by geodetic meridians and therefore give the direction of true north and south. If you use either of these lines as a north–south reference when determining true azimuths from your map, you'll be right on target. Almost.

The direction of true north is not constant across a given map because the meridians converge toward the north (see figure 13-6). So if you want to know the precise direction of true north for a specific area of the map sheet, you'll have to plot a line of longitude across it. That's easy enough—just connect the tick marks of equal longitude at the bottom and top map borders and you'll have a true north–south line. The direction of true north indicated in a standard declination diagram is accurate *only* for the center of the map sheet.

Invariably, the neat lines at the map borders are good enough. The error from map edges to center seldom amounts to more than 2 degrees. Don't make the mistake of assuming that the grid lines run true north–south. They almost never do! On the Aylmer map they point 3 degrees to the east of true north (as defined by the direction of the 108°00' line of longitude).

Now that you have a true north–south reference line, you can use your orienteering compass or a plastic protractor to compute true map azimuths. You may then use the declination information in the map margin to *change these true azimuths to magnetic ones that can be set on your compass.*

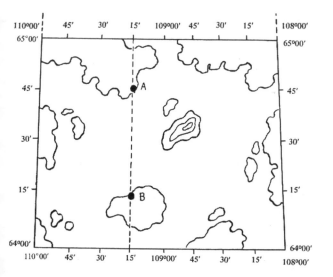

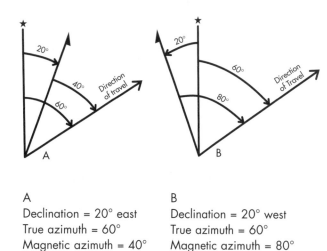

A
Declination = 20° east
True azimuth = 60°
Magnetic azimuth = 40°

B
Declination = 20° west
True azimuth = 60°
Magnetic azimuth = 80°

Figure 13-6. The actual true north direction is not constant across a given map but varies with the direction of the true north meridian as shown above. Any two points, such as A and B, selected on a common meridian should be on a true north line within the limit of map accuracy standards.

Figure 13-7. If you want to know the precise direction of true north for a specfic portion of the map sheet, simply plot a line of longitude across the map.

There are several ways to make the conversion:

- **The rhyme method:** Just apply the rhyme *Declination east, compass least; declination west, compass best.* Translation: If the declination indicated in the diagram is *east*, subtract its value from your true azimuth. If the declination is *west*, add it. Reverse the rhyme to convert magnetic azimuths to true ones.

  For example, assume you're located at point A on the Aylmer quadrangle. You've computed a true map azimuth of 160 degrees to point B. The declination is 32½ degrees east (we'll call it 33). Subtract 33 degrees from 160 degrees and you get 127 degrees—the value you should set on your compass and follow on the ground (lake).

  Similarly, if the declination were west, you'd add it for a value of 193 degrees (160° + 33° = 193°).

- **The diagram method:** Draw a representative diagram whose mathematics reflect the rhyme.

  Consider diagrams A and B above (figure 13-7).

The declination of A is 20 degrees east and the true azimuth determined from the map) is 60 degrees. The magnetic azimuth equals the difference—40 degrees. Since the declination flag is to the right (east)of true north, you'd get the same answer by applying the rhyme Declination east, compass least. Sixty degrees minus 20 degrees equals 40 degrees. The opposite situation is shown in diagram B.

If you remember that azimuths are *always measured clockwise,* you'll have no trouble with your diagrams.

- **Mechanical means:** I'm no math wizard, and when faced with the complexities of big lake travel, I need all the help I can get. That's why I stubbornly cling to my Silva Ranger compass, which has a built-in mechanical device for offsetting declination. I turn a tiny screw, which takes only a second, and the declination for the area is locked in to the compass. Problem solved!

- **Makeshift mechanical means:** You can adjust any orienteering compass for declination by sticking a narrow piece of tape across the face of the dial at an angle equal to the value of the declination.

For example, if the declination is 30 degrees east, set the tape so it passes through the 30-degree and 210-degree gradations on the compass dial. If the declination is 30 degrees west, apply the tape cross the 330-degree and 150-degree lines.

Use the compass per instructions to compute true azimuths from the map, then convert them to magnetic readings by aligning the compass needle with the tape rather than the printed arrow in the capsule (be sure you match the north end of the needle to the north end of the tape). Your compass will now point to your *magnetic* azimuth. If you have an orienteering compass, try the procedure. It's much less complicated than it sounds.

■ **Adjusting the map for declination:** This is easy enough—just draw lines across the map that are parallel to the direction of magnetic north. Then use these lines as magnetic north–south reference lines when you determine map directions. This will enable you to compute magnetic azimuths directly from the map without doing any mathematical calculations. Consult figure 13-8 for an example.

Declination lines are overprinted on all competitive orienteering maps.

My recommendation is that you buy a compass with a mechanical declination adjustment, or learn the rhyme. Either way you can't go wrong.

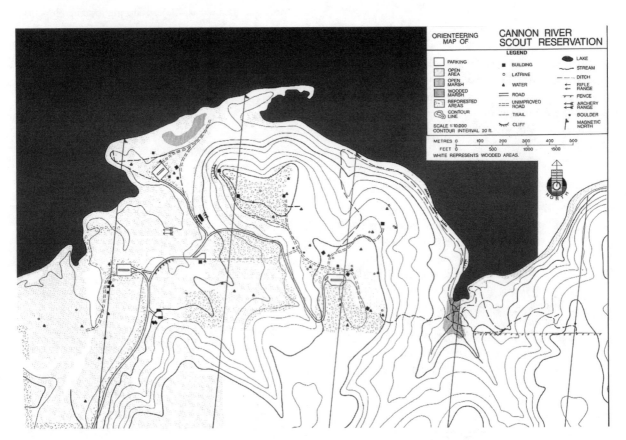

Figure 13-8. Competitive orienteering map adjusted for a magentic declination of 6 degrees east. Note the angle of the declination lines in relation to true north.

Updating the Declination

The magnetic poles are constantly moving. Their location changes from year to year (and minute to minute). Movements are subtle, however; they're generally small enough that only surveyors interested in extreme accuracy need worry about them.

Still, the problem will surface if you're working off a very old map like the Aylmer quadrangle shown in figure 13-3. Note that the declination information given in figure 13-3 is more than thirty years old (1963) and its value is *decreasing* 7$\frac{1}{2}$ minutes each year.

To update the data for 2001, multiply 7.5 minutes by 38 years. The answer is 285 minutes. Divide this figure by 60 minutes to convert it to degrees: 4.75 degrees. If you're canoeing in the boxed zone (declination 32.5 degrees), subtract 4.75 from 32.5. You get 27.75 degrees, or simply 28.

Remember, 1 degree of compass error equals 92 feet per mile of ground error. A 5-degree error over a 1-mile distance could cause you to miss your objective by 460 feet. That may be enough to send you down the wrong channel if you're threading your way through thick fog.

There's a common misconception that due to the large declinations in the Far North, magnetic compasses are generally worthless. Hogwash! It makes no difference if the variation[4] is 3 degrees or 30—*as long as you know what it is and apply it correctly.*

Granted, there's some inconvenience when values vary considerably across a single map sheet. Even so, the difference seldom amounts to more than 5 degrees—nothing to worry about if you keep your compass shots relatively short (less than a mile or two) and aim off to minimize errors.

AIMING OFF

Aiming off is an orienteering term. The idea is to introduce a calculated error in a *known direction* into your travels. For example: Assume you're located at point A on the Aylmer map (figure 13-3). Your objective is X—the rapid-filled river.

Let's face it. The best way to get around the horn to X is to proceed directly to W then follow the shoreline of the land mass south and west, jumping the wide bays.

But wait! You've heard that the northwest tip of the island at C has a marvelous *level* campsite—room for a dozen tents! That's worth going a bit out of your way for. The lake is dead-calm and the weather is foggy but stable, so you plot a beeline to the middle of the island at B. Why B? Shouldn't you strike a course directly to C?

Look at the map scale. The island is nearly 8 miles away-too far to see from your location, fog or no fog. And the limited visibility definitely complicates matters; there's some likelihood you could pass the island without seeing it if your azimuth to C is even a few degrees in error to the west. To be safe, you should aim off for the center of the island B rather than its easy-to-miss northwest corner. When you reach the island, just paddle west along the north shore until you come to C. You can't go wrong![5]

Aiming off is an important navigational procedure. It enables you to rely heavily on your watch. If you figure a travel speed of 4 miles per hour (reasonable for a loaded wilderness canoe), you should hit the island in very nearly two hours. If your ETA passes and there's no island in sight, put ashore immediately and try to determine where you goofed. If you continue to paddle down the lake, you'll only compound your error.

Getting from C to X is academic. Simply plot a compass course from one recognizable attack point (island, peninsula, bay) to another. Then follow your course religiously and keep accurate track of your time. Reaffirm your position at each attack point and you won't get lost!

You may want to check your own navigational skills by computing the magnetic azimuth and travel line to the alphabetical attack points on the map. Answers are on the next page.

TRIANGULATION

Assume you're lost somewhere in Whigam Lake (figure 13-9). To find your position by triangulation, shoot magnetic compass directions to two or more points that you can identify on both the map and ground (a hilltop, channel, bay, the mouth of a river, end of an esker, fire tower, gravel bar, or the like) and plot the *reciprocal* azimuths of these points on your map. You're located where the lines cross.

In the example: The magnetic azimuth to island A with its large identifiable hill equals 70 degrees. The magnetic azimuth to the high hill at B equals 119 degrees.

[4]Variation is a seafaring synonym of declination.

[5]This example is for illustrative purposes only. It would be much safer and almost as fast to proceed to C via M–N–O–P–B than to cut straight across the lake as suggested. It's never a good idea to span large sections of open water in a canoe, even when the weather is favorable.

TABLE 13-1

From	True azimuth	Magnetic azimuth (2001 decl. equals 28° E)	Distance (miles)	Travel time/hours (4 miles per hour)
A–B	161°	131°	8	2 hours
B–C	Follow shoreline	—	—	—
C–D	229°	201°	5	1 hour 15 minutes
D–E	Follow shoreline	—	—	—
E–F	278°	250°	2.5	About 40 minutes
F–G	270°	247°	2	30 minutes
G–H	Follow shoreline	—	—	—

First, convert these magnetic azimuths to true azimuths so you can plot them on the map. By reverse application of the rhyme *(Declination east, compass least)*, you get:

A: 70° + 22° (value of the declination) = 92°
B: 119° + 22° = 141°

Now plot the *reciprocal* of these true azimuths on the map.

Reciprocal of 92° = 272° (180° plus 92°)
Reciprocal of 141° = 321° (180° plus 141°)

Draw the lines. You're located at O.

For greatest accuracy choose triangulation points that are at least 30 degrees apart. And the more points you can shoot at, the more precisely you'll pinpoint your position.[6]

Free Triangulation

Establishing your location along a river is easier than on a lake, because the river provides a free triangulation line. For example, assume you want to determine your position along the river in figure 13-10. Your compass reveals that the large hill to your right is at a magnetic azimuth of 34 degrees. Convert this value to a true direction by adding the declination (34° + 22° = 56°). Then determine the reciprocal (56° + 180° = 236°) and plot it on the map. You're located where the line crosses the river.

Let's summarize what we've learned:

■ If you don't want to get lost on a complex lake, know exactly where you are at all times. Check your map

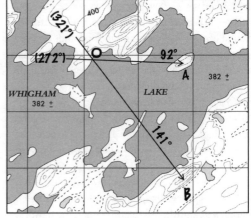

Magnetic declination = 22° East.

Figure 13-9.

1. Determine *magnetic* compass azimuths to two or more recognizable points.
2. Convert the readings to *true* azimuths by reverse application of the rhyme.
3. Plot the *reciprocal* values of these true azimuths on the map.
4. You're located where the lines cross.

[6]Once you become skilled in using the orienteering compass, you'll discover you can draw triangulation lines without making mathematical computations. See my book *Basic Essentials: Map & Compass* for the mechanics of this procedure.

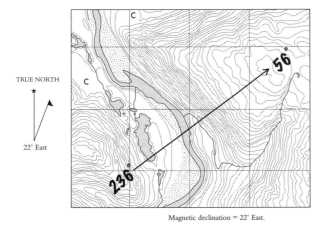

Magnetic declination = 22° East.

Figure 13-10. Free triangulation: You're located where the line crosses the river.

and compass frequently; you can become confused easily in fog or by paddling around or between islands.

- Don't expect to correctly interpret ground features that are very far away. A mile is about the limit of accurate perception, even in good light.

- Keep your compass shots as short as possible, and aim off to minimize the chance of error.

- *Believe* your compass. It won't fail you if you use it correctly and apply the appropriate declination. Contrary to popular belief, a compass is reliable in the Far North.

USING UTM COORDINATES AND YOUR GPS

If you've ever tried to plot a GPS position on a map to the nearest 100 yards using degrees, minutes, and seconds of latitude and longitude, you know it isn't easy. That's because latitude and longitude are not a rectangular grid—the distance between longitude lines varies as you go north or south. Of course, there are tools (templates) that will help you interpolate intermediate numbers, but they're a hassle to use and one more thing to lose on a canoe trip. It would be far easier to plot a precise fix if the grid lines were rectangular (no convergence).

Enter the Universal Transverse Mercator (UTM) grid. It is perfectly rectangular, and coordinate values are in meters. UTM coordinates are referenced and/or overprinted on all U.S. and Canadian topographic maps. Almost any GPS—even the least expensive models—can be set to read them.

Figure 13-11. Universal Tranverse Mercator grid.

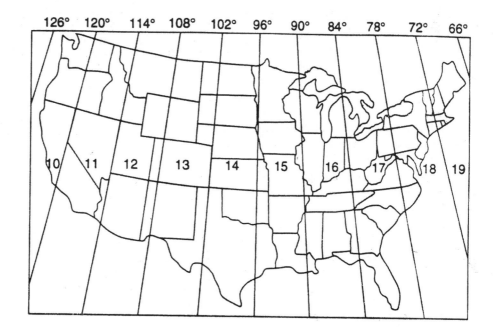

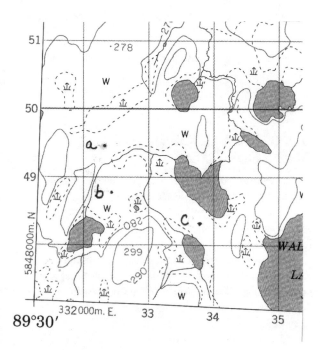

51
·278
W
50
a.
W
49
b.
W
299
c.
290
W
332000m. E.   33   34   35
89°30'
5848000m N

Figure 13-12.

What Is UTM?

UTM divides the world into sixty zones. Each zone spans 6 degrees of longitude and 164 degrees of latitude (it covers from 80 degrees south latitude to 84 degrees north latitude). Zone 1 lies between the 180-degree and 174-degree west meridians, and the zone numbers wrap eastward around the earth. Zones 10 through 19 cover most of the U.S. and Canada (see figure 13-11). Lettered bands of latitude (not shown in figure 13-11) divide the zones. Bands N through X (skipping O to avoid confusion with zero) are in the Northern Hemisphere. The letters increase alphabetically as you go north. A central meridian runs through the middle of each 6-degree-wide zone and is assigned an arbitrary (false) easting value of 500,000 meters (to avoid using negative numbers). Thus the grid values to the west of each central meridian have

an easting value of less than 500,000 meters; those to the east of each central meridian have an easting value of more than 500,000 meters.[7]

To specify a point you give its distance in meters from the false east origin (easting), and from the equator (northing).[8] All this is unnecessarily academic. To use your GPS with UTM coordinates you simply need to know the *hemisphere and zone in which you are traveling,* the *horizontal map datum,* and *how to read the coordinates.*

Zone Numbers

You'll find the zone number in the margin of every map. It is expressed as a number (for example,16) on U.S. topographic maps, and as a number followed by a row letter on U.S. military maps and Canadian topographic maps. For example, the map section shown in figure 13-12 is in Zone 16U, which is in Ontario, Canada. If you use map coordinates to initialize your GPS or program a waypoint, you'll have to specify the zone *number and hemisphere* (northern or southern). Some GPS units allow you to set the complete zone designation (16U, for instance).

Map Datums

A datum is part of a shape that best fits the part of the world that's indicated on your map. The earth is not a uniform ball, so certain datums provide a truer picture than others for some portions of the earth's surface. Essentially, the map datum tells your GPS what "earth shape" the map is using. The datum is printed on the bottom of all topographic maps. The three most popular datums are *North American Datum 1927* (NAD 27), *World Geodetic System of 1984* (WGS 84), and *North American Datum 1983* (NAD 83). There are hundreds of datums, and most GPS units will read the most popular ones. If you use the wrong datum, your GPS won't provide an accurate fix. If you set up your GPS to use latitude and longitude, a datum error may result in a map error of as much as 200 meters in North America. But a datum error with UTM coordinates is more serious—up to 300 meters in North America. In short, you'd better use the right datum, especially if you use the UTM system.

[7] The false east origin is a line exactly 500,000 meters *west* of the zone's central meridian. Within each zone the same coordinate value can represent either the Southern or the Northern Hemisphere—that's why you must specify the hemisphere when you use your GPS.

[8] Points south of the equator are handled differently: In order to have northing values increase going from south to north (and to avoid negative numbers), the equator is given a false northing value of 10 million meters. So in the Southern Hemisphere, the northing value represents the distance of the point (in meters) from a false origin that is 10 million meters south of the equator.

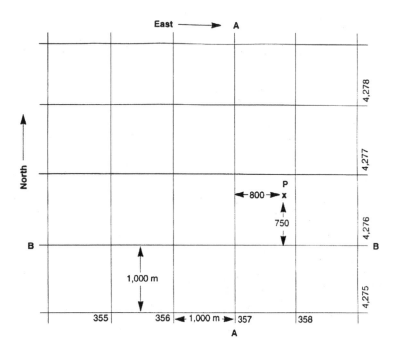

Figure 13-13.
Reading the coordinates

When you enter a waypoint on your GPS, the GPS puts it into memory under the WGS 84 datum (its default datum) after first converting it from the datum you have currently chosen. If you later choose a different datum, your GPS will translate the coordinates and display them in the new datum you selected.

Reading the Coordinates

Figure 13-13 illustrates how to read the coordinates. The grid value (easting) of line A–A would be reported as 357,000 meters east (A–A is actually 143,000 meters west of its central meridian). Line B–B is 4,276,000 meters north of the equator. Point P is 800 meters east of line A–A and 750 meters north of line B–B.[9]

Thus the complete UTM designation of point P (to the nearest meter) is 357800E / 4276750N.[10] If there are an odd number of digits, it's because the preceding zero in the easting value has been dropped. The zero will appear on the display of your GPS. Some GPS units will also display the complete zone designation (such as 15T). The rule is to read it *right up*, which means you should read the easting value first and the northing value second. Strangely, some GPS units list the northing values first.

See if you can determine the UTM coordinates of points a, b, and c on the map in figure 13-12. Eyeball them—don't use a metric ruler or coordinate roamer.[11] (You probably won't have one when you're canoeing.) Note that the first easting digit and the first two northing digits on the map are smaller than those that follow. These secondary numbers represent millions and hundreds of thousands of meters, so they are reduced in size to eliminate confusion. They are omitted on military maps, which use the Military Grid Reference System (MGRS), a slight modification of UTM.[12] The downsized numbers will automatically show up on your GPS.

Answers:
a) 332300E / 5849500N or [03]32300E / [58]49500N.
b) 332400E / 5848800N or [03]32400E / [58]48800N.
c) 333800E / 5848300N or [03]33800E / [58]48300N.

---

[9] I am indebted to the U.S. Geological Survey for use of this diagram, which appears on Fact Sheet 142-97.

[10] Technically, a complete UTM designation would include the zone number.

[11] For precision plotting, use an inexpensive plastic coordinate scale. Some orienteering-style compasses have UTM coordinate scales printed on the base plate.

[12] The military drops the small digits and uses a two-letter identifier to indicate the 100,000-meter square of operation.

The beauty of the UTM system is that you get a reasonably accurate canoeing fix by plotting just three numbers. Consider the position of point a: The boldfaced numbers 323/495 (33**32**300 / 58**49**500) indicate that you are three-tenth's (0.3) of a grid square east of line 32 and five-tenths (0.5) of a grid square north of line 49.

You'll go through batteries fast if you leave your GPS on for continuous positioning. Better to turn on the machine only when you need it. For example, suppose you've been on course for an hour but suddenly become confused among some islands. Just turn on the GPS and read the important three easting and northing numbers; you'll know right where you are.

If you mount your GPS on a stern thwart and keep your map beside it as suggested in chapter 6, you can fix your position without taking your hands off the paddle.

Checklist for Setting Up Your GPS

Initialize your GPS according to instructions. In the setup menu:

1. Define the coordinate system (UTM or latitude and longitude). I prefer UTM.

2. Select the correct horizontal datum for the map you are using.

3. Select which north—true or magnetic—your receiver will use as a reference. I prefer true north because GPS bearings (to waypoints) are in true map perspective. However, if you are confused by declination, select magnetic north. Then you can set the bearings that your GPS computes to waypoints directly on your thwart-mounted running compass without messing with math.

4. Set your GPS to read the same units (feet or meters) as your map. All Canadian maps are metric. Most American maps are in feet.

Reminder: Be sure you have programmed into your GPS the hemisphere and zone number (or complete number-and-letter zone designation) in which you are operating.

Tips and Concerns

■ Don't take GPS elevation readings seriously. The earth blocks enough important satellites to prevent accurate readings. Elevations can be off by several hundred feet! If you want accurate elevations, use the contour lines on your map.

■ Your GPS will convert UTM coordinates to latitude and longitude and vice versa. All you need to do is change the coordinate system in the setup menu. If you'll be doing a lot of conversions, you may want to use a computer program such as Tricon (Windows 95) or Geocon (DOS). These can be downloaded for free (http://rockyweb.cr.usgs.gov/software).

■ If you want to share UTM coordinate information with someone, be sure you reference your eastings and northings to the map sheet you're using. Technically, you should provide the horizontal datum, complete grid zone designation, and full easting and northing; for example, "NAD 27 /16U / 332,300E / 5,849,500N."

■ Most sailors and bush pilots don't understand UTM coordinates. Always use latitude and longitude when you report a fix to a floatplane pilot or powerboat captain. You can change latitude and longitude to UTM in seconds by redefining your coordinate preference in the setup menu of your GPS.[13]

BEAVER STREAMS AND MOOSE TRAILS

Finding your way through a maze of beaver streams and moose trails calls for resourcefulness. Modern maps are made almost entirely from aerial photos. And if you can't see the sky because of a too-dense tree canopy or tall grass, the plane-mounted camera certainly can't see the stream. Therefore, in these areas your map may be in error, though the general flow of the watercourse—minus the switchbacks—is usually accurate.

The heads and mouths of small streams are almost always plotted correctly, but deciphering the maze in between

---

[13] I am indebted to Michael Ferguson for his help in preparing this section. Michael's book *GPS Land Navigation* (Glassford Publishing, 1997) is the definitive text on GPS navigation.

often calls for a ready compass. Moreover, streambeds are constantly changing, and these changes will not be reflected on a topographic map that is many years old.

Some hints for navigating small meandering streams:

- Where a stream forks, take the route with the strongest flow even if it looks more restrictive than a broader channel. If there is no discernible current, note which way the grass bends in the channel and follow.

- Check your compass frequently; don't rely on your map, especially if it is many years old.

- If you come to a dead end and see a portage trail, scout it without your canoe and gear. Your "portage" may be an animal trail leading to a connecting tributary or a dead-end point.

It's beyond the scope of this chapter to provide a complete course in navigation. Even the advanced basics require more space than these pages provide. If you're really serious about canoeing complex waterways, you'll study one of the excellent books listed below. Then you'll get out and practice!

As you gain experience and develop your map interpretation skills you'll become less dependent on your compass for precise directions and more confident in your own visual acuity. But you'll never dismiss the importance of your compass or diminish its value as a route-finding aid.

Map, compass, perception, skill, confidence . . . these are the tools that ensure a confusion-free canoe trip.

SUGGESTED READING

Basic Essentials: Map & Compass, by Cliff Jacobson.
Canoeing and Camping: Beyond the Basics, by Cliff Jacobson.
GPS Land Navigation, by Michael Ferguson. This is by far the best book on GPS navigation.

Figure 13-14. Dead end. Following a moose trail in the Boundary Waters Canoe Area.

Be Expert with Map and Compass, by Bjorn Kjellstrom.
U.S. Geological Survey Fact Sheet 142-97, September 1997. Available from the USGS. For complete information on all these resources, see appendix B.

CHAPTER 14
PORTAGING

If a man can pack a heavy load across a portage, if he can do whatever he has to do with-
out complaint and with good humor, it makes no difference what his background has been.
And if he can somehow keep alive a spark of adventure and romance as the old time voyageurs
seem to have done, then any expedition becomes more than a journey through wild country. It
becomes a shining challenge and adventure of the spirit.

—Sigurd Olson, *The Lonely Land,* 1961

The ax-blazed spruce that juts from the riverbank indicates we have arrived at the portage. A 2-mile carry will see
us safely around the thundering cascades below. Dead-tired,
we haul the canoes and gear up the steep muddy bank to the
small clearing above. There is no argument where to camp.
This is the only level place around and it's near sundown.

Rain. We rig a hasty tarp, stack the packs beneath it ,
then all crowd in for a hit of schnapps and a hand in the decision making process. The consensus is to carry the boats and
food packs over the portage and pitch camp when we return.
Maybe by then the rain will have stopped.

I pick up the canoe and take off down the down the trail.
My friends follow close behind with the other canoe and
packs. It's easy going; we should be there in thirty minutes.
The path merges into a logging road that 1/4 mile later ends in
a tangled web of other roads. I drop one arm from the gunnel
of my canoe and pull out my compass. The map says to head
east, so I pick a road that runs roughly in that direction.
Thirty minutes pass with no sign of water. We continue
another fifteen minutes. Still nothing. At 8:30 P.M. we stop and
climb a small hill nearby for a better look. In the distance is
the river, but it's beyond a mass of tangled alders and swamp.

What we say now is unprintable. We've come too far—
way too far! Disgusted and weary, we shoulder our outfit and
backtrack the entire 2 1/2 miles to camp. We set up the tents in

total darkness and persistent rain. By mutual agreement we
refuse to discuss the portage. It can wait until tomorrow!

We find the trail easy enough the next day. It's just a
matter of careful map reading and diligent searching, unencumbered by canoes, pack, or the threat of darkness.

In the near-wilderness of the BWCA and Quetico, it's
common practice to carry the canoes and heavy packs over
the portage first and return for the lighter packs second time
around. On a wilderness river, where the trail is less sure,
you'll want to reverse this procedure or, better, partially (or
wholly) scout the way without a load.

If the trail looks good from the start, carry a light pack
and a couple of paddles across. This will give you freedom to
search out short cuts and alternate routes around obstacles
like fallen trees, washouts, and mud.

Portages are not always easy to find in remote country,
though the trend (unfortunately) is to mark them with
brightly colored metal signs or garish paint. Either method is,
in my opinion, an intrusion into the sanctity of the wilderness and my own sanity.

In places where there are no signs you'll find an ax blaze,
jutting pole, wide clearing . . . or garbage. I've seen ice cream
buckets, paint cans, plastic ribbons, broken paddles and
canoes, discarded boots, underwear, and, once, an old parking
meter used to mark portages. Humans are very creative.

Figure 14-1. The author portages his canoe around a dicey drop along the Burnside River, Nunavut, Canada.

The location of river portages as given in government trip guides often calls for considerable interpretation. For example, at high water the head of a portage may be dangerously close to the rapids below, while at low water you may have to clamber hundreds of yards over a dry boulder bed to reach it. Written descriptions of the specific whereabouts of portages must be tempered by an understanding of this relationship.

Searching out portages on a complex lake requires careful map reading, good compass skills, and a bit of luck. Portages are frequently plotted incorrectly on maps, so you'll want to aim off generously when you shoot compass bearings to them.

If you get confused on a large lake, head toward the nearest dip in the horizon that's in line with the suspected direction of your portage. Dips indicate channels or ravines, hence connecting links (portages) between waterways.

Being on the correct side of a dangerous river in your approach to the portage may be a matter of survival. Mix a $1/4$-mile-wide river with a 6- or 8-mile-an-hour current (quite common on tundra rivers during the summer runoff) and the ordinarily simple task of crossing from one bank to another takes on monumental proportions. You may be in real trouble if you've put ashore just above a major falls only to discover that the route around it is on the opposite bank. An error like this may mean an hour of upstream tracking (if the shoreline permits it) and a dangerous ferry across.

If your map shows a portage just ahead but gives no clue as to which side of the river it's on, select the shore with the lower relief (elevation) and/or lesser amount of vegetation. Rationale: Portages have been in use for centuries by Natives and explorers who, like you, had to get around obstacles in the river. Indians and voyageurs were no better at scrambling over canyon walls than you are. They took the path of least resistance, and so should you.

More often than not you'll find portages on the *inside* bends of rivers. This is merely a matter of energy economics: the shortest way to cut off a loop is from the inside. Only if the short route is very unforgiving do people purposely select the long way around.

PORTAGE LOGISTICS

Packs

Pack in *odd* units—that is, three or five packs per canoe, not two or four. This will equalize the number of trips you and your partner must make over the portage. Some canoeists can carry a pack and canoe at the same time, but it's a killer and a sure recipe for a sprain.

The same applies to double-packing—carrying two packs, one on your back, the other over your chest. Double-packing works well enough on the groomed trails of the BWCA and Allagash but it's out of place in the rough entan-

Figure 14-2. Portaging around Tipi Falls on the North Knife River, Saskatchewan.

Figure 14-3. Double-packing is dangerous because you can't see your feet or the trail ahead.

glements of a river portage. Indeed, you're aching for an accident if you carry something on your chest that obscures your view of the immediate trail. My rule on canoe trips is that everyone must be able to see his or her feet!

Paddles

Paddles should be hand-carried over the portage, not hauled inside the canoe as recommended by some experts. The reasons include:

- Weight. At around one and a half pounds per paddle, you'll be shouldering an additional four and a half to six pounds (three or four paddles per canoe). Doesn't sound too significant, but over the long haul it is!

- It's hard on canoe paddles. Every time you jam a paddle between seat and thwarts, you scrape off some var-

nish. Minor, perhaps, but still not the best way to treat fine equipment.

- Brightly varnished or painted paddles become highly visible markers for your gear when you set it along the portage trail. Drabness is a major reason why things are left behind or lost on portages. There's not much color among the scrub vegetation on a northern river. Set an olive-drab Duluth pack just off the trail in a maze of olive-drab vegetation and you may have a real search on your hands to locate it later.[1] But jam a paddle upright through the pack straps and you'll have an eye-catching flag to guide the way.

By the way, brightly colored equipment—packs, canoes, and clothing—is important in the North Country. It provides an edge against loss and brightens up your photographs.

Accountability

Each team should take responsibility for the gear in its canoe and inventory it at the end of *every* portage. To avoid confusion as to who has what, *don't* shift items from boat to boat after each carry. Instead, make equipment assignments on a daily basis. (See color figure 14-4.)

Loose Items

Except for camera bags, fishing rod cases, paddles, and gas cans,[2] there should be none! Shirts, rain gear, and the like should all be stuffed solidly into a pack sack or jammed under loops of shock cord strung through canoe thwarts. Unsecured gear is a sure recipe for loss on the portage trail or in a capsize.

Habits

Develop an unyielding system of packing and portaging equipment. If you always carry your two paddles and camera over the portage and always set your camera behind your seat, don't vary from this procedure. Clint Waddell reports that he and Verlen Kruger left the tail section of their canoe cover along a portage in northern Canada some 3,000 miles into their 7,000-mile trip. Two thousand miles later they forgot a folding saw when they broke camp. In both cases the men violated a habit. In the first instance it was dark and they

[1]Duluth Pack offers packs made from bleached white canvas on special request only. These packs are every bit as tough as the unbleached versions but are easier to keep track of on land and in the green of the river.

[2]I prefer to carry stove fuel in a plastic can *outside* my pack.

were in a hurry—Verlen assumed Clint had packed the cover, while Clint, who ordinarily took responsibility for it, thought the opposite. In the second case Verlen changed his packing system slightly one morning, which left no place for the saw he carried. He assumed Clint would get it.

Assumptions have no place on a wilderness canoe trip. Each person must communicate his or her intentions and stick solidly by them. Good habits are essential to prevent loss of equipment and ensure that you can find specific items when you need them.

COMFORT

You'll discover you can ease the pain of portaging if you occasionally drop one arm to your side as you carry the canoe. This transfers some of the weight of the canoe to the shoulder of the outstretched arm and gives your other shoulder a rest.

Another trick is to keep your outstretched arm straight, with the hand *reversed*—fingers touching the inwale, thumbs against the outwale. This position puts more muscle tissue in the critical zone and makes for a less painful carry.

Granted, my techniques—dropping an arm, reversing the hand, straight elbow—are aimed at the small-frame person who needs every portage advantage possible. Big men with brawny shoulders may rightfully scoff at my suggestions, though even they will gain some extra comfort by occasionally practicing these procedures.

There are times when portaging is downright drudgery—all you can think about is getting over the trail quickly! But often as not a portage is a welcome break from long hours of tedious paddling and the mental strain that accompanies running long stretches of difficult rapids. Portages are usually less numerous on the big rivers of the Far North than on the small waterways of the BWCA and Quetico. In fact, it's not uncommon to canoe for days on some northern routes without making a significant carry.

Even a really bad portage is seldom as ominous as trip guides and the testimonials of past voyageurs suggest. Canoeists have a long, proud history of exaggerating the difficulties (and dangers) of rivers. Perhaps it is the passage of time that clouds our view of reality when we report how things are. Or maybe we're just describing the river as we wish it was. (See color figure 14-5.)

CHAPTER 15
THE JOY OF SOLO CANOEING

It's silent, awesomely silent. And swift. With a mere touch of the paddle it turns. Instantly, precisely. It leans when you lean, slips aside willingly, goes on command. Like a dragonfly it skims across quiet water. Its bow entry, quick and sure, produces only the faintest murmur of parting water.

Confidently it twists its way down rock-strewn mountain streams, between the snags and deadheads of lazy river backwaters. Two and a half inches of water is enough to float it, cargo, crew, and all. And where the water ends and land begins it carries easily—thirty-five or forty pounds light, a load handled by anyone.

It goes where no other canoe can go, does what no other canoe can do. It has grace, style, and elegance unlike any other watercraft. It is, quite simply . . . the solo canoe.

The first two rapids indicated on the map were runnable. Just big waves, no problem. But shortly the mood of the river changed. Below us lay twelve pitches (about a mile) of substantial white water. The map indicated a gradient of 50 feet per mile!

"Let's line it on the left," suggested Paul. "No," I answered authoritatively; "let's portage on the right." After a heated debate we parted company—Paul to line, I to portage.

The portage trail wound tortuously upward—impossible to carry even my solo canoe over. For a short time I hauled the boat behind me with its bow tracking line, like a dog on a leash. It skidded over the rocks, hung up between trees. I sweated and strained. Cussed. It began to rain. For the first time mosquitoes appeared.

Finally I had had enough. Paul was right! Enviously, I watched him 75 feet below line the first pitch successfully. I was burning with sweat, delirious for a drink of cold water. I could take no more. I then did something very stupid. I decided to run the entire rapid—blind! Anything to get off this awful mountain. I strained my ears and listened for the roar of a falls, the hollow drone of a ledge. There was none. I again checked the map for signs of hidden dangers. It looked okay. This accomplished, I slid the canoe down the bluff into a

small eddy below. I adjusted the nylon spray cover then cautiously but determinedly paddled into the foamy white of the river.

The first drop was the largest—an exhilarating Class III run with big waves, unclear passages, and hundred of rocks to avoid. I drew hard, pulling the boat sideways to get into a clear channel ahead. But an unseen rock caught me dead-center at the port bilge. Instantly the canoe swung sideways and grounded on the rock. Then I heard a terrible cracking sound! But no panic. I kept the upstream gunnel high and forcefully pushed off with my paddle. Sluggishly the canoe slid forward to freedom. I looked down into the fiberglass walls of its hull. There was no leakage!

I raced through the rapids, drawing, prying, ferrying to cross currents. I discovered the trick of laying the boat on its side to pass safely between close rocks. I quartered (ran nearly sideways) the bigger waves to gain buoyancy. In a few minutes it was over—a mile of white water behind me. I drifted into the quiet pool below, shared knowing glances with Paul (who'd been waiting for me there for an hour), and silently began to sponge the accumulated water from my canoe.

It was a glorious run—stupid, dangerous, but nonethe-

Figure 15-1. Solo canoes are more seaworthy than most people think. Here, freestyle expert Charlie Wilson plays in a rapid in his Bell Flashfire.

less glorious. I had come through it all without incident. My boat was totally predictable, reliable, eminently stable in the biggest waves. The rain subsided and the bugs disappeared. A golden sun streamed beckoningly through clouds of twisted gray. There was no need for further words. Drained and gratified, we quietly drifted the last 5 miles to Lake Superior.

EVOLUTION

It began in 1975, when friends Bob Brown, Darrell Foss, and I agreed to build solo canoes. Darrell responded with a wood-strip version of an old British touring kayak, while Bob made a 13½-foot open canoe of his own design. Being somewhat less creative in these matters than my friends, I constructed from plans the only solo canoe available at the time—the 14-foot MCA (Minnesota Canoe Association) Model.

Plans for this and more modern solo canoes are available from the Minnesota Canoe Association (appendix B). In 1988 the MCA released its new *Canoe Building Book,* which is, in my opinion, the best source of information for wood-strip/fiberglass canoe builders. MCA membership costs $22 a year. You get *Hut,* the monthly magazine, and a set of canoe-building plans of your choice.

After months of casual paddling on quiet streams, we were ready for the test—a four-day BWCA trip. Despite miserable weather, we were hooked. From then on it would take more than casual prodding to get any of us into the bigger boats.

But our canoes were less than perfect. Though fast, the kayak was a pain on the portages and during loading and unloading operations. And Bob's canoe and mine were simply too slow for efficient touring. So back to the drawing board we went. The idea? To design a wilderness tripping canoe that with two weeks' worth of gear aboard would be fast on the flats yet turn with precision. One that was seaworthy in chop, waves, and rapids through Class III. A forgiving craft that was comfortable to paddle and portage.

Henry Rushton built boats like this a century ago, though none were big enough to suit our purposes. Nevertheless, maybe we could learn something from his designs.

After months of study and dead-filed plans we produced our version of Rushton's traveling canoe. Built to my specifications, it measured 15½ feet long, 11 inches deep, and a scant 30 inches at the rails (maximum beam). Weight? Just thirty-six pounds![1]

"Too big," said Darrell, as he watched me stripping it up.

"They always look big on the forms," I chortled. "Wait'll you paddle it!"

But Darrell had other ideas. In just ten days he completed his canoe—a scaled-down version of my boat, a 14½-footer of profound grace and beauty. (Plans for building this canoe are available from *Canoe and Kayak* magazine [appendix B]. This boat was a forerunner of the once popular Mad River Slipper.)

Finally, the new canoes were ready. Several weeks of field-testing on local waters suggested they were just what we wanted: snappy yet forgiving; equally at home in fast water

1The fiberglass-Kevlar facsimile of this canoe (dubbed the CJ solo) was first manufactured by Old Town Canoe Company, later by Bell Canoeworks. The CJ was a good boat for its time but can't compare with the best modern designs. Currently the 14-foot Bell Wildfire (designed by David Yost) is my favorite tripping canoe. My wife, Sue Harings, prefers the sportier 13-foot Flashfire (another Yost design), which is essentially a scaled-down version of this boat. Bell's new 15-foot Merlin II is another fine back-woods tripper. It turns more easily than the original Bell Merlin, which makes it better suited to beaver streams and rapids. Bob Brown and I designed the 14½-foot Lady Slipper (later renamed Slipper) for Mad River Canoe in the mid-1970s. The Slipper is largely out of production now, but it's still a fine canoe, though less sporty than the Bell models I've described. If you want a Royalex solo that does it all, check out the 14-foot, 44-pound, Bell Yellowstone solo. It's similar to the popular Wildfire. For long solo expeditions you can't beat the Verlen Kruger–designed Sea Wind (www.krugercanoes.com).

Figure 15-2. Sue Harings, the author's wife, paddles her Kevlar Mad River Slipper on a small Minnesota river in early spring.

and flat. Light and sweet they rode the waves, like a yellow leaf in autumn. We discovered the incomparable joy of paddling alone . . . together. Our tandem canoes gathered dust in the garage.

But deep down we wondered how our little boats would perform in the real wilderness. Were they strong enough to withstand the rigors of a major trip? Big enough to ride over the large waves and rapids we were sure to encounter? Fast enough? Sufficiently maneuverable to twist down a beaver stream? Would they carry the load?

DIFFERENT STROKES

Then there was the matter of learning to paddle alone efficiently. The solo canoeist lacks the symmetry enjoyed by a tandem team. Perhaps we should consider use of the double paddle. At the turn of the century when soloing was in its heyday, almost everyone used double paddles. Virtually all of Henry Rushton's solo canoes were designed to be paddled with twin blades.

In the end only friend Paul Swanstrom liked the idea of a double paddle. But Paul discovered that the traditional kayak paddle was too short, so he made a special 9-footer from a pair of canoe paddles. I let him use my old and slow MCA 14-

foot canoe for the trip. Without the twin blades he'd never have stayed with us.

Darrell and Chic[2] adopted the snappy Minnesota switch (racing stroke), which they used almost exclusively. But I stubbornly stuck with the time-honored C-stroke (see appendix A).

We argued a good deal about which stroke was best. Ultimately, we agreed that the Minnesota switch—which is basically a short, fast bow stroke (you take three or four strokes on one side of the canoe; switch sides and repeat)—was most efficient. Since there's no steering component (rudder) to this stroke, the canoe describes a slightly erratic path in the water. The Minnesota switch is mindless, boring, and ugly, but it moves you along with less effort (and skill) than the classic C, especially when you use a bent-shaft paddle.

Nonetheless, the C is the traditional way to paddle alone. It's a dynamic, precise stroke—the canoe barely wavers as it runs. Olympic flat-water canoeists use the C to propel their shallow, straight-keeled racing hulls. Over the *short haul* the C may be the fastest way to paddle a solo canoe.

I grew to love the C and learned to use it hour after hour without tiring. And in rapids the stroke blended nicely into the bow draw and low brace (appendix A). But could I maintain the pace day in and day out on a long wilderness voyage?

Granted, our little canoes were delightful to paddle—like touring the back roads of America in a vintage sports car. But could they meet the challenge of a wild northern river? Experienced canoeists we talked with were skeptical. And reference to these craft in the canoeing literature was limited to messing around on quiet ponds. There was no mention of using them for serious trips.

It was up to us, then—a small circle of friends—to prove it could be done. All we needed was to finalize the details of packing, portaging, and paddling . . . and find an isolated, awe-inspiring route that offered enough variety— large lakes, meandering beaver streams, substantial rapids, and more—to produce a meaningful experience from which we could draw conclusions. Tough portages didn't scare us. After all, our heaviest canoe (my old 14-footer) weighed only forty-three pounds!

[2] Unfortunately, Bob couldn't join us for the trip. In his place went Chic Sheridan—a talented sixty-one year-young precision welder and jack-of-all-trades. At first Chic was apprehensive about keeping up wth us "young boys," but in the end we were frequently the ones who trailed behind.

Figure 15-3. The author's Bell Wildfire solo canoe "rigged for running." Note clamp-in yoke, kneepads, sponge, and seat pad.

CARRYING THE CANOE

We wouldn't carry our solo canoes the traditional way—with a gunnel perched on one shoulder. Painful experience taught us that a true yoke, like the one recommended in chapter 6, was essential for comfort over the long haul. But the yoke must be removable so it wouldn't interfere with the centralized solo paddling position. The answer was to clamp[3] rather than bolt it to the gunnels.

THE ROUTE

After studying scores of maps and trip guides, we settled on the Steel River circle route. Our 1980 topo maps indicated it had everything we wanted: unsurpassed beauty (bluffs to 700 feet), extreme isolation (no roads crossed the river anywhere), lots of good rapids, and a short (10-mile) auto shuttle. More important, the river was located only 500 miles from home.

Easy shuttle, fabulous scenery, challenging rapids. There must be a reason why the Steel River wasn't overrun with people.

There was. The portages! Even the easy ones required

more than casual perseverance. And the worst came at the start. For example, the government trip guide stated: "Unfortunately the canoeist will be facing the steepest and longest portage (a bit over a mile) the first day out. Portage #1 is a climb up over a steep ravine (it gains 400 feet) that will test the mettle of even the most ardent outdoor enthusiast. Packing light and being in good physical condition are prime requisites."

PORTAGING

We had it all carefully worked out and weren't intimidated. We'd each carry two packs in our canoe—a number 3 Duluth, loaded to weigh forty-seven pounds, and a small day pack of fifteen pounds (we used a bathroom scale to evenly distribute every ounce).

First trip over the portages we'd carry the big Duluth, our two paddles, camera, and life jacket. Second trip we'd tote

Figure 15-4. The author prepares to do some "pond hopping" along the upper reaches of the Steel River in Ontario. The canoe is a Mad River Slipper.

---

[3] A simple hardwood bracket and wing nut work fine. Or if you want a really slick outfit, get a removable solo yoke from Bell Canoeworks (appendix B). I'm proud to say I had a hand in its design.

the day pack and canoe. Average weight per trip would be around fifty-five pounds—pure luxury when you're used to manhandling eighty-pound canoes and sixty-five-pound Duluth packs on traditional canoe trips.

We set the heavy Duluth pack just forward of our feet, belly-down. It made a fine foot brace and fit nicely under our fabric splash covers. The day pack—which was crammed with rain gear, wool shirt, wind jacket, and other frequently used essentials—reclined at arm's length behind the seat. The trim was perfect![4]

We had all the procedures down pat. All that remained was to get to our river and convert principle to practice!

Our first mistake was breakfast. We parked the van along deserted Santoy Lake Road the night before our departure with the intent of having our contact person (the owner of a local motel) shuttle it the next morning. But when we arrived at the motel the following day, our man was gone—out cutting wood. Had he forgotten about us? No matter, we'd get breakfast at a restaurant and find someone else to drive the van.

After breakfast I asked D. E. Miller, proprietor of a small cafe, if he'd shuttle our vehicle. "Sure," said D. E. "Ten bucks plus two bucks a day to store the van." That seemed reasonable enough, so we agreed.

I opened my map and showed Miller our route. Methodically he ran his forefinger along the thin red line that represented Highway 17. "Here's where you wanna start," he said, tapping his finger repeatedly on a point about 5 miles west of our intended Santoy Lake put-in. "That Diablo Lake portage'll kill ya."

Then he told us about a great trail—a "two-lane highway," he called it—built by a youth works program a few years ago. "Hardly anyone knows about it," he said. "Not on the maps. That Diablo portage'll kill ya!"

I studied the map. It was 2, maybe 3 miles (if the trail ran straight) to Diablo Lake—three times farther than the MNR-recommended route. And the cumulative gain in elevation was close to 800 feet! "How do you know this route's better?" I asked feebly. Miller faced me squarely and with a condescending voice replied, "I live here, don't I?"

I mumbled a polite reply and meekly nodded approval. Long experience in the Canadian bush had taught me to trust the locals.

A three-minute drive from the restaurant brought us to the trailhead, which, snuggled in dense alders, was impossible to spot from the road.

We unloaded canoes and gear, said good-bye to Miller, and began the arduous hike skyward to Diablo Lake.

The trail was anything but a two-lane highway. Barely wide enough for our solo canoes, it was a network of tangled brush, roots, and downed trees. Unyieldingly the path climbed steadily upward. It would cross two lakes, two beaver ponds, and several creeks before it terminated at Diablo Lake.

Seven hours of arduous portaging brought us to the first pond. A two-minute paddle and we continued again—another mile. Then came ten minutes of open water and another portage, this time nearly straight up through thick brush. Along the trail we met a man carrying a bright red chestnutwood-canvas canoe. He'd begun the portage *the day before!* A smug smile flashed across my face as I passed him by. I was beginning to discover the joy of tripping in a solo canoe.

It was 7:00 P.M. when we slid our canoes into the dark, slick water of Fishnet Lake, a mile from our destination (Diablo Lake). Nine hours of nearly continuous portaging had brought us only 2 miles. Tired and drained, we made camp on a small island just offshore.

In the morning we awoke to a thick, penetrating fog. I fired up the big Optimus stove and prepared bacon and pancakes. Within ninety minutes we were waterborne, paddling north into the fog in search of a portage whose location we could only guess.

We found the portage easily but the scenario of the day before repeated itself. We horsed our boats through thickets, snaked them between threes, hopped from rock to rock. Occasionally there were short stretches of water to paddle. But mostly there were portages.

We kept reminding ourselves that this was fun! Still, we were becoming weary and angry. We began to talk openly about finding some way to abort the trip. Halfway through a swampy portage, we paused to rest. Darrell spread open the map sheet, which we all stared at in disbelief. Though Diablo Lake was just ahead, we would need to carry our outfit at least another mile beyond it to reach the first real lake that had significant open water.

---

[4] The seat on most factory-built solo canoes is mounted with the leading edge 4 inches aft of dead-center. This results in perfect trim with the paddler but no weight aboard (the weight of the paddler makes no difference). If, like us, you plan to carry two packs of unequal weight, and your canoe does not have a sliding seat, you'll have to remount the seat 6 inches in back of center to compensate for the heavier pack. To balance the canoe for day trips, simply set a five-pound weight (a light day pack works fine) in the bow.

Figure 15-5. Sue Harings runs a rapid along Ontario's Steel River. The canoe is a Kevlar/carbon fiber Bell Flashfire.

Chic reached into the side pocket of his day pack and withdrew our store of peppermint schnapps. We said nothing—just gloomily passed the bottle around, again and again. We'd had it!

At 3:00 P.M. on the second day, we nosed our little canoes into a quiet bay that marked the southern end of beautiful 12-mile-long Cairngorm Lake. We had carried our canoes and gear for more than sixteen of the first eighteen hours of our trip to reach this lake. We were ecstatic—a giant load (literally) had been lifted from our shoulders. We stripped our clothes to zero and plunged headlong into Cairngorm's crystal-clear waters. We swam and played, washed our shirts and socks (no soap, of course). Then we lunched on a sloping lichen-splashed outcrop, Kosher bagels, hard salami, cheese, salted nut rolls, and lots and lots of Wyler's lemonade. Oh joy!

The discussion became strangely philosophical. Was it worth all those hours of portaging to get into this positively gorgeous lake? It was unanimous: absolutely not! "Thank God for little boats," we chorused. "Can you imagine carrying your

eighty-pound Old Town Ranger over those portages, Cliff?" asked Darrell. We passed around our carefully guarded bottle of schnapps. Another chorus of "thank God for little boats."

CANOE STRENGTH

Our two real fears about soloing on the Steel were wind and the questionable strength of our wood-strip canoes. Our experience on local streams suggested that the areas that receive the greatest abuse on a solo canoe are the bow stem (at the waterline) and center bottom, just beneath the seat. So prior to the trip we reinforced these areas with layer after layer of fiberglass cloth.[5] It paid off! Not only when I solidly smacked that rock on the final descent to Lake Superior, but also in the boulders of "Darrell's Mistake."

Darrell was in the lead when we hard the muffled sound of rushing water. He put ashore at the head of the rapid to check it out. I back-ferried into an eddy to wait for his decision to run or portage.

"Hey Cliff, come take a look," he called.

[5]Fiberglass-covered wood-strip solo canoes that weigh less than forty pounds may not be strong enough for tough trips. Thirty-eight pounds is about minimum for all-fiberglass construction. Kevlar-composite hulls are a different story: My Bell Wildfire weighs thirty-two pounds in Kevlar/carbon-fiber construction and it's stronger than most people will ever need. Ultralight Kevlar-composite canoes are worth their high price!

"Nyah," I answered lazily, "doesn't sound too bad. What d'you think?"

"Looks okay . . . straight shot . . . should be easy," said Darrell. "You go ahead, I'll follow."

"Sure," I muttered. "Let's put the scratches on *my* boat!"

I started down the rapid confident there would be no problem. Then I saw it—a gradually sloping 5-foot drop with one boulder after another, and only a few thin ribbons of water between. No way! I thought. But it was too late. I swept, drew, pried, cross-drawed, lurched, skidded, and screeched. In a second it was over and I was safely floating in the pool at the base of the drop. I was hopping mad and amazed that my fragile stripper had survived the beating. I gained a new respect for wood and fiberglass!

I reached for my whistle to warn the guys. Then I stopped short. "Like hell," I said to myself. "Let's see how tough their boats are!" So I just leaned back in the canoe and waited for the inevitable.

It was a comedy of errors—one wipeout after another. *Everyone* had to get out and walk, to drag their canoes over the boulders, to cuss and complain. *All except me.* I loved it!

PADDLES

In retrospect I'd have to attribute my good fortune in navigating these and subsequent rapids more to the extra-long paddle I used than to any superior skills. Whenever I heard the sound of rushing water, I put aside my 56-inch paddle and grabbed an old but sturdy 60-inch solid-ash beavertail. The unwieldy ash paddle seemed out of place in my modern strip canoe, but it was much more efficient in rapids. The shorter stick just didn't have enough leverage to spin the boat quickly around obstacles.

This realization came as a shock to all of us who for years had snubbed our noses at long paddles. We'd been brainwashed by the pro racers into believing that short paddles were always better. Fact is, you need plenty of length for solo slalom maneuvers. The old Red Cross canoeing manual was right on target in this respect.

Once through the rapids, however, you'll want to return to a shaft with a more reasonable length. A 56-inch straight paddle, or a 54-inch 12- to 14-degree bent-shaft (I prefer 12 degrees), is about right for traditionally styled solo cruising canoes. After years of experimenting I've settled on a 54-inch, ten-ounce carbon-fiber Zaveral paddle for most of my solo canoeing. I switch to a 58-inch Bell Straight paddle for rapids

and beaver streams. The Bell Straight model—which is made by the Grey Owl company (appendix B) in Canada—was designed by freestyle expert Charlie Wilson. It's strong enough for serious rapids but light enough for messing around. And the price is too good to be true.

WIND

We came to appreciate the shallow 11-inch depth of our canoes and the low 15½-inch ends. Paddling into a headwind was hard work, but controlling the boats wasn't. We plunged ahead through the biggest waves—even the 2-footers we later encountered on Santoy Lake near the end of our run. As near as we could estimate, our traveling speed was about 80 percent of what we might have expected to make in larger tandem boats.

Note: Considerable evolution has occurred in solo canoe design since the early 1980s. Today's state-of-the-art cruisers will *outrun* the average tandem canoe on all types of water and will negotiate heart-throbbing rapids with nearly equal aplomb—that is, if your skills are up to the challenge. There are, of course, a number of specialized white-water solo designs, but these boats are too slow on the flats for wilderness travel.

PHYSICAL PROBLEMS

I alone suffered physical problems on the trip: My hands kept falling asleep! The tingling began after two very strenuous eleven-hour days of rough upwind paddling in the big rollers of 30-mile-long Steel Lake. The culprit was my unyielding use of the solo C-stroke. Evidently, the constant twisting action of my wrists and iron-clad grip strained the muscles in my hands until there was a physical overload. It was quite frightening at first. The solution was to eat crow and adopt the Minnesota switch along with my friends. By trip's end my hands were back to normal and I settled into a modified style of paddling—a few moments of C, some switching, back to the C again, and so on. For long-distance touring—solo or tandem—variety is essential!

I might add that tendonitis, which was a serious concern in the days when everyone J-stroked with long, straight paddles, is now largely a thing of the past. I you value your health over the long haul, you'll use a bent-shaft paddle and switch sides frequently. I wouldn't dream of going on a canoe trip—solo or tandem—without my bent-shaft paddle. Bent paddles are, as Martha Stewart would say, "a very good thing."

JOY

We enjoyed a freedom in soloing unmatched by the togetherness of a bigger boat. Though we traveled as a close-knit group, we were often separated by hundred of yards. There were long periods of time when no one spoke, when no one competed with the silent majesty of the wilds. Perhaps that's what made this trip so memorable: Good friends were near to share joys and hardships, yet each of us was very much along and in command as we paddled along. There was never the cramped feeling you get when paddling bow in a fine-lined tandem cruiser. Even with ten days' worth of gear aboard, we had plenty of room to stretch out. And our full two-piece splash covers made canoeing in wind and rain a joy.

To be sure, we were somewhat slower than the big canoes on open water. But we were much faster in rapids and portages. Loading and unloading the little canoes at the base of a rocky landing was easy: There was never the awkwardness that's generally associated with manhandling longer, heavier craft.

Despite the magnificence of our surroundings, our conversation invariably returned to our canoes. How could we improve their designs to make them faster without sacrificing load capacity and the critical need for quick turns? What was the optimum fiberglass layup for a lightweight wood-strip canoe that would see use in the wilds? By trip's end we had no final answers to those questions—only strong opinions. However, we agreed unanimously that solo canoes work as well in the backcountry as conventional tandem craft and are much more fun to paddle.

Because we pared clothing, food, and equipment to the bare minimum to save as much weight as possible, we traveled over land and water with a lightheartedness seldom experienced in big canoes. But most important was the joy of skillfully paddling a sweet, responsive canoe. And that, plus an increased awareness of the sights and sounds of the river, has kept us coming back for more.

Soloing is addictive . . . it rejuvenates both body and spirit.[6]

---

[6]Those bitten by the solo bug will find a wealth of specific information and paddling procedures in my books, *Canoeing & Camping: Beyond the Basics* and *Basic Essentials: Solo Canoeing* (appendix B).

CHAPTER 16

COMMERCIAL CARRIERS AND THE LONG DRIVE

Travel agencies suggest that getting there is half the fun. We know better! After long hours (or days) of elbow-to-elbow confinement within the padded walls of a passenger car—packs, paddles, life jackets, and sundries wedged into every corner, canoes with their network of ropes strung overhead, road dust everywhere—canoeists are more than ready for whatever freedom and tranquillity the river has to offer.

About all that can be said in favor of the long drive is that it's *usually* the cheapest way to get everybody—and everything—to the water's edge.

Our six-man crew traveled in style to the Hood River in the Northwest Territories in 1982: We shared the comforts (and cost) of a small motor home! And despite the horrible gas mileage, the ride was sheer luxury and worth every penny we spent.

Even if you can find a vehicle that's large enough to carry everyone, though, you'll still need a trailer to haul your gear. You'll find suggestions for building a good one in the next section.

CAR-TOPPING YOUR CANOE

Many years ago I was gassing up at a service station when a car with a new aluminum canoe on top pulled alongside. One questionably tight belly rope plus a bungee cord at the bow and stern precariously held the craft to the slick metal overhead racks. My friend Marc Hebert—a Native American—pointed to the rig and said, just loud enough for the driver to hear, "My people have a saying that each day spent canoeing adds a day to their life. Naturally, this assumes they'll get to the river alive!"

"Yeah," I agreed, sarcastically. "That canoe is a disaster waiting to happen."

The poor man looked wonderingly our way. He didn't have a clue.

Now, in the vestiges of middle age, I regret that snobbish encounter. Today I would be kinder and more helpful. It's been twenty years and I still wonder whether that canoe became a highway UFO.

Every accomplished paddler I know has had at least one close encounter with a canoe that nearly became a kite. Fortunately the Great Spirit has usually intervened at a critical moment and saved the day, for even recklessly secured canoes—like the one Marc and I witnessed that day—seldom fly off cars. Those that do commonly land out of harm's way with only broken hardware to evidence their flight. Hardly anyone ever gets hurt.

Nonetheless, good paddlers don't tempt fate; they know it pays to rack their canoes right.

Good-Bye Rain Gutters

Canoeists still mourn the passing of rain gutters, which accept all manners of clamp-on devices. No current system is

Figure 16-1. Driving the Mackenzie Highway to Yellowknife, Northwest Territories.

as secure as racks that bolt directly to the drip eaves of the car. My 1986 Chevy van has rain gutters—and, like most canoeists, I plan to keep it forever. I'm convinced that the world's first closed cars had rain gutters because they were designed by canoeists for canoeists!

Regrettably, the days of the wonderful generic racks that attach to a car's drip eaves are over. With the exception of full-sized vans and a few SUVs, all of today's vehicles have air-plane-style doors that require specially fitted brackets. Thule and Yakima (appendix B) lead the way in gutterless designs and offer racks to fit nearly every car model.

Caution: The load brackets that come with gutterless carriers are built to fit the rooflines of specific vehicles. Do not jury-rig them to fit cars for which they weren't designed!

Even if you don't plan to buy a second canoe, you may need to shuttle a friend's (and his friend's and his friend's!), so be sure to order double-length (80 inches) crossbars. The standard 48-inch carrier is too short to carry paired canoes.

Expect to pay around $200 for a quality-built cartop carrier and tie-down accessories. Locking bars are essential to prevent theft. Even then, many paddlers prefer to remove their expensive racks and store them inside their cars when they're on the river.

Never set canoes on hard, unpadded carriers—the gunnels are sure to be damaged. Here's how to protect your canoe, your car, and your peace of mind:

- Sew or duct-tape scrap carpeting around the crossbars. This ancient low-tech method is still the best way to protect fine woodwork. Most "show" canoes ride on old-fashioned carpeted racks. Carpeting tells the canoe world you're a real canoeist.

- Yakima, Quik-n-Easy, and a few other companies use tubular aluminum conduit (Yakima covers its with plastic) crossbars. Some canoeists armor the conduit with rubber heater hose, which slides on easily if you lubricate the rubber with brake fluid.

- You can bolt L-shaped plastic gunnel brackets (an optional accessory) to the crossbars. These brackets provide a wide, protective bearing surface for the canoe's gunnels and prevent the craft from shifting in wind—a safety advantage. If your canoe has wooden rails, you may want to glue scrap carpeting to the hard plastic faces of the brackets.

Straps or Ropes?

Most experienced canoeists prefer ropes to straps. Leave them tied to the racks while you're on the river and no one will steal them. Load your canoe and throw them over the top of the car—there are no heavy buckles to damage the finish. Will ropes loosen on a long trip? Very little. Polypropylene, polyester, and natural fibers stay drum-tight in any weather. Nylon ropes stretch slightly when they get wet. But cinching them takes seconds, if you use the right knots. You may want to review the power cinch in chaper 12.

Carrying Fragile and Paired Canoes

- You can break the back of a fragile canoe if you snug its ends too tight. For this reason many canoeists prefer to tie only the bow. Racers *never* tie down the tails of their ultralight canoes!

- Whenever you carry two canoes side by side on an overhead rack, always pad the outside of one of the canoes so the finish won't be galled if the two craft shift and touch.

- If you carry two canoes on a double rack, place the lighter and more fragile on the passenger side of the carrier. This will allow the sturdier and more rigidly tied craft on the driver's side to take the abuse of high winds generated by passing trucks.

Rules for Safe Travel

- Use padded carriers that fit your car. Expect to pay big bucks for a reliable setup.

- Tie down each canoe separately. Run *two* ropes or straps over the canoe's belly and secure each to its respective crossbar. Don't string one long rope from crossbar to crossbar—it could loosen at highway speeds, and the canoe could come off the car.!

- Add *two* lines to the bow and *two* lines to the stern of each craft. Secure each line to eye bolts in the bumpers, to padded S-hooks that ride in secure notches under the bumper, or to loops of webbing secured to bolts under the hood (figure 16-2). Pull the webbing up through the crack between the hood and fender when you need it. Never wind ropes around bumpers: Sharp bumper edges (even plastic ones) can cut or abrade them.

- Don't use your polypropylene lining ropes to tie down your canoes. Polypro takes a permanent set and will coil itself into impossible configurations. Lining ropes should be carefully coiled and used only for their intended purpose.

- Never use rubber ropes or elastic bungee cords to secure canoes on cars!

- Check the tightness of straps and ropes every time you stop for gas. If you carry multiple canoes, mount the fragile ones on the passenger side of the vehicle. Pad the sides of paired canoes if you don't use gunnel clamps.

- If you observe an unsafe cartopping situation, politely call it to the attention of the driver.

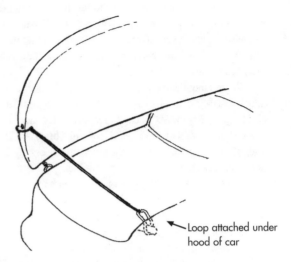

Loop attached under hood of car

Figure 16-2. Secure your nylon webbing (for tie-down lines) to a bracket or bolt under the hood of your car.

Three's Company—Ten May Be a Record!

Canoeists commonly carry three or more canoes on a rack built for two. It's a game we play to impress our friends. My personal record is five canoes on a Jeep Wagoneer; a friend boasts ten on a vintage van!

It's not hard to carry multiple canoes on a double rack. Just mount 'em in pairs and tie each one separately. Span the bellies of the paired canoes with a pair of carpeted 2-by-4s. Tie the ends of the 2-by-4s (drill tie-down holes through them) to the crossbars of the racks. Now mount the second tier of canoes, and so it goes—the sky's the limit.

Frankly, I feel uneasy whenever I carry more than three canoes on any vehicle. If I need to haul more than three boats, I use a trailer.

Building the Canoe Trailer

Stick with canoeing long enough and you'll want—no, need—a canoe trailer. There are some commercial designs, but none is built for rough-road use. The typical factory-built canoe trailer has a wimpy tongue and spaghetti-thin cross-bars, cushy springs, and 12-inch wheels that bottom out in the ruts of every logging road. Running lights and a cargo box? These are extra-cost options or do-it-yourself projects. If you want a good trailer, you'll have to build it yourself or contract the job out.

Everyone who has trailered canoes for very long has a wealth of horror stories to share. Here are a few.

The school district for which I work once built a heavy-duty convertible trailer that could haul canoes in summer and ski equipment in winter. By removing some bolts, the tongue could be shortened or lengthened—a great idea, or at least so it seemed.

Within the first year the tongue snapped off while the trailer was being towed behind a busload of kids. The driver hit the brakes and the momentum rammed the canoes a yard through the back of the bus. Fortunately, no one was injured.

Another case: I was driving 60 miles an hour when the tongue snapped on my friend's home-built trailer. The trailer flipped over and ground to dust the enclosed box, along with my beautiful wood-trimmed Royalex canoe. I just eased off the gas and let the heavy Chevy Suburban drag the remains along until the momentum subsided. Incredibly, there was a commercial welder at the next gas station who got us rolling in a matter of minutes.

Those who are new to canoe trailering may suggest that I'm either jinxed or careless. I can assure you that I am neither. Trailering canoes on even well-built trailers is dangerous business, as every knowledgeable canoeist will attest.

The late Karl Ketter, whose mother Betty Ketter (she passed away in 1999) owned a commercial outfitting business

EXPEDITION CANOEING

in Minnesota, once told me he had yet to see any canoe trailer that would last more than seven years. "No matter how you build 'em, the tongue always breaks," said Karl. Herein lies the problem: The long, whippy tongue, which characterizes the canoe trailer, eventually succumbs to stress. And as I discovered, simply welding on more iron isn't the answer. Overkill can kill! It's something to do with the harmonics of vibration, I'm told.

Designing a Trailer That's Right for You

First, answer these questions:

■ How many canoes do you plan to haul? If your tow vehicle is a light truck, it's best to limit capacity to four or six. Six canoe trailers stand awkwardly high, especially when built for today's deep-hulled trippers. They need a heavy undercarriage or a weight-filled cargo box for stability. If you need six-canoe capacity, it's better to trailer four and cartop two than to manage a six-canoe-high kite in a wicked crosswind.

■ Do you want a cargo box? If so, limit your capacity to four canoes so the trailered load won't be too high.

■ Will you pull the trailer long distances over unimproved roads? If so, you'll need big wheels and enough spring travel to keep from bottoming out. This means heavy-duty construction all around and a finished weight of around 1,000 pounds—more if you include a cargo box and spare tire.

Figure 16-3. Driving the Wollaston tote road from LaRonge, Saskatchewan, to Wollaston Lake. Note the two spare tires and nylon door covers on the author's trailer.

It follows that for light loads on asphalt and good gravel, a medium-weight (650-pound) trailer with a 2,000-pound axle rating and 12-inch wheels is good enough. But for pounding the back roads of Canada, a heavy frame matched to a 3,500-pound axle and 15-inch wheels, is better.

Whether your trailer is lightweight or heavy, construction methods are similar. You'll vary the size and thickness of components, and perhaps the mountings, but that's all. Let's examine the structure of a heavyweight four canoe trailer, equipped with cargo box.

Building the Frame

Materials: Don't try to save money by using old auto axles and scrap steel, whose history is uncertain. Five hundred bucks will buy a new axle and all the new steel you'll need to assemble a reliable rig.

Your life rides on the tongue, so don't skimp. I specify $1/8$-inch-thick, 3- by 3-inch tubular steel stock for heavy- and lightweight trailer tongues. Reinforcement of tongue and frame should be $3/16$-inch angle steel or better. The schematic shows one proven layout (figures 16-4 and 16-5).

Concerns: The tongue should be reinforced on the top and sides as illustrated. Use a horizontal brace *and* an X-brace to stiffen the canoe tree, as illustrated. You'll weaken the frame's side rails if you cut, bend, and weld them to the tongue. It's better to make a solid rectangular frame, then weld on separate side braces.

Be sure to add removable, vertical struts on the canoe tree as shown in figure 16-6. Without them the tree will eventually break welds and shake loose. This is almost a certainty if you drive bumpy roads without the canoes on board. Loaded canoes act as horizontal braces that stabilize the cross members and deaden the vibrations that cause welds to fail.

Springs: Match the spring weight to the maximum load you'll carry. Springs that are too light will cause the box to bottom out. Those that are too heavy will transfer shock to the trailer and stress both welds and metal. If you commonly carry 300 pounds on a rig that's designed to haul 1,500, you'd better consider shock absorbers. Otherwise your well-built frame may shake apart at the seams.

Case in point: A few years ago, a friend and I both had identical heavy-duty trailers built by the same man. Each was designed to haul around 1,500 pounds of canoes and gear.

Twelve hundred pounds of equipment is a common load for me; 300 pounds is average for my friend. My trailer has negotiated the Trans-Canada Highway to the Northwest

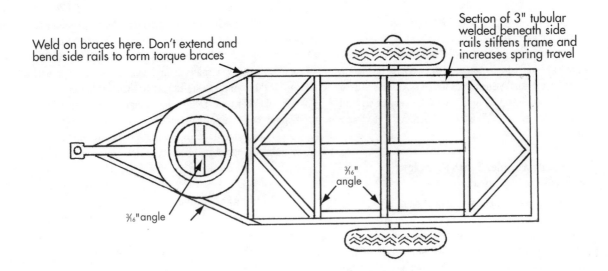

Figure 16-4. The canoe trailer.

Weld on braces here. Don't extend and bend side rails to form torque braces

Section of 3" tubular welded beneath side rails stiffens frame and increases spring travel

³⁄₁₆" angle

³⁄₁₆"angle

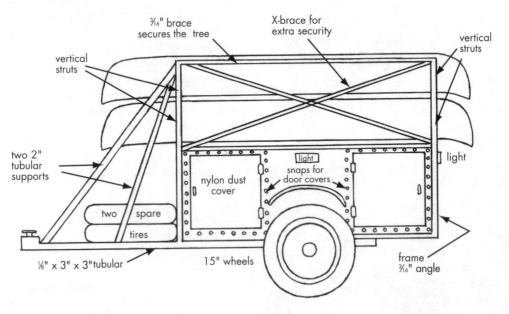

Figure 16-5. Proven trailer layout.

³⁄₁₆" brace secures the tree

X-brace for extra security

vertical struts

vertical struts

two 2" tubular supports

light

light

snaps for door covers

nylon dust cover

two spare tires

⅛" x 3" x 3"tubular

15" wheels

frame ³⁄₁₆" angle

Territories four times and has logged more than 10,000 miles on fist-sized gravel. The first year I lost the surge brakes when the hydraulic line sheared on a rock. The following summer a spring mount failed and had to be rewelded at a bush plane hangar deep in the wilds. I also broke a shock absorber.

Otherwise, no problems.

After just 3,000 miles of driving on light-duty gravel roads, however, the huge 3-inch tubular tongue on my friend's trailer gave way right behind the hitch. Evidently vibrations set up stresses that caused the steel (not the welds) to fail. An

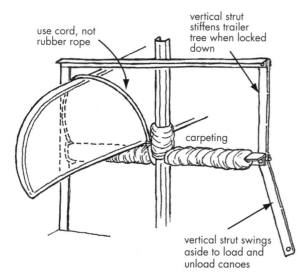

use cord, not rubber rope

vertical strut stiffens trailer tree when locked down

carpeting

vertical strut swings aside to load and unload canoes

Figure 16-6. Canoe tree with vertical struts.

engineer told me that shock absorbers or lighter springs would have prevented the fracture. Moral? Bigger is better only if it's sprung right!

Fenders: A backroads trailer needs at least 4 inches of spring clearance. So mount fenders high, even if they look comical. The first time you bottom a fender well on the tread of a fast-spinning tire, you'll see why!

Cargo box: A cargo box should be water- and dustproof and easy to access when the canoes are loaded. Most cargo boxes are built from treated plywood, which warps no matter how you brace it. You can futz with this—and you will—or adopt a simpler, method that will cover the ever-widening cracks. I simply close the hinged doors then snap a fitted waterproof nylon cover over them. The cover is made oversized so that it'll go over the hinges and doorjamb.

The roof of a cargo box is even more vulnerable to the elements than the sides. You *must* seal the wood with fiberglass, or cover it with shingles, tar paper, or aluminum siding to prevent buckling and delamination.

It is absolutely essential that the tow vehicle have generously sized mud flaps on the rear wheels. Without them canoes and trailer will be sandblasted to pieces on gravel roads. There should also be a double-thick plywood apron on the front of the cargo box to absorb the flying stones that get

by the mud flaps. I drive about 2,000 miles a year on bad gravel and need to replace my stone shield every three years.

Spare tires: Once, far from help, I got two flat tires in one day. Naturally, that wiped out all my spares and left me stranded till I could make repairs. This cost me a day of travel. But I learn fast: My trailer now has two spares stack-mounted on the tongue. The five-hole Chevy wheels match my van, so I have still another spare if needed.

Lights: Waterproof boat trailer lights are essential on a rig that will overwinter in snow and rain. Be sure to get the deluxe package, which has bright amber running lights on the side.

Warning: When you're securing electrical wires to the frame, use tape sparingly. When my trailer once flipped over in Canada, I discovered that the tongue had broken at a place covered with duct tape. Had I used narrow electrical tape instead, I would have discovered the crack immediately.

Brakes are desirable on any trailer, though frankly I've learned to live without them. Twice now low-slung bush roads have ripped the hydraulic cable on my surge brakes. Three years ago, after much frustration, I finally pulled the shoes.

The real problem with surge brakes is that they lock up solid when you back uphill—a frequent occurrence in the backcountry. Of course you can stop the vehicle, get out, and disengage the brake clutch when the need arises, but this is often awkward or dangerous. For example, say you're building momentum while backing through thick, black mud when the rear end suddenly locks up. So out you go in ankle-deep mire to release the clutch . . . sure you do!

Nonetheless, if your trailer's gross weight is more than 2,000 pounds, then you should probably have brakes (many states require them!). Electric brakes are the sensible option.

Storage

Most canoe trailers are necessarily left outside year-round. Sun, rain, and snow beat on the plywood box; in a few years warping and delamination occur. Even well-primed steel rusts quickly. What can you can do to prolong the life of your trailer, short of storing it indoors?

■ Thoroughly wash the metalwork at the end of the season and spray it with oil or WD-40. Breakfree—available at gun shops—is an excellent metal preservative, but it's very expensive.

■ If you build an enclosed box, seal the top with waterproof material such as fiberglass, tar paper, or tin.

Failing this, apply a good grade of light-colored (to reflect heat) epoxy paint.

- Trailer tires usually fail from rot and weather checks, not from wear. Wooden boards placed under the wheels will keep tires from contacting damp ground or cement. Drape fabric from the fenders to shield tires from sunlight.

- The ball is a frequent source of concern. Vibration over the long haul may cause the nut to work loose, creating a dangerous situation. It goes without saying that you should check tightness at every stop, but this may not be enough. One solution is to permanently weld the ball onto the hitch—a bad idea if you change tow vehicles and need to up- or downgrade your ball size to match the hitch. I apply Loctite, a liquid sealant available at gun shops and hardware stores. Loctite prevents nuts and bolts from loosening due to vibration, yet allows them to be removed with heavy force.

- A 3-foot length of steel pipe makes a handy wrench extension if you need to remove a damaged nut or hitch ball. Other essential tools include a heavy steel hammer, pipe wrench, and giant crescent wrench. Be sure to include WD-40 or other metal lubricant.

Maintenance

Each spring I repack the wheel bearings on my trailer and check the tongue and frame for hairline cracks. It makes sense to carry spare wheel bearings and seals, cotter pins, grease, and the tools you'll need to pull wheels and make repairs. A couple of 2-foot-long pieces of scrap steel (the same stuff you used to make the frame) and a 6-foot length of chain (figure 16-7) will keep you going if a tongue breaks.

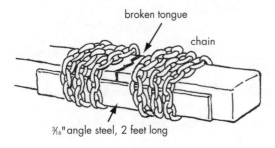

broken tongue

chain

³⁄₁₆" angle steel, 2 feet long

Figure 16-7. Scrap steel and chain can repair a trailer tongue.

THOSE WONDERFUL CANADIAN RAILROADS

It was a sweltering 98 degrees the day we arrived at Moosonee on Arctic tidewater. The map indicated that the train station was less than a mile across town, an easy portage. But it was dreadfully hot, so we casually inquired about taxi service. Almost immediately a burly red-haired man drove up in an ancient one-ton stake truck. "Taxi?" he asked. "You bet," I replied, and in a flash we loaded canoes and gear onto the bed of the old truck and piled aboard. A short dusty drive along pulverized gravel brought us to the well-kept station that marked the end of the line for Ontario Northland's famed Polar Bear Express. A polished diesel engine with a white polar bear emblazoned boldly on its sides clanged confidently in the glaring sun while a team of twenty cars waited silently in tow.

We unloaded our outfit and inquired at the ticket counter. The fare to Cochran was $8.75: canoes rode for slightly more.

"Eighth car back," said the agent, pointing to the hulking train. "Use the pushcart over there." We nodded our thanks and shuttled our three canoes and twelve Duluth packs down the track to the appointed car. A railroad employee saw us and jumped off a flatcar, eager to help. We gratefully declined the offer so he walked alongside and chatted, curious about our trip.

We stacked our gear neatly into one corner of the near-empty boxcar, fastened the necessary baggage tags, and retired to the passenger compartment. Inside the car the temperature was a scorching 110 degrees! A round-faced conductor took our tickets and apologized for the breakdown in the air-conditioning. "Is there a lounge?" I asked. "Yes sir," he replied, "three cars back. Only place aboard that's cool." We bolted from our seats intent on beating the crowd. An eight-hour ride in a sweltering metal box was not our idea of a good time.

The conductor was right. The lounge was cool, clean, plush ... and virtually unoccupied. We settled in for the night and round after round of that famous Canadian beer.

If you've never ridden a Canadian bush train, you've got a pleasant surprise in store. The experience is almost as much fun as the canoe trip itself.

Much of northern Canada is still dependent on working trains to bring goods and services to remote communities. As a result you'll rub shoulders with the heart and spirit of the

Northland—loggers, miners, Indians, prospectors, trappers, and wilderness travelers like yourself. The bush trains are a thrilling melting pot of personalities, occupations, and dreams.

In addition to regular service at established stations, trains will often stop at any mile marker to accommodate canoeists and their gear. But don't expect fancy porter service or dazzling pullman decor. Railway employees are friendly and helpful, but they do expect you to help load and unload your own gear.

In remote areas trains frequently run in different directions on alternate days—and not all trains will stop for canoeists. So be sure to write for an up-to-date timetable.

Most of the passenger train service in Canada is consolidated under Via Rail, which makes getting specific information about schedules, procedures, costs, and the like relatively easy. A phone call addressed to Via Rail (appendix B) will bring prompt, courteous answers to all your questions.

Canoes accompanied by their owners are usually considered excess baggage rather than freight and travel for about the same price as a passenger.

Some railroads won't handle canoes longer than 18 feet in standard baggage car service. There seems to be no logical reason for this regulation, because there's usually plenty of room in the boxcars. And a 20-foot aluminum canoe weighs no more than an 18-foot wood-canvas one. However, the rules get bent a lot in remote areas, so there's real likelihood you'll be allowed to board with whatever you're paddling. But to be safe, check the length requirements before you commit yourself to your beloved 18½-footer. The alternative might be a lonely ride home on a passenger train while your canoe travels unescorted on a freight train!

Freight trains, by the way, haul freight: passenger trains carry people. Still, there are exceptions. I know of several cases of friendly freighters picking up canoeists by appointment . . . and otherwise. The bush trains are marvelous!

Virtually every Canadian railroad has a wealth of materials free for the asking. And when you receive them, you'll understand why Canada's trains are surviving while ours aren't. The tourist packet I received from Via Rail weighed a full five pounds! Included was a wonderfully informative tour book that listed major cities, points of interest, historical information, mile markers, maps, and much more. there was also a volume of provincial and city brochures, plus a surprisingly detailed guide to canoeing Manitoba rivers.

Materials supplied by Algoma Central, though less volu-minous, were equally useful—including a number of high-quality canoe routes accessible by rail.

Regrettably, things are changing fast in Canada. A decade ago you could flag down a bush train and, if space permitted, climb aboard. Now centralization through Ottawa has made things less personal. Unless you have a prepaid ticket and so are on the computer roster, even remote country trains may fly right on by, despite your frantic waves and hopeful look.

Nonetheless, if you make advance arrangements through Via Rail, or the station nearest your bush departure point, you'll have no trouble. And again, once you're in the backcountry, the rules change. Railroad folks are usually very friendly and accommodating to all they meet along "their" track. If there's room aboard, they'll probably take you on, even if the city bosses (what they don't know won't hurt 'em!) don't agree.

CHARTER PLANES

High noon and mist gray. An icy wind ships gentle whitecaps across the 40-mile lake. the wind stops: the rain (snow?) begins. I stare unbelievingly at the thin column of mercury in my pocket thermometer. Thirty degrees. Exactly! Hard to believe it's the eighteenth of August. Clad in layered woolens and bombproof rain gear, I'm warm. Barely. I shiver slightly and search longingly into the menacing sky. Nothing. Will he come? Perhaps he's forgotten us. I snug the parka around my face and nestle against a half-full Duluth pack. We wait!

Minutes blend to hours. Still no sign. At last I hear the sound, muffled at first, then louder. Finally an amorphous speck of silver appears on the horizon. The speck grows larger. Pontoons, twin props—a turbo Otter! The plane cuts power and drops gracefully to the water's surface. A long glide, pause . . . a turn. Slowly it chugs our way.

The engines stop and the metal floats settle gently on the sloping gravel beach by our camp. The door opens and a grinning heavyset man wearing sunglasses emerges. "Sorry I'm late, boys," says the man, "Had to pick up a load in Uranium City." But no apology is necessary. The long wait provided ample time to dream of chairs with padded backrests, tables to sit at, ice-cold beer, McDonald's hamburgers . . . pizza. "Let's hit it, guys," calls someone. It's back to reality—and to work!

Fitting three 17-foot Old Town Trippers into the belly of the Twin Otter isn't easy. We stack 'em opposite the side door, tails against the back wall. We twist, turn, grunt . . . the third boat fits. Luckily, the pilot makes no comment even though the stem of one canoe rests just inches from the instrument panel.

All aboard and ready to cast off. Wait—the money! Seven hundred twenty-six dollars for 220 air miles. Expensive but worth it. We peel off the fare in Canadian traveler's checks, settle into the thinly padded folding seats opposite our canoes, and fasten our seat belts. The pilot revs for take off. There's no upholstery to deaden the sound. The noise is deafening!

I watch the "copilot"—a boy in his late teens. His forefinger moves methodically across the map. He looks out the window, checks the compass. His finger advances a few millimeters across the map.

Those in front are warm, but back where I sit it's downright cold. Hard to believe this is a million-dollar airplane. Then the jolting begins. Rough weather, sleet ahead. I study the faces of my friends. No one looks too well. The talking stops, the queeziness begins. Ultimately we level out and the ride—and our stomachs—smooth. I'm grateful now we've got the Otter and not a pair of Cessnas. The Cessnas would be cheaper, to be sure, but less safe. For me that's enough.

Minutes later we set down in a protected cove. It's over and we're homeward bound.

Almost everyone who lives and works in the vast roadless regions of the Far North has access to some sort of aircraft. There are Cessnas, Beavers, Navahos, Lancers, Otters, a variety of helicopters, and more. Finding an aircraft to haul you to and from the river is easy: All you have to do is match what's available with what you can afford to pay. Alas, this is invariably more difficult than it sounds.

The Provincial Bureau of Tourism can supply the names and addresses of charter aircraft companies that service the area of your interest. Write for specifics and get a firm commitment before you leave home.

A Cessna 185 is the cheapest way to fly for a party of two—that is, if the pilot will carry your canoe. Before 1980, 185s routinely carried canoes on their pontoons. Now changes in provincial regulations and insurance coverage have prohibited many of these aircraft from carrying external loads, at least with passengers on board. There are still some 185 pilots who will carry canoes, but the list is shrinking. Most pilots I've talked with agree that Cessna 185s are simply too small to safely accommodate two passengers, gear, and a canoe. Check out the load calculation in Table 16-1 and you'll see why.

A single-engine Beaver or Otter is better than a Cessna if you have a lot of gear or an 18-foot canoe, and a Twin Otter is best for large parties with two or three canoes. A Twin Otter is a big plane and, with careful packing, can easily accommodate a crew of six, a month's supply of gear, and three 17-foot canoes, although you might have to explain this fact to some disbelieving Twin Otter pilots.

Packing a Twin Otter

The big twin is a twenty-one passenger airplane, though with canoes on board, fifteen of its twenty-one fold-down seats are out of commission. Whether you carry one canoe or three, there's only room for six passengers. If you put three canoes inside, select modes with similar shapes and shearlines so they'll nest slightly when the yokes are removed. For ease of loading, remove the center thwarts (yokes) from two of the boats. Have your own tools available; the pilot will simply watch. And figure on a maximum length of $17\frac{1}{2}$ feet per boat. Three canoes much longer than this simply may not fit. (See color figure 16-8.)

Costs are ordinarily computed on a per-mile basis, which means you pay for each mile the airplane flies from its *sea base* to your location and return. Prices vary slightly from one air service to another, so it pays to shop around.

Figure 16-9. These Inuit children at the hamlet of Bathurst Inlet on the Arctic Ocean (population about thirty) prepare to board the "school bus"—a Single Otter on floats—which will fly them to the boarding school at Cambridge Bay. In the foreground the author and his crew wait patiently for their chartered plane, which is on the way.

Figure 16-10. Inside a Twin Otter—packed for a long trip.

considerably, increases gasoline consumption, and creates problems during takeoffs and landings. Nevertheless, a lot of canoes are flown on the struts of airplanes . . . safely!

Table 16-2 gives the vital statistics and 2004 charter costs of some of the most popular bush planes. Prices will certainly be dated by the time you read this, but comparative relationships won't.

Considerations

Maximum Load

The amount of weight an airplane can *actually* carry depends on the distance traveled (the amount of gas required), the presence or absence of an external load (a canoe), and the length of the waterway (runway).

The useful load of an aircraft is reduced substantially when a canoe is carried on the pontoons. For that reason the rule is to *double the weight of the canoe when determining load capacities, though some pilots increase it much more than that.*

Some conservative air services *halve* the useful load when a canoe is carried outboard, which by this calculation would leave only about 300 pounds payload in the cabin.

Practices vary among charger companies, so get all the facts before you commit!

Some companies have an external tie-on charge of $50 or more for securing your canoe to the floats of the aircraft.[1] There may also be an additional per-mile charge for the drag incurred on the plane from the pontoon-mounted canoe. Generally floatplane pilots are less than enthusiastic about carrying canoes outside aircraft. The canoe reduces speed

TABLE 16-1

A Sample Charter Weight Calculation for a New Cessna 185

Basic empty weight average (plus oil and survival gear)	2,247 pounds
Pilot	+175 pounds
Operational empty weight.	2,422 pounds
Assume total fuel weight (round trip) is	+300 pounds
	2,722 pounds
Gross weight of the aircraft is	3,320 pounds
useful load, or 3,320, minus 2,722	598 pounds
Subtract weight of 80-pound canoe	-160 (canoe weight doubled)
Amount of weight you can put in the cabin	438

[1]Not all floatplane pilots are expert at tying on canoes. You'll want to oversee the procedure with a wary eye and use your own superior knot skills. Canoes do sometimes fall off airplanes!

TABLE 16-2

2004 Charter Costs and Characteristics of Some Popular Bush Planes

Name of Airplane	Number of Passengers*	Payload** (pounds)	Cost/Per Mile*** (Canadian dollars)	Comments
Cessna 185	3	800	3.50	Wheels or floats. One canoe may be carried externally. Some Cessna pilots wil not carry canoes. It's generally agreed that canoes longer than 17 feet should not be carried in this aircraft.
Cessna 206	3	900	3.50	Same payload as a C-185 but more space in the cabin, which allows a bulkier load.
DeHaviland Beaver	4–5	1,200	6.50	Workhorse of the North! Carries two passengers and a month's load of gear in the cabin. One canoe up to 18 feet long can be tied on the floats. Some Beaver pilots will carry two canoes on the floats for a short distance.
Cessna 208 Caravan	9	3,000	7.25	Wheels only. One canoe up to 16 feet long can be carried inside the aircraft for extended trips (bulkhead and copilot's seat must be removed.) Huge payload.
DeHaviland Single Turbo Otter	10	2,400	7.50 / 9.00	One canoe up to 18 feet long is carried on the floats. A few pilots will carry 20-footers. Some pilots will carry two canoes. It's hard to overload this airplane for a canoe trip.
DeHaviland Twin Otter	21	2,600	10.20	Wheels or floats. Will accept three 17-foot canoes or two 18- to 18-½ footers inside. You can't carry enough gear on a normal canoe trip to overload this airplane. External loads are not permitted. Cheapest way to fly for six people.
HS 748 Sidley Hawker	40	10,500	20.80	Wheels only. Twelve people and six canoes can easily fit inside.

*Number of passengers (or weight of gear) must be reduced when a canoe is carried on the pontoons.
**Includes the rough weight of the pilot but no gas.
***Costs vary from air service to air service. Long trips, light loads, and early bookings may earn discounts. It is usually less expensive to charter a wheeled airplane than one on floats; payloads of floatplanes are necessarily less than on wheels.

Money

Air charter services prefer to be paid in cash (Canadian or U.S. dollars) or by a certified check drawn on a Canadian bank. Most will also take American Express traveler's checks and Visa. A few will accept MasterCard. I don't know any air service that accepts American Express or Discover credit cards. Visa is, by far, the best credit card if you're doing business in Canada. Personal checks? Even people I've done business with for years won't take them!

The pilot expects to be paid in full when (or before) he or she picks you up, so plan accordingly. If the company doesn't take Visa, you'll need a certified check or cash. Given the option, I usually go with cash, much as I hate to carry it. If your plans change or for some reason your air service can't honor its flight commitment, you're stuck with a certified check. Cash, of course, is good anywhere. An inconspicuous money belt is probably the safest way to carry large sums of money.

By booking your flight as least six months in advance, you may get a guaranteed rate—insurance against next season's inflation. Get a commitment in writing before you head north.

Figure 16-11. Helicopters are available, but pricey! Along the Fond du Lac River, Saskatchewan.

Split Fares

If you're in no particular hurry (can wait around a day or two on either end of your trip), the flight dispatcher may be able to arrange a split fare with another customer. The savings can amount to several thousand dollars. It's always wise to ask about split fares, even if they only occasionally materialize.

Finally, it's been my experience that charter air companies don't like to answer mail. Invariable, the quickest route to success is by phone. So first call and get a price and commitment. Then follow up with a letter of confirmation. You'll receive an answer ... eventually. And always phone a week or two ahead to reconfirm your intent to fly. The personal follow-up pays rich dividends.

If you lose your money on the river and can't afford to pay, the pilot will surely fly you out anyway. No self-respecting bush pilot would consider leaving anyone stranded in the bush, even if they have to foot the bill. However, there's no guarantee they won't leave your gear sitting by the water's edge if they suspect you don't intend to pay!

Bush pilots are generally very considerate and understanding. They know their airplane is your link between life and death—a responsibility they accept willingly and with an air of flamboyance that commands admiration and respect.

BY BARGE OR BOAT

If your trip terminates at a roadless settlement that receives scheduled air and boat service, you may be able to ship your canoes to a port that you can later drive to. This way you can save a bundle by flying out aboard an inexpensive commercial airline. The disadvantage of this, of course, is time—it may take several weeks or months for your canoes to arrive at the port of call where you can pick them up.

Northern Transportation Company (appendix B) operates a tug and barge service based in Hay River, Northwest Territories, for the northern and Arctic communities. Settlements receive scheduled service during the June through September shipping season. The company's Web site has route maps, sailing schedules, and just about everything else about the operation. Arrival times are approximate and depend upon business and the weather. The company is licensed to carry freight only; it does not accept passengers. For information on current rates and schedules, call or e-mail the cargo office in Hay River.

Whether or not you'll save money by barging your outfit depends entirely on how much time you have, the number of canoes in your party, the weight of your gear, the availability of low-cost commercial aircraft, and the distance you have to drive to the port of call.

PROTECTING DELICATE GEAR ON YOUR TRIP NORTH

You are en route to a remote Canadian river. Your camera, GPS, and expensive carbon-fiber canoe paddle will ride in a crowded van or be wedged among camping gear in a floatplane. On the way home they will bounce in a bumpy train. How can you keep fragile items safe until you're on the river and in control?

Optics

Hard cases aren't enough: You must provide for stupidity and the unexpected! My camera and GPS ride nearby me in the van. I take them into the restaurant at lunch stops (mostly to avoid heat buildup in the vehicle). If we take a motel room, these items do, too. Dry bags should not be sealed until you're on the river—and then they should be opened (to discourage condensation) at least once a day. Always hand-carry optical gear on floatplanes and trains.

Figure 16-12. Powerboat shuttle on Hudson Bay. At the mouth of the Tha-anne River, 50 miles south of Arviat, Nunavut, Canada.

Eyeglasses

A hard case is a must. The best I've found is the waterproof Witz model, which is bright yellow and can be snapped to a D-ring or pack strap.

Canoe Paddles

My expensive carbon-fiber paddle is always a concern on a rugged canoe trip. Treat it wrong and it may snap like a newly cut diamond. Naturally, I take precautions:

On the drive up: Careful placement and a cushy paddle bag are enough.

In the floatplane: Time is money, and pilots are in a hurry. Your gear is considered cargo and treated accordingly. Loose items are dangerous in an airplane, so paddles are locked in tight—usually stacked under or alongside heavy packs.

I personally carry my bent-blade aboard the aircraft and hold on to it, if the pilot allows. Otherwise I pack it last—after everything and everyone is loaded.

On commercial airplanes: Commercial airplanes usually won't accept loose (individual) paddles. Those that do may count them as extra luggage, subject to a surcharge. The solution is to bundle paddles and tape them together. Bundled paddles are seldom handled with a loving touch.

If I don't have a paddle bag, I wrap my bent-shaft with newspaper, plastic poly bags, or the plastic groundsheet from my tent. I've used plastic Duluth pack liners and dirty field pants. Anything that provides bulk and softness (your life jacket) will work.

On trains: The conductor is usually happy to let you help load the train, which means you have control over the placement of paddles and delicate items. Well, sort of. The problem with trains is that people get on and off at every stop and gear is moved around. Canoe paddles sometimes get munched.

You can keep your paddle in the passenger car with you or take a chance on the baggage car. I usually bundle blades and go the baggage route. The key is to have a big, heavy bundle that won't be bothered.

Color counts: Brightly colored gear is less apt to be lost or damaged. Barren land canoeists often paint paddles so they can see them on the tundra. Normal paddles blend in.

If you don't want to muck up a pricey blade with paint, apply brightly colored plastic tape. Or tie pink surveying ribbon to the shaft. My wife, Susie, lost her graphite paddle when we capsized on the Hood River in 1992. Hours later we saw a flash of pink in an eddy—it was her paddle.

In camp: When you arrive in camp, the safest place for your paddle (bent-blade or otherwise) is alongside your tent, not under an overturned canoe. Always set bent-shaft paddles *blade-up* so they won't break if stepped on.

FINAL THOUGHTS FOR U.S. CITIZENS WHO ARE TRAVELING IN CANADA

Bob O'Hara, whose testimony you read in chapter 5, offers these final thoughts for U.S. citizens who are traveling in Canada:

- Have a passport if you're coming from the eastern United States. A birth certificate and photo ID are enough if you're from the Midwest.

- If you're driving, get a Canadian Insurance Card (yellow) from your insurance agent. Have proof of adequate finances—cash, traveler's checks, credit card.

- Handguns are illegal (as mentioned earlier). Long guns must have a trigger lock. You must have a hard case for your firearm if you are flying on a commercial airplane. Ammunition must be stored separately from the gun.

CHAPTER 17
HAZARDS AND RESCUE

To canoe a remote northern river without incident requires know-how, perseverance, and a lively appreciation of what it means to suffer an injury or lose a canoe when you're 100 miles from the nearest help. It requires many years under fire plus occasional "upsetting experiences" to develop the proper respect for a wild river. First, you acquire essential paddling skills, learn the basic maneuvers, and coordinate with a partner. You know your limitations and are extremely cautious. You take no chances. Yet!

In time you get the mechanics down pat. You can do a fast forward ferry into an eddy, pivot smoothly around a mid-stream boulder in a Class III rapids,[1] twist confidently down a mountain stream. You can handle whatever the river throws at you, alone or with a partner. You're almost as good as you think.

Then one day, far from the nearest road, you run a tough drop your friends elect to portage. "Walk around it," they urge. "We're too far from home to take chances." But the die is cast. You'll show 'em! So down the river you go, confident of success. But you miss the clear channel; the hydraulics were more than you bargained for. The result is a cold swim to shore and a damaged canoe. It's more than just embarrassing—your heroics have endangered the welfare of the entire crew. You vow you'll never pull a stunt like that again in the bush.

Surprisingly, the ones most likely to get hurt on a wilderness canoe trip are neither overcautious beginners who realize their limitations, nor practiced trippers who know they can't conquer a river. It's usually the paddle-competent, over-confident hot dog who becomes the statistic. And high-tech white-water skills are not the equalizer. Avoiding the dangers of the river is!

In the pages that follow I'll probe some of the hazards

you're likely to encounter on northern canoe routes. The anec-dotes you'll read are real. However, I urge you not to overreact to the implied dangers. Northern rivers are very safe places for those with good skills and mature judgment. Of course there's always the unexpected, the unpredictable. And that, good or bad, is what makes wilderness canoeing such an exciting ball game. Invariably, if you play by the rules you won't get hurt!

OVERRELIANCE ON THE MAP: THE CONTOUR-INTERVAL TRAP

You're a week into the trip and so far the days have been uneventful. You've run some substantial rapids without prob-lems, taken the cautious route, and portaged the questionable drops. Your maps, with their detailed profiles, have been your lifeline. You're doing a fine job as a trip leader.

Now there's time to relax. Neither your map nor trip notes suggest there are imminent dangers. The river is at peace; only the occasional skitter of a dragonfly across its mirror-smooth green surface breaks the tranquil laziness of the moment. You want to lay back and float a while, just take it easy.

Your friends paddle alongside, eager to go. They don't share your views of slowing down. "We'll go on ahead, get a good campsite, have coffee on when you slugs arrive," says the fast team.

You check the map again. The contours are uniform; there's no hint of danger. Surely it's okay to break the rules and separate the party for a few hours. Why not let your friends exercise their muscles? But wait! Fifty miles from the nearest road is no place to take chances. You reluctantly make the decision—"We'll pick up the pace and stay together."

---

[1]See appendix E for a review of the international white-water rating scale.

Ahead the river narrows and bends sharply to the right. The current quickens and produces a barely audible gurgle. Maybe a Class I rapid, you muse. Certainly nothing stronger than that. Your friends are chomping at the bit. They pull ahead.

"Hold up," you call. "Let's check this blind corner." "Aw, it's just a swift" is the reply. But you're unsure. You decide to go ashore and have a look. You tie your canoe to a tree and struggle through thick underbrush to cut off the riverbed. Ultimately, you push aside a small sapling and step into the blazing sunlight. Nothing. Just the same persistent gurgle. Then you see it—a sheer 10-foot drop over glass-smooth granite. And barely a sound! The falls is not a killer, but it is a canoe eater for sure. Run it and you'll have a long walk out.

Triumphantly you work your way back through the undergrowth. "Falls!" you call sharply. "Let's portage!"

There's no portage trail or hint of one. Getting around the falls means horsing canoes and gear through tangled vegetation. Later you walk out to the flat rock above the ledge and study the map again. You're hopping mad. How dare the cartographers miss a dangerous spot like this! Then your eyes wander to the map margin. *The contour interval is 100 feet!* Suddenly everything is quite clear: A 10-foot fall is insignificant when the distance between contours is that large.

Until now I've suggested that a good map and detailed profile will keep you out of trouble. As the case in point indicates, it won't always. Maps with generous contour intervals are next to worthless for identifying subtle dangers.

The lesson is academic: Don't assume the way is clear just because the map says so. If you can't see around a bend and feel a gnawing uncertainty in your gut, then get out and look, even if it means climbing a hill or bulldozing your way 1/4 mile through dense alders. Certainly you should rely heavily on your map for basic information; just *don't take too literally what you don't see!*

FALLS

It's late June on the Missinaibi River in northern Ontario. For more than an hour, the six canoeists have been intimidated by the awesome roar of Thunderhouse Falls—a canoe-length slot in hard granite through which the entire volume of the Missinaibi thunders fearfully. Immediately beyond Thunderhouse Falls are two more substantial falls of near-equal fury. The total drop is more than 40 feet!

In the turmoil below Thunderhouse Falls stands conjuring house—a solitary vertical pillar of stone once held in awe and superstition by the local Indians. The men are excited. They are about to experience the highlight of their trip.

The Ontario trip guide indicates that the 1-mile portage begins at the head of a small rapid on the west bank. Information received from previous parties who've run the river suggest the portage is well marked . . . and well used! Everyone fully understands the dangers of getting too near the falls.

As the men approach the small rapids above the falls they spot the portage marker on the left. But the white water beyond looks easy and there's a large pool below—plenty of room to pull out.

The trip leader starts down first. The rapids is easy going; all goes as expected. He paddles the length of the pool and puts ashore a safe distance above the falls. Then he prepares to carry gear and canoe up the steep bank to the portage trail above. In a moment the second canoe snugs to shore against the first with the third boat close behind. The result is a classic canoe jam-up—everybody falling over each other and everything. Disgusted and impatient, one canoe decides to paddle out into the pool to wait, and perhaps get a better photograph of the head of the falls. The crew ferries into midstream and nonchalantly back-paddles to hold position. The bow man puts down his paddle and fetches his camera. He stands up in the canoe and begins to shoot. Evidently entranced by the majesty of his surroundings and confident he's in full command, the stern man also rests his paddle. Neither one realizes that the current is gently but forcefully carrying them toward the lip of the falls. Suddenly there's an awakening! The men back paddle for dear life. Again and again. But it's too late: The silent strength of the slick tongue carries them into the rocky chasm below. One man swims to shore; the other perishes in the succeeding cascades.

You initial reaction to the tragedy is probably "don't mess around above waterfalls." But the error goes much deeper than that. First, the clearly marked portage began *above* the pool for a reason—safety! Neither the trip guide nor map indicated that it was okay to go beyond it. Nevertheless, it was safe enough to continue downstream into the pool if you pulled out well above the falls. The crew leader's real mistake was not that he went too far, it was allowing his less experienced crew to join him. However, he might still have saved the day had he advised everyone of the dangers and admonished them to hang tight, paddle upstream, and hold to shore until each canoe was unloaded. But he didn't, and the result was disaster.

On a different river the scenario might have been played differently. Burr Falls on the Fond du Lac River begins in the middle of a low canyon that's preceded by a ¼-mile-long pool. Above the pool is a short stretch of fast water with a small island at its head. A well-marked portage begins just upstream of the island. (Note the similarity between this and Thunderhouse Falls?)

Below the pool the river narrows and drops without warning. Once you're into the quickened flow, there's no escape—the canyon walls are sheer and at least a dozen feet high. Total drop is about 30 feet. I doubt you'd survive the fall!

Only the small rapids and quiet pool are evident from the top. When we arrived the wind was blowing strongly downstream and masked the sound of the fury below. We could hear nothing from our holding point on the island.

We put ashore on the island to study the map. We knew the falls was just below. Somehow we'd missed the portage, though we'd been searching diligently for it. The trip guide indicated that the path was a few yards above our location on the east bank of the river. I searched downstream with binoculars. There was no hint of danger. All signs suggested we could proceed safely into the quiet pool. Perhaps it was the canyon wall that stopped us—and the knowledge that once committed, escape was impossible. Or maybe it was our sixth sense that suggested something wasn't right. But our real concern was the location of the portage—*above the island!*

We applied the rule, "If the carry starts here, there's a reason!" and backtracked accordingly. Had we violated our instincts I doubt you'd be reading these words now.

Proceeding beyond marked portages isn't always safe, even if it appears so from above!

WIND

In case you missed a subtle point, the direction and intensity of the wind are critical in sensing—or failing to sense—a falls. A good upstream wind out of a canyon can make a 3-foot ledge sound like Niagara Falls, and a downstream breeze can hush the most violent drop. So keep in touch with your map. *Know where the falls is!* And continually check the relative position of ground features to the river. If dead ahead, the tree line abruptly drops off, there's a reason! Get ashore and check it out.

DAMS

Dams are much more dangerous than falls. The hazard lies in the uniform drop and accompanying backroller (eddy) at their base. Float a small log over a dam and watch it tumble over and over, trapped in the turbulence below. Now picture your canoe doing the same thing. Broaching at the base of a dam may be certain death. Your only recourse in an upset may be to abandon the craft *and your life jacket,* swimming down under the eddy to the current beneath—a frightening maneuver that calls for cool determination and a realization of what's happening.

If, heaven forbid, you find yourself being swept over a dam with no recourse but to obey the flow, then drive the canoe forward with all your strength. Your only salvation may be to get enough forward speed to breach the dangerous backroller. Running a dam—even a low one—is a life-threatening situation!

STRAINERS

A strainer results when a river flows between the branches of a submerged tree. If you get sucked into one, there may be no escape—especially not if you're wearing loose clothing or a bulky life vest that catches in the debris.

Strainers are every bit as dangerous as dams—maybe more so, because they don't look very ominous from above. As with other canoeing dangers, your best bet is to avoid them in the first place, in this case with an evasive maneuver called the back ferry.

If you spot a strainer ahead, tuck your tail toward shore (inside bend) at an angle of about 30 degrees and back-paddle for dear life. The combined vectors—forward velocity of the river and reverse speed of the canoe—will move you sideways toward shore (figure 17-1). This procedure is identical to that used by old-time ferryboat captains to cross strong currents. Only experience can suggest the best ferry angle.

You can also spin the canoe around and cross-ferry with your nose upstream (the forward ferry). This maneuver is more powerful than the back ferry and is the best way to cross fast currents that have dangerous obstacles below.

Space does not permit me to treat evasive maneuvers and paddling techniques here. If you want a solid background in the basics of canoeing white water, see these books: *Path of the Paddle* by Bill Mason and *Paddle Your Own Canoe* by Gary and Joanie McGuffin (appendix B).

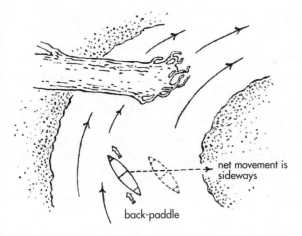

Figure 17-1. The back ferry. If you spot a strainer ahead, tuck your tail toward shore at an angle of about 30 degrees and back-paddle! Your net movement will be sideways.

CANYONS

The dangers in running a canyon are twofold. Most obvious is the inability to get out if you capsize. Second is the difficulty of determining the *real height* of waves from a vantage point on the canyon rim. Waves tend to flatten when viewed from above. And the higher you are, the flatter they appear. Even a dozen feet makes a difference. Binoculars (not a monocular!) help put things into proper perspective but still require you to interpret the difference between sheer magnification and wave size.

There's no second-guessing once you start into a canyon. Either you make it or you don't. Canyons are one place where the rule "if in doubt, portage" should be applied religiously!

ICE-COLD WATER

Perhaps the greatest danger in canoeing northern rivers is capsizing in cold water. The hazard lies in the shock of initial dunking and the hypothermia that follows.

Hypothermia is a medical term that means "low temperature." Symptoms change as the body temperature falls:

99–96 degrees F.—Victim shivers intensely.

95–91 degrees F.—Shivering worsens, slurred speech, amnesia.

90–86 degrees F.—Shivering stops and muscles stiffen; skin becomes blue or puffy.

85–81 degrees F.—Increased severity of the above symptoms.

80–78 degrees F.—Unconsciousness, erratic heartbeat.

Below 78 degrees F.—Death.

Canoe upsets invariably occur in rapids where even a good life jacket won't always keep your head above water. So you can't assume the recommended huddle position to conserve body heat and wait patiently in the freezing froth for a friendly watercraft to speed to your rescue. Every second is precious. You must get to shore quickly—a feat that's next to impossible if your arms and legs are immobilized by cold.

Layered woolens covered with waterproof nylon help conserve body heat both in and out of water, but not nearly enough. Only a neoprene wet suit cuts the cold and keeps it out. Wet suits, however, are uncomfortable, time consuming to put on and take off, and generally impractical under typical field conditions. Far better to wear the time-proven woolens—and your life vest—and not capsize at all!

An ice-water dunking requires immediate treatment *even if the victim disagrees.* Dr. Forgey, in his book *Wilderness Medicine* (see appendix B), recommends the follow procedure:

Remove the victim from wind and place him in the best shelter available. Replace wet clothing with dry clothing if possible. Insulate the victim from the ground and add heat . . . strip the victim and place him in a sleeping bag with a stripped rescuer. A hypothermia victim alone in a well insulated sleeping bag will simply stay cold. If he is conscious, give him warm drinks[2] and candy or sweetened foods. If no sleeping bag or fire is available, have a party huddle together. Avoid use of alcohol.

One real danger in treating hypothermia is aftershock—a condition that may result if the outside of the body is warmed too fast. The effect is to dilate the surface blood vessels and thereby shuttle cold blood from the extremities into the already cold interior core of the body. Since the temperature of the blood in the hands and feet may be *dozens* of degrees below that of the inner body, the consequences of pumping it to the heart and brain are obvious—death in a matter of minutes!

[2]Here a thermos of soup is indispensable. Firing a stove and waiting for water to boil may be a luxury you can't afford.

A hypothermic must be rewarmed gradually and evenly. The strenuous exercise advised by some "experts" may speed death by placing an additional load on the heart. A hot drink and the sleeping-bag treatment is the most reliable procedure.

It's interesting to note that Dr. Richardson—surgeon on Sir John Franklin's ill-fated journey up the Hood River in 1821—prescribed the sandwich treatment for a voyager who had capsized in a bad rapid. The account reads:

Belanger was suffering extremely, immersed to his middle in the center of a rapid, the temperature of which was very little above the freezing point, and the upper part of his body covered with wet clothes, exposed in a temperature not much above zero, to a strong breeze.... By the direction of Dr. Richardson, he was instantly stripped, and being rolled up in blankets, two men undressed themselves and went to bed with him; but it was some hours before he recovered his warmth and sensations.[3]

The sad irony is that Arthur Moffat (see chapter 4, Loose Threads) might have survived his dunking on the Dubawnt River had his crew understood the nature of hypothermia. Evidently Moffatt's friends believed his authoritative cries of "I'm okay, I'm okay," and simply placed him in a sleeping bag inside a tent. There was no sandwich treatment or hot drink.

I urge those who canoe frigid waters to read Dr. Bill Forgey's authoritative book *Hypothermia, Death by Exposure*. Dr. Forgey's book dispels common myths (such as the belief that even dead pigs and watermelons exhibit aftershock!) and provides field-realistic alternatives to treating hypothermia in a wilderness environment.

POOR COMMUNICATION; NO SUPPORT CANOE

Two experienced canoeists were lining their 18-foot Grumman around a rapid on the Kanaaupscow River in Quebec when, without a word, each simultaneously let go of his line momentarily. The canoe, now free, slipped quietly away and out of sight down the rapid. The disgruntled canoeists walked the shoreline of the river and carefully searched the rapid for signs of the canoe. Nothing! Did the craft dive for the deep currents and become wedged between rocks? The pair had sat down at the edge of the pool below

the drop to contemplate their misfortune when the canoe, bone-dry and virtually undamaged, mysteriously floated to shore within a few feet of where they were sitting. Joyously, the men climbed aboard and smugly waited for their friends upstream to finish the $1/2$-mile-long arduous task of lining the rapid.

A similar case ended differently: Two young men traveling alone on a remote river in the Northwest Territories halted their canoe near a small island to check a rapids below. Each man had a firm hold on some willow branches that jutted from the island. Cautiously they let the canoe downstream, working their way from branch to branch. Then without a sound, each man let go of his branch and leaned over to grab another. The unbalanced canoe capsized and floated away, leaving the men stranded on the island without food, shelter, or warm clothing.

The pair were rescued two weeks later only because the HBC manager in Yellowknife had persuaded them to register their route with the RCMP before they left. When the two were long overdue, the mounties initiated an air search.

In each case the near-tragedy could have been averted if each man had simply told the other what he planned to do *before* he did it. In the first example there was a rescue canoe that could have chased the lost boat if necessary. In the second case there wasn't. The Far North is no place for fuzzy thinkers or those who travel without a support crew. Two canoes are the *minimum* for safety; three are much better!

CAPSIZING ON OPEN WATER

It was early July when the two inexperienced teenagers set their 17-foot canoe into the icy waters of Reindeer Lake (Saskatchewan). For several days they paddled along without incident, gaining confidence as the hours passed. When a substantial tailwind came up, the boys rejoiced and adjusted their course toward open water to take advantage of it. Soon they were riding the waves, surfing along, making wonderful time. Unaware of the dangers, they let the wind push them farther and farther into the teeth of the menacing sea. When at last the pair realized their predicament, they were $1/2$ mile from land. They panicked, tried to turn upwind, and capsized. Though both wore life jackets, one lad died in the frigid water—a victim of hypothermia. The other boy made it safely to shore, where he was later rescued by fishermen.

Their mistakes included traveling without a support

---

[3]From "Narrative of a Journey to the Shores of the Polar Seas in the years 1819, 20, 21," by Sir John Franklin, Charles E. Tuttle.

canoe, getting too far from land, misjudging the weather, and inexperience in handling a canoe in rough water. Capsizing far from shore on a rolling lake is serious, especially if the water is very cold. Under these conditions even a support canoe may not be able to help: Its paddlers will be too busy attending to their own problems.

The recommended procedure for running rough open water is to stick tightly together, parallel, one or two canoe lengths apart. If a canoe upsets, your first responsibility is to get your friends out of the cold water immediately. The canoe-over-canoe rescue touted by the Red Cross and Boy Scouts is generally impossible to perform in a running sea. Far better to forget about the swamped canoe and gear and put your efforts into rescuing the paddlers.

If there's only one support canoe, rescue may mean throwing some packs overboard to provide room—and essential freeboard—for the victims. If you have two support craft, they can work as a team and share responsibility. In either case there's real danger of swamping the upright canoes when those in the water climb aboard. And even if you are able to perform a safe rescue, it's doubtful you'll ever recover the gear you tossed into the lake.

The worst canoeing disaster of all time occurred on June 12, 1978, when four replica North canoes (20- to 24-foot freight canoes of eighteenth-century vintage) carrying a total of thirty-one people capsized in 4- to 6-foot waves at the headwaters of the Ottawa River. Twenty-seven teenagers and their four adult leaders had just embarked on a sixteen-day canoe trip into the wilds of Quebec when it happened. Far from shore, one canoe capsized in the big waves, spilling its occupants into the icy water. A second canoe tried to help but it, too, upset. The remaining two canoes put ashore to dump packs then set out to rescue those still in the water. But the victims panicked and capsized the canoes as they climbed into them. Thirteen people died!

In retrospect: All the canoeists wore life jackets and were good swimmers. The boys were reasonably skilled in the art of paddling and self-rescue.

There are no procedures guaranteed to save you in a rough-water upset. Staying ashore and calmly waiting for the weather to pass is your best insurance.

LIGHTNING

In 1980 I was canoeing the Gull River in Ontario with a group of teenagers when lightning suddenly lit up the sky and rain came down in buckets. Rain fell so fast and furious that I could barely see my bow partner.

The Gull was barely 50 yards wide at that point, and the shoreline was choked with trees to the water's edge. There was no safe landing in sight.

The distance of a lightning strike can be estimated by dividing the number of seconds between the flash of light and the thunder boom by 5. For example, a ten-second delay indicates that the lightning is about 2 miles away. I get pretty scared when the count drops below five seconds.

At the two-and-a-half-second strike, my friend Al Todnem turned his canoe sharply toward shore and poured on the coal. I stayed in the middle of the river and yelled for him to come back, but he couldn't hear me above the roar of the storm.

When Al's canoe was just offshore, lightning took the top out of a tall birch at the river's edge. The top exploded into flame and showered sparks in all directions. The burning top—which must have weighed half a ton—splashed down an arm's length from the canoe!

The point is that getting to shore when lightning strikes is a good plan only if there's a safe landing spot away from tall trees.

A cone of lightning protection extends from the tallest object in an area about 45 degrees in all directions. My experience suggests that the best plan is to stay within this protected zone but far enough away so that lightning can't jump from a tree root to you. Lightning can jump a dozen feet or more, so 50 to 100 feet from shore is probably the best place to be.

NOT SCOUTING A RAPIDS YOU'VE RUN MANY TIMES BEFORE

It's early June on a rapids you've paddled many times. Pangs of conscience tell you to check the pitch from shore before you proceed. But you arrogantly dismiss the warning and plunge confidently ahead.

Then you see it—a storm-downed sapling that blocks the way. "Back!" you scream. But it's too late. The canoe spins suddenly sideways and overturns. You and your partner escape to shore just in time to watch the golden Kevlar hull break up on a midstream boulder.

It happened just like this to me on a Canadian river I'd paddled *five* times before. I thought I knew every rock and eddy in the watercourse. But it hadn't rained for weeks, and

Figure 17-2. Here's the price the author paid when he didn't check a rapids he'd run many times before! The canoe is a 16½-foot Kevlar Mad River Explorer.

my ordinarily clear channel was a dry boulder bed—a discovery I made when I wrecked my boat (figure 17-2).

Whenever I head to northern Canada to paddle a river I haven't done before, friends chide me about going into harm's way. I explain to them that I'm always very careful on routes I haven't canoed before. It is on familiar runs that I take things for granted and let down my guard. Not scouting a rapid you've paddled before can be a recipe for a long walk home!

FAILURE TO HEED THE ADVICE OF LOCALS

Grand Rapids on the Mattagami River (northern Ontario) is more than 1 mile long and ¼ mile wide. When the water is high, the rapids are quite lively and produce a hollow

<hr/>

[4]The Pas is located on Canada Highway 10 about 150 miles south of Flin Flon.

drone that can be heard for several miles upstream. Nevertheless, the rapids are relatively easy if you choose the correct side of the river and stay alert.

When the two young lads on their way to James Bay came to the rapids, the bow man stood up, cast a long glance downstream, and purposely selected a route *opposite* that advised by local residents of Smoky Falls, some 30 miles upstream. Their aluminum canoe went over a ledge, swamped, and wrapped around a rock. Unable to salvage their canoe or gear, the boys ended their trip and walked the shoreline back to town, which took them nearly three days.

The antithesis is taking the advice of local residents too literally. Our two-day portage on the Steel River (chapter 15—The Joy of Solo Canoeing) testifies to what can happen when you seek advice from a noncanoeist. Nevertheless, you can get reliable information from nonpaddlers if you compare the input from several sources. For example, Santoy Falls was a major obstacle on our 1981 descent of the Steel River. We'd heard that the falls was a killer and that the portage around it began dangerously close to the drop. Naturally we were intimidated, so we asked some fishermen on the lake about its location. Seven of the eight people we surveyed authoritatively reported that the carry began just west of the falls in a small bay. It did, and there were no problems.

POOR PLANNING; INEXPERIENCE

It was 1968 and the man was a high school teacher with a free summer. His friend was a businessman who had precisely fourteen days of vacation. The idea was to paddle about 200 miles of Manitoba's South Seal River. To save time they'd drive to The Pas[4] then fly commercial air to Lynn Lake. There they would charter a floatplane to the put-in. The canoe would be sent by rail from their home in Minneapolis to Lynn Lake ahead of time. Fast and neat; the canoe would be waiting for them when they arrived. Or so they thought!

First stop, Lynn Lake train station. "What, no canoe?" Checking revealed that customs authorities had impounded the craft for payment of duty. "The canoe was being shipped to a Canadian, *wasn't it?*" No matter; the misunderstanding could be cleared up in a few days. *A few days* indeed! Precious time was ticking by. The businessman didn't have a few days.

So the men went shopping for a canoe. A thorough search turned up the only canoe in town—an old but relatively sound 17-foot wood-canvas Chestnut. The craft weighed at least one hundred pounds and had a deep fin keel along with a square stern. But it *was* a canoe, and it cost only $80!

The teacher was hopping mad. Everything was going wrong. He looked at the bright yellow fabric cover he had made for his Alumacraft. It wouldn't fit the Chestnut, but it might come in handy for *something!*

Problems compounded. Instead of averaging 25 miles per day, as they had anticipated, they were making only 10. They had the wrong footwear, the wrong rain gear, the wrong canoe . . . and the wrong attitude. Only the teacher's insistence that they bring a small Optimus stove saved the day. Without it they'd have been miserable in the incessant rain.

What worried them most was that they were falling drastically behind schedule. So to compensate they took to paddling well into the evening. They grew impatient and careless. At around 9:00 P.M. on the ninth day, they encountered the rapid. It looked easy enough from the top, so they decided to run it blind. The moment of reckoning came quickly: Man-sized rollers at the bottom swamped the canoe and the boulder field took out the keel and one gunnel. The old Chestnut was wrecked beyond repair. The trip was over!

The men salvaged the gear and struggled to shore. An inventory of their food revealed a seven-day supply. The river was too fast and narrow to land a floatplane on, so the next day they carried their outfit about 6 miles overland to a small lake that had a sand beach. There they devised elaborate signals, making a huge SOS on the beach and cutting flags from their yellow canoe cover. And each afternoon the men flashed their signal mirror hopefully across the empty skies.

Twenty-one days later they were picked up by a search and rescue plane. It was the flash of light and yellow flags that caught the pilot's eye. "Good thing you boys registered with the mounties . . . otherwise we'd never have found you," the pilot told them.

Total cost of the rescue came to nearly $3,200 (a fortune in 1968), which the men paid sheepishly but gladly.

The errors speak for themselves: inexperience in running white water, impatience, poor planning, and lack of a support crew. The one thing the men did right was to register their trip with the authorities. Wilderness rivers bear no malice toward the unprepared, but neither do they grant immunity from error!

FOREST FIRES

July 1994. Week two of a nine-week canoe trip in northern Canada. We were on the Little Partridge River, which is located just south of the Northwest Territories.

It was midafternoon when we saw the smoke and crackling flames! My husband, Mike Wevrick, and I climbed an esker and walked upriver for a better view. Fires burned across the river as far as we could see, and they moved along at alarming speed: I feared the flames would jump across to us at any second. The expression paralyzed with fear took on real meaning.

Mike and I had experienced other fires earlier in the summer. But all had been confined to a lakeshore where we could simply paddle away. Now we were on a small river from which there was no escape. We kept our EPIRB nearby with distant hopes that, if we activated it, a rescue plane would come in time.

We had been watching fires for several weeks and learned there was a pattern: In the morning flames were localized and columns of smoke were well defined. As the day progressed the columns blurred to hazy smoke that blanketed the sky. We agreed that it would be best if we arose at first light and made time before the wind came up and the fires grew. Thank goodness our plan worked or you wouldn't be reading this today!

—Sara Seager

As a forester in Oregon many years ago, I fought several good-sized fires. And I have been canoeing when the woods were ablaze all around me. If you're caught in the canoe country with a raging fire in progress, here's the recommended survival procedure according to Walt Tomascak, Fire Management Officer for Minnesota's Superior National Forest:

If you smell smoke or see a convection column rising in the distance, remain calm and evaluate the safety of your position. Generally, fires move in a predictable direction so you may be able to outflank it by moving perpendicular to its path, that is so long as you can stay on or near water. If the fire has reached the lake you're on, move to the opposite shore and stay near the water's edge. If the shoreline is burning all around, get out in the center of the lake and stay there. Wet down your clothes, hat, and

Figure 17-4. Forest fires! Little Partridge River, Saskatchewan.

life jacket. Remove all nylon clothing! Flaming nylon produces the most severe burns—instantly!

If sparks are flying badly, overturn your canoe in the middle of the lake and get under it for protection. The canoe will retain a large air bubble inside in which you can breathe and talk normally.

An intense crown fire often generates its own winds. In extreme cases these winds may reach speeds in excess of 100 miles an hour! If that happens you may be in trouble whatever you do. Generally, though, you should be able to survive even very large fires if you're at least 100 yards from a burning shoreline.

I would not recommend leaving your canoe under any conditions since it offers a means of eventual escape as well as protection from radiant heat. Its best use, as I've suggested, is as a heat and ember shield when overturned in the water.

Under some conditions, forest fires may jump ½ mile or more—another reason why you should stay put near a large body of water. If you must travel through an area that is burning, wait until the fire activity is lowest, which is generally late evening through midmorning.

ICE

You can portage or line around difficult rapids or wait out a running sea, but the only thing you can do about an ice-

Figure 17-5. Bob O'Hara pushes through the ice on Aberdeen Lake, Nunavut, Canada, on July 17, 1969.

Figure 17-6. Ice! Aberdeen Lake, Nunavut, Canada.

The men waited. And waited. Entertainment was provided by the shortwave radio they carried. "I remember sitting on a big rock staring into the sky while the radio blasted out the incredible news we'd landed two men on the moon. And here we were landlocked by a mini glacier," said Bob.

Ten days passed and still no wind. Then the crew crossed paths with a wildlife biologist and Inuit who were also iced in. The worry now was food. Would there be enough to last the trip?

Fortunately the crew had a rifle, which the Inuit man used to kill a caribou. The six men consumed the entire animal in less than two days!

Finally, on the twelfth day, wind broke the ice free and the men continued on to Baker Lake. "We hit an ice fog on Shultz Lake," recalls Bob. "Visibility was zero so we ran compass and dodged floes the whole day. It was pretty tricky . . . and dangerous weaving between those heaving ice masses."

O'Hara followed the ice out of Shultz Lake—an exhilarating experience. He said "It was a helluva ride! We clicked off 60 miles in four hours—took us two days to do that on the Dubawnt [River]. The run was so fast we damn near passed Baker Lake right by."

No one can give you advice on how to handle an ice-locked lake. It's something you look at, think on, then act . . . or sit, as the case may be. There are hazards. Most serious is getting behind schedule and perhaps running out of food down the pike. On a very long trip, your concern may be finishing up before you're pelted by the snows of winter.

Traveling in broken ice is a perilous procedure. Leads open and close quickly as wind blows the ice around. If you get caught between floes—a real possibility if the wind is up—there may be no escape. And the effects of capsizing in frigid water are obvious. For all these reasons you'll plan your trip to ensure ice-free water. And if your plans are thwarted by a quirk of nature, just be sure to carry enough food (a ten-day supply is recommended) to weather the inconvenience. Bring along an extra measure of patience, too, plus a flexible schedule so you can complete the run without rushing mindlessly through it and thereby endangering your safety.

TIDES

The Kellet River begins about 20 miles north of Wager Bay at the edge of the Arctic Circle. It's a remote, challenging river that to date has not been canoed. The problem is ice. Lots of it. Bob O'Hara and a friend attempted the river in

choked lake is stay put and pray for a good wind to break things free. Sometimes the wind comes, sometimes it doesn't. If it doesn't, you wait, gripe, and exhaust your food supply for no gainful purpose.

In 1969 Bob O'Hara (see chapter 5) and crew flew into the junction of the Thelon and Hanbury Rivers with the intent of paddling the Thelon to the community of Baker Lake. On July 17 they nosed their canoes into Aberdeen Lake . . . and broken ice 4 feet thick! Aberdeen was jammed shut. It would take a strong north wind to blow it free.

For two days the men made what time they could by skirting the shore, sliding, dragging, and pushing their canoes over the ice. Tempers flared, muscles ached, everyone became physically and emotionally exhausted. Their weary bodies needed huge quantities of precious food to maintain the pace. They were making no time at all and were consuming food at an alarming rate. Bob stopped the work and put everyone on half rations.

Figure 17-7. A 20-foot Grumman canoe stranded on the tidal flats of Wager Bay. Tides of up to 14 feet inundate this area every twelve hours.

their 20-foot Grumman canoe in 1980, but were unsuccessful.[5] The path to the Kellet remained ice-choked the entire season.

Bob also experienced unusual tides in the area. "I didn't have an up-to-date tide table, so we used what we had," he commented. "One afternoon we stopped for lunch on a rocky outcrop in Wager Bay, tied the canoe to a boulder, then went

Figure 17-8. Going ashore at hide tide. Hudson Bay, about 40 miles north of Churchill, Manitoba.

off to explore. When we returned a few hours later the tide had gone out. I mean *really* out! There was ½ mile of huge boulders between the canoe and open water. So we just sat and waited for the water to return."

O'Hara learned that tides of up to 14 feet inundate Wager Bay every twelve hours. After their first tidebound experience, the two men made it a practice to always stop (and camp) on a high hill that had a near-vertical drop to the sea. "That way we could lower the canoe to the water if necessary—like dropping into a swimming pool," said Bob.

O'Hara also discovered that tidewater sometimes moves rapidly and forcefully. "Once on a side trip down the river we lined around a good-sized ledge. Later, when we followed the tide back upstream, we rode a full-blown rapid hell bent for leather. The ledge was completely washed out!"

If Bob O'Hara had been new to the Arctic, this episode might have ended tragically. Bob's best advice? Get a current tide table and learn to use it. And bring an accurate watch!

Some things to remember about tides:

- There are two high tides per day (twelve hours apart) and two low tides per day (also twelve hours apart). It takes six hours to go from high tide to low tide, and vice versa.

- Tidal cycles occur fifty minutes later each day, which means that if high tide is at 1:00 P.M. today it will be at

---

[5]Bob originally planned to canoe the river with a crew of six in two 20-foot canoes, but four men dropped out during the final planning steps. His partner for the trip was an experienced canoeist and an M.D.

1:50 P.M. tomorrow, 2:40 P.M. the next day, and so on.

■ If you've ever watched the tide roll in or out, you may have observed that the water moves very slowly near the times of high or low tide. But when the tide is halfway through its cycle, the water moves much faster. This has to do with the position—and gravitational effect—of the moon (and, to a lesser extent, of the sun). The important thing to remember is that the period of greatest tidal change (tidal velocity) occurs during the *third and fourth hours after high or low tide*. So if you have to cross a wide bay, you'll want to paddle during the slowest tidal flow, which occurs an hour on either side of high or low tide.

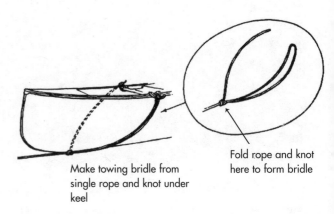

Make towing bridle from single rope and knot under keel

Fold rope and knot here to form bridle

THE ART OF LINING

Around the bend you see the dancing horsetails that mark the rapid. There's no question: You'll have to portage. You put ashore just above the drop then probe through thick alders in search of a portage trail. Half an hour of diligent scouting fails to reveal the slightest trace of a path. Getting around the rapid will mean horsing the canoes through hundreds of yards of tangled vegetation.

What about the other bank? Not a chance. A sheer rock face stretches tirelessly the full length of the pitch. There's no way to get around it, save for hauling the boats over the top

Figure 17-9.

with ropes, mountaineering style.

Running the drop is out of the question. And so is portaging. You'll have to line!

Canoeing texts make lining sound like a lark: Just attach ropes to the ends of your canoe, walk along the shore, and the canoe will naturally follow. If you tuck the bow to shore and angle the tail slightly outward, the side wash of the current

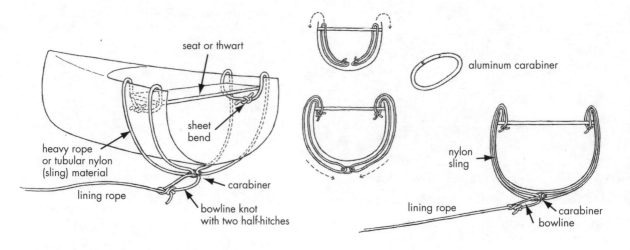

seat or thwart

sheet bend

heavy rope or tubular nylon (sling) material

lining rope

carabiner

bowline knot with two half-hitches

aluminum carabiner

nylon sling

lining rope

carabiner

bowline

Figure 17-10. You can make a reliable lining harness from tubular nylon sling (mountaineering) material.

Figure 17-11. Lining the lower canyon on the Porcupine River, Saskatchewan. The author holds the bow line. The canoe is a Dagger Venture.

tightly woven material around the core). It's soft, not slippery, and holds knots securely. You can buy this rope by the foot at marinas or prepackaged in 50-foot lengths at some hardware stores. Twenty-five feet of rope on each end of the canoe is all most canoeists can handle. If you need more rope, use a double sheetbend to tie on the extra piece.

The side wash of a rapid exerts tremendous pressure against the hull of a canoe. For this reason you should secure your lining ropes as close to the keel line as possible. The lower the connection, the safer the system. Most canoeists (myself included) simply tie to a hole drilled midway down the canoe stem. But more cautious types rig a Bill Mason–style harness around the *upstream* portion of the hull, as illustrated in figure 17-9.

You can also tie about 3 feet of 1-inch-wide tubular nylon sling material (available at mountaineering shops) to each gunnel, or around the stern seat, and join them at the keel line. Tie or clip (use a carabiner) your lining rope to the sling loops and you'll have a secure harness that pulls right from the keel. When you've finished lining, remove the rope and haul the nylon webbing into the canoe (figure 17-10).

Lining is a daily (often hourly) routine on wilderness rivers, and rigging a harness is a hassle. Consequently, most wilderness travelers just tie to holes in the canoe's stems. PVC-reinforced holes (as suggested in chapter 6) are safer than fittings because they can't get sheared off or bent.

will push the craft into the main stream. Reverse the angle on the canoe and the river will scoot it back to the bank. Simple as pie.

Don't you believe it!

In the process of writing this book, I questioned dozens of wilderness canoeists about problems (if any) they had encountered while lining. Answers were unanimous: Lining was perceived as an art—one that is frequently difficult and dangerous. Working a canoe along the edge of a powerful rapids with a pair of ropes while hopping nimbly from rock to rock calls for skill, determination, surefootedness, and coordination.

Here's how to get the job done without an upsetting experience.

Attaching the Lines

For my lining rope I prefer brightly colored, $^3/_8$-inch-diameter kermantle-style polypropylene (there's a sheath of

Procedure

The object of lining is to work the canoe down the edge of the rapids, maneuvering it around boulders, logs, and ledges. One person usually controls the bow line, the other takes the stern, though it's possible to do the job alone. The stern person provides the judgment and control; the bow paddler follows the stern person's commands and tries to keep the boat from sideswiping rocks. The cardinal rule is *never* to let the stern drift out beyond the bow. If this happens, the canoe may suddenly swap ends, capsize, and float on downriver. The power of the current is enormous—no way will you be able to haul the swamped canoe ashore with lines!

For this reason the most experienced partner controls the tail line. Nearly all lining accidents (capsizes and swampings) are the fault of a too-meticulous bow person who refused to lighten up on his or her line!

You need surefootedness and athletic ability to expertly line a canoe down a tough drop. The scenario requires that

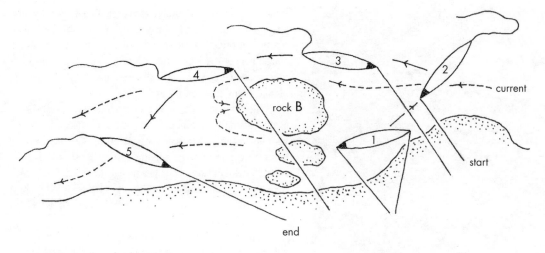

Figure 17-12. Lining around an obstacle (rock).

you run along the shore at *current speed,* jumping confidently from rock to rock while watching the canoe, *not your feet!* If you dally and snub the canoe at a critical moment, tail wash may pour in over the stern and swamp the boat.

Problem: You're lining down a tough rapid when the stern swings too far out into the current. The side wash threatens to capsize the hull. Which of these is the correct maneuver?

   a) Pull the stern line hard and snap the canoe quickly to shore.

   b) Command the bow person to let out his or her line.

   c) Let go of the stern line and allow the craft to spin around in the current.

Answer: Except in rare instances, as when you're crossing awkward eddy lines (see the discussion of pinwheeling below), "b" is correct. You should remember that nearly all control of the canoe rests in the hands of the person upstream!

Lining Alone

One way to prevent the dreaded situation of the canoe's tail getting too far out in the current is to line the canoe alone, using a *single* stern line—a good idea if your bow person is very inexperienced, nonathletic, or won't follow directions. The downside of this practice is that your canoe will probably bang into and hang up on every rock in the river!

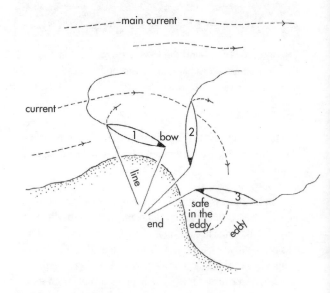

Figure 17-13. The canoe is being lined around the rock shelf on the right. There's a very strong eddy line below the shelf. As soon as the bow crosses the eddy line, the stern line will be released and the bow line hauled in. The canoe will make a fast 180-degree turn into the eddy. Setting tail-first around the rock shelf (as is usually recommended) doesn't work in this scenario.

Figure 17-14. Lining requires teamwork. Here the author (left front) and crew line the canoe over a jutting rock to avoid a dangerous hole.

Pinwheeling

Pinwheeling is a useful technique for working the canoe around obstacles near shore. It's also useful for crossing strong eddy lines that have nasty curling waves you must avoid.

Problem: Your canoe is sitting in a quiet eddy (figure 17-12). You must line it around rock B. When you push the bow of the canoe out into the river in an effort to clear B, the current forces it back to shore. The water is too deep and swift to walk out to B. What to do?

Solution: Pinwheel (reverse) the canoe and float it around rock B. Use your lines to ferry the canoe back upstream and out into the main current. Let go of the stern (upstream) line and allow the current to pivot the craft out and around rock B. This is essentially an eddy peel-out with no paddlers aboard. Be sure you have good hold of the bow (downstream) line when the tail swings around.

Another example is illustrated in figure 17-13. There was a very strong eddy line below the shelf. We tried setting around tail-first, as recommended, and nearly lost a canoe. Then we tried a classic eddy turn, which worked just fine.

Here's the pinwheel procedure: As soon as the bow crosses the eddy line, the stern line is released and the bow line hauled in. The canoe will make a fast 180-degree turn into the eddy. This tactic is useful when working space is tight or there are obstacles (trees) that halt the lining process.

Rules

Don't put monkey fists or loops on the ends of your lining ropes. If you goof and the canoe upsets, the knot or loop may become wedged between obstacles in the river and cause the craft to wrap. In the words of the late Bill Mason: "Keep a knife handy when working around lines!" I know of several cases where canoeists became entangled in lining ropes and were reluctantly dragged to sea. Wear a sheath knife or clip-on river folder whenever you are lining canoes. And *always* wear your life jacket!

Successful lining requires team coordination and a shoreline that's relatively free of vegetation. If you've got to pick your way between overhanging trees, you might as well portage. Lining down a major rapid—one that'll eat up your canoe if you goof—takes practice, patience, and athletic ability. It's not a skill you can learn from a textbook!

TRACKING

Tracking is the opposite of lining. Here the idea is to haul the canoe upstream. Tracking is just like ferrying. To get around obstacles near shore, simply pull the tail line smartly inward, which sets the nose of the canoe on an outward tack. Then you walk (run!) upstream and let the side wash ferry the canoe around the obstacle. The greatest danger is allowing the bow to get too far out into the current; if it does, the stern person must instantly let up on the line.

Figure 17-15. Tracking is the opposite of lining.

For greatest safety you may want to rig a towing harness around the *upstream* end of the canoe. You'll lose some leverage with the harness (the rope pulls from the keel, just forward of the bow seat), but the canoe won't capsize if you yank hard on the line to haul in a bow that's out of alignment with the current.

SALVAGE

It had been only four days since our four-man canoe team arrived by helicopter at the headwaters of the South Nahanni River. Gordon Lightfoot and I were lining his new Old Town Voyageur canoe through some very turbulent water down a drop between two boulders when, without warning, the canoe spun broadside to the current and swamped. We pulled the packs from the canoe just as it submerged and watched, horrified, as the canoe bent backward and wrapped tightly around the boulder. All that was visible was one gunnel and side of the hull. This demoralizing scene brought to mind Gordon's hit song "The Wreck of The Edmund Fitzgerald," but in this situation it was our own wreck and a hopeless predicament.

We spent the balance of the day trying to salvage the boat, but it was no use. The combined strength of four men, a strong rope, pry bar (log), and sophisticated applications of all the physics we knew were to no avail. After hours of frustrating failure, we gloomily retreated to the head of the rapid to set up camp and develop our strategy for the immediate future. We were now four men with one canoe. Things couldn't have looked worse!

It was then that we met a party of five canoes led by Dr. Brian Gnauck of Marquette, Michigan. Now there was new hope! Could the combined strength of fourteen men pull the canoe free? I remained skeptical. Fourteen or forty—what difference could it make?

But Fred Nelson, one of the new arrivals, produced a block and tackle, which we hoped could provide the edge. We combined forces and attached the block and tackle to our bow line, which we had wrapped around the hull. The idea was to pull the canoe away from the boulder against the full force of the current—a near-impossible task without the aid of pulleys. Perhaps if we also pried with a large log as we worked the winch line . . . but I was pessimistic. Even if we succeeded in retrieving the canoe, it would be irreparable. Or so I thought.

Together we pulled, pried, pulled some more. In an instant it was over and the canoe popped free, like a cookie from a mold. We pulled the canoe quickly up the rocky shore then watched in amazement as its grossly distorted shape, now free of the pressure of the pounding water, slowly returned to its original form. Only a small wrinkle on each side of the hull gave any indication the canoe had been abused.

Truly, ABS Royalex is a miracle material.
—Fred Gaskin, 1980

If you pin a canoe on a boulder on a remote river, you've just got to find a way to free it. If weight and space are minimal concerns, your best bet is to carry some bona fide retrieval gear—block and tackle, 100 to 200 feet of braided ³/₈-inch rope, and so forth. The water pressure on a pinned canoe is at least a ton, which means you'll need a pulley with a mechanical advantage of three to one or better to budge it. (See color figure 17-18.) If you don't have pulleys, you should rig a multiple power cinch like the one shown in figure 17-19. This hitch makes a powerful winch despite the great amount of friction in the system. Some pulley principles are illus-

Figure 17-16. Paul Pepperall (right) pries while Ted Anderson (center) and well-known singer Gordon Lightfoot (left) use a large stick as a tourniquet to shorten the rope.

trated in figure 17-20.

Salvage ropes should always be attached *around the hull* of the canoe—never to seats, thwarts, or lining rings, which may break loose. Position ropes on the canoe to take advantage of the force of the current. Often you can free a pinned canoe by jockeying it around only a few inches.

Nearly every North Country canoeist has at least one horror story to tell about a rapids that was "almost linable." Fred Gaskin's South Nahanni near-disaster is not unique. My files are filled with similar cases.

Wilderness canoeists know they're tempting the patience of the river when they line a difficult drop, so they proceed with caution and give the river the respect it demands.

If you're going into harm's way, you may want to pack along a copy of Les Bechdel and Slim Ray's excellent book, *River Rescue* (appendix B).

CONCLUDING SPLASH

The canoeing literature is rich with advice on how to avoid disaster. To wit: Don't paddle when the wind is up; stay close to shore on big lakes; line or portage dangerous rapids; and much more. This stock advice is hammered home in all canoeing texts, including mine. Still, experienced paddlers would be lying if they said they always do the prudent thing.

Case in point: In 1998 I led a canoe trip down the Tha-

Figure 17-17. Pepperall (left) and Lightfoot (right) attempt to lift the canoe while Anderson (not shown) pries from the upstream side.

anne River in Canada's Northwest Territories. Eric Morse, the famed Canadian canoe man, disliked Hudson Bay rivers because of their nasty, unpredictable weather. If there's an axiom in the area, it's that the wind always blows upstream—

and it's usually accompanied by rain. As expected, headwinds wreaked havoc with our schedule all the way.

The lower Tha-anne is a mess of huge (Class III to VI) rapids and falls that begin just beyond Hyde Lake, which canoeists must cross. Hyde Lake is shallow, and there are few islands to break the wind. A small breeze produces big waves. It's 6.8 miles to the far shore if you canoe straight across. In calm weather you can canoe that far in about two hours. But it's much safer to paddle 25 miles around the north end of the lake and hug the shore all the way. Once you leave Hyde Lake it's a rigorous two days to Hudson Bay.

The wind was blowing bloody murder when we arrived at the headwaters of Hyde Lake, so we camped and hoped for a clear sky in the morning. Two days remained to make the

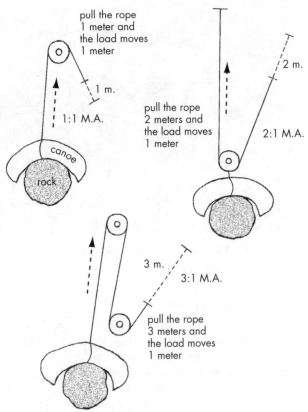

Figure 17-20. Pulley principles.

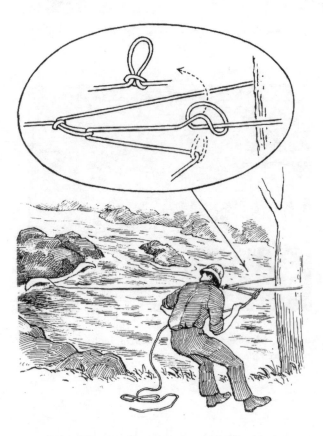

Figure 17-19. The multiple power cinch makes a powerful winch for retrieving a pinned canoe. See chapter 12 for instructions for making the basic knot.

bay, where we had arranged for charter boats to pick us up. The wind continued to blow all that night and the next day. When it finally quit at 3:00 A.M. on our last day, we found ourselves in a serious predicament. Hyde Lake, plus 22 miles of rapids and falls, lay between us and Hudson Bay. Could we do it all in one long day? It seemed impossible.

We studied the map. Prudence suggested that we paddle around the lake, which would take at least seven hours and foil our plans to make the bay on time. A thin fog and barely perceptible tail breeze suggested that if we made a beeline across the lake right now, we'd be out of harm's way by sunrise. What to do?

A vote was taken and we agreed to power straight across

the open water. I programmed the outlet of the lake into my GPS and determinedly paddled into the mist. An hour later we had completed 5 miles and the shoreline loomed ahead. Suddenly a squall came up and we steered into the teeth of it, grateful for our full splash covers. Seconds later the squall passed and the sun came out. We continued downriver and arrived at Hudson Bay at 10:40 P.M., minutes before the sun went down. We had been in the saddle for nineteen hours, longer than any of us had ever paddled.

The point is that there are serious pressures associated with being where you have to be when you have to be. Here's why we thought the beeline plan was best:

- The sky was clear and the weather looked stable.

- We were experienced paddlers and had full splash covers on our big Royalex canoes.

- It was too far and too foggy to see the outlet of the lake but we knew exactly where to go. GPS doesn't lie! We could run a straight, unerring course all the way.

- The slight tail breeze would speed our progress. We figured we could easily make the run in less than two hours. We loaded our canoes slightly stern-heavy to ensure control if the wind picked up.

The moral is that you will discourage danger if you have all your eggs in order. We had apparently stable weather, an experienced crew, splash-covered canoes, an unerring route, and two hours till sundown. Still, we took a chance, and we should be thrashed for doing so.

PATIENCE

Patience is like a secure eddy in the middle of a raging rapid. It's gives you time to formulate a plan before you dash dumbly downstream. Most modern paddlers don't have much patience. They offer these reasons why:

Bad weather/behind schedule. Gotta keep truckin' or we'll lose our layover day at the falls or miss our float plane.

A macho attitude. Why portage? Other parties did these rapids, so can we!

We're prepared for the worst! Whitecaps ahead? No problem; got spray covers.

At the outset, I should make it clear that I am usually not a patient man. When I taught school (thirty-four years), I would sometimes call the shots before all the facts were in. Such a flippant approach would have killed me on a canoe trip. Here are some examples of how patience pays:

Behind Schedule

The wind was blowing bloody murder when we arrived at Otter Lake (Fond du Lac River, Saskatchewan), so we put ashore to wait it out. The waves continued through supper, so I suggested we camp and try again tomorrow. We were snuggled under a tarp, sharing hot buttered rum and popcorn, when we saw two canoes—wind in their face—plugging toward our camp. I waved them in and suggested they share our camp. They said they were behind schedule and had to keep going.

The wind quit around noon the next day and we paddled off with a smile, determined to make up lost time. The sun sets around 11 P.M. at this latitude (59 degrees), so we agreed to canoe till dark. Sometime that day we passed their camp. Everyone was asleep so we chose not to linger. We logged 31 miles that day and 29 the next, which put us ahead of schedule. We never saw the other canoe party again.

Moral? Nature rules! Stop when you must; run when you can.

Big Bear

We had just finished breakfast when I heard someone scream, "Bear! Big bear!" Sure enough, a huge cinnamon-colored black bear was circling our camp. I hollered and blew a whistle. He didn't even look up. So I grabbed my rifle and amassed everyone into a tight group. He circled closer. When he was 50 feet away, I fired a warning shot over his head. He just sniffed the air, then ambled down the bank and came in from another direction. He paused behind a large rock and stood up to see us better. He was just 20 feet away.

I was plenty scared, even with a powerful rifle in hand. But I did not want to kill this gray-whiskered old boy. So we talked. I looked unthreateningly into his eyes and told him I didn't want to hurt him, we'd be gone soon, and he could have his way. I said I respected him and wanted him to go on living. But I emphasized that I would have to shoot him if he came over that rock.

We stared at one another for some time. I could sense the wheels turning in his head. There was no fear or animosity. Only the question of what to do next. Then, after what seemed like an eternity (I learned it was just two minutes), he turned and walked away with dignity. As soon as he was gone, some crew members said they would have shot him long before he got so close. But as the fear wore off, all agreed that my patient plan was the right one.

CHAPTER 18
BARREN-LAND TRAVEL

There's a land where the mountains are nameless
And the rivers all run God knows where;
There are lives that are erring and aimless,
And deaths that just hang by a hair;
There are hardships that nobody reckons;
There are valleys unpeopled and still;
There's a land—oh it beckons and beckons,
And I want to go back—and I will.

Robert Service,
"The Spell of the Yukon"

Tundra. Amorphous gray rock, copiously splashed with lichens and dwarf willow—and not a real tree in sight. The view is hardly compelling. But wait! On the far shore there is a hint of motion. I squint wonderingly through a milky haze of late-afternoon sun. Yes, there they are; I see them. My God, there must be thousands. Tens of thousands! I reach for my binoculars and within seconds the world comes into unbelieving focus.

Caribou! The herd stretches across the endless tundra as far as I can see. Occasionally one looks up toward me in my green Old Town canoe. Only a curious clicking sound, produced by movements of their anklebones, reveals their presence.

I beach the canoe, pull it well up the stony shore, then excitedly scamper up the bank for a closer look. Once on top I casually work my way toward the animals. Using my "lost-wallet technique" (I look down and pretend I'm not interested in them at all), I'm able to come within a dozen feet of the herd's perimeter. A giant bull stares numbly my way—his double-shovel rack must weigh at least fifty pounds. I have no need for the telephoto on my camera; he stands just a canoe length away. I emit a low whistle, to which he responds with a

long questioning look in my direction. Unconvinced that I am completely harmless, he lopes off at half speed into the safety of the herd.

The tundra is rich with the feel and smell of the caribou. A city-bred man, I stand in awe of this timeless sight—the annual migration of 90,000 animals from Bathurst Inlet on the shores of the Arctic Ocean to warmer wintering grounds in Saskatchewan, the relative south.

Life is hard on the barrens. There are wolves and grizzlies to avoid. A limited food supply and the unrelenting assault of billions of blackflies will take their toll. The Arctic lakes are ice cold; the rivers contain thrashing rapids that must be breached. Only the fit will survive the southward march. The weak, the old, and the stragglers will perish before the first snow.

The tundra is as it was. The rituals of a thousand years are repeated again and again. Only my presence reveals the incongruity of the moment. Excitedly, I snap picture after picture until I've exhausted my supply. Three rolls of thirty-six exposures and two hours of stalking are enough for now. I think I'll wander back to the canoe and take a nap. The caribou will continue to cross my path for days. There'll be time

Figure 18-1. Caribou crossing Point Lake, Nunavut, Canada.

for more photos later.

I sling my camera and methodically plod toward the lake and the comforts of my canoe. The knee-high cotton grass bends with each breath of the persistent north wind. It reminds me of Nebraska. The Arctic desert is in full bloom—bright flowers dot the bleak landscape and give a splash of needed color to this stark land of little sticks.

I climb a small knoll then pause to rest. In the distance are three dark shapes partially concealed in the heather of the tundra. Muskox? I descend to all fours and inch toward them, my heart pounding for a better look. When I am within 100 yards, I stand, committed.

Sensing my presence, the shapes also rise. My God, they are grizzlies! Three of them. Mama and two nearly full-grown cubs. Momentarily I stand frozen with fear. My instinct is to run, but I know better. A full-grown grizzly can manage speeds of 40 miles an hour. I can do 10! Besides, there are no trees to climb, no places to hide. I am at the mercy of the bears.

One hundred yards away are the caribou and my friends

with their still-clicking cameras. As the adrenaline flows, I'm reminded of a bear encounter that an acquaintance experienced along the Koyukuk River in Alaska. When, in the distance, Tom saw a large brown bear galloping curiously toward him, he dropped his pack, shucked off his boots and reached for his running shoes.

"Why you puttin' on your tennies?" asked the partner. "You know you can't outrun a grizzly!"

"Yeah . . . I know," came the answer. "But I don't have to outrun the bear. All I have to do is outrun you!"

This sad humor, and an air of desperation, prompts me to try a similar ploy: "Hey, you guys . . . bears!" I called out at the top of my lungs, hopefully my friends will heed the cry and capture the bruins attention long enough so that I may quietly disappear into the tundra. No luck. My friends are too far away and too engrossed in their picture taking to notice me.

Until now the bears have merely stood erect and observed me curiously. Grizzlies are very nearsighted; it's doubtful these can see me clearly, let alone interpret my

Figure 18-2. A huge lake trout that was caught in the estuary of the Burnside River on the Arctic Ocean. This big fish was photographed and released.

intentions. I am downwind, but my senseless chatter has given away my position. Their prey targeted, the animals drop to all fours and lope determinedly toward me.

Figure 18-3. Muskox along the Hood River, Nunavut, Canada.

I can neither speak nor swallow. Thoughts move muddily through my mind, probing for a solution. There is none. In desperation I melt into the tundra, hands clasped solidly behind my neck, knees pulled tightly to my chest: the fetal position.

"Oh please, God, don't let me die in the tundra," I pray. I close my eyes and await the final moment—the feel of hot breath and piercing fangs.

For an eternity, time stands still.

Then, through a mental fog, I hear someone calling. I learn that the bears came within 50 feet before shyly wheeling away. Slowly the world begins to turn again and the realization of my near-death takes hold. Silently, I thank God for intervening on my behalf.

Still floating high on a cloud of disbelief, I amble awkwardly on rubber legs toward the safety of my canoe. I arrive in time to see the alpha male (leader of the caribou herd) break into the chilling lake water. Caribou are followers: In a flash there are hundreds—no, thousands—in the water, swimming neck and neck toward the opposite shore, a mile away. Ten thousand hooves thrash the icy water, which, by my thermometer, reads 36 degrees. The roar is deafening. Had I not known otherwise, I'd suspect a major falls just around the bend.

Marc and I exchange glances. There is no need for words. Together we push the big canoe into the scalloped waves in pursuit of the swimming caribou. I paddle while Marc photographs. Click, click . . . again and again. In an instant he's shot a roll of thirty-six.

Marc leans hard on his paddle and we power ahead, soon overtaking the oblivious creatures. The canoe glides alongside a yearling; affectionately, I stroke his back with my paddle.

Ten minutes later it's over. We pull the canoe onto the stony beach then walk to a high outcrop to view the spectacle. Marc pulls a flask of peppermint schnapps from his pack and we each take a long sip. Then we turn to stare at the lean brown shapes that crowd the water.

Together we stand on the shores of Point Lake, deep in the heart of the Northwest Territories of Canada. Our destination is Bathurst Inlet on the Arctic Ocean. We will spend thirty-one days and nearly $5,000 for charter airfare to pursue our dream. It is the fourth day of our canoe trip and already we have received more than our money's worth.

Whenever I mention that I'm returning to the Arctic for another canoe trip, I'm greeted with either envy or skepticism. There is no middle ground. To some the barrens are a place of indescribable beauty and wonder. Others perceive this as a stark, foreboding land of lichen-covered hills, where ice, polar gales, pounding rapids, and near-freezing water are expected hazards; where isolation is absolute; where danger, physical hardship, and uncertainty are daily companions. A silent awesome scape of endless tundra where skill, common sense, resourcefulness, and even luck are essential ingredients for making a safe, adventure-free canoe trip.

Why on earth would anyone want to canoe a barren-land river?

Reasons are diverse and often impossible to relate. There is the great thrill of seeing and photographing some of the largest and most interesting animals in North America. The barrens are home to the solitary tundra grizzly—which, though often portrayed as foreboding and aggressive, is usually quite timid in the presence of humans; the dazzling white Arctic fox and wolf; the shaggy muskox—remnant from a prehistoric age; and the plentiful caribou.

Along the Arctic Ocean there is an abundance of unusual marine life, too. From mid-July to the end of August—heart of the canoeing season—you may encounter herds of playful whales, seals, and even a walrus or polar bear.

The bird life is equally fascinating. There are bald and golden eagles as well as peregrine falcons, whose diving speed has been clocked at over 100 miles an hour! Gyrfalcons, snowy owls, jaegers, fulmars, terns, ptarmigan, kittiwakes, ivory gulls, loons, and many more. In all, nearly 300 species of avians call the barrens home, making this area one of the richest havens anywhere for bird fanciers.

Fishing is inevitably a prime attraction. Even a rank amateur with rod and reel can, within an hour, catch a daily limit of grayling, char, or giant lake trout.

Everywhere in this vast roadless region there are bountiful fish, birds, and animals. The tundra is a mecca for the biologists, birders, anglers, and everyone who feels an affinity for the unspoiled wild.

As inseparable from the land as its fish and wildlife is the Inuit. Though now confined to outpost settlements, these once nomadic people still depend heavily on fish and wildlife resources for their livelihood. They routinely hunt caribou, seal, and bear, and build their ingenious igloos during their winter travels.

Arctic explorers have described the Inuit as "unspoiled man." Carefree, proud, and unquestionably honest, these kindly people willingly share their homes and sustenance with complete strangers in need. Traveling with an Inuit family for a few hours or a few days provides an eye-opening glimpse into a world forgotten by the hustle and greed of modern man.

Some tundra rivers abound in Inuit sign—decades-old tent rings (circles of water-smoothed rock once used to hold caribou skin tents in place), inukshuks (human likenesses made by piling up rocks and designed to scare caribou toward awaiting hunters), food caches, and artifacts. The thrill of camping at a traditional Inuit site or of finding relics is profound and everlasting. Genuine artifacts are of course protected from theft and vandalism by Canadian regulations, but no self-respecting canoeist would think of stealing or obliterating them. (See color figure 18-4.)

You cannot canoe an Arctic river without developing a deep concern and respect for the land and its inhabitants.

Not to be overlooked is the challenge of canoeing a brawny, demanding waterway. Though many Arctic routes are technically no more difficult than ones deep within the timberline, they are generally free of the traffic of other humans. To canoe the barrens is to be utterly alone and dependent

Figure 18-5. Remains of a 200-year-old Inuit dwelling built entirely of caribou antlers. Nadlak, an island along the Burnside River, Northwest Territories.

Figure 18-6. Inuits camped along the shore of Dubawnt Lake, Northwest Territories, during the early part of the twentieth century.

upon your own resources and knowledge. And it is this feeling of self-sufficiency, of individual challenge, that is to many the greatest lure. The rivers of the high Arctic are to the wilderness canoeist what the Himalayas are to the obsessive mountaineer. To experience the solitude, the dangers, the raw untamed beauty . . . and to live in harmony with the land without incident is for many the supreme accomplishment.

SKILLS

There are few second chances in the barrens: A serious map-reading error may send you scurrying down the wrong waterway into subsequent disaster. Overturning in a rapid or swamping far from shore in the rollers of an icy wind-tossed lake could cost you your canoe, your equipment, and possibly your life! A polar gale may keep you pinned down for days, at best playing havoc with your schedule, at worst shredding your tents into a mass of useless nylon. In the Arctic there is no turning back once the floatplane drops you off. The only way out is usually downriver!

For these reasons only the best canoeists with the best skills and equipment should canoe the northern reaches of the Northwest Territories, Nunavut, Alaska, and Labrador. To suggest otherwise is to minimize the hazards and invite disaster.

If you are uncertain of your skills, make your first trip with an experienced guide who understands the need for cau-

Figure 18-7. A modern camp along the Hood River, Nunavut.

Figure 18-8. Wind on the tundra. The author and his wife batten down their tent in preparation for the coming storm. Thlewiaza River, Nunavut.

tion. If you have a good basic canoeing background, can turn the other cheek to bad weather and persistent bugs, and have a high tolerance for the pain of portaging long distances and paddling many hours without sleep you'll get along fine under a competent tutor. But select your guide with care. Get testimonials from others who have canoed with him or her. And shun parties larger than eight or ten. Large parties are unwieldy on a dangerous river. The logistics of getting everyone through the rapids safely, of maintaining control among canoes in heavy seas, of locating enough level tent sites, and much more become increasingly difficult as the group size enlarges. As I've suggested in chapter 3 (Picking a Crew), six people are the logical choice for safety.

You'll find fully outfitted and guided commercial trips advertised in the classified pages of outdoor magazines, notably *Canoe and Kayak* and *Kanawa*. You may also want to join the Minnesota Canoe Association and the Wilderness Canoe Association, and subscribe to *Che-Mun* (see appendix B). Club newsletters are the best place to look for a crew who is trying to fill out a trip. You may also try the science and natural history museums in your area. For example, the Science Museum of Minnesota offers scores of trips to exotic places. For many years I outfitted and guided many of its canoe trips. (See color figure 18-9.)

Perhaps the hardest lesson to master if you're new to the Arctic is that nature controls your plans. Time is usually short, no matter how generous your schedule. For example, when we discovered that were three days ahead of schedule on our 1984 Hood River canoe trip, we slowed down to fish and hike. Then bad weather struck and we lost five days. We had to put in long hours to make Bathurst Inlet and our float-plane on time.

Similar scenarios played out on the Caribou River (Manitoba) and the Tha-anne (Nunavut). On the other hand, we enjoyed great weather—and lots of playtime—on the Seal (Manitoba) and Burnside (Nunavut) Rivers. You never know what lies ahead on a tundra route. And you can never plan too much time. If in doubt, shorten your route!

Some specific canoe skills you should master include the following.

The Forward and Back Ferries

These tactics are essential when you're negotiating rapids and muscle sections of Arctic rivers. When the river races violently, you'll need to stay on the inside of all bends (the place of slowest flow and, usually, lowest waves) to avoid being swept into the violent outer currents. If the river is very wide, staying inside curves may mean making frequent cross-stream ferries in accelerated water. Ferrying across a ¼-mile-wide fast-moving river while a substantial rapid looms ahead requires good judgment and precise control of your canoe. A foul-up and subsequent broadside in icy mid-stream can be disastrous.

Practice ferry maneuvers *with your partner* before the wheels roll north!

Eddy Turns

Eddies are a safety valve: They provide a place to take out above a falls or rapids, a spot to rest before you proceed into the dangerous waters below. Be well practiced in both bow upstream and bow downstream eddy-in, eddy-out procedures.

You need a good coordinated canoe team to paddle an Arctic river. A skilled bow partner is a necessity, not a luxury. You can't horse a heavily loaded canoe around boulders by sweeping or prying from the stern. Both canoe partners should be darn good!

EQUIPMENT

Arctic rivers seldom give second chances, so there is no room for equipment failure. Canoes, tents, clothing, and footwear suitable for use down home may not be the best choice for the demanding conditions of the barrens. Take canoes, for example: The testimonials you read in chapter 5 all honestly suggest that above all else, you need a very strong, high-volume canoe. Considerations regarding speed, light weight, and aesthetics are all secondary to the basic premise that *your canoe is your lifeline!* It must get you safely through mile after mile of punishing rock fans, across heavily running seas, and through difficult rapids. The water temperature on Point Lake at the start of our 1982 Hood River trip was a scant 39 degrees. It never warmed beyond 47 degrees on the Hood. An upsetting experience cannot be taken lightly when you're working with such low water temperatures. This is why a high-volume, intensely seaworthy canoe (and by this I mean a boat that keeps the water out!) is the logical choice.

Some canoe writers suggest using a fine-lined skinny canoe with full fabric cover for negotiating Arctic waterways. Certainly such a boat may be used to advantage if your route contains few rapids or rapids that are wide open and uncomplicated. More than likely, however, you'll encounter nicely runnable drops that simply require intensive maneuvering—something that may be difficult if you have a canoe that doesn't turn. Canoe stems—especially square ones—may take a terrific beating in the rocky Arctic shallows, another consideration when selecting your canoe.

The ice-cold water of a tundra river dictates that you use extreme caution when running rapids. Even if your fabric canoe cover keeps the water out, the bow person is apt to get drenched in the bigger waves, a major reason why the vote goes to canoes with enough forward volume to keep the partner up front reasonably dry.

Any rapid you feel you should wear a wet suit for is a rapid you should be portaging or lining around! The typical scenario on most Arctic canoe trips is: You canoe in blazing sun for hours, then you portage or line for a while. It's back into the canoe again for a short run down a nice rapid, then you're back to quiet water. Soon a storm blows up and you put on your rain gear. An hour later the sky clears and bugs come out. On most canoe trips you'll broil in your own juices if you wear a wet or dry suit for very long. And putting on and taking off a wet or dry suit several times a day will drive you nuts!

On the other hand, it's not a bad idea to bring along a waterproof Gore-Tex paddling shirt (see chapter 8), which can be stuffed into a thwart bag. I sometimes put on my paddling shirt before I run cold, dicey rapids. The shirt comes off as soon as the danger has passed.

While portages tend to be infrequent on Arctic rivers (troublesome areas are usually lined), the ones you do make may be long and punishing. For example, our longest carry on the Hood River in 1983 was 3 miles, around Wilberforce Falls. On our 1988 descent of the Burnside River, we hauled gear 4 miles to bypass the Burnside canyon and it unrunnable falls. Be sure your canoe is set up for a comfortable carry (has a good yoke). If you rent canoes, bring your own yoke!

Lining is a way of life on tundra rivers, and there are few second chances if you screw up. So rig your canoe with lining holes at cutwater, as explained in chapter 6, or rig a rope harness around the hull—to pull right from the keel, Bill Mason fashion—when the need arises. Keep your lines coiled and secured under loops of shock cord on the deck as I've recommended. And practice lining with your partner in the spring freshet of a local river before you head north. A little practice here will pay dividends later on.

Tents

As I suggested in chapter 10, your tents should be large enough for prolonged comfort and to ensure that there will be sufficient shelter to sleep the crew if one tent is destroyed in a gale or lost in an upset. This means three- or four-person (6 feet by 7 feet for larger) tents should be used to sleep each pair. Most important is a reliable high-altitude design that will withstand persistent gale-force winds.

On our Hood River trip, we were once tentbound for sixty-two hours—pinned down by icy rain driven by an unrelenting wind that raged at 50 miles an hour. Fortunately, our Cannondale Aroostook tents never failed us.

For nearly three decades I've relied on Cannondale Aroostook tents. In fact, my original 1974 Aroostook is—albeit with a few patches—still in operation. The Aroostook is unique: Its fly and canopy are connected and the pair are baffled at the ends (thermos bottle construction). The tent

Figure 18-10 and Figure 18-11. The Cannondale Aroostook (the author's favorite tent). Along the Burnside River, Northwest Territories.

has two integral 6-foot vestibules and twin entries. Two shock-corded aluminum poles and four stakes secure the tent in winds of up to 35 miles per hour. Add six more stakes and you're set for a gale. The Aroostook can be *pitched alone* in less than three minutes in a 40-mile-per-hour wind . . . without bending poles or shredding fabric. Try this with any other tent!

The Aroostook cost nearly $300 when it first appeared in the early 1970s. Sales lagged and production stopped around 1980. Now these tents are jealously guarded relics. A new Aroostook today would probably cost more than $600.

If I had to choose a tent for canoeing the Arctic today it would probably be a North Face VE-25 (geodesic dome) or one of the sophisticated Moss designs.

Some of the best woodland tents just aren't windproof enough for use on the barrens. You might get away with a low-to-the-ground two-person version of a good forest tent, but I don't recommend it. At the risk of snobbery I'll suggest that if you can't afford a good high-altitude tent, you probably can't afford to canoe the barrens. The Arctic is no place to second-guess the weather and what it may do to your equipment.

Cookware and Stoves

Double up on cookware and stoves. Carry a backup set of both in another canoe, just in case. And don't put all your stove fuel in the same boat. Allow *at least* one gallon of gasoline per week for a crew of four. If this sounds extravagant, remember that Arctic waters are much colder than those in the south, and hence require more heat energy to boil. Fitted pot cozies (see chapter 11) save stove fuel and keep food hot long enough for seconds.

Medical Kit

On the tundra, more than anywhere else, you should have a complete medical kit that includes a variety of wide-spectrum prescription antibiotics. Shortly after the start of our Hood River trip I developed a throat so sore I could barely swallow my food. Fortunately, we carried a half-dozen different antibiotics. The right drug seemed to be erythromycin, which I took on a regular schedule for nearly a week. In a few days I was fine.

Stress to your family doctor that you will be *totally* isolated and you'll probably get the prescriptions you need. And be sure to carry enough tablets of each drug so that the affected person can rely on them for at least seven to ten days.

Equally important, make sure at least one member of the crew is skilled in the use of everything in the medical kit. On a long trip it's essential to have someone along who has much more than a casual acquaintance with intricate first-aid procedures.

With the exception of Band-Aids and moleskin, and the one instance mentioned above, I've never had to resort to the sophisticated underpinnings of a complete medical kit. Nonetheless, it's only common sense to be prepared! For kit examples and ideas, see appendix D.

Clothing

The suggestions I've given in chapter 8 (Gearing Up), though quite complete, may be enhanced in the Arctic by these few considerations:

- **Fabrics:** *Wool, fleece,* and *nylon* are the key words for everything except long underwear (I still prefer wool), which may be polypropylene or polyester—but never cotton. A cotton-polyester T-shirt and a pair of light nylon river pants may be useful on hot days. Some people bring shorts (really!). Fleece can substitute for wool but it's bulkier (consumes more pack space), less strong, and it doesn't repel rain. Wet wool is warmer than wet fleece, and it breathes better on hot days.

- **Hats:** I bring four hats: a wide-brimmed canvas Tilley for hot days, an Outdoor Research Sahale Sombrero for rain, a knitted wool stocking cap, and a fleece balaclava. Except for the stocking cap and balaclava, all my hats have chin straps. On cold, windy days I often wear one hat over another. Loss of a warm hat can be serious; everyone should have a spare.

- **Gloves:** I've tried all types and still prefer leather-faced woolens. Wool retains heat better than synthetics when it's wet. For really bitter days I switch to insulated Gore-Tex or neoprene wet-suit gloves. Some paddlers like choppers (wool mittens with leather shells); others prefer fingerless wool gloves, like those trout anglers wear. My fingertips get cold in these, so I've never become a fan. Choose gloves that please you—and be sure to bring one or two extra pairs!

- **Socks and undershorts:** Five or six pairs of good wool socks are enough for a three-week canoe trip. Ditto lightweight polyester or nylon undershorts. Most paddlers wear thin wool or synthetic liner socks inside heavy wool ones. *Tip:* You'll get fewer blisters if you wear the liner socks inside out, seams away from your skin.

- **Fleece neck warmer and balaclava:** These are almost essential for trips above the tree line. My wife, Susie, often wears both these garments together.

- **Footwear:** The only footwear that makes much sense on a tundra river are 16-inch-high fully waterproof boots. For years I wore knee-high rubber marsh boots (still a good choice), but now I am sold on Chota neoprene mukluks, which are lighter and more flexible and won't flood if you step over the top. On a long trip, I bring four—yes, four—pairs of shoes: Chota mukluks, Chota Quetico Trekker portage boots, felt-soled booties for wading and swimming, and sandals for

Figure 18-12 Laundry day on the Tha-anne River, Nunavut.

those rarest of days when it's horribly hot and not buggy.

On the other hand, my wife, Susie, prefers a different system. She brings Chota mukluks, Tingley rubber overshoes (see chapter 8), tennis shoes, and floppy sandals. On cold days in camp, she inserts wool felt snowmobile liners into her Tingley boots and wears this combo over her stocking feet.

I don't know of any footwear that feels great when you wear it day after day, mile after mile. I've found that two sets of waterproof boots (like the Chota mukluks and felt-soled booties), plus a dry set for camp and shoes that are cool and airy, are the most comfortable way to go. Sometimes a blister will begin to develop partway through a long portage. That's the time to stop and change shoes. You'll be amazed at how this simple practice will save your feet.

Gore-Tex socks can make any leather boot waterproof, or so say the manufacturers. My experience is that Gore-Tex socks develop holes over time (it takes about a week). They get wet and stay that way for the duration of the trip. However, they're nice for day trips and overnighters if you don't have to line or portage.

- **Severe outerwear:** It's surprising how cold it can feel on the wind-blown tundra when the thermometer registers relative warmth. For example, I remember waiting out a fierce north wind on Takijaq Lake in the Northwest Territories while wearing the following: Thin wool long johns *and* Damart long underwear, wool shirt and trousers, down ski jacket and nylon wind shell, wool gloves, and heavy stocking cap. Though the thermometer hovered at a balmy 43 degrees, I was only comfortably warm.

Perhaps it's the sustained exposure to chilling weather or the physical letdown that accompanies the end of a tough day. Whatever the reason, you need plenty of warm clothes for Arctic canoe travel.

Handy Items

■ Generally the only firewood along tundra rivers consists of pencil-thin branches from scrub willows and alders. For this, a saw or ax is useless. A pair of compact rose clippers will enable you to collect a surprising amount of deadwood in a short time. (I'm indebted to Alex Hall, famed Arctic canoe guide, for this useful tip).

■ A small wood-burning stove is useful. For tundra trips, where there is minimal wood, I use a forced air (battery-operated) Super Sierra stove (see chapter 11) to burn garbage. In wooded areas where thick duff makes a campfire unsafe—I rely on the Littlbug (www.littlbug.com) stainless steel stove. It accepts small logs and puts out as much heat as a roaring campfire.

■ Some canoeists carry emergency locator transmitters (EPIRBs) and/or shortwave radios. Everyone should bring emergency signaling gear—mirror, smoke, flares. Smoke grenades and mirrors are most practical, while flares have little value in a land that receives more than twenty hours of sunlight a day in summer. You'll find a detailed discussion of these emergency signaling items in chapter 8.

■ Without trees to break the wind or a fire to keep foods warm, the temperature of hot water in a metal pot reaches equilibrium with the environment minutes after you've shut off the stove. The solution is for each canoe team to carry a one-quart stainless-steel vacuum bottle. As mentioned in chapter 8, I prefer to carry two small one-pint bottles because they're easier to pack.

As soon as the stoves are silenced, boiling water for tea and dishwashing is poured into the vacuum bottles and saved for later. The extra weight of the steel bottles is more than compensated for by the fuel you'll save in cooking—not to mention the joy of a hot drink in the comfort of your tent on windbound days.

MAP INTERPRETATION

The northern regions of the Arctic generally receive less than a foot of annual rainfall, so except in spring when the ice goes out, water levels in the small rivers are apt to be too low for canoeing. Almost without exception, wherever a waterway narrows to a single line on a 1:250,000 scale map, you're in for a long walk. If your routine includes many of these single lines, be sure you have sturdy hiking boots. You'll need them!

PORTAGING

If you're accustomed to portaging along well-marked trails within the timberline, carrying your outfit overland on the tundra will be a unique and generally pleasant experience. Since there are no trees on the barrens, portage trails don't exist. You merely strike-off cross country in the appropriate direction.

Where you must portage into a lake some distance away, your best bet is to follow a marked drainage (you better know how to interpret contour lines) or plot a compass bearing to the objective. As I've pointed out in chapter 13, compasses are very reliable in the Arctic as long as you apply the declination correctly.

When the direction of travel has been determined, the crew strikes off *together*, completing each leg of the carry in approximately 1/2-mile increments. At each rest stop the gear is placed in a tight pile, paddles strung through pack straps, blades skyward for good visibility (it really helps to have brightly painted blades). Then the crew returns for another load. The portage is continued in this manner—the crew moving in a continuous phalanx—until it is completed.

There are several important benefits to portaging as a group.

■ It prevents loss of gear in the drab heather of the tundra.

■ By maintaining an advancing set of markers, you ensure a direct beeline to your destination.

Figure 18-13. Reb Bowman "double-packs" the 3-mile portage around Wilberforce Falls, Nunavut, Canada.

■ Overland travel is perhaps the only time when you might encounter a grizzly bear. Grizzlies, as I've indicated, are usually quite timid and will ordinarily run

from humans at the first whiff. But if you're downwind and the bear fails to sense your presence until the distance between you and him is a matter of feet, there can be dangerous consequences. By traveling together you keep the noise level—and "nose level"—high. I might add that bear bells, so popular in western mountains, can be used to advantage on the tundra if you're worried about a bear encounter.

In reviewing this chapter, my first impression was that I had been too dogmatic in my suggestions—for in most ways canoeing an Arctic river is no different from paddling any challenging waterway within the timberline. But as my thoughts began to meld, I realized that the one thing that makes the barrens much different from most Canadian and U.S. routes is remoteness. *Absolute awesome isolation!* This fact, coupled with the ice-water temperatures and polar winds, demands that canoeists exercise extreme care.

Adopt a humble rather than hot dog approach to the water and weather, do your homework well, equip yourself with the best equipment you can afford, plan a route of reasonable length, and you'll make an enjoyable adventure-free canoe trip. But watch out: Arctic fever runs high. Tundra rivers are addictive. They'll capture your heart.

There's a whisper on the night-wind,
there's a star agleam to guide us,
And the wild is calling, calling . . . let us go.
—Robert Service, "The Call of the Wild"

CHAPTER 19

SOME INTERESTING MODERN CANOE TRIPS

In this chapter you'll follow four adventurers as they descend major rivers in northern Canada. Each story is written in the author's own hand and has a different emphasis and rationale.

Read carefully between the lines and you'll discover, again and again, the appliation (and occasional misapplication) of skills and procedures I've suggested throughout this book. You'll also come to realize that these modern-day voyageurs have a deep love for the river and its human and animal inhabitants. They are sincere in their desire to protect wild places from the encroachment of civilization and human pollution. They subscribe dogmatically to the ethic, "Leave only footprints!"

DOUG MCKOWN:
THE MACFARLANE RIVER, SASKATCHEWAN

Doug McKown's account of the MacFarlane River appeared as an "Expeditions" piece in the spring 1999 issue of Che-Mun. *It is re-printed here, with the author's permission and slight editing. For more on this canoeing expert and author, see chapter 5.*

I chose to share the MacFarlane trip with you because it is a remote and challenging river, yet one within the capabilities of intermediate-level wilderness paddlers who have good judgment. The wonderful thing about the MacFarlane is that you won't run into other people—and, you won't have to sell the farm to pay the floatplane bill.

The very remote location of the MacFarlane River drew us to it. The river rises in the center of northern Saskatchewan, about 30 miles north of Cree Lake. From here the MacFarlane flows north through a vast, unpopulated area for about 225 miles to the lonely shore of vast Lake Athabasca. There are no houses, fishing camps, or permanent settlements

along the route. A 2.2-mile portage around the lower canyon of the river makes most canoe outfitters think twice about bringing groups to the area. However, a major drawing card for us was the unique sand-dune formations that are found along the south side of Lake Athabasca at the mouth of the MacFarlane. So unique are these areas that they have been protected with the formation of the Athabasca Sand Dunes Provincial Park. This unique 743-square-mile park has no campsites, roads, buildings, trails, signs, or people.

After a seemingly endless drive from Banff, Alberta, my wife Donna and I met our paddling partners Keith Webb and Heather Dempsey at the floatplane docks in downtown Fort McMurray, Alberta, which is the end of the road for those driving to the MacFarlane River system.

Our starting point was the headwaters of the MacFarlane River, at the west end of Lazenby Lake, 160 air miles away. After a long but smooth flight over the green carpet of the boreal forest, our pilot landed the little Cessna on the calm waters at the west end of the lake. As we unstrapped the canoe from the pontoons, I searched the sky, hoping that the second plane would be able to find the same spot in this endless maze of lakes and streams. Sure enough, a few minutes later the blue-and-white Beaver splashed down and we set up our first camp on the river.

We were up early, eager to begin our trip. As we finished breakfast Heather spotted a black bear ambling out of the forest. The bear was 100 meters away feasting on blueberries in a recently burned-over area. We hoped this sighting was an indication of more to come. We watched the bear for a while then left him to his breakfast as we loaded up and paddled away. At the exit of Lazenby Lake, the MacFarlane River is a small, shallow stream flowing through the continuous boreal forest. Its banks lined with willow bushes, the river flows

Figure 19-1. Heather Dempsey and Keith Webb running a small rapid on the upper MacFarlane.

through the alluvial sand and sandstone formations of northern Alberta and Saskatchewan. The sandstone is largely overlaid by an extensive sand deposition. This sand results mostly from an extensive glacial lake that existed in this area at the end of the last ice age. Lake Athabasca, itself 156 miles long, is but a remnant of this once vast body of water.

The river flows with considerable current as it leaves Lazenby Lake. Initially we were quite careful in our travel because we questioned the dependability of the 1:50,000-scale topographic maps we carried. When we were planning the trip, we discovered that there is no exit shown on the map to connect Lazenby Lake to the rest of the MacFarlane River. While many rapids were indicated on the topo maps, some rapids were not where they appeared to be; others were not shown on the map at all! We soon realized that just about any narrow place shown on the map would have a rapid.

The MacFarlane is a beautiful river. The appearance of the boreal forest is ever changing, with older growth, young forests, and recently burned areas. This is a continuous cycle of burning and regeneration on which all the flora and fauna depend to maintain a healthy ecosystem.

Everywhere that the river had eroded through the sand to the underlying rock there was a swiftly flowing rapid over smooth sandstone ledges and exciting continuous rock gar-

dens. Campsites were plentiful. Whether it was open jack pine forest with a soft floor of crispy reindeer moss or rocky ledges overlooking a rapid, we were never disappointed.

We took a chance on low water levels and chose to run the MacFarlane late in the summer. Late-season trips have advantages: The bugs are usually less ferocious, and the blueberries are ripe. We had blueberry pancakes, blueberry scones, blueberry granola, or blueberry muffins almost every day. Every campsite provided berries free for the picking.

The ripe berries also brought out the bears in force: As we came around a point, I spotted a bear among the jack pine. I shouted and the bear stood up on it's hind legs and looked straight at me. Then it stood up for another look and ran down the shore toward our canoe. It took a few steps into the water, as if undecided whether to continue investigating. It lost interest in us as we floated away. This behavior surprised us. We were all used to seeing bears around our homes that ran instantly at the sight of humans. It was refreshing to see a healthy, inquisitive bear that had never seen canoeists before. It was also mildly disquieting, because this bold behavior was repeated many times during our trip.

The next day we rafted the canoes together along a quiet stretch of river and allowed a light breeze to push us along. We were all sprawled out when I glanced over Heather's

Figure 19-2. A waterfall in the lower canyon of the MacFarlane.

shoulder and saw a black bear about 12 feet offshore, maybe four canoe lengths away. Its ears were perked up and it was swimming toward us as fast as its paws could paddle. As I dove for my camera, the bear hesitated then evidently decided we were too noisy for comfort. He turned back to shore, took one last look at us, then ambled into the woods. After that we became concerned that a bear might visit our campsite, so we were very careful to keep a clean camp. We carried pepper spray and had contingency plans for night encounters. However, of the thirteen bears we saw on our sixteen-day canoe trip, not one ever came into camp. I think the bears were more inquisitive than hungry. With endless supplies of blueberries, bearberries, and bunchberries, the bears had plenty to eat. It might have been a different story if we had come earlier in the season.

Bears were not the only wildlife we saw. Waterfowl were always making noisy exits, splashing and flying in front of our canoes. We saw Canada geese, mergansers, mallards, loons, terns, and sandhill cranes. One morning we surprised twenty-six snowy white pelicans above a small rocky rapid. They took off in a blur of white wings and large dark eyes. On several occasions a family of otters surrounded us. Lifting their sleek bodies high out of the water, they would snort and huff at us as we floated by. We also saw muskrats, beavers, mink, and moose. Once we saw seven moose in one day! They would lift their great heads at us, with a mouthful of dripping greens hanging from blubbery lips. At their leisure they would slowly turn and canter off in an awkward but rapid gate.

Many of the rapids of the MacFarlane rate Class I and II and could be scouted from the canoe. (See color figure 19-3.) All the major rapids occurred at ledges where waterfalls roared down. The MacFarlane is one of those delightful rivers that have many rapids but few portages. The river drops about 948 feet over the approximately 190 miles that we canoed. In this distance there was only one lift over and three portages. While there were a number of wide places in the river, 12-mile-long Davy Lake was the only big body of water.

We paddled through the last turns of a broad estuary into the wide expanse of Davy Lake on a beautiful, dead-calm evening. We camped on an exquisite little island a mile or so from shore. A beautiful beach and no bugs or bears made this an unforgettable campsite.

That night the wind began to howl and we awoke to a storm that kept us windbound all day. The following morning we arose early and headed toward the first of three major canyons. The first canyon was ¾ mile long and passed two dramatic ledges and a spectacular waterfall. The portage ran through open forest and, except for a steep descent near the end, was quite pleasant. Thirteen miles downstream we came to the dreaded middle canyon and made a 2-mile carry around it. This middle canyon is truly spectacular: Huge ledges and steep rapids rush between towering canyon walls for nearly a mile. The river drops about 260 feet as it descends the canyon, below which is a magnificent three-ledge waterfall. Just downstream are three more wild waterfalls. We hiked along canyon walls that were broken and cracked into weird and wonderful shapes.

There were about 3 miles of continuous Class II and III rapids from the end of the middle canyon to the final lake. It was great fun to run these rapids but also a little distracting, since this was the first time we got a clear sight of the major sand deposits of the dunes. As we paddled out into the little lake, sand ridges interrupted the trees and signaled the end of our trip. We chose to end our trip on this sheltered lake because we thought that Lake Athabasca—which was barely 4 miles downstream—was too wide and windy for a float-plane to land.

We were able to spend some time exploring a huge area of sand dunes on the west side of the river before our float-plane came. The vegetation ranged from dry desert grasses to carnivorous sundew plants and trees with roots that reached down through the air in a desperate stretch to reach the ground. This area is the most northerly formation of active sand dunes in the world. In our static, almost instantaneous observations, we could see where an enormous dune, 45 feet high, was in the process of engulfing a living forest. On the other side of this dune, we walked among the tops of long-dead trees in an ancient forest that was again being slowly exposed by the ever-shifting sand. One morning we saw a wolf in the middle of a vast sand plain. After a bold and curious look in our direction, he trotted off into the forest.

The dawn of our last morning broke windy and clear. As we waited patiently for our plane, we watched impossibly long lines of Canada geese in their stately V-formations, heading south for the winter. It made us realize that even on this pleasant warm day, there were signs that this brief summer was coming to an end.

CLIFF JACOBSON:
THE WILBERFORCE FALLS AFFAIR

Tripping into Marriage on the Hood River, Northwest Territories

Sue Harings and I live in a restored, nineteenth-century French-colonial-style farmhouse just outside River Falls, Wisconsin, where Susie teaches home economics/Quest to seventh- and eighth-graders at nearby Meyer Middle School. It's a seventeen-minute drive to Hastings, Minnesota, where I have taught environmental science at the middle school since 1971. Each summer Susie and I canoe wild places together.

We were married on August 12, 1992, at Wilberforce Falls on Canada's Hood River. The event was described in Canoe and Kayak *and* Outdoor Canada *magazines,* Che-Mun, *and in my book* Campsite Memories, *which is out of print.* Canoeing North into the Unknown *by Bruce Hodgins and Gwynth Hoyle (appendix B) says our wedding is the only recorded one at Wilberforce Falls. This story is about two people who are in love, wild places, and the magic of canoes.*

When adventurer Sue Harings graduated from college in 1971, she set out to explore the world alone. A middle school teacher from River Falls, Wisconsin, Susie, as she prefers to be called, has scuba dived the Great Barrier Reef; hiked in Alaska, Glacier National Park, Australia, New Zealand, Grand Cayman Island, and the Orient; and paddled scores of wild rivers all over Minnesota and Canada. Competent, friendly, and charming, forty-six-year-old Susie is at home wearing pile and green wellie boots or "girl clothes." Dubbed FRU (Frivolous, Ridiculous, Unnecessary) queen of the Minnesota Canoe Association, because she brings too much gear on all her trips (but—to her credit—carries it all), Susie ties passion-pink surveying ribbon to everything she owns. That and her infectious smile are her trademarks.

"I like to be feminine and have pretty things around me," says Susie. "I won't go anywhere without my earrings and makeup!"

Figure 19-4. An original drawing of Wilberforce Falls by Sir John Franklin (1819–1821).

EXPEDITION CANOEING

I met Susie in 1986 when she joined a canoe trip I was leading for the Science Museum of Minnesota. She proved a capable paddler and amiable partner. Her smiling, upbeat nature earned her the respect of the crew and the title of Trip Clown. When I called her a "forty-year-old teenager" or a "walking garage sale," she simply smiled coyly and said something clever that made everyone laugh. Susie refused to grow up: She screamed in the rapids, laughed during thunderstorms, and, like a little kid, did everything possible to get out of camp chores. She was the hit of the party and everyone loved her.

Years passed and our friendship and respect for one another grew. Our relationship centered on canoeing and camping and was purely platonic. I was happily married to Sharon and Susie liked—no, loved—her single lifestyle.

Then on December 11, 1990, tragedy struck. Sharon suffered a massive asthma attack and died on my living room floor. She was barely fifty years old. For the next two months I wallowed in self-pity. Both kids were away at college, my ten-year-old Shelty dog had died a month earlier, and for the first time in twenty-four years I was completely alone. Admittedly, Susie was not my first choice of dating partner. She was too much a friend—one I didn't think I could get serious about. But I missed her happy smile, so I asked her to dinner at a fine Italian restaurant.

From then on we were constant companions who shared one adventure after another. Together we walked the snow-capped trail to Devils Den on the Kinnikinnic River, broke March ice in our solo canoes, snowshoed the Outback during a blizzard, winter-camped along Lake Superior, and hiked a mile into the woods at midnight to sleep near a wolf den.

Ten months after our first date, Susie agreed to marry me . . . on the condition that the wedding would be another great adventure.

Susie knew that I would be leading a canoe trip down the Hood River in the Northwest Territories of Canada during the summer of 1992, so she begged to go along. The highlight of the trip was Wilberforce Falls—an awesome cataract that drops 160 feet through a 3-mile canyon. The highest waterfalls north of the Arctic Circle, Wilberforce would be a perfect wedding site. "I'll wear a fur-trimmed wedding dress and my green wellies," Susie laughed.

I liked the idea but unfortunately, the trip was filled; there was no space for a bride. Perhaps she could charter a floatplane from Yellowknife (capital of the Northwest Territories) to Wilberforce Falls, 350 air miles away. But when costs were computed, it was out of the question. The one feasible option was to put her aboard the weekly commuter flight from Yellowknife to Bathurst Inlet Lodge on the Arctic Ocean. From there lodge owner Glen Warner could fly her about 40 air miles to a tundra lake three miles from the falls. Then Susie would pack her wedding dress, accoutrements, and nonessential FRUs across the tundra to the marriage site, where she would wait alone for two days until we arrived by canoe. "It'll be my most remote solo trip!" grinned Susie.

Then just weeks before the great adventure, a man dropped out of the expedition and Susie joined the crew. She was the only woman among nine men, but it didn't bother her at all, not even when she discovered that the bridesmaid would have to be a man.

Destination: Yellowknife, NWT, 2,311 miles from River Falls Wisconsin. Five people in a van and forty-six hours of nonstop driving. Pavement stops at the Mackenzie River. From here to the territorial capital you eat dust, road oil, and fist-sized gravel. Graders are an endangered species; flat tires, flying stones, and oil-caked mud are not. The sign WELCOME TO YELLOWKNIFE means it!

Our first stop was the only carwash in town. Thirty Canadian dollars buys enough bug and tar remover, scrub brushes, and time to make the rig touchable. With eight pairs of hands working, the wash job takes just thirty minutes. Then it's off to Air Tindi, where floatplane service in to the Hood River system has been arranged for more than a year. Over the growl of a landing Twin Otter, dispatcher Bill Gawletz, who has a genuine liking for canoeists, hails a hearty welcome to our crew. Plans are finalized, $16,000 Canadian changes hands, and takeoff is scheduled for 7:00 A.M. tomorrow.

A shower and nap at the Discovery Inn and we're off to experience the wonders of Yellowknife. There's Eskimo and Indian art to buy, a wondrous museum to see, and, for Susie, me, and "marriage commissioner" Charles LeFevere, a date with the marriage division of Vital Statistics.

A pretty young woman named Vickie Joan Hickey enthusiastically ushers us into her office. There are forms to sign and fees to pay, but in the end it's legal. Charlie is certified to perform the wedding on August 12, 1992. The signings and instructions take about an hour. Though the Northwest Territories is about one-fifth the size of the United States, there are only 55,000 inhabitants, most of whom live in Yellowknife and surrounding "southern" communities. People—especially priests and ministers—are rare above the tree line. That's why there are marriage commissioners.

At 10:00 A.M. on August 1, two Twin Otter floatplanes settle into a quiet bay above the first rapids on the Hood River. It's raining and confusion abounds. Thank God there are no bugs! Minutes later the plane revs for takeoff. There are waves and long solemn looks and the customary last flyover. Packs are muscled into canoes and the brightly colored nylon splash covers are attached. "Where's the wedding pack?" I call. Dead silence. Again, "Where's the wedding pack?"

"Okay, you guys, who hid it? Who's the clown? . . . It's not funny," yells Susie, hysterically. Again, no answer. Susie and I exchange doleful looks: The white canvas Duluth pack that contains her ermine-trimmed wedding dress, a guaranteed-to-stay-fresh-for-a-month wedding cake, bridal bouquet of dried flowers made by local businesses, my white shirt, red bow tie and cumberbund, and all the treats are either on the disappearing plane or at Air Tindi's loading dock, 310 air miles away.

"Both of us are doorknobs. We deserve each another," cries Susie. Then, with great theatrical flair, she screams: "I can't get married without my dress and cake! We'll have to wait till next year and get married on the Thelon. I won't be married without my dress. I won't. I won't. I won't!"

Charging grizzly, foot-stomping muskox, whirlpool rapid: Nothing can match the fury of a thwarted woman on the tundra. Ultimately Susie comes to her senses, apologizes, and politely informs everyone that she must sulk for three days. We try to assuage her by offering to construct a dress from white plastic poly bags. "You can use my head net for a veil," someone offers weakly.

Fortunately, the rain, rapids, excitement of the tundra, and intense physical punishment of the portages encourage perspective and when, at 8:00 P.M., camp is pitched, the loss has become a numbing but distant reality.

Under the multicolored 14-foot tarp, I prepare hot buttered rum and Oriental stir-fry while the crew administers to other chores. The blowtorch whir of the two Optimus 111B stoves obscures the hollow sound of distant engines.

"Twin Otter comin' in," yells someone. Sure enough, it's a twin—flaps down and wing dropped; he's circling. Richly emblazoned on the side is the AIR TINDI logo. I stop the stir-fry and grab the small, handheld radio: "Air Tindi Twin Otter, Air Tindi Twin Otter, this is the Cliff Jacobson party. Can you take a message to base for us? Over."

There is no answer. Instead the plane zooms in and drops to what, from our perspective, is crash altitude. It banks slightly and the copilot kicks something out of the door. It's the pack—the white wedding pack! With flair and precision the twin climbs skyward and wig-waggles a fond good-bye.

Considering the fall, pack and contents are in surprisingly good shape. There's a small tear in the double canvas bottom and wide cracks in the plastic containers that hold the pudding cake and frosting. Susie's dress, flowers, and condiments are intact. Everyone cheers and waves as I order a round of Pusser's rum and toast Air Tindi!"

After the trip I learn the story from dispatcher Gawletz: "Michael Peake (who was waiting for another flight) found a white pack on the dock that had a DULUTH PACK logo and CLIFF on the flap. It was so light I figured it contained town clothes, but when I opened it, I discovered a wedding cake and dress. I knew you guys wouldn't rest till you got that pack, so I put it aboard a northbound twin and asked the pilot to drop it off on the way home. Would've been nice if we could've found some open water to land, but the guys have kicked stuff out the side door before."

How's that for going the "extra air mile"?

For the next ten days, we bask in the joys of the river. There are rapids to run and caribou and muskox to photograph, and an interesting bear encounter.

Three bends south of Wilberforce Falls we come upon an abandoned mine occupied by two Canadian geologists, whom we invite to attend the wedding. It's barely 3 miles from the mine to Wilberforce, so the men enthusiastically agree to come.

Wilberforce Falls: bold, compelling, spectacular. Highlight of the North, it drops 160 feet in two successive pitches. By comparison the American Niagara Falls drops 167 feet. It has been a dry summer and the water level is very low. Indeed, the west channel—normally a thundering cascade—has been reduced to a picturesque dry coliseum of balconies and caves. The view from on top is breathtaking. To the east, west, and south are hundreds of miles of uninhabited tundra. To the north is a water-carved river valley of immense proportions, and the Arctic Ocean. A deservedly spiritual place, Wilberforce Falls is a perfect wedding site.

"Better come here, Cliff. Got a rare archaeological find," calls a voice excitedly. Sure enough, in a sun-parched cove, its eight legs weighted firmly with smooth stones, is a partially inflated, green plastic octopus. Nearby are a note and poem that express good wishes from a Canadian group that passed by three weeks ago. Ollie the octopus is now our official mascot and will be an honored guest at the wedding.

Figure 19-5. The wedding procession at the "chapel of the blue dome."

The wedding day—August 12, 2:00 P.M. sharp. Unbeknownst to Sue and me, the crew has prepared a wedding extravaganza. Bridesmaid Brad Bjorklund has scoped out a cathedral-like ceremonial site (which he calls the chapel of the blue dome) at the upper falls, where Susie can be hidden from view until the wedding march announces her grand appearance. Clad in a flowing black robe, marriage commissioner Charlie LeFevere—or His Excellency, as he has come to be known—solemnly approaches a tripod of canoe paddles that serves as the marriage pulpit. Seconds later I appear, clad in newly washed wool trousers, white shirt, red bow tie and cummerbund, L. L. Bean hunting shoes, and a clean white Tilley hat. At least one guest notices that I have shaved for the occasion. Another questions the real purpose of the sheath knife on my belt.

On my right, nervously clutching the ring—a brilliant green chrome tourmaline stone set in a rich gold Tiffany setting—is best man Biff Kummer. Trip physician and philosopher Jerry Noller has provided the guests with formal attire—tuxedo T-shirts.

In unison the witnesses stand and face the pulpit. One man opens a tiny music box, which plays "Here Comes the Bride." Escorted by bridesmaid Brad, Susie, carrying a mixed bouquet of Wisconsin dried and fresh tundra flowers, steps forward in time with the music. She wears an ermine-trimmed full satin dress with flowing train and green wellie rubber boots. Bright red lipstick, gentle eyeshadow, and soft

facial makeup complete the picture. By any account, she is beautiful. It is 73 degrees; there is a slight breeze and *no bugs!*

Just before the vows are taken, a powerful omen appears. A huge raven, jet black and preened, flies into the cathedral and perches on a flat rock a dozen feet away. Proud and unafraid, the bird just stands and watches. As the ceremony begins the raven flies casually away; seconds later a white gull takes his spot. Everyone—even those who are not religious—is touched by this favorable omen, which Dr. Noller says, is "extremely powerful medicine." Later Jerry reads about ravens from an Indian spirit book entitled *Medicine Cards* by Jamie Sams and David Carson:

Raven is the messenger that carries all energy flows of ceremonial magic between the ceremony itself and the intended destination. . . . It is the power of the unknown

Figure 19-6. The wedding ceremony at the chapel of the blue dome.

at work, and something special is about to happen. Raven magic is a powerful medicine that can give you the courage to enter the darkness of the void, which is the home of all that is not yet in form. . . . Great Spirit lives inside the void . . . raven is the messenger of the void (and the Raven's black color is the color of the void).

For me the meaning is brilliantly clear: Sharon has come to tell me that what is about to happen here is good and right. In a final act of love, she unselfishly gives her blessing.

Charlie reads the script we have prepared and we end the ceremony with the traditional kiss, after which bridesmaid Brad leads us to the reception site. Spread on a silver space blanket within yards of the thundering falls are all manner of condiments—smoked oysters, kippered herring, pepperoni, and sardines; mixed nuts, mellow mints, and rich Dove chocolate bars. The centerpiece of the display is a white, richly frosted, two-layer pudding cake with a plastic wedding couple on top. Here, near the top of the world, in this land of little sticks, it is all quite unbelievable.

As I pour the wedding cognac, the two geologists stroll forward with a large box wrapped in newspaper and bound with orange surveying ribbon. "All we could come up with on such short notice," says the older man, who also produces a bottle of 151-proof rum with which to spike the cognac.

Susie tears open the box and unbelievingly stares at its

Figure 19-7. The bride and groom cut the cake at the top of Wilberforce Falls.

contents. "It's a toaster, a real toaster!" she screams. Sure enough, it is a toaster, and a four-slice model to boot. "Honest, we can really use it," I mumble as I walk my new wife to the pinnacle of the falls for a photograph. As the picture is snapped, a stark white Twin Otter, bearing the words AIR TINDI on the side, zooms out of nowhere and buzzes the falls, clearing the upper ledge by a matter of yards. The plane climbs powerfully upward, circles broadly, then wags a salute and turns toward Yellowknife. Later I learn that it is my friend Bob Dannert, en route home from a trip down the Simpson River.

"I could see it all," said Bob later. "The white dress, red cummerbund, and gourmet layout. By the way, was that really a toaster?"

Addendum: Our marriage was registered in Yellowknife, Northwest Territories, Canada, on August 18, 1992.

HAP WILSON:
LAND WHERE THE SPIRIT LIVES

Here Hap Wilson—author, artist, environmentalist, wild and woolly adventurer, and teacher (he taught actor Pierce Brosnan how to canoe for the 1999 Canadian-made film Grey Owl*)—shares his love for Manitoba rivers and provides insight into the making of his guidebook* Wilderness Rivers of Manitoba. *Hap Wilson's complete biography is in chapter 5.*

The splits on my fingertips were getting worse; in fact, when I paused momentarily to catch my breath I saw that they were now bleeding, and the blisters that had long worn off had blistered once again. My feet were no better off. I put the lining rope down and flexed some feeling back into my finger joints. Everyone needed a rest.

Stephanie and I had been paddling nonstop since ice-out in early May. With back-to-back expeditions we had little chance to slow our pace or to even take a few days off to let our bodies repair themselves. There was a good distance to cover in order to complete the Manitoba rivers survey, and already it was late July. We were five weeks into a barren-land trip and had three more weeks to go. Deep down we wondered if our aching bodies would last the trip.

This Arctic fringe roller-coaster ride, up one river, down the next, up another to gain access to yet another downstream course, finally led us to an intermittent, undignified fluvial ditch called the Roberts River. More rock than water, the shores were defended by an impenetrable fortress of willow and alder. Today put our relationship with our Swiss friends

Figure 19-9. A lone caribou on the Caribou River.

and paddling companions, Walter and Jori Von Bolmoos, to the litmus test.

The options we faced were all unfavorable: We could take our lumps hauling canoes over and between rocks in the river, or hoof it alongside following a scrabble of stunted spruce and boulder fields, trying to keep the wind from sending our canoe airborne like a kite; or we could sit on the riverbank and wail.

In the end we chose "all of the above." The Roberts River was just a glorified spring spillway where the winter melt flushed quickly over the permafrost, leaving the waterway expunged barely enough fluid to float a leaf, let alone two 17-foot canoes. I'm sure Robert must have died somewhere along this route! Lining was impossible; wading up to your crotch in icy water was the only solution. (See color figure 19-8.)

The river was fairly deep between slime-encased boulders, but the space between rocks was never more than half a canoe length. This spawned an array of tactics that included

tugging, jerking, grunting, and cursing, all the while watching the vinyl skin on our Royalex canoes peel off in little curls on top of the rocks.[1]

But Walter and Jori never complained—at least in English. But the day was wearing on all of us and the 650 kilometers that lay behind us had taken a toll in hardship. I could tell without asking that this day was finished!

We found a break in the shore sedge where there had been much caribou activity not long ago. Until this point we had seen only scattered small groups and individual animals roaming the tundra. There was a flat rise above the river, so we set up camp there. The wind was resolute, making it difficult to set up the tents, but fortunately (for once) there were few blackflies. A rather high sand and gravel esker rose up to greet the waning sun, casting a longer-than-usual dullness over the evening camp. Nobody talked. We just tended our wounds.

We were behind schedule; not that I particularly like to

[1] I can unhappily report similar experiences on Roberts Creek (after much cussing, my party and I downgraded it to creek status). Roberts—located near the headwaters of Manitoba's Caribou River—is every bit as awful as Hap says.

adhere to any formal timetable, but in two days we were to meet the rest of our crew at the headwaters of the Caribou River and get reprovisioned. If we didn't show up on time at the rendezvous site, the others might fly back to Churchill—and we, of course, would be seriously short of food. We had eaten up our rest days and progress was pitifully slow; we had only made 5 kilometers (3 miles) in eight hours today. Our rendezvous point was still 20 kilometers (12 miles) away. It was one of the lowest moments I can remember. The isolation, the aloneness, the fatigue, and the abuse to our bodies exacted a high toll, and doubts echoed solemnly in our souls. We climbed into our wind-rattled tents not at all looking forward to the next day. I recall lying there, body aching and mind sloughed and despondent.

The deep funk had broken when we heard a strange clicking sound, intermingled with what sounded like Canada geese, faint at first, but slowly rising above the din of the wind and flapping tent.

"Caribou!" I heard Walter yell. "Lots of them!" Zippers unzipped and we all rushed out of our tents to have a look. There were hundreds of them across the river, no more than 100 meters away, filing slowly past, presumably looking for a place to cross the river.

Unknowingly, we had pitched our camp at a caribou crossing. It was wonderful to watch them, to listen to them talking, not frightened in the slightest; and now the whole weight of our journey and the heavyheartedness that was

Figure 19-10. Lunch on a quiet esker along the Caribou River.

internalized through sheer exhaustion was lifted. My soul had been retrieved by this encounter, which made my aches and woes seem inconsequential and trivial. Life was good and tomorrow would bring new wonders.

A wilderness trail is seldom straight; if it were, then it would not be nearly as interesting or provocative. Our modern, pampered lifestyles often lock us into paradoxical tedium, constrained by monotonous and repetitive tasks. We crave wild things and the adventure of exploring twisting, unpredictable paths.

In Manitoba there are no straight lines, at least for the canoeist. Beyond the grain elevators and prairies of the south there is a paddling paradise of over 100,000 lakes and rivers, which are wilder than most native Manitobans can imagine.

While researching seventeen of Manitoba's wildest rivers over a four-year period, I encountered fewer than twenty other paddlers. Native Manitobans know their province largely in consumptive terms—resource extraction, hydro development, grain export, and the like. Few realize the extent of the wilderness and how many wonderful rivers there are to canoe.

The motive behind my book *Wilderness Rivers of Manitoba* was not an exploitative pursuit to sell out sacred or yet-unmolested wilderness, but rather to proffer some kind of protection through the notoriety of eco-adventure possibilities. Canadian politics dictate a "use it or lose it" management philosophy. I'd rather bump gunnels with other like-minded paddlers than have to portage around yet another hydro dam!

The Cree and Ojibway people referred to *Manitou-ba* as the "Land Where the Spirit Lives," derived from the whimsical nature of Lake Winnipeg. Canoeing this spirit land conjures up many images: The long drive to Thompson; a native Dene village on the edge of wildfires; hand games and the drummer's chant; endless miles of rapids and wet bandannas wrapped around our faces to protect us from the acrid smoke; paddling among beluga whales and a night sail down the Hudson Bay coast; spirit pictures painted on stone and ancient waymarkers across the tundra; wet feet and the warmth of dry socks; "bull-dogs," mosquitoes, and blackflies; chromatic sunsets and the silhouette of caribou against the sky; long treks across the tundra; a clay pipe found in a rock crevice on the Hayes River, and a half-buried rusted cannonball on the beach at York Factory; the smile of a Dene child riding in the back of a pickup truck over a road that goes nowhere; Arctic grayling frying in a pan over the fire; a soaring bald eagle and howling wolves; northern lights and a mid-

Figure 19-11. A tundra camp along the Povungnituk River.

night paddle and stars so close you could touch them. Manitoba is a place that time has forgotten and man has not yet tainted with his meddling, and my own heart yearns to go back there—where the Spirit lives.

MICHAEL PEAKE: POVUNGNITUK RIVER IN THE FOOTSTEPS OF FLAHERTY

Michael Peake is one of Canada's best-known explorers. He and his brothers Geoffrey and Sean have been featured on a number of television programs, notably Anyplace Wild. *Michael's complete biography is in chapter 5. In 1992, when Sue Harings and I were married on a canoe trip on the Hood River, Susie's wedding dress was in a white pack inadvertently left behind on the floatplane loading dock. Michael Peake found the pack and convinced Air Tindi to deliver it to us on the river (see The Wilberforce Falls Affair earlier). Susie later confided that she might have postponed the wedding till she got her dress. Michael, I owe you.*

There are few areas in Canada as alluring and mysterious as the Ungava Peninsula, now known as Nunavik at the top of Quebec. Except for a handful of Inuit coastal villages, this lonely land remains untouched by the face of progress.

Bounded on three sides by icy Arctic waters, this barren, rugged spline of rock has escaped the forward thrust of modernization that has engulfed so much of the North in the last three decades, largely due to its stark and forbidding climate. Buffeted by the fierce storms from both Hudson and Ungava

Bays, the vegetation resembles the high Arctic tundra. At the very apex of this plateau lies the Nouveau-Quebec Crater, a 2-mile-wide, 1,300-foot-deep hole that was blasted into the solid granite bedrock thousands of years ago.

Our trip began in the summer of 1988 at the headwaters of the Povungnituk River, a mere 20 miles from Hudson Strait. Our Hide-Away Canoe Club group included myself and brother Geoffrey, Peter Scott, and Peter Brewster. The Povungnituk is the most northerly and least known of all the major rivers in Ungava. In its 300-mile course that nearly bisects the peninsula, the river falls almost 2,000 feet. We chartered a Twin Otter from Kuujjuaq on July 16, flying north 250 miles to the crude landing strip at Raglan Lake, headwaters of the Povungnituk. This was a dormant mine site then but is now a large and active facility that ships out all its ore to the coast for processing in the south.

Summer comes late to Ungava, especially this year. We landed at the airstrip in a snowstorm. The lake was almost entirely frozen, and much of the surrounding land was snow covered. The pilots of the Twin Otter took photos of our now apprehensive-looking group, surely thinking they would be of value when we never returned! The high elevation combined with the proximity to the ocean makes the ice-free season very short here. Spring had been a cold one, and the so-called summer was delayed three weeks or more.

The land around the headwater plateau is exceedingly barren and stark. There is little vegetation—just mosses and lichens barely an inch high. The Povungnituk for the first 30 miles scarcely deserves the name *river*, with a midchannel depth of sometimes 6 inches, barely enough to float our Old Town Trippers, fully loaded with thirty days' worth of food. The river finally becomes large enough to offer some real rapids where it makes a sharp bend to the west. We had left the higher plateau and the bulk of the snow behind. The Povungnituk passes within 12 miles to the north of the crater. As we approached we could see the rim from many miles away, though it looked just like a normal ridge. The northeast rim of the crater rises to 2,150 feet, the highest point in Ungava. As we neared, the Povungnituk became larger still and the rapids continuous. One stretch went for over 2 miles without a break as the river cut its way off the plateau.

We left the Povungnituk at the 35-mile mark and headed up a small creek that would take us to the crater by way of a chain of lakes. On our fifth day of paddling since Raglan Lake we crossed out of the Povungnituk watershed and into the Vachon River system (which empties into Ungava Bay). We

Figure 19-12. Portaging one of the many rapids on the Povugnituk River.

the others. The *National Geographic* (January 1952) article describes the extreme difficulty of reaching the crater over a sea of shattered boulders, and we had prepared ourselves for the worst. The eastern approach is clear of all debris and was a pleasant hike, if you don't mind wet feet.

Our first view of the crater was superb. The sky was clear, and the crater stretched out over 2 miles across the gorge. It was so big you could not get it in frame even with a very wide-angle lens. The crater's lake was still frozen. This lake, 400 feet below the rim and 800 feet deep, is incredibly pure and clear. Unfortunately we were not able to check this firsthand, as it had only thawed a couple of feet out from shore. We spent the next couple of days exploring and enjoying one of the continent's more unique campsites.

One of the few advantages of this harsh climate and lack of vegetation in Ungava is the total absence of bugs. Usually any trip to the North is cursed with hordes of blackflies and mosquitoes but we hadn't seen even one yet. We were able to enjoy the luxury of eating outside without head nets, and even leaving the tent doors unzipped if we so desired.

Our route now headed southward toward Nantais Lake, a distance of 50 miles. This section had the most overland travel to it, as we followed a sporadic chain of lakes connected by shallow, rock-filled streams. The larger lakes still had thick ice, and we easily sledded our canoes across their level surface. We then headed due south over some long and occasionally very rocky portages and on July 25 reached Nantais Lake,

paddled to the closest possible point to the crater, which was still 4 miles distant, and then cached the canoes and hiked in with enough food for the next three days.

The land is mossy and wet and rolls gently uphill toward the crater. The force of the impact was so severe that there are "ripples" of land emanating from the crater marking the force of the blast. We were heading for the lowest point of the crater rim on the eastern slope, which bears a marked contrast to

Figure 19-13. Ice! Above Nantais Lake.

EXPEDITION CANOEING

more than 30 miles long and indented with many bays and channels. Not surprisingly the lake was still dotted with the clinking mats of rotting candle ice, which we were unable to paddle through (despite a Herculean effort—it's like cement), so we took the long way around. Fortunately our route lay across the narrowest section of the lake, a distance of less than a mile. Nantais is drained by the Arpalirtuq River, and the next 10 miles of river was the crux of the trip.

The Arpalirtuq drops over 400 feet—an incredible falls for such a short distance. We were worried that the river would be totally unrunnable. As we approached the outlet of Nantais, we could clearly see that the water levels were still very high, usually a good sign. The upper Arpalirtuq has cut a small canyon through the soft limestone that acts as a snow trap and in winter gales must almost fill with snow, because there were sheer snowdrifts 10 to 15 feet high following the river's bank in places. We were acutely aware of what an upset in the icy water would mean.

The next day we cautiously headed into the canyon, scouting at every corner. We were able to run almost everything because the high water allowed us to stick to the shores closely. The river dropped relentlessly, and we ran some of the best white water we have ever experienced. As the day wore on, we grew bolder. Peter Brewster and Geoffrey swamped near the end of one tricky set, but their spray covers kept them dry.

Figure 19-14. On August 8, high winds shredded our tents. We were lucky to be alive. Aftermath of the storm.

As the river descends toward Klotz Lake, the topography changes. We found ourselves lining down foaming, churning rapids with large standing waves and heavy turbulence. The last drop into Klotz is the toughest and required all our skill in lining to avoid mishap. As we paddled away and looked back upon that raging white demon, we could scarcely believe we had just come down it and were very glad we were not heading up.

We now entered the historical part of our trip, retracing a portion of a trip made by Robert Flaherty in 1912 across the Ungava Peninsula. Flaherty, whose 1922 landmark film *Nanook of the North* was shot in Ungava, was among the first nonnatives to explore the region's interior. He named the river he paddled the Povungnituk. Since that time that name has been applied to the northern branch of the river, and Flaherty's route is still unnamed on modern maps. Part of our trip was to prove that Flaherty indeed traveled this southern route, the true Povungnituk River and the route the Inuit used to get to the interior.

Most of the remaining way is lake travel, interspersed with short river sections. We headed west and crossed the divide between the Ungava and Hudson Bay watersheds. With 230 miles left to go from Klotz Lake and two weeks to complete it, we felt fairly confident of finishing the trip on schedule. Yet from this point to the very end the prevailing westerly wind was relentless. We were slowed to a snail's pace some days and winded in on three occasions. And then came the great storm—but more on that later.

As Flaherty had promised, the upper river is largely unnavigable, being more a series of falls and heavy rapids—unlike the upper Povungnituk, which runs in a smooth gradient for miles. We had a number of portages around canyons that were quite unrunnable. The water is incredibly clear, as Flaherty had noted. Our battle with the wind did not fare well and we soon felt like the head of a nail as the wind hammered on. In addition, the river became much larger, and the rapids less runnable.

Below large, round Lac Couture we had one good day of rapids with only a few portages, our best day on the river yet. We also noted the spot where Flaherty took a picture of a great falls, proving (if there was any doubt) that this was indeed the route he traveled. Not long after that moment, we were blessed with a rare tailwind! A strong east wind pushed us along at an almost breakneck speed. This was the only time all trip we had a tailwind, and unfortunately it heralded the arrival of a major storm that was building off in the purple clouds over Hudson Bay.

We noticed very strange cloud formations in the evening that were very dark and turbulent, boiling and swirling the way coffee does when you add cream. These, we later learned, are called mamma clouds and indicate the coming of extremely unstable and violent weather. Had we known this we might have chosen a more sheltered campsite. We were very exposed to the wind from almost every angle (although there is very little natural shelter up here anyway), and our tents had withstood winds of up to 50 miles per hour before so we felt secure.

That night was a rarity—a thunderstorm raged most of the night, making us all feel more than a little vulnerable with almost nothing for cover and the lightning striking at fairly close range. About 12:30 A.M. Geoffrey had to secure one of our canoes that the wind had rolled over. By 5:30 A.M. the wind picked up to 50 miles per hour and turned broadside to my tent. Sleep was fitful, waking every 10 or 15 minutes. By 6:30 the wind increased to just over 60 miles per hour and we became seriously concerned that our tents wouldn't hold.

At exactly 6:47 A.M., the first pole snapped on my tent. Minutes later, when we were in the process of moving it to a more protected spot, a crushing gust snapped four of the aluminum poles on Geoff's tent, and it blew apart before our eyes. The next sixty minutes were surreal. You had to scream to be heard, and only by someone a few feet away. A partially loaded pack exploded into the air and was carried down the lake with fuel bottles and excess gear. We dismantled the other tent, stuffed ourselves and our gear under the canoes, and waited it out. The wind blew the tops off the 6-foot waves and drove them into the air as blasts of spray. Sand, lichens, and mosses were torn from the ground; even small rocks became airborne if we threw them into the air. We had to struggle to walk against the wind. It was an awesome display.

The wind screamed steadily at over 60 miles per hour. for several hours. We finally made ourselves some soup, filled with flowing lichens. By evening the wind had subsided enough for us to cook dinner, and Geoff was able to repair his tent using lots of duct tape. As we sat in stunned silence marveling at the strength of that incredible storm, we realized the date. It was August 8th. 8–8–88!

The next morning we were on the water at 6:20 *a.m.* in a race to Povungnituk, still 60 miles away. The storm had churned up the lakes and deposited a great deal of silt in the water. We were in push mode. Early rising, late to bed. Our final day on the river was no different from the others: more slogging into the wind. We finally joined up with the main branch of the Povungnituk we had left so many miles before. When we arrived in the town of Povungnituk we learned that the town had lost twenty-three of their large freighter canoes in the great storm, as Hudson Bay had surged 12 feet. The boats vanished without a trace!

CHAPTER 20
MENDING THE TEARS

A Primer on the Art of Modern Canoe Repair and Maintenance!

I began my research for this chapter by contacting a number of canoe companies and canoeing gurus. From Marathon Canoes came instructions for fixing tempered aluminum; from the Minnesota Canoe Association and Eugene Jensen,[1] tips for repairing fiberglass-covered wood-strip canoes; and from Mike Cichanowski (owner of We-no-nah canoes),[2] procedures for repairing and reinforcing fiberglass-Kevlar canoes. Coleman and Old Town provided instructions for mending polyethylene hulls, and Blue Hole and Old Town suggested ways to patch Royalex canoes. The art of canoe repair, I learned, has come a long way since furnace tape and fiberglass.

Included in this chapter, then, are tips for making field and permanent repairs to all the new synthetics in addition to the venerable old aluminum and fiberglass canoes. The Red Cross canoeing manual contains enough information about wood-canvas craft to let me omit it here.

Frankly, I hope you'll never have to use any of the techniques contained herein on a canoe—at least not *your* canoe! But in the event your good judgment fails in a bad rapid, there are the recommended repair procedures.

FIBERGLASS/KEVLAR

Many years ago I watched what appeared to be a new fiberglass canoe scrape its way down a rapid I'd portaged around. I hailed the man and asked him how he could subject a beautiful canoe to such abuse.

"I just hope I live long enough to wear it out," he grinned.

Later that summer I saw the man at a canoe event. His bright green Sawyer canoe looked like new. He said he learned how to repair it by attending a seminar sponsored by the U.S. Canoe Association. I joined the organization that day and soon became a canoe fanatic just like him.

You don't need special skills to fix fiberglass/Kevlar canoes. I use the two terms interchangeably because repair procedures for both materials are the same, except for some cosmetic concerns that I address later (Kevlar). Patching fiberglass/Kevlar canoes is easy work, and there are lots of second chances if you mess up. Once you get the hang of it, you can usually mend minor gel-coat damage in an hour and major breaks in half a day.

Generally it's best to stick with duct tape for field repairs, saving serious patching for the controlled conditions at home. Fiberglassing along a riverbank without the proper tools—such as sharp scissors and a power sander—may later complicate a proper job. The following pages thus address permanent fiberglass/Kevlar repair work done at home.

Terminology

Fiberglass cloth is composed of twisted strands of fiberglass that are woven at right angles to one another. Cloth has the highest glass-to-resin ratio (about 1:1) of all fiber-

---

[1] Eugene Jensen is one of North America's best long-distance canoe racers. Though now moderately retired from racing, he continues to design and build canoes. Jensen-designed canoes are manufactured by at least half a dozen performance-minded companies.

[2] Check out We-no-nah's excellent new *Canoe Repair Video,* which contains step-by-step procedures for mending modern fiberglass-Kevlar hulls. It's available from the We-no-nah Canoe Company (appendix B) and We-no-nah Canoe distributors.

glass materials, and also the greatest strength. Six- or 7.5-ounce-per-square-yard cloth is the most practical weight for mending canoes.

E-glass and S-glass: E-glass is the common boatbuilding fabric and the one you should use for most canoe repairs. S-glass—a patterned material—is much more abrasion resistant and expensive.

Episize biaxial tape: Two layers of fifteen-ounce-per-square-yard nonwoven E-glass are lightly stitched together at a 45-degree angle. Biaxial tape comes in 4-inch-wide, 10- and 20-yard rolls. The material is bound at the edges so it's easy to apply along a keel line. For invisible repairs, cover biaxial tape with one layer of six-ounce E-glass.

Kevlar cloth: This incredibly strong, very expensive aramid is used in police flak vests and as a tire cord fiber. All the best fiberglass canoes use some Kevlar to reinforce delicate areas. Kevlar is *much* stronger and more abrasion resistant than fiberglass cloth.

Mat: Chopped, cross-linked glass fibers that are held together with a dried resin binder. Glass-to-resin ratio is about 1:3, which makes mat one-third as strong as cloth. Mat becomes very stiff as it absorbs resin, so it's often used in canoe bilges to improve rigidity. Many layers of fiberglass cloth will stiffen an area as well as mat, and the resulting repair will be lighter and stronger.

Gel coat is a microthin, waterproof resin on the outside of most fiberglass and Kevlar canoes. It resists light abrasion but it breaks when the canoe hits rocks. You can replace broken gel coat, but not without a fight. Gel coat is difficult to apply and almost impossible to color-match perfectly. The section on Mending Gel-coat tells you how to make cosmetic repairs without using gel coat.

Colloidal silica is used to thicken epoxy resin. I use it to fill deep cuts and gouges. Colloidal silica is very strong and it sands easily. *Caution:* Always wear a dust mask when you work with colloidal silica. The particles are very light and may go deep inside your lungs.

Resins: There are polyester, vinylester, and epoxy resins. Epoxy is the strongest and best for repairing canoes. Special boatbuilding epoxies such as Ad-Tech, System Three, and West System (appendix B) are worth their high price (more than $80 a gallon). They come with accurate measuring pumps so you won't waste resin by pouring more than you need.

MEKP: Methyl-ethyl-ketone-peroxide. The hardening agent used for polyester resin. It comes in small plastic tubes and smells awful. It's dangerous stuff—it'll blind you if you get it in your eyes! You don't need MEKP if you use epoxy.

Fiberglass/Kevlar Repair Kit

- Very sharp long-blade scissors
- Orbital and rotary power sanders
- Saber saw
- Plastic squeegees (like those used for body work on cars)
- Polyester resin (for epoxy boats, choose fast-curring epoxy)
- Clear tin cans with friction caps, or glass or polyethylene containers (for storing resin)
- Tube of MEKP (for polyester)
- 1-inch-wide paintbrush
- 7.5-ounce fiberglass cloth
- 50-grit sandpaper
- Dixie cups (for mixing resin; *never* mix resins in a container that contains uncured resin!)

Safety Concerns

- Laboratory safety goggles, plastic gloves, and dust masks are essential when you're making fiberglass/Kevlar repairs. You'll use lots of gloves and masks, so you might as well buy 'em by the box.

- Always mix and apply resins in a well-ventilated (outside!) area, and wear a *good* dust mask when you sand fiberglass. Use a new mask for each sanding project.

- Using a protective skin cream (barrier cream) helps protect your skin from contamination by resin or solvents that get through gloves.

- You'll need special solvents to remove resin from tools. Acetone is the standard for polyester; epoxy thinner for epoxy. *Always* wear barrier cream *and* gloves if you use these dangerous solvents! West System 855-16 biodegradable Tool Cleaning Solution works well for cleaning uncured epoxy spills. You'll find mail-order sources for these and other canoe repair materials in appendix B.

- Household vinegar is fine for cleaning tools, *but not skin!* Vinegar dissolves epoxy just enough to allow it to go deep inside the subdermal tissues of your skin. This increases the chance of an allergic action—and who knows what later on?

- If fibers get in your hair or on your skin, washing with soap and water seldom removes them. In fact, washing may drive the glass particles that cause your skin to itch deeper! Try using a vacuum cleaner to swoop up abrasive dust. If discomfort persists, apply masking tape to the affected area then gently pull the tape off—as if you're removing lint from clothes. This usually works. Some waterless hand creams will remove some resins from skin. You can also wash the affected area with a good hair conditioner, which seems to lubricate and smooth the fibers. Rinse your skin thoroughly after you've applied the conditioner, as you would for hair.

Scratches

Shallow scratches can often be polished out with auto buffing compounds. Use a light touch on the buffer—bear down hard and you may cut into the glass or Kevlar below!

Deep scratches are best left alone, unless they are so deep that they abrade the glass or Kevlar beneath. If fiberglass or gold furry stuff (damaged Kevlar) protrudes from the scratch, you'll want to make repairs. If the damage is light, simply flow epoxy resin into the cut. When it has hardened, polish it out and paint it.

Heavily scored or broken Kevlar should be covered with a fiberglass patch. Fair the edges of the hardened patch into the surrounding hull, then paint it. Be sure to use fiberglass; Kevlar *cannot* be sanded!

Mending Gel Coat

One trip down a rocky river and you'll need to repair the gel coat on the nose of your canoe. Gel-coat repair kits do a good job if you're very patient. The book procedure calls for filling the break with color-matched liquid gel coat (which is runny and hard to contain), then sanding and polishing to blend the repair. This is slow, frustrating work, and it's almost impossible to get a perfect color match. The following procedure, on the other hand, is easier and faster and the finished repair is invisible. You'll need:

Figure 20-1. Pick out the shards of damaged gel coat. Then catalyze the polyester putty (use extra MEKP for a hot mix) and work it into the break to overflowing. If you're using epoxy, stir in colloidal silica until you get a peanut-butter-thick mix that won't run.

Figure 20-2. When the resin has cured, sand it level.

Figure 20-3. Finish to silky smoothness with 400-grit wet sandpaper.

Figure 20-4. Paint the patch. Later, use a mixture of paste wax and pumice to blend the paint to the hull.

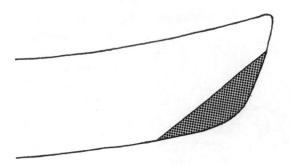

Figure 20-5. If you have a canoe whose color you can't match, mask a short, artificial waterline along the bow and stern.

- White polyester putty (available at marinas) or gray auto body putty. Use epoxy if you want a stronger repair. Thicken the epoxy with *colloidal silica,* as suggested in step 2 below.
- 60- and 100-grit dry sandpaper, and 200- and 400-grit wet-dry finishing paper.
- Matching auto acrylic or epoxy paint.
- Fiberglass *boat* wax (it contains a mild abrasive) or paste wax and pumice.

If you have a natural gold Kevlar canoe, or one whose color you can't match, repair the gel coat as described above—then mask a short, artificial waterline along the bow and stern (figure 20-5). Paint the masked area an attractive color. The paint will hide your repair.

Skid Plates

Some paddlers glue thick Kevlar skid plates on the ends of their canoe to protect them from damage. Here's why this may not be a very good idea:

- Kevlar skid pads may absorb a pint or more of epoxy resin, which increases the weight of the canoe by several pounds. This weight is added at the extreme ends of the canoe, which affects its swing weight, or ability to carve and check turns. If you want to turn a high-performance canoe into a barking dog, just add some weight to its ends. You'll notice the flywheel effect immediately.

- You can't sand Kevlar, so the harsh edges of the thick felt pads won't fair in to match the contours of the hull. The result is increased wetted surface and noise.

Here's a better plan: Lightly sand the area to be patched and cover it with one layer of biaxial tape. Saturate the fabric with resin (a plastic squeegee works better than a brush), then lay an oversized cover piece of six-ounce E-glass or S-glass on top. Work resin into the material until the cover patch is saturated. When the resin is dry, fair the edges and lightly sand the surface of the fiberglass until it's smooth to the touch. Spray-paint to match the hull.

Patching with Fiberglass

You'll be able to handle almost every fiberglass canoe repair problem once you know how to apply:

- An emergency field patch to a damaged area that's accessible from both sides of the hull.
- An emergency field patch to a damaged area accessible from one side.
- A cosmetic patch to an area accessible from two sides.
- A cosmetic patch to an area accessible from one side.

Before I examine the specific procedure for patching, there are some general considerations you should be aware of. First is the matter of strength. Canoes flex much more than other watercraft, and they occasionally hit rocks! Consequently, a repair that's strong enough for a fishing boat may not be durable enough for a canoe. Second is aesthetics. Many paddlers are very conscious of how pretty their boat looks. With care you can make a patch that is both strong and beautiful. However, invisible patches, which result when you lay up layers of fiberglass cloth over gel coat from the inside of the hull (no locking outer cover patch), may not be strong enough for a canoe and are therefore not recommended by the Minnesota Canoe Association building chairman.

Emergency Patch to an Area Accessible from Both Sides of the Hull

1. Trim away the broken pieces of fiberglass with a sharp knife. This will leave a jagged hole, though one with structurally sound edges.

2. Sand off the gel coat about 2 inches back from the edges of the hole.

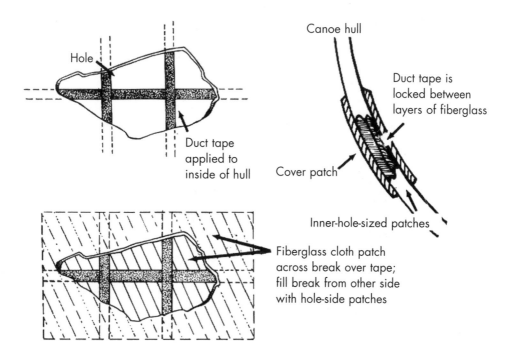

Hole

Duct tape
applied to
inside of hull

Canoe hull

Duct tape is
locked between
layers of fiberglass

Cover patch

Inner-hole-sized patches

Fiberglass cloth patch
across break over tape;
fill break from other side
with hole-side patches

Figure 20-6.

3. Sand the area around the inside edges of the hole.

4. Mix the polyester or quick-curing epoxy according to directions and lay two or three layers of patches across the inside hole. Add an outside patch or two. For greater strength, fill the area between the inside and outside patches with smaller hole-sized pieces of fiberglass cloth.

5. Paddle the boat home, cut out the patch, and do it right (see the instructions for applying a cosmetic patch below).

If the hole is very large (several inches across), you'll have to provide support for the fiberglass until the resin sets up. The easiest way to do this is to place thin strips of duct tape across the hole on the *inside* of the hull. Lay two or three fiberglass patches over the duct tape and fill the break with hole-sized patches. Cover the hole-sized patches with a large piece of fiberglass cloth to lock them in place (the tape will remain imprisoned between the layers of fiberglass). This patch is ugly, but it will keep out water and stay put until you get home.

[3] You may have to cut out some flotation foam to provide a working area behind the hole.

Emergency Patch to an Area Accessible from One Side Only

About the only time you could have a problem like this is if a break occurs adjacent to a flotation element at the bow or stern (another reason why canoe makers should use suspended flotation in canoes).

If you're in paper birch country you can make a form of birch bark and patch the hull according to the directions given for making a cosmetic patch. Otherwise you'll have to wall in the hole from the inside one strip at a time, as follows:

1. Wet out two fiberglass strips (2 to 4 inches wide) and poke them through the hole with your fingers.[3] Work each strip flat along the edges of the hole (as always, first cut out badly damaged glass and sand the inside edges of the hole) so that about half the width of each strip is supported by sound fiberglass.

2. Overlap another pair of fiberglass strips at right angles to the first set. Keep this up until only a small hole is left in the center of the damaged area (figure 20-7).

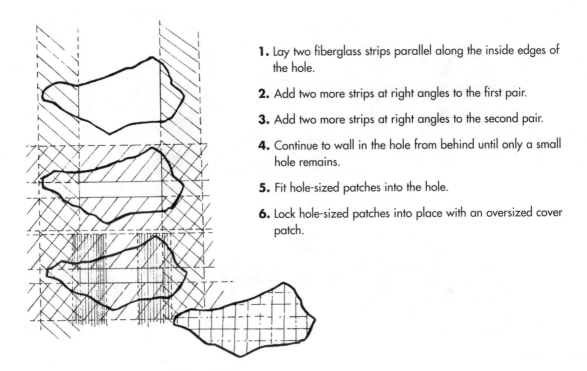

1. Lay two fiberglass strips parallel along the inside edges of the hole.

2. Add two more strips at right angles to the first pair.

3. Add two more strips at right angles to the second pair.

4. Continue to wall in the hole from behind until only a small hole remains.

5. Fit hole-sized patches into the hole.

6. Lock hole-sized patches into place with an oversized cover patch.

Figure 20-7. Emergency patch to an area accessible from one side only.

3. You may have to allow these layers of glass to set up before you can proceed to the next step.

4. Carefully fit several fiberglass patches *into* the damaged areas. The patches should seal the small hole left from overlapping the strips and extend to the edges of the damaged area.

5. Lock the fitted patches in place with an oversized patch. (Be sure to sand off all gel coat in the affected area or the outside cover patch won't stick.)

6. Sand the edges of the patch to blend.

Cosmetic Patch to an Area Accessible from Both Sides

1. Cut out the splintered glass with a fine-toothed saber saw.

2. Feather the inside edges of the hole with small rotary grinder.

3. Place plastic wrap, waxed paper, or aluminum foil over a flexible piece of cardboard (be sure there are no wrinkles in the wrap) and tape the cardboard—wrap-side against the hull—to the canoe (figure 20-8).

4. Use sharp scissors to cut several fiberglass cloth patches to fit into the hole from the inside of the hull. Cut each patch slightly larger than the previous one to accommodate the increased taper (feather) of the hole (figure 20-9).

5. Wet out the patches on a board and place them into the hole—smallest one first, then the next smallest, and so on—until you've reached the level of the inside hull.

6. Cut a large patch to seal the smaller patches. This patch should extend beyond the last patch at least 1 inch all around. (Be sure the area around the hole has been sanded thoroughly.)

7. When the patch is dry, remove the cardboard form and sand off the gel coat, about 2 inches back, all around the repaired area.

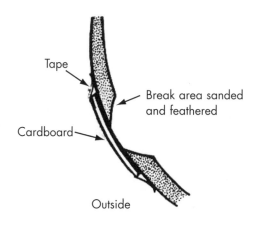

Figure 20-8.

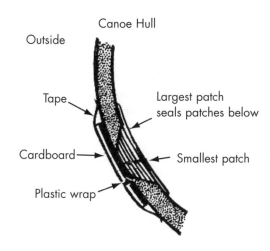

Figure 20-9.

Because gel coat is difficult to work, many canoeists prefer to simply paint the area with color-matched epoxy paint. Gel coat, however, produces a nicer-looking patch.

If you want a really pretty patch, leave off the outside locking patch and apply gel coat from the *inside* of the hull directly to the plastic wrap (or foil or whatever) before you lay up the patches (the gel coat must be hard before you begin patching).[4] Don't think you've erred if the color of your hardened gel coat doesn't match perfectly the factory color of your

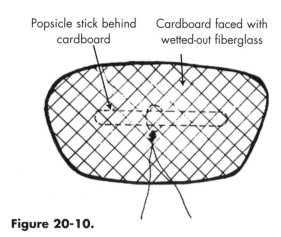

Figure 20-10.

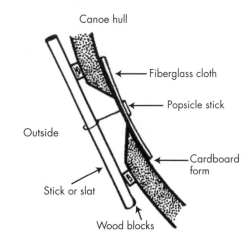

Figure 20-11.

8. Apply an oversized fiberglass cloth patch to the outside of the hull.

9. When dry, sand and feather the inner and outer cover patches until they blend in with the contours of the hull.

10. Mask around the outside patch and apply color-matched gel coat. Sand and feather the gel coat to the contour of the canoe (use progressive grits of abrasive).

[4]Inner and outer locking patches are recommended for strength. These large patches will have minimal effect on the appearance of the boat.

boat. No one has yet found a way to get a precise color match.

Cosmetic Patch to an Area Accessible from One Side Only

1. Cut out the bad glass and feather one edge of the hole.

2. Cut a piece of cardboard to the approximate shape of the hole, but slightly larger and more oval in shape.

3. Cut a couple of fiberglass cloth patches the size of the cardboard, place them on the cardboard, and wet them out with resin.

4. Run a small copper wire through the center of the cloth and cardboard around a Popsicle stick, and back through the glass-covered cardboard (figure 20-10).

5. Force the wet glass/cardboard form into the hole (you'll have to bend the cardboard slightly) and align it so the cloth butts against and overlaps the inside hole edges.

6. Pull on the wire to tighten the form firmly against the inside of the hull; wrap the wire around a wood stick or slat and block the stick at the ends to provide pressure for the patch until it dries.

7. When the patch is dry, snip off the wire and complete the repair from the outside hull as for a cosmetic patch accessible from both sides. The cardboard form and Popsicle stick will remain inside the boat (figure 20-11).

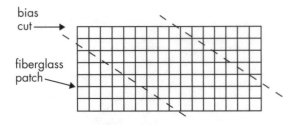

Figure 20-12. If you cut fiberglass patches on the *bias* (diagonal cut), they'll lay easily into tightly curved areas.

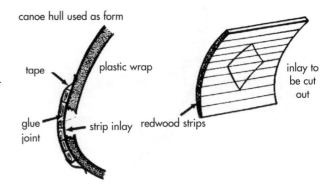

Figure 20-13. Using the hull of the canoe to make a strip inlay.

Kevlar

Kevlar boats are repaired just like fiberglass ones, except an invisible patch is harder to make. This is because Kevlar doesn't sand well. In fact, if doesn't sand at all—it just fuzzes up and makes a mess. This means you can't feather the edges of the Kevlar patch to blend in to the contours of the hull. For this reason most canoeists prefer to patch Kevlar canoes (at least on the outside) with fiberglass instead of Kevlar. It's less hassle, and for small areas the loss of strength is insignificant.

However, if you need to repair large sections of material, you'll have to use some Kevlar. Fiberglass may not be strong enough. In 1987 I wrapped a Mad River Kevlar Explorer canoe around a midstream boulder in a lively rapids. Amazingly, the rails held (which saved the boat from breaking up), but the hull broke in five widespread places. Fortunately, the break did not go through all the layers of Kevlar.

With the help of six friends, we peeled the boat off the rock, popped the hull back into shape (a light boot kick did the trick), and paddled it home, sans duct tape. Later I began the arduous repair, which required two full days. Since the interior walls of the canoe were sound (though the Kevlar was hinged), I simply reinforced the outside with 7.5-ounce fiberglass and West Epoxy. The repair looked and felt okay, but it later broke in three places on a canoe trip down a rocky river.

The solution was to wall up the inside with a single layer of Kevlar, over which I placed some six-ounce fiberglass cloth (to permit cosmetic sanding of the edges). Since the addition of the Kevlar cloth, the old Explorer, which I've lovingly nick-named Patches, has remained sound, and despite tough use, no further repairs have been necessary.

It's important to realize that patching invariably creates a hull section that's stiffer than the surrounding material. When a canoe impacts an obstacle, the unyielding area usually breaks first. It's here that the extra strength of Kevlar cloth will be most appreciated.

If your canoe has oiled ash rails, keep them *well oiled* with Watco marine finish. Ash will break rather than bend if it dries out. If the gunnels break during a canoe wrap, the show's over!

WOOD-STRIP CANOES

You can patch a wood-strip canoe just like a fiberglass one, but if you want an unnoticeable repair, you won't get it! A stripper is the prettiest watercraft afloat; the last thing you want is to destroy its beauty with an ugly fiberglass patch.

Damage to strip boats tends either to be superficial (just through the outer layer of glass cloth) or catastrophic (major structural damage). Superficial injuries are simply repaired by sanding and applying polyester or epoxy resin to the affected area. A final sanding and rubdown with extra-fine steel wool and pumice will restore the hull to a semblance of new. Deep scratches may be partially removed by progressive sanding and buffing.

Catastrophic damage calls for resourcefulness, since it's almost impossible to restructure large areas of broken-out hull with matching wood strips. Your best bet is to cut out the damaged area and install a wood inlay.

Obtain a contrasting piece of ³⁄₈-inch-thick wood (most strip boats are laid up with ¼-inch-thick strips) slightly larg-er than the damaged area. Trace an attractive pattern on the wood (perhaps a fish or diamond) and cut it out with a saber saw. Sand and smooth the inlay and trace it onto the hull around the hole. Carefully saw out the tracing (this will remove all the damaged wood) and glue in the inlay with epoxy. Sand the inlay to the level of the hull on both sides and lock it into place with a fiberglass cloth patch on each side.

Sand and buff the glass patch and apply several coats of paste wax. This repair will be very attractive.

If the hull has been damaged along a severe curve, such as a section of extreme tumblehome, the repair process will be more complicated. Because of the curvature at the break, a solid inlay won't work (unless, of course, you use a very thick board and sand away great amounts of material). The solu-tion here is to use the curve of the hull as a temporary form for laying up a strip inlay that will fit into the damaged area (figure 20-13). Edge-glue the strips with Elmer's glue as shown in the diagram, and secure the strips to the form (canoe hull) with tape. All glue joints will be covered with fiberglass so there's no danger of the Elmer's glue dissolving in water. The form should be heavily waxed or covered with plastic wrap so the edge-glued strips won't stick to it.

When the strips have dried, remove them, saw out the inlay, and glue it into the damaged area. Finally, cover each side of the inlay with fiberglass cloth.

If this method sounds like too much work, simply saw out the damaged strips and replace them with new strips of approximate matching colors.

THERMO-FORMED PLASTIC BOATS

Though thermo-formed plastic boats (ABS, Royalex, and polyethylene) have been around for some time, only a handful of people have had much experience repairing them. This is because molded plastics are very strong; they seldom break, even when severely impacted against a rock. And that's fortu-nate, for tears in these plastics are not at all easy to repair.

Royalex

Royalex is a laminate of cross-linked vinyl, ABS plastic, and ABS closed-cell foam.

Dents

Royalex is very strong, but it dents. Shallow dents visible only on the outside of a Royalex hull will usually disappear in time. You can help this along simply by exposing the dented area to warm sunlight for several hours. The heat from the sun will cause the dent to level itself somewhat.

Deep dents that are visible on the inside of the hull are reparable (with some effort) by applying *moderate* heat to the dented area. An electric iron adjusted to a "rayon" setting, 75-watt lightbulb, hair drier, or commercial heat gun will work fine. Where extensive reshaping is required, a bank of two to four heat lamps and a friend is recommended.

Apply heat slowly to the dented areas. Don't let the vinyl outer layer get too hot. Royalex is an excellent insulator, so if you apply too much heat too fast, you'll broil one side of the material without even warming the other.

When the dent is soft enough to be moved, gently push it back into shape and hold it there until it cools.

Holes

The standard procedure for mending holes in Royalex is to fill them with epoxy putty or epoxy resin and microballoons. If you undercut the ABS foam around the hole, the epoxy will bond more strongly. Wipe off excess resin (putty) from the vinyl surface with a wet rag. When the epoxy is dry, paint it with polyurethane or acrylic-base enamel, or use fuel-proof model airplane dope (excellent!).

There are dozens of epoxy formulations. Some types bond tightly to ABS, while others don't bond to it at all. The general-purpose epoxies sold at marinas are fine for emergency repairs, but they may not be the best for use where high strength and long-term durability are required. Royalex canoe makers will sell you the proper repair materials in kit form, or they'll suggest specific adhesives that you can buy locally. You'll find some recommended epoxies in appendix B.

Tears

Bob Lantz of Blue Hole Canoe recommends the following procedure for mending a tear in Royalex with epoxy:

1. Cut out the ragged edges of the tear with a knife and undercut the ABS foam to provide purchase for the epoxy.

2. Apply Epoxybond epoxy putty (available at most hardware stores) to both edges of the tear and press the edges together.

3. Sand the vinyl around the tear lightly and clean it with rubbing alcohol.

4. Apply two layers of fiberglass cloth to each side of the hull over the tear.

5. When the repair has dried, sand the patch to blend into the contours of the hull and paint it.

A fiberglass patch correctly applied with the proper epoxy probably exceeds the tensile strength of the surrounding undamaged hull material. However, it's doubtful that this or any other patch will restore the damaged area to its original flexibility. In all likelihood only remolding the break (virtually impossible) can do that.

It's interesting to note that the best epoxies for bonding

ABS may stick poorly (or not at all) to the outer skin of a Royalex boat, and vice versa. So if you want a first-class repair job, you should probably either grind off the vinyl surface of the hull and use ABS-proven adhesives throughout, or use two different adhesives—one for bonding the ABS, and the other for gluing the fiberglass cloth to the vinyl. I've had good luck bonding fiberglass to vinyl with the epoxies listed in appendix B.

Ribbed ABS Canoes

Ribbed ABS canoes have gone the way of the passenger pigeon, and for good reason. They were badly designed, difficult to repair, and not really inexpensive. Nevertheless, a few of these old hulks are still around (and intact), so a word about their repair is in order.

For field repair use duct tape. Solvent-bonding with MEKP/ABS glue or ABS-specific epoxy and fiberglass cloth is the best way to make permanent repairs.

Polyethylene Canoes

Polyethylene canoes[5] are touted by their makers as the toughest watercraft afloat. They'd better be, because it's impossible to repair them in the field and only slightly easier at home.

About all you can do for a break in the skin (rare in polyethylene hulls) is cover it with duct tape and pray it doesn't get worse. Holes—which might result from hitting sharp granite or a spike in a bridge piling—are more likely. One manufacturer (Hollowform) suggests you fix a small hole by installing a steel bolt through it (a watertight washer should be placed on each side of the bolt)!

Coleman, however, advises use of its special repair kit, which consists of three flat pieces of Ram-X for patching a two-part adhesive, and instructions that must be followed *exactly!* Things get interesting when you realize that the plastic must be flame-treated with the *oxidizing* (not reducing) flame of a propane or *butane* (not gasoline) torch before the adhesive is applied.

Since Coleman was kind enough to send me a repair kit, I gave the procedure a try. I can report that the technique requires some skill but is not difficult. Patching a curved surface with this outfit, however, borders on the impossible.

Fortunately for Ram-X owners, Coleman has found that

---

[5]Some trade names for polyethylene canoes include Coleman (Ram-X), Hollowform (Xylar), Keewadin (K-Tek), and Perception (Marlex).

tears along curves and hard-to-reach areas can be mended by welding polyethylene into the break with a nitrogen torch. To accommodate owners of broken canoes, Coleman has set up a number of nitrogen welding stations around the country. Contact Coleman for information about the welding station nearest you if you have a Ram-X canoe that requires this type of repair.

Repairing an Old Town Discovery canoe is similar to, but easier than, mending Coleman Ram-X. First you sand the mating surfaces of the hull, then perform the blow-torch flame treatment described above. The tear is then patched with fiberglass cloth and special epoxy resin provided by the manufacturer.

Out of curiosity, I repaired some damage on one of my Discoveries with material supplied by Old Town. A second small rip in another fleet boat was fixed with West epoxy and Kevlar. Both canoes have been in tough service for years since the repair, and they're doing fine.

Another way to repair polyethylene is offered by Dick Steinke, senior chemist for the H. B. Fuller company in St. Paul, Minnesota. Dick suggests melting parent polyethylene into the hole or break with a medium-hot flatiron. This method takes some skill to effect a neat repair, but it welds the break and thus restores the area to its original strength.

A final tip: Be careful how you handle any plastic boat in ultracold weather. An acquaintance of mine once witnessed the demise of an ABS (not Royalex ABS) hull that was accidentally dropped from the top of a van in minus-28-degree northern Minnesota cold. The canoe shattered into an undetermined number of pieces!

In case you're wondering why anyone in his right mind would be messing with a canoe at these temperatures, I can report that the boat was purchased as a Christmas present for a fourteen-year-old boy. The canoe was being taken home for the holiday!

CANOE MAINTENANCE

Regular maintenance goes a long way toward preserving your investment. These tricks will keep your canoe looking like new.

Oiling Your Brightwork

Oiled wood rails are easier to maintain and more flexible (less likely to break in a wrap-up) than varnished ones. Strip away varnish and rub in a good grade of exterior marine oil.

I've tried just about every formulation, from Watco and Djeks Olay to traditional linseed oil and quick-drying gunstock finishes like Birchwood Casey and GB Linspeed. On rigorously maintained canoes, one oil works about as well as another, though a tougher finish often results when high-gloss linseed and tung oil formulations are used on top of deep-penetrating marine oils. Here's an easy way to get a rich, furniture-grade shine:

1. Strip or sand away all factory varnish. Then remove dents and gouges by "whiskering" the wood. Here's how: Saturate a cotton rag with water and wring it dry. Fold the damp rag several times and set it over the dent or gouge. Use a hot steam iron (no steam) to firmly press the cloth over the damaged wood. Continue to iron the cloth until it no longer steams. Whisker again, if necessary, to fully raise the wood grain to the surface. If wood fibers are broken, the dent may not surface completely, in which case you may need to level the void with epoxy.

2. Sand (use 80- to 120-grit paper) the bare wood to a soft, even patina. If your canoe has factory-oiled rails, a light sanding with 120-grit paper will prepare the hull.

3. Pour the finishing oil into a bottle that has a flip top or rotating dispenser cap. Keep the bottle nearly full of oil to prevent long-term oxidation and age-thickening of the oil. You may want to mix in a small amount of walnut or oak-colored stain to give the wood a more pleasing color. Ash and spruce, for example, usually have an anemic look unless stained. Mahogany and cherry, on the other hand, should never be stained.

4. Apply a liberal coating of oil to the wood with a lint-free rag. As soon as you've finished coating the wood, *immediately* wipe off excess oil with a dry cotton rag (an old T-shirt works well). Lightly polish the wood with the cloth as you work. Leave the canoe right-side-up with its trim exposed to the sun for an hour or two before you store it away.

5. *One or more days later,* wipe on a thin coat of oil and lightly polish it with a soft, lint-free cloth. This should take less than five minutes. Repeat this step at your convenience as often as you like for several weeks or months. The wood grain will eventually fill and take on a deep, rich look.

Note that the finish is built up slowly over a long period of time. If your canoe came from the factory with oiled rails, the initial sanding should require barely fifteen minutes. After that, each application of oil takes only a few moments.

Restoring Weathered Woodwork

To restore gray, weathered woodwork, sand it well and then apply trisodium phosphate (TSP) cleaner, available at hardware stores. Wearing protective gloves, work in the TSP with a stiff brush. Rinse completely, let dry, then sand to silky smoothness. Afterward, apply a quality finishing oil in successive coats as suggested above.

Removing Stains and Scum

Occasionally use a commercial hull cleaner (I've had good results with Star Brite) to remove scum lines and stains from fiberglass and Kevlar gel coat. Paste wax will brighten and protect the hull, but it will also increase resistance (wax is hydrophobic) to the water. Canoe retailers often wipe on 303 Protectant before they display their canoes in the store. I use 303 on a regular basis on all my canoes. The product hides scratches, imparts a deep sheen, and protects against ultraviolet damage—important if you store your canoe outside.

Keeping Wood-Trimmed Canoes from Coming Apart at the Seams

The gunnels and decks of modern wood-trimmed canoes don't have drain holes like those on traditional cedar-canvas craft. As a result, bilgewater runs down the inwales (inside gunnels) of the canoe when it is turned over and becomes trapped in the ends, beneath the deck plates. The accumulated water remains here until evaporation sets it free. Meanwhile, the thin wood at the apex of the decks rots and warps, and the canoe eventually comes apart at the seams. Over the years I've owned four wood-trimmed Mad River canoes, all of which have separated at the ends.

Unfortunately, most canoe makers are insensitive to this problem. Those who aren't usually drill an ugly vertical drain hole through the top of each deck. An equally easy—but more aesthetic—solution is to drill a $1/8$-inch-diameter drain hole horizontally through each stem just beneath the deck plate. This hole is invisible unless you view the canoe at eye level, head-on.

The final touch is to varnish the inside decks and inwales where they meet. The best procedure is to stand the canoe on end (lean it against your house) and pour varnish

into the constricted area. The excess should run out the hole you drilled. Wipe off pooled varnish and, later, clear debris from the hole with a tiny rat-tail file. Do this on your new wood-trimmed fiberglass or Kevlar canoe and it will never warp and come apart at the seams!

Aluminum Canoes

Flat black paint will cut glare off the decks of aluminum canoes and give these craft a custom look. Prime the metal with vinegar before you paint. Allow the vinegar to set overnight so it will have time to etch the aluminum.

Your aluminum canoe will slide over rocks with barely a murmur if you apply a heavy coat of Johnson's paste wax to the hull. There's no need to polish the wax.

To repair major damage: A riveted patch is stronger than a weld. Rivet kits and instructions are available from the Marathon Canoe Company (appendix B).

WINTER STORAGE

Winterizing your canoe is mostly common sense: clean out debris, wash and polish the hull, repair damage, apply an ultraviolet protectant to plastics, oil or varnish the woodwork, uniformly tighten bolts, and store your treasure in a weather-protected, well-ventilated area, out of reach of small animals. Get your boat ready before the snow flies and you'll be ready to climb aboard when the rivers run again.

Canoes should be stored *upside-down* on sawhorses, wood 2-by-4s, metal bars, or nylon slings. Bars should be carpeted, especially if the canoe has wood rails. Some paddlers suspend their canoe from thick dowels tethered to the ceiling joists of their garage. This trapeze lofts the canoe above vehicles and saves space.

If you must store your canoe outside, try to find a shady place that's not in the path of high winds. Fiberglass/Kevlar, Royalex, and polyethylene canoes can be safely stored outside if you've applied an ultraviolet protectant. Wood-canvas canoes and all other canoes that have wood trim should be protected from the weather. Some paddlers use car covers made from DuPont's Tyvek material.

A 50-mile-per-hour wind will turn an unsecured canoe into a kite, so tie down any canoe that's stored outside. If you keep your canoe on sawhorses in your backyard, stake both the horses and the canoe to the ground.

Do brush off snow as it accumulates. A heavy snow load can bend or break the back of almost any canoe.

Storing Royalex Canoes in Frigid Temperatures

Owners of wood-trimmed Royalex canoes are advised to remove the gunnels (near the decks) of canoes that will be stored in subfreezing weather. It's believed that uneven rates of material expansion cause Royalex to crack.

Over the years, I've owned more than a dozen wood-trimmed Royalex canoes and just two have suffered cracks. There appear to be two reasons for the cracking:

First, cracks seem to develop more often when canoes are used in cold weather, then turned over and put away wet. Bilgewater seeps into the wood rails and screw holes, where it freezes and cracks the adjacent Royalex. Solution? If you use your canoe in transitional weather, sponge out accumulated water before you turn the boat over.

Second, Royalex shrinks as it ages. Maximum shrinkage appears to occur after about five years—which explains why old canoes crack more frequently than new ones. This procedure will prevent cracks:

Remove the first six screws at each end (and on each side) of the canoe and pull the outer gunnel away from the hull.

Enlarge the screw hole (about 50 percent) in the Royalex hull (just the Royalex, not the rails), or route a $^3/_8$-inch-long horizontal slot in the screw hole. The slot will be parallel to the keel line. The screw hole will now appear as a horizontal slot.

Screw the rails back on. The Royalex won't bear against the screw when it shrinks, and your canoe won't crack.

CHAPTER 21
ADVICE FROM THE EXPERTS

If there's an axiom about wilderness canoeing, it's that you never quit learning. Each new trip—even those taken over old, familiar ground—sets new ideas in motion. No one has a monopoly on good ideas, so I've asked the experts— some of whose biographies and canoe testimonials you read in chapter 5—to share some hard-earned advice with readers of this book. My question was: "What advice can you provide for a paddler who is about to make his or her first wilderness canoe trip?" Some experts responded with generic suggestions that are appropriate to any canoe trip, anywhere. Others keyed in to the unique challenges presented by the unforgiving barren-land routes north of 60 (the 60th parallel).

ALEX HALL

Alex Hall's biography appears in chapter 5.

Remote wilderness canoe trips should never be dangerous if you follow these rules:

1. Be prepared.
2. Never take chances.
3. Remember that Mother Nature is always in charge.

The first two rules are self-explanatory; the third suggests that you can't fight bad weather, big winds, and dangerous rapids. You must bend like the willow before a breeze, and know when to take cover when the weather deteriorates. This may mean camping earlier in the day than you expected, or sitting tight in your tent for several days till a storm passes through. If you've planned your time too tightly, it may even mean missing your pickup boat or charter floatplane. Many have perished because they took chances to meet a deadline. A humble, respectful attitude is the right attitude for canoeing the cold rivers of the barren lands. Many have perished thinking they were up to all the challenges that nature could unleash.

BILL SIMPSON

Bill Simpson's biography appears in chapter 5.

I carry something in my kit that always brings stares, questions, and snide comments. It's called a fire hose, and it's a 30-inch length of flexible surgical tubing. You simply position one end at the base of the campfire where the coals are, blow vigorously through the other end, and watch the flames leap to life. It does give you a rather heady feeling, especially at altitude, but no harm is done. The tubing can be purchased from any pharmaceutical supply company. Or ask your doctor.

ANTONI HARTING

Toni Harting is a freelance writer and photographer who specializes in canoe-related topics. He edits Nastawgan, *the quarterly journal of the Wilderness Canoe Association, based in Toronto, Ontario. An avid wilderness paddler, Toni has written scores of articles, published numerous photographs, and is the author of* French River: Canoeing the River of the Stick-Wavers *(Boston Mills Press, 1996) and* Shooting Paddlers: Photographic Adventures with Canoeists, Kayakers, Rafters *(Natural Heritage Books, 2000).*

■ An extendible slide pole like that used by window cleaners to get at high windows is extremely useful. I've used mine as a center support for a kitchen tarp, as a pole to keep my canoe off the shore when tracking upstream, and as a high monopod for my camera.

The slide pole can be extended up to 4 meters, which provides a nice vantage point for photographing campsites and rapids.

- Given today's emphasis on "leave no trace" travel, I am reluctant to suggest bringing along a machete. Still, it can be a very useful tool, especially on small, tag-alder-choked Ontario bush rivers that aren't paddled much. Most Ontario bush rivers do not have established or government-maintained campsites. The few open spots that do exist quickly become overgrown. That's when a machete comes in handy. Rest assured that that tangle of alders you clear for a tent spot will grow back in a season.

BOB HENDERSON

Bob Henderson teaches canoe-tripping skills as part of the Outdoor Education Program at McMaster University in Hamilton, Ontario. He writes a heritage column for the Canadian Recreational Canoe Association's journal, Kanawa. Bob likes the long portage trails of Algonquin Park, but his favorite destination is Labrador.

I cut my teeth on long, mean portages, like those in Ontario's Algonquin Park. The Grand Portage (9 miles!), which runs along the Ontario-Minnesota border, was my longest carry. I don't like conventional canoe yokes. Instead, I prefer to portage with a thinly padded center thwart and a leather tumpline. This setup is far more comfortable than any yoke I've tried. A yoke is comfortable for about five minutes, then the pain sets in. You are locked into the position between the pads and there are no adjustments you can make for comfort.

A thwart and tumpline spreads the weight of the canoe over a wider area than a yoke alone. You can flick the tumpline on and off your head at any time, or change its location on your head.

It's important that you don't pad the thwart too heavily. You need to feel a healthy connection to the canoe if you move with any speed. A couple of wraps around the thwart

with a closed-cell foam sleeping pad is enough. Don't use open-cell foam; it's too mushy.

Some canoeists tie their paddles across the thwarts to form a simple yoke, which may be dangerous if you trip (the tumpline could snap your neck). I also feel that the confining paddles provide too much connection (which means you can't escape!) to the canoe.

The logic behind a lightly paddled thwart and tumpline asks you to consider the end of the portage rather than those first "feel-good" minutes at the start. It also speaks to the merit of a traditional plan that has stood the test of time.

SARA SEAGER AND MIKE WEVRICK

Sara Seager and Mike Wevrick have canoed in Ontario, Quebec, the Northwest Territories, Saskatchewan, Manitoba, New England, Labrador, and British Columbia. She says she intends to "paddle every ecosystem in Canada." Sara and Mike travel with their dog, Kira, who loves the wilderness as much as they do.

- **Stove lighting:** Use a long-barreled spark lighter (the type used for igniting Bunsen burners and propane torches) to light your stove. It works better in wind than matches, and you won't burn your thumb. Most hardware stores have them.
- **Bug shirt:** Sew up the front and cuffs of a man's lightweight, cotton-polyester dress shirt. The thin dress shirt is cool in the hot sun and it dries fast. Blackflies can't get in, and deet can be applied to the cuffs and neck. Don't sew too high up the neck or you won't be able to get the shirt over your head. You'll find old dress shirts at Salvation Army stores and garage sales.
- **Traveling with a dog:** You need a crate for your dog if you're flying on a commercial airplane (chartered bush planes usually accept uncrated dogs). Most small communities in the Far North don't have pet stores or veterinarians, so they don't have dog crates. Don't trust commercial airlines to supply a crate—they often don't have one. We fly or drive to the put-in, then mail the crate to our destination. The Canadian Postal Service has a size limit, but a large crate, where the two halves are nested together, fits the limit. Call ahead to check on your crate.
- **Insect repellents for dogs:** Deet should not be used on animals. Instead, use biodegradable pyrethrums or permethrins. You'll find these in tick and flea spray,

which you can get in hardware stores and western tack shops.

BILL HOSFORD

Bill Hosford has canoed so many Canadian rivers that it would require a full page to list them all. Notable descents include the Thelon, Nahanni, Mountain, Coppermine and Burnside (Nunavut), and the Whanganui in New Zealand. Bill is an engineering professor at the University of Michigan.

■ **Flotation:** I watched my daughter's splash-covered canoe capsize in a rapid she was lining on the Nahanni River. Covered canoes usually float belly-down when they upset, so I was surprised to see the boat right

Figure 21-1.

itself. She recovered the canoe at the bottom of the rapid and found less than a cupful of water in it. She had attached her gear to the canoe with D-rings on the bottom. This kept the load (and center of gravity) low.[1]

■ **Portages:** At Ringham Canyon on the Pukaskwa, there's a miserable 3-mile portage. We scouted the drop and decided it could be run if we lowered the canoes around a falls at the head of the canyon. A few hours later we met two bedraggled men who had completed their first carry across the portage. When they learned our plans, they decided to follow suit. The problem was that they had carried their paddles to the other side of the portage! Moral? Save two paddles per boat for the *last* carry!

■ **Sailing:** You can really make time in a tailwind if you have an efficient sail. We carry sails made from a trapezoidal piece of ripstop nylon (see figure 21-1). You insert canoe paddles through the sleeves (grips up) and set the blades on the floor or seat of the canoe. This sail rigs quick and drops fast. You can even tack (somewhat) with it if you vary the angle of the sail. The sail weighs less than six ounces and is very compact.

ALAN KESSELHEIM

Alan Kesselheim is a well-known canoeing writer.

If I were limited to one salient piece of tripping advice, it would be to give yourself plenty of time in the itinerary. A rushed trip is a hassled, unhappy, and potentially dangerous trip. When the deadline looms, it's tempting to cut corners and take chances. Most important, hurrying through a wilderness journey negates the very reasons we go in the first place. Solitude, reflection, comradeship, relaxation, rejuvenation . . . all of it gets lost if you have to rush.

My planning rule of thumb is 15 miles per day for a trip average. On a river with steady current you can do better, but on a trip with a variety of paddling conditions, potential for weather delays, and a handful of portages, 15 miles is comfortable. Besides, if you get ahead of your itinerary, lighten up, kick back, remember what you came for in the first place!

---

[1]If your packs come a few inches above the gunnels, as recommended to support your three-piece cover—see chapter 7, Covers Aren't Just for Whitewater—they'll lock in solidly with gunnel cords.

BOB DANNERT

Read Bob Dannert's biography in Chapter 5.

Every successful canoe trip is the result of good planning. I never leave even the smallest detail to chance. I consider an adventure an unplanned emergency. For me, planning is also an integral and enjoyable part of a canoe trip. Planning is a process that begins months in advance, not a few weeks before you begin!

Good planning means you have every piece of gear you need and not one thing more. Everything should be multipurpose on a canoe trip—try to make one item do the work of two.

The bottom line: You have thoroughly researched your river and have marked on your maps the dangers that they reveal. You have first-aid, repair, and survival equipment. You are prepared for the hordes of insects you know you *will* encounter. You have adjusted your schedule so that you will arrive at your destination on time, even if you are windbound 20 percent of the time, which is the rule on Arctic rivers. You carry at least 10 percent extra food in the event bad weather slows you down or your bush plane doesn't pick you up on time. You anticipate what could go wrong and you plan ahead. Planning continues even as the wheels roll north.

You may be an expert on canoeing rivers within the timberline, but barren-land routes require much more care. There is less room for error in the barrens, and help is seldom available if things go wrong. You must make sure your crew understands the extra demands imposed by canoe travel in a remote, treeless region. Everyone must be prepared to continue in spite of wind or rain, bugs or blisters, cracked, dried skin, or sore muscles—high water, low water, or no water. I tell my crews that they will have some of the best times in their life and some of the worst—and the two might be just hours apart.

I also believe it's important to be in good physical shape. This means pretrip workouts. By being in shape you are less tired, and as a result you can do more and still have fun. An Arctic trip is much more than paddling a canoe. There's fishing, hiking, photography, and a myriad of other things to see and do.

KENT FORD

Kent Ford is one of the top white-water paddlers of all time. He's an American Canoe Association instructor trainer and the former director of instruction at the Nantahala Outdoor Center. He was a member of the world-champion C-1 team in 1983, 1985, and 1992. Kent has hosted and written a number of superb instructional materials, including Whitewater Self Defense *and* Solo Playboating. *His video* Drill Time *is a must-see for those who play in big rapids. Kent Ford's books and videos are available at most paddling shops. You'll find more tips on his informative Web site (www. performancevideo.com).*

I have occasionally caught myself abbreviating standard safety practices when I am on the river with a group of friends—especially on a multiday river trip. We assume a lot of knowledge, and it would be easy for one very inexperienced person to join the trip with virtually no safety-oriented instruction.

I think it is important for the most experienced members of the trip to set up an open dialogue on safety, explaining what hazards might lie ahead, and what can be done to avoid them.

Many people fear white water and view it as extremely dangerous. This leads to fear that, if not addressed, can compromise both safety and enjoyment. You can abate fear if you review the things that contribute to accidents, and discuss ways to avoid them. For example, a huge percentage of white-water accidents involve flooded rivers, hypothermia, and no PFD. Make sure your group understands how to guard against these dangers. Create a list of hazards, then review each one, stressing the procedures for playing it safe.

Everyone should be comfortable with these procedures:

■ **Swimming in white water:** Right after an unexpected swim, get on your back and point your feet downstream. Keep your feet up to avoid getting them trapped between rocks. Your PFD should protect your body from shallow rocks as you float downstream. In this eyes forward position, you can clearly see and evaluate what lies ahead.

Keep your body lined up with the current and use your legs as shock absorbers if you hit rocks. In shallow water arch your back to keep your feet high. Turn your head and time your breathing to take in air between waves and holes. Correct timing requires concentration.

Keep your feet near the surface and never try to stand in water that's deep enough to float you. If you catch a foot between rocks, the water may bowl you over and hold you under water!

Caution: Don't let embarrassment, frustration, or cold make you hunt for footing.

When you see a hazard to avoid or a place you want to go, angle your body in the direction you want to go and backstroke upstream. This is just like back-ferrying a canoe—your head points in the direction you want to go.

- **Swim aggressively if you need more power:** Swim aggressively (roll on your stomach and use a crawl stroke) if you need more power. The crawl/aggressive swim is the best plan for rivers with deep, turbulent water—it enables you to get to where you want to go as fast as possible. Try to breathe on the downstream side to avoid inhaling water. You'll tire fast, so use short, intense bursts. A breast- or sidestroke will improve your visibility but slow your progress.

- **Barrel-roll across an eddy line:** The easiest way to swim out of an eddy is to do barrel rolls over the eddy line. This technique helps you break through the current differential, which tries to spin and reject you.

- **Swim headfirst over a strainer:** If you find yourself being unavoidably drawn into a strainer, somersault to the head-downriver swimming position and kick flat to launch up and over the top of the debris. The goal is to keep your head *up*. The normally recommended feet-first swimming position is too passive for strainers!

- **Dropping over a falls:** The best plan is to ball up, to avoid washing into a foot entrapment. This is a real concern with sheer drops of several feet or more.

- **Exiting a pour-over hole:** If you get stuck in a pour-over hole, you may have to change your shape to enable the hole to spit you out. Swim aggressively for the sides where water rushes by, or swim upstream to a current that will flush you out from below.

- **Swimming long rapids:** It is best to avoid a swim on long stretches of continuous white water, especially in cold, flooded rivers lined with trees and strainers. But if you do have to swim, be superaggressive in getting to a safe place. Watch the currents to decide if it's safer to stay with your boat or to abandon it and swim aggressively to shore. In big flows you will probably need help getting to shore, and you'll be grateful if your group has the skills to assist.

BEVERLY AND JOEL HOLLIS

Beverly and Joel have paddled more than 8,000 miles in Canada. They have made nineteen trips, each of which lasted about a month. Generally they go by themselves in their Old Town Tripper or Scansport Pakboat folding canoe. Their favorite rivers include the Kuujjua, Thomsen, Nahanni, Coppermine, Horton, Kazan, Natla/Keele, Mountain, Thelon, and DePas/George.

- **Frequent flier points:** We use airline frequent flier points to defray the cost of flying to the Canadian Arctic. For 25,000 points each, we have flown from Boston to Inuvik, NWT, and back. In 1999 we flew from Boston to Inuvik—then canoed the Bell/Porcupine/Yukon Rivers—then flew from Anchorage, Alaska, to Boston for 25,000 points each. Our only cost was $180 for excess baggage.

  We have found it best to join the Canadian Airlines and Air Canada frequent flier programs and fly their partner airlines, such as United or American Airlines, to gain points. We earn extra points by using our Diners Club and American Express credit cards.

- **Roof rack for your canoe:** As backpackers-turned-canoeists we use pack frames with a built-in shelf to carry our bags of food and gear on portages. We use duffel bags lined with two heavy-duty plastic bags for carrying food. These bags weigh between sixty and seventy pounds when full.

  When paddling, we attach the pack frames on top of our spray cover with bungee cords. On top of the frames we carry our lunch, fishing gear, map, throw bag, and so on. For laundry days we string bungees between the pack shelves and hang our clothing out to dry. On several occasions we have placed moose or caribou antlers or muskox skulls that we have found on top. On tundra rivers we keep a plastic bag on top to store wood that we collect during the day for our evening cooking fire.

- **Barging canoes:** We save charter floatplane dollars by shipping our canoe around the Northwest Territories/Nunavut by barge. It is very inexpensive if you make arrangements a year or two in advance.[2] For example: When we did the Kuujjua River in 1998, we shipped our canoe from Inuvik to Cambridge Bay by barge the year before. We ended our trip at Holman just in time to meet the barge—which, fortunately for us, was a month late. This allowed us to ship our canoe back to Inuvik immediately rather than waiting for next year's barge.

- **Folding canoes:** Another option is to buy a folding canoe and bring it with you as excess baggage on the airplane. We have a 17-foot Scansport Pakboat that we have used on two of our last three expeditions with great success.

SHARON CHATTERTON

Sharon Chatterton came to wilderness cabin life and canoe guiding in her late thirties. Twelve years later she writes and lectures, teaches college classes, paddles the mountain lakes, walks the boreal trails, and is gloriously free to follow her wilderness dreams. She and Dick Person are life partners. Together they share a self-sufficient lifestyle and a remote cabin in the Yukon Territories of Canada.

- **Carry and comfort kit:** A fitted thwart bag provides fast access to bug dope, sunblock, binoculars, silk scarf, and wind shirt. It can hold a compass and extra

matches. Mine carries notebook and novel, glasses, hand cream and hairbrush, and a washcloth to dry hands and splashed equipment or to give me wake-up. The bag is my survival-gear "pick-up-and-carry" and comfort kit. Attach it to your belt and it carries basic survival gear for short hikes.

- **Lapboard or backboard:** A portable flat surface is a boon on a trip. A 10-inch by 12-inch piece of ³/₈-inch-thick, unfinished marine plywood makes a lightweight lapboard for eating, reading, writing notes, sorting picky repair bits, laying out small specimens, and cutting food. Clip your map to it or slide it against a rigged rod to buffer the hook against damage. Heated to smoking against the fire, it's first-rate ecstasy under a cold bottom or lap. Adjust your own back support angle when it's propped against a tree as a chair. Imagine it hot on a sore back. We never go without a lapboard apiece.

- **Guide to health and good eating:** Carry a medicinal and edible plant guide. Learn to steep tea, boil up a decoction, and apply a plant topically. Learn a painkiller, an antibiotic, an anti-itch, a wound closure, and an insect repellent. Examples: Conifer sap makes fair tea, a great wound closure, and an antibiotic. Mild Labrador tea calms you and your stomach.

- **Allow the wilderness to teach your children:** Children don't need modern games or toys on a canoe trip: The wilderness will educate and entertain. It helps if youngsters have a map; compass and binoculars; film canisters and sandwich bags for collecting things; a magnesium fire stick and matches; stout cord and sharp saw; and sturdy knife to cut cord, make bows, and whittle cups and what-nots. Go as silent adviser more than parent. The bush will teach everything else, if you let it.

LAURIE GULLION

Laurie Gullion is a certified American Canoe Association instructor, wilderness guide, and popular author. She has paddled thousands of miles in Alaska, Canada, Norway, and Finland. Her complete biography is in chapter 5. Laurie's decision to abort a canoe trip on the flooded Coppermine River commands deep respect and a hard look in the mirror.

[2]Check out the NTCL (Northern Transportation Company Ltd.) Web site in appendix B for sailing schedules and pricing.

■ **Hard decision:** Three feet of water covering the shoreline bushes raised some concern when our group of experienced American canoeists, ranging from forty-five to seventy-seven years old, landed on Point Lake, at the headwaters of the Coppermine River. We had twenty-eight days to canoe the Coppermine River to the Arctic Ocean, and nearly two weeks to reach the first technical rapids. We figured (hoped) the water level would drop significantly by then.

On the twelfth day of our trip, we encountered the first rapids that demanded serious scouting. We watched the waves dancing in riverside bushes and flowing so high into the spruces that they prevented us from fully scouting the crux corners and drops.

The Coppermine is considered a high-volume river, and as we would learn later in Yellowknife, the western Arctic was experiencing its highest water levels in eighteen years. A cold and demanding river under the best conditions, it was now at its worst, with water flowing well above the banks and into the trees. Any swims would be long and dangerous, given the height of standing waves and limited shoreline access for towing people and boats to shore.

The river did not look safe at all and we began to wonder if we should continue on. Before inching our way down the rapid's top section, we discussed our options—including the possibility of returning to the upper lakes where we knew floatplanes could land. Ahead of us the Coppermine flowed through steep-sided canyons and valleys, and we questioned whether a floatplane could land on the river in an emergency. If we went on, we would be committing ourselves to a 250-mile-long swollen river with an unknown number of rapids and portages.

After some discussion we decided to descend through the next few rapids to get a better sense of the river, knowing that we could still return upstream to the lakes if necessary. As we discovered later that day, our well-supplied group did not portage quickly, and we faced the possibility that some of the longer portages downriver might put us way behind schedule. Additionally, our group was already dealing with fatigue and a troubling injury to a group member that could affect performance in rapids as well as safety on portages. However, other issues complicated our decision whether to continue on, and a fascinating and painful experience in leadership and followership dynamics emerged.

First, there was disagreement about the actual level of danger. Second, the two oldest members of our team had envisioned this trip as possibly their last independent adventure before they might need to rely upon the support of outfitters. The younger members of our crew knew that it would be emotionally devastating to their older friends if we failed to reach the Arctic Ocean as planned. But the high, cold water suggested that we should not go on. Our decision to turn back—fraught with tension and tears—was not an easy one.

Later reports from the Coppermine revealed that cold, rainy weather did shadow those groups that descended during July, including a Swedish team of six that lost one boat, nearly lost a second one, and straggled into Kugluktuk out of food. As one of two people in quasi leadership roles who advocated that we turn back, I feel relieved about the rightness of the decision for safety's sake.

I had had to change three of seven previous Arctic trips when bad weather or low water forced us to abandon our goals. The Coppermine was my fourth northern experience that proves that nature—what I call the Demon—runs the show. But I cannot ignore how a decision to turn back can so deeply impact others whose goals and perceptions are different than mine.

■ **Maps:** I dislike map cases because they can crack in cold and destroy expensive maps. Instead, I laminate my topographic maps after folding them in half and trimming off the excess paper edges. First I mark them (with Sharpie pens) with helpful information. I highlight rapids, falls, and contour lines crossing the river, and put red distance dots every 3 miles along my route so that I can quickly count up mileage. I paste any necessary scale, ruler, and legend information onto the map section, where it won't obscure my route. I take the indelible pens along on my trip to add information (wildlife sightings, weather, wind, and so on). After the trip I have a colorful record that corresponds to my journal.

■ **Women's hygiene:** Privately, women often ask about how to handle tampons in the backcountry. I drop used herbal tea bags in my collection baggie for short-term deodorizing and burn tampons as soon as possible over an extremely hot trash fire (necessary for complete burning). If a lack of dead and downed wood prevents trash burning for a while, then I definitely store this bag in a bearproof container even if I'm not in bear country. Even small mammals like to play kickball with these items and will chew through packs and tent walls to do so.

HAP WILSON: MAPS

Canoeist and author Hap Wilson is one of North America's most proactive wilderness advocates. His guidebooks are prized for their accuracy, intimate detail, and artistry. Indeed, wilderness route finding would be far easier if government maps were as detailed and accurate as the ones in Hap's books. Read Hap's full biography and "favorite canoe" in chapter 5, and his touching story "Land Where the Spirit Lives" in chapter 19. You'll find more good map ideas in these articles by Hap Wilson, which appeared in the July 1995 issue of Canoe and Kayak *magazine: "Mapping Canada's Wild Rivers" and "History of Mapping in Canada."*

Bad maps can cause big problems on a dangerous wilderness river! Indeed, tragic deaths have been attributed, at least in part, to closely following a map that was out of date or just plain wrong.

Canadian topo maps were initially conceived for political reasons—to designate ownership—and later for military use, resource extraction, and development purposes. They were never intended for recreational travel. They still aren't! Much of the available published material and canoe route brochures distributed by provincial governments—even for established parks and heritage rivers—are inaccurate and out of date.

Before you head out, scrutinize any resource material, especially government maps and surveys. Check out reputable trip reports and guidebooks. Do the location of rapids, portages, and other obstacles match those on your map?[3] Most important, learn how to read, interpret, and *appreciate* topographic maps for what they provide—and what they don't!

MICHAEL PEAKE

Michael Peake is one of Canada's best-known explorers. His biography is in chapter 5.

Do your homework. We used to joke that 90 percent of a trip's work was in the planning. And the other 90 percent was actually doing it! The point remains—plan your trips well. Research the historical aspects of the route—even if it's not in the Arctic. Make sure you have your equipment both on paper *and* in the packs.

KAY HENRY

Really, is there anyone who hasn't heard of Kay Henry and Mad River Canoes? Kay and her former husband Jim founded Mad River Canoe Company in 1971, with a bold new idea: Produce a line of affordable high-performance canoes that look as good as they paddle. The company started with just three boats (the Malecite was the first); they now have twenty-five! Mad River has won several national industry awards for construction excellence.

Kay is a very competent and enthusiastic paddler. A former canoe racer, Kay and her partner were the first Americans to win the grueling five-day, 350-mile Arctic Canoe Race in Finland as well as several U.S. National Whitewater Open Canoe titles. Kay has canoed dozens of tough rivers in northern Canada and tries to manage at least one wilderness river trip each year. She also skis, hikes, and enjoys other outdoor activities near her Waitsfield, Vermont, home.

- Never feel squeamish about scouting a rapid in the wilderness. It's a long way home if you lose a boat or gear.
- When wilderness paddling with children, I always take a large bag of unshelled peanuts. Besides being a healthy snack, it takes time and concentration to shell the nuts, so the snack lasts a long time and can occupy youngsters during those more difficult moments.

FRED GASKIN: THE OCEAN IS NO PLACE FOR A CANOE!

Every canoeing season I do battle with canoeists who think it's safe to canoe on James and Hudson Bays. After all, scores of canoeists (including me) have paddled Arctic tidewa-

---

[3]The serious map error shown on figure 2-6 in chapter 2 illustrates the point. Mantiou Falls on the Fond du Lac River is misplaced by nearly ¼ mile! Fond Du Lac River trip guides—written by paddlers who have canoed the river—have it right.

ter without incident. The rationale for doing so is that canoeing the Bay to your take-out point is invigorating and a whole lot cheaper than chartering a powerboat or floatplane. The fact is that canoeing on James and Hudson Bay is extremely dangerous. If you want chilling accounts of those who didn't make it, contact the Canadian Mounted Police in Churchill or Moosonee. They are the ones who will call your loved ones if you don't arrive alive!

Fred Gaskin has had as much experience canoeing Arctic rivers as anyone. He loves a fair challenge but he won't take chances with his life. I suggest that you take his good advice seriously! See his canoe testimonial in chapter 5.

It is very dangerous to canoe on Arctic tidewater. You're far safer to charter a floatplane or powerboat. An example is the Harricanaw River in Quebec, which empties into James Bay. It's a two-day paddle from the mouth of the Harricanaw to Moosonee—that is, if you survive the experience!

I've done two trips on the Harricanaw River. On the first trip we paddled the bay and nearly had a deadly accident. At one point we were 2 miles from shore in very shallow water when a squall came up—we were belted by huge waves and three giant waterspouts all at once! Fortunately, the water was only knee-deep so we got out of the canoes, knelt low, and desperately hung on to the gunnels waiting (hopefully) for the storm to pass. We were very lucky to have survived.

James Bay, and parts of Hudson Bay, are very shallow, so you can't paddle close to shore. You're in big trouble if you're ½ mile out and a storm blows up!

Experience is a wonderful teacher. The second time we canoed the Harricanaw we arranged a floatplane pickup from the mouth of the river back to our base. No more Arctic tidewater for us. In the future we will always charter a plane, if available, and carry a radio phone to confirm our location and time of pickup.

BOB O'HARA

See Bob O'Hara's complete biography in chapter 5. In 1971 I attended one of his multiscreen slide presentations and became hooked on Arctic rivers. I have learned many things from Bob over the years, and I am pleased to share with you twenty-five of his coolest ideas.

1. Lining ropes should be shorter than 50 feet. Longer ropes are hard to handle.

2. Bring one or two 100-foot-long ropes for special situations.

3. When I stop for the day along a tundra river, I don't unpack my canoe. Instead I pull it up on shore and leave the packs—and splash cover—on the boat. I remove essential items (and packs) as they are needed. This saves wear and tear on the packs and my body—and the extra weight (in the canoe) keeps the canoe from being blown across the tundra by high winds.[4]

4. Don't bring an expensive canoe to the Arctic unless you are willing to spend a fortune to fly or barge it out. Good used canoes or inexpensive new ones can be left with the Natives and replaced for less than the cost of freighting them home.[5]

5. High-topped rubber boots are essential for canoeing tundra rivers.

6. Blackflies will not bite you if you are in a tent. Instead they will climb up the walls to the top in an effort to find a way out.

7. Small items can fall out of pants pockets or break from rough handling. I carry important items in the zippered front pocket of my anorak.

8. Compared to the total cost of a trip, film is cheap. Take lots of it and use an ASA of 400 or better.

9. Your pictures should tell the complete story of your adventure—crew, equipment, camp, cooking, eating, fishing, wildlife, flowers, departures, and arrivals. Get some close-ups of everyone in your crew.

10. A foot-operated bilge pump works better than a bailer—and you can keep paddling while you pump!

11. Crew dynamics are often overlooked in the planning stages and may cause difficulties later. Make sure everyone has time on task and time off. Be clear in your duty assignments. Share the load equally.

12. Drink more water than you think you need.

13. Bring thirty-pound-test line for that special fish.

14. Bring spare parts for your stove.

15. Always carry a tarp for wind and rain.

---

[4] I heartily recommend this practice!

[5] There are customs regulations (and duties) that govern the sale of U.S.-bought canoes to Canadian citizens. Canadian customs officials can provide details.

16. Bright colors are important on the tundra—you want to be seen by aircraft.

17. Keep your wallet in your day pack, and your day pack strapped to the boat when you're canoeing.

18. Keep prescription medications in a waterproof container, and carry an extra supply in another canoe.

19. A good windbreaker is one of your most important garments.

20. Clothes are the best bug dope you can buy.

21. Mark your maps daily. Indicate where you camped and what you did.

22. Take soup spoons and insulated mugs.

23. Bring a backrest of some sort.

24. Permafrost is cold: Use a full-length sleeping pad.

25. Just for fun, bring a kite.

DICK PERSON: ON SURVIVING A WILDERNESS EMERGENCY

Fed up with civilization, Dick Person emigrated to Canada in 1969. He lives largely as a hunter-gatherer and earns a modest income by lecturing and teaching workshops on all phases of life in the outdoors. Dick and his partner, Sharon Chatterton, share a log cabin on the shore of Teslin Lake in the Yukon. You may contact him for presentations by snail mail or e-mail (appendix B). Naturally, he has no phone. A more complete biography is in chapter 5.

You have survived the capsize, but you are alone and your canoe has disappeared downriver. Your wet clothes and the lowering sun suggest you'd better act fast before hypothermia sets in.

The kind of clothes you are wearing (they better be *wool!*), and what you have on your body, along with your state of mind and survival skills may determine whether you live or die.

A situation like this generally brings a level of shock and confusion, so you must fight the urge to panic. Calm assessment of your immediate needs will lead to an effective course of action.

You should have these items in your pocket or attached to a lanyard on your belt: strike-anywhere wooden matches in a waterproof case; a sharp belt knife (I prefer the Grohmann 1); a Swiss Army Knife or multitool; and 25 feet of nylon parachute cord.

Most whitewater PFDs have pockets where you can store small items. My Lotus vest has a removable minipack on back that holds a fair amount of stuff. I keep these items inside the pocket: spare matches, a butane lighter, a Silva Guide model compass, a small container that has 30 to 50 feet of different-weight monofilament nylon fishing line, BB lead shot weights, two small spoon-type lures, two Colorado spinners, various-sized hooks, red fluorescent yarn, and plastic fish eggs. I always have a whistle handy.

I pack emergency food in the form of dried fruits, nuts like almonds or Brazils, and homemade granola. No candy bars—their high-sucrose sugar gives a flash of energy that provokes a quick insulin rush and a depressed energy state.

You can go crazy or die if you allow insects to have their way. I pack bug dope and the Original Bug Shirt, which is made in Canada. Seal the Bug Shirt and draw your arms inside and all skin will be protected while you sleep.

Water purification tablets are essential in some areas and should be included in your kit. A stainless-steel cup serves as cup, cooking pot, and water purifier. If you keep calm and have the skills to use the tools you have along, you'll survive till help arrives.

GEORGE DROUGHT: THE TUNDRA TUNNEL

George Drought is one of Canada's best known wilderness canoe guides and outdoor photographers.

When bugs and bad weather threaten the day, my crew retreats inside a floorless (safe for cooking) 20-foot by 9-foot by 6-foot-high waterproof nylon tundra tunnel, which my friend Rae Ford and I designed for barren-land canoe travel. The four main poles are from the Eureka Expedition 5 tent. The two vestibule poles are fitted 4 feet apart at one end to form a conical shape (great for storage) that will spill winds of up to about 60 miles per hour. Large snow flaps all around enable the tunnel to be weighted with rocks and securely guyed. There are three large no-see-um-screened windows with internal storm covers on each side, plus two at the front door. The tunnel seats twelve and weighs twenty-eight pounds, pegs, poles, and all. I wouldn't do an Arctic canoe trip without it!

Figure 21-2. George Drought's tundra tunnel.

BOB FISHER

Bob Fisher has over forty years of canoeing, hiking, and skiing experience. Bob and his son Graham—who is a certified ORCA Level III canoe tripping instructor—offer two- to five-day guided canoe adventures for adults and families in the Georgian Bay region of Ontario, Canada.[6]

Figures 21-3 and 21-4 illustrate how to make Bob's kitchen hooks rope and paddle pole pockets. Commercial versions are available from Outdoor Solutions in Toronto, Ontario (appendix B).

- **Kitchen hooks rope:** Here's a slick way to hang kitchen utensils, water bags and stuff sacks on a tree without sawing branches or pounding nails (horrors!). You'll need a yard of light rope, four or more closed 1¼-inch S-hooks, and a metal or nylon ring.

  Close one end of each S-hook and thread the closed ends on the rope. Tie the ring to one end of the cord and tie a large knot in the other end of the cord. The knot should be small enough to pass through the ring but large enough to retain the S-hooks.

  Run the rope around the tree and pass the knotted end of the cord through the ring. Sung the cord and secure it with a quick-release knot. Now hang your stuff on the hooks.

Figure 21-3. Kitchen hooks rope.

- **Paddle pole pockets:** Paddles (straight- or bent-shafts) can be used in place of poles to rig a rain tarp if you have pole pockets. We make them from Cordura nylon, sized to fit blades up to 8 inches wide. Nylon straps with buckles secure the paddle blades; Velcro tapes hold the shafts. The paired pockets are adjustable for length—the maximum pole length with 58-inch paddles is around 8 feet. Tip: Protect the part of the paddle that touches the ground (grip) with an old sock or glove, or sew up a sock from Cordura or canvas.

ANNIE AGGENS

Annie's biography is in chapter 5.

Never take the map at face value. I've seen Class V rapids that were simply marked as "moving water," and I've paddled ripples that were marked as long sets of big rapids. Maps are

---

[6] You may contact the Fishers by phone at (416) 487–2950 or by e-mail at upthebay@sympatico.ca.

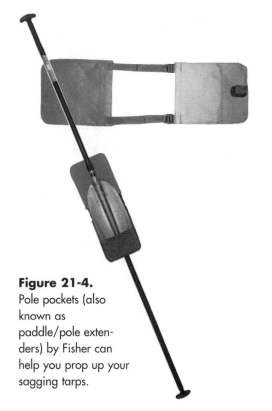

Figure 21-4.
Pole pockets (also known as paddle/pole extenders) by Fisher can help you prop up your sagging tarps.

just one of many tools: The others are listening (you won't be able to hear rapids very well in a following wind), scouting, and taking corners cautiously.

There are big differences between maps that were made during low-water years and those that were made in high-water years. It's great if you can get samples of each and compare them. Low-water maps may clearly show islands that vanish mysteriously when the water is high. And low-water rapids may wash out with increased flow—or they may be formidable to canoe. It's important to know that water levels often change when you change watersheds. Once I paddled a stretch that was 3 feet below normal; then I did a watershed crossing of 25 miles and encountered water that was 3 feet higher!

VERLEN KRUGER:
THE EXTENDED EXPEDITION

Verlen Kruger has canoed more miles than anyone on the planet. He and Steve Landick are the only canoeists who have ever paddled up through the Grand Canyon! A more detailed biography is in chapter 5.

It takes more than skill and strength to prepare for an expedition. *Good judgment* is your best assurance for a successful trip. Do your homework thoroughly—both mentally and physically. Begin with small trips close to home, then branch out to bigger ones. Climb to the top of the ladder one step at a time. Remember that no two trips, even on the same river, are the same experience. Here are some tips that will help you prepare for your big dream:

- Join an active canoe club. You'll meet other paddlers and share ideas.

- Subscribe to canoe magazines. Articles will keep you abreast of what's happening in the canoeing world.

- Read all the good books about canoeing that you can find. I feel this one's the best.

- Spend a year in the marathon racing circuit. This will increase your paddling efficiency, break mental barriers, and help you get into shape.

One of the most stressful things you'll have to face on an extended journey is friction with your partner. Traveling by solo canoe lightens the mental load, as you can each break off for a while and go your own pace. Still, there are many decisions that must be jointly made, such as when to start and stop, where to camp, and so on.

Steve Landick and I adopted the Captain for the Day system. On odd days Steve was the captain; on even days I was captain. This allowed each of us to exercise our best judgment and to feel involved. This simple plan eliminated many arguments.

BUCK TILTON:
MEDICAL TIPS

Buck Tilton has an M.S. degree and a WEMT certification. He is the cofounder of the Wilderness Medicine Institute, now officially the Wilderness Medicine Institute of NOLS (National Outdoor Leadership School). Buck has authored more than 750 magazine articles and twenty-two books. I especially recommend his classic work, Medicine for the Backcountry *(appendix B). Buck is a special friend, and one who always makes me smile. These tips are a small sample of what you'll find in his exhaustive articles and books.*

- Remove a bee stinger as soon as possible. You can scrape it out with a stiff object like your fingernail or blunt knife edge, or you can grab it with your finger and jerk it out. Tests have proven that both ways are equally safe and effective.

- Lips can't tan! They burn easier than true skin, not only because they lack melanin, but also because they dry out from sun and wind and get licked a lot, and moisture increases the chance of burning. The more lips burn, the faster they age and wrinkle, and the more at risk you become for lip cancer. Paddlers should always use a protective sunscreen on their lips!

- Serious cases of bacterial infection have developed in wounds washed in freshwater lakes. Better to clean all wounds with water you're sure is safe to drink. If possible, boil the water or use a purifier.

- Salt tablets are a gastric irritant not recommended for human consumption. A pinch of salt to a liter of water seems to help prevent and treat heat problems—a pinch being too little to taste.

- Toss an average paddler into ice water and he or she will survive for approximately an hour and a half before hypothermia causes death. But rapid cooling of the muscles from an icy dunking will predispose you to a quick drowning—that's why you should always wear your PFD when canoeing frigid water.

- After a near-drowning, resuscitated victims often develop serious complications, usually due to the absorption through their lungs of nasty things that were in the water. All resuscitated victims should be evacuated to a medical facility as soon as possible.

- Take your drinking water from the middle of a still lake, not from a moving current. Currents stir up bacteria and protozoans that may cause disease. Better yet, filter (use a purifier) or boil your drinking water.

GARY AND JOANIE MCGUFFIN

Gary and Joanie McGuffin are among the premier adventure-paddlers/writer-photographers of all time. It would take several pages to describe all their accomplishments. Indeed, only Verlen Kruger can boast more miles paddled. Joanie and Gary are sincere (and internationally respected) environmentalists. You'll find their complete biography in chapter 5.

- **Help save a river:** Write a letter in support of preserving a wilderness area or wild river. Don't let a lack of information and facts about the issues discourage you. Speak from the heart as a paddler. You represent the huge and growing paddle-sports industry with considerable economic clout.

  Suppose you've just returned from a wilderness canoe trip. There was a stretch of river where an obnoxious ATV trail ran along the riverbank. At one campsite the latrine had been dug within several feet of the river and the take-out was strewn with garbage. Describe your feelings. Tell where you come from and the impact your visit had on the local economy (canoe rental, one hotel night, two restaurant meals, purchase of groceries for trip, and so on). Request a reply as to how this situation will be remedied. Don't be discouraged by the first government red-tape answer. Just return the reply letter and your original correspondence and keep asking how and when the problems will be fixed.

- **Compatibility and goals:** If you are planning a long journey with friends, be sure that everyone knows— and is comfortable with—one another's goals. Structure your trip around the skill levels and objectives (hiking, photography, fishing, white-water thrills) of your crew.

- **Choose rugged gear you can fix with simple tools:** Being lovers of long-distance wilderness travel, we know that strong, durable, well-constructed gear and the ability to repair and improvise makes for a safer, more enjoyable, smoother-running journey. Do not compromise strength for light weight, or for the sake of acquiring a bargain.

CHAPTER 22
A PLEA FOR CONSCIENCE

Every river has places that are special. These may be awesome mist-filled chasms, musty beaver ponds, high lake-locked bluffs, or just your own perception of something very ordinary. What and where these places are is not important. That they exist in your own mind is what counts.

When you find your special place, you'll know. Then the weeks of planning, the exhausting drive up, the blackflies of the day before will all be eclipsed by the beauty of what you see. And even if you're not a reverent person, you may find yourself softly whispering, "Thanks, God, for letting me be here."

The magic of your special place is everywhere—in the lush green of the forest, the champagne-clear sparkle of the water, the crisp persistent breeze. You experience deep satisfaction—privilege—in being here alone, if perhaps only for a few fleeting moments.

Your eyes casually wander to a small open area and the charred remains of a fire. You know others have camped here before. But no matter. Does the revelation make this place any less beautiful for you than them?

Then you see it, the thoughtless refuse of voyageurs who preceded you—rusty cans, a broken whiskey bottle, lengths of parachute cord, scraps of paper, the rotting viscera of fish. Suddenly this place is no longer special. It is an abomination, a trash heap, an insult to man and God. You stare in disbelief at the mess scattered about and feel a deep gnawing pain growing upward from the pit of your stomach. The pain surfaces as rage, and you swear loudly, determinedly, again and again!

What kind of people have done this? you ask. Surely they must be big-city. Hardly! Slobs come from all walks of life, from cities large and small, from suburbs, from exclusive country homes, and from the depths of the wilderness itself. Regardless of background, they share a common attribute—ignorance of the simplest ecological relationships; their lack

of knowledge about the fragility of the land, its water, fish, and wildlife is absolute. Most are amiable people with warm hearts and a good sense of humor. Their failing is that they've never been taught the *proper way* to do things outdoors.

That, friends, is our job!

Many years ago I sat on an island campsite along the Minnesota-Ontario border and watched with growing anger a man on a nearby peninsula scrape and wash his dishes in the lake. His actions created a small but determined raft of suds that a gentle breeze pushed my way. The longer I watched, the madder I got. I was about ready to jump into my Sawyer Cruiser, paddle in hand, both barrels blazing, cuss words flying, when I remembered the old cliché, "You can catch more bears with honey than guns." So I calmed down, forced a smile, and in a stately fashion canoed to the peninsula.

When the man saw me he waved, smiled, and mumbled something about coffee. Then he stepped candidly into the water and helped me disembark from my canoe. "Don't wanna scratch that pretty blue boat," he said cheerfully.

My hostility melted to confusion. This was a really nice guy!

For an hour I shared the man's fire and hospitality. I told him tactfully how organic wastes increased bacterial levels in the water; why soaps—biodegradable or not—kill essential microorganisms; how improperly disposed-of feces leach into the water and pollute it; how fires can creep hundreds of yards underground and spring to life when conditions are favorable; how it may take dozens of years to replace a tiny patch of lichens which a thoughtless camper picked because "they looked pretty"; that forest service and park personnel have neither the time nor budget to pick up the garbage of campers.

We had quite a talk, he and I.

The man freely admitted his ignorance of ecological relationships. "I'm willing to learn," he said honestly. "But

Figure 23-1.

where do you learn this stuff? Why didn't the forest service or my outfitter tell me these things?"

"Yes," I agreed. "Why didn't they!"

Over the years I've run into scores of polluters, many of whom, like the man I met along the border, were unaware of the impact of their actions. I've cussed out a few to their faces, reported some to authorities, and once even pretended I was a conservation officer and threatened to write a citation. But mostly I've used the "honey rather than guns" approach.

You'd think that overcrowding of canoe routes, and the accompanying scars it leaves upon the land, would be limited to local streams and popular places like the BWCA, Quetico, and Allagash. Not so. Virtually all the great northern rivers—from Ontario to the Northwest Territories—are now paddled regularly . . . and trashed regularly by canoeists who should know better.

The day may come when all who use the backcountry will have to be licensed and show competency in ethical land- and water-use practices. I view that day with mixed emotions. On the one hand, I yearn to be free to enjoy my wilderness pursuits unencumbered by bureaucratic regulations designed to protect the environment.

But I am weary of being my brother's keeper. So I plead for conscience and an army of knowledgeable outdoorspeople who care about the future of our wild places. The answer lies in education—by schools, government, commercial outfitters, guides, youth camps . . . you—not in the impersonality of blind regulations.

There are still hundreds of free-flowing unspoiled rivers in North America that have not yet felt the darkening influence of humans. Whether these rivers will continue to exist in their unpolluted form in the next century depends on all of us—our attitudes, our beliefs, our willingness to get involved. Fortunately, we are born of a well-educated, concerned generation—one committed to chartering a new course toward environmental responsibility and action.

APPENDIX A
A REVIEW OF CANOE STROKES

These are the basic strokes. Space precludes the inclusion of all the variations and sophisticated maneuvers. For a complete course on white-water paddling, see the paddling books listed in appendix B.

KEY TO PADDLE DIAGRAMS

Back side of paddle blade

Normal power face of paddle

TANDEM STROKES

FORWARD STROKE (BACK STROKE)

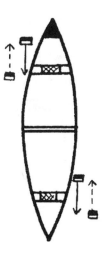

Paddle is brought straight back *parallel* to keel line. Paddle should not be carried beyond your hip.

Useful turning strokes for flat water. Not enough power for white water.

(A) Reverse Sweep
(B) Forward Sweep

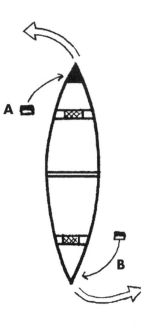

DRAW

Your most powerful turning stroke. Paddle is submerged and pulled rapidly toward the canoe. Use an aerial recovery.

CROSS-DRAW

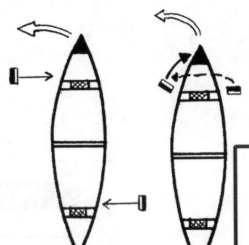

Use in *bow* only. Very powerful stroke for turning canoe away from bow person's paddling side. An excellent stroke for use in shallow water.

J-STROKE

Essential stroke in stern of canoe. Keeps Canoe tracking straight. A reverse form of this (the *reverse J*) is used by the bow paddler to keep straight course when back-paddling.

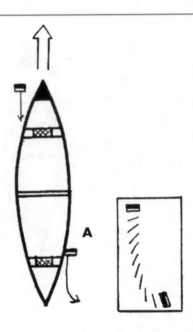

A

DIAGONAL DRAW

By varying the angle of the draw from the perpendicular, a variety of moves is possible.

Note: Paired diagonal draws on the same side would unbalance and possibly upset the canoe. Except when paddling in a crosswind, it's never a good idea to paddle on the same side as your partner.

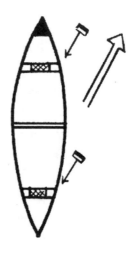

SCULL

Useful in bow, stern, or center of solo canoe. Turns canoe in direction of scull. Excellent shallow-water stroke with good bracing action in white water. Maintain same power face throughout scull. A *reverse scull* can be performed by using opposite power face.

Paddle remains in water throughout stroke.

BOW PRY

Paddle is pried forcefully around bilge and over gunnel. Greatest power—and least control—results when both hands are above the gunnel. This stroke has a stabilizing effect in heavy water, but the paddle can catch on rocks and upset the canoe in shallows.

In shallows the preferred bow stroke for turning offside is the cross-draw. Use an *underwater* recovery for the pry; an *aerial* recovery for the draw and cross-draw.

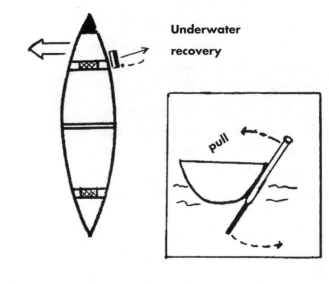

Underwater recovery

pull

STERN PRY

A powerful stroke for turning to the off-side. Paddle is pried smartly over gunnel and underwater recovery is used. Unlike the bow pry, the paddle is angled to the waterline as indicated.

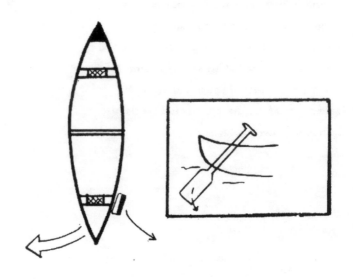

LOW BRACE

Used in both bow and stern to stabilize (brace) canoe and keep it from capsizing in heavy water. Flat of blade is nearly parallel to the water. Stroke requires powerful downward thrust.

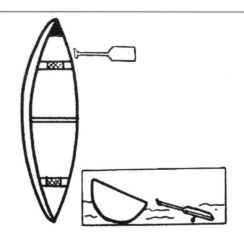

HIGH BRACE

A combination brace and draw. Paddle is held stationary, its face against current or at a strong climbing angle to it. The success of this stroke depends on speed (either paddling or current) and a strong lean. Useful for making eddy turns and as pure bracing stroke when paddling solo.

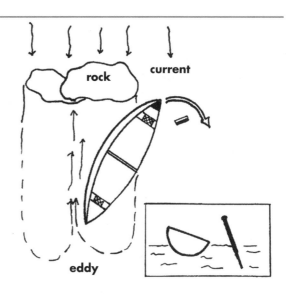

HUT STROKE (not shown)

Instead of using the conventional J-stroke to maintain a straight course, just switch paddle sides on cue. The hut is used by every serious canoe racer in North America. It is the fastest way to move a canoe, and just what you need for trucking into the waves of a wind-tossed lake. Switching cadence is generally six to eight strokes per side. A bent-shaft paddle of 52 to 55 inches is the preferred hardware.

SOLO STROKES

All the typical tandem strokes above may be used with varying successes in the solo canoe as long as you realize that:

- The net movement of the boat is in true line with the direction of the stroke, since the paddler is located at the enter of the craft.
- Many strokes, such as the cross-draw, bow draw, and sweeps (and of course, braces), require a strong lean for good effect. For example, it's very difficult to turn a fine-lined straight-keeled solo canoe without leaning it considerably and using the rocker in the sidewall. Some small solo canoes will lift their stems clean out of the water and pivot sharply when laid down in this fashion.

The accomplished solo canoeist blends a variety of hard-to-define (and diagram) strokes and techniques into a free-flowing show of grace and beauty. Paddling on open solo canoe in traditional fashion is an art form—one that requires years of practice to master.

The modern solo paddler who scorns tradition—and the customary C-stroke—will use a short bent-shaft paddle and take three or four strokes on each side of the canoe. This switching procedure (called the Minnesota switch or hut stroke) is remarkably efficient in keeping the canoe on a straight course. Through ugly to watch, it is the only practical way to paddle alone for long distances, especially upwind.

The *complete* canoeist should know and appreciate both methods! *Some* of the paddle strokes unique to the solo canoe are shown below.

BACK STROKE

A powerful stroke for going backward. Often completed with a pry off the gunnel at A.

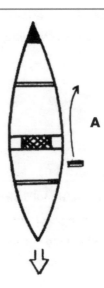

C-STROKE

The soloist J-stroke—used to keep the canoe tracking straight when paddling on one side. The paddle is nearly vertical to the water, the blade brought under the hull. Some paddlers finish the stroke with a pry off the gunnel. The arc described by the paddle is actually less severe than shown.

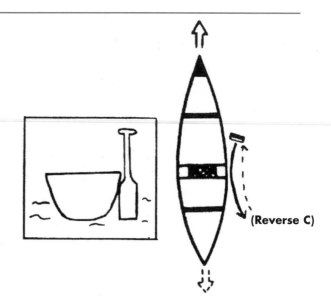

(Reverse C)

ACUTE DRAW (BOW DRAW)

This one takes practice because of the awkward hand position (the wrist of the top hand is turned so the thumb is down). Throw your shoulders into the stroke. This is your most powerful stroke for turning the canoe toward your paddle side.

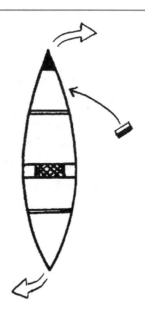

CROSS-DRAW

Identical to the tandem cross-draw. Mentioned here because it is your most powerful stroke for turning to the offside.

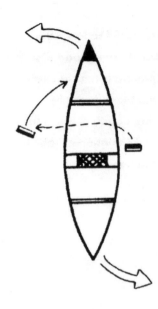

CROSS BACK STROKE

When you need a powerful back stroke and turn at the same time, rotate your shoulders and flip paddle across the canoe as for a cross-draw, only more severely. The canoe may be backed straight by angling the paddle outward at the start of the stroke.

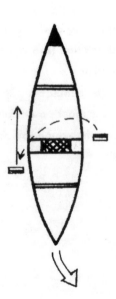

COMPOUND BACK STROKE

This requires twisting your upper body more than 90 degrees at the start of the stroke. The power face of the paddle is reversed partway through the stroke. The procedure is thought by some to be more powerful than the standard back stroke. Some paddlers finish the stroke with a pry off the gunnel at A.

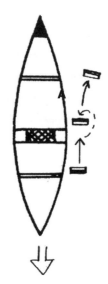

OUTSIDE PIVOT

Part cross-draw, part sweep. Looks impressive but is actually less efficient than two cross-draws, which can be done in about the same time. Useful for picking your way among obstacles in quiet water.

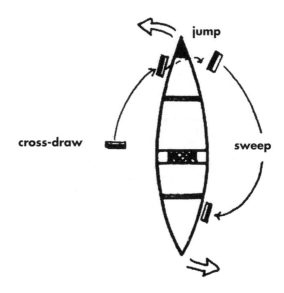

PRY

Useful in heavy water for moving the canoe sideways from your paddle side. Identical to the stern pry except the paddle shaft is more vertical to the water. Power should be applied at or just behind the center of the canoe.

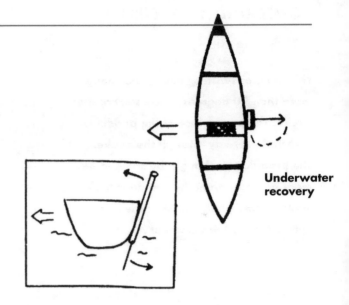

Underwater recovery

INSIDE PIVOT

A combination reverse sweep and bow draw. Used to turn the canoe sharply toward your paddle side. Actually, it's no more effective than two bow draws, which can be done in about the same time. The advantage is that the reverse-sweep component can be blended with a back (low) brace for stability when turning in heavy water.

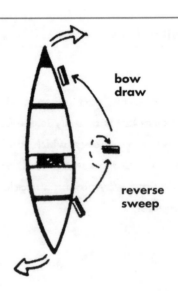

bow draw

reverse sweep

APPENDIX B
ADDRESSES

CANADIAN MAPS, AERIAL PHOTOS, CHARTS, AND TIDE TABLES

Canada Map Office
615 Booth Street
Ottawa, ON K1A 0E9
(800) 465-6277 or (613) 952-7000
www.maps.nrcan.gc.ca
Order indexes to topographic maps (but not maps) from here. The office will provide a list of U.S. and Canadian dealers that sell topographic maps.

Department of Fisheries and Oceans
Hydrographic Chart Distribution Office
1675 Russell Road, P.O. Box 8080
Ottawa, ON K1G 3H6
(613) 998-4931 or (613) 998-1217
www.charts.gc.ca
Free catalog of Canadian marine charts and tide tables. Orders must be placed through a Canadian map dealer.

Federal Maps, Inc.
52 Antares Drive, Unit 1
Nepean, Ottawa, ON K2E 7Z1
(613) 723-6366; fax (613) 723-6995
www.fedmaps.com
Largest regional distributor of Canadian government maps and charts produced by the Canada Map Office, including all available scales of topographic maps, aeronautical charts, and thematic maps. Generally ships within two working days.

Geomatics Canada
(613) 992-8118; fax (613) 947-2410
http://ess.nrcan.gc.ca/geocan/index_e.php
Lists dealers that sell Canadian topographic maps.

Magnetic Declination Calculator—Canada
www.geolab.nrcan.gc.ca/geomag/cgrf_e.shtml
On-line calculator allows you to determine current magnetic declination for anyplace in Canada.

National Air Photo Library
Canada Map Office
615 Booth Street
Ottawa, ON K1A 0E9
(613) 995-4560
www.maps.nrcan.gc.ca
Here's where to get Canadian aerial photos. NAPL prefers that you e-mail your request (specify location coordinates).

World of Maps
1235 Wellington Street
Ottawa, ON K1Y 3A3
(613) 724-6776; fax (613) 724-2776
www.WorldofMaps.com
Mail-order source of all Canadian topo maps, charts, and travel books. Fast, personal service—they go the extra mile.

INUIT LAND ADMINISTRATION OFFICES

Contact these offices if your canoe trip takes you through Inuit-owned land. A Web search by region will reveal weather, community information, and local news.

Baffin Region
(867) 979-5391; fax (867) 979-3238

Kivalliq Region
(867) 645-2810; fax (867) 645-3855

Kitikmeot (Arctic Coast/Cambridge Bay) Region
(867) 982-3310; fax (867) 982-3311
www.polarnet.ca

Labrador Inuit Association
12 Sandbanks Road
Nain, NL A0P 1L0
(709) 922-2941; fax (709) 922-2931
www.nunatsiavut.com

Northwest Territories
Land Administration Office
Box 1500
Yellowknife, NT X1A 2R3
(867) 669-2671; fax (867) 669-2713

Nunavut Land Administration (INAC)
Building 918, Box 100
Iqaluit, NT X0A 0H0
(867) 975-4275; fax (867) 975-4286
www.fishingdestinations.ca/info/nunavutregs.htm
Nunavut fishing information—licenses etc.

TRUCKS, TRAINS, AND BARGES

If you finish your trip at a remote settlement, you may be able to ship your canoes south by truck, train, or barge. Patience is a virtue, however; shipping time may be a matter of weeks or months.

Alaska Railroad
327 West Ship Creek Avenue
Anchorage, AK 99501
(907) 265-2494
www.akrr.com

Northern Transportation Co. Ltd.
42003 MacKenzie Highway
Hay River, NT X0E 0R9
(877) 770-NTCL or (867) 874-5128
Fax (867) 874-5103
www.ntcl.com
Tug and barge service. Services Arviat, Baker Lake, Chesterfield Inlet, and other remote communities.

Via Rail, Canada, Inc.
101-123 Main Street
Winnipeg, MB R3C 2P8
(888) 842-7245
www.viarail.ca
Largest railroad system in Canada. View fares, book tickets (save money by booking in advance).

TRUCKING COMPANIES IN NORTHWEST TERRITORIES THAT WILL CARRY CANOES

Byers Transport
2840 76th Avenue
Edmonton, AB T5J 2J1
(403) 440-1000
www.byerstransport.com

Grimshaw Trucking & Distributing
11510 151st Street
Edmonton, AB T5M 3N6
(403) 452-5820
www.grimshaw-trucking.com

Northwest Transport Ltd.
(800) 661-6992
www.nwtl.com

AMERICAN MAPS, AERIAL PHOTOS, CHARTS, AND TIDE TABLES

Magnetic Declination Calculator—U.S.A.
www.ngdc.noaa.gov/seg/geomag/magfield.shtml
On-line calculator allows you to determine current magnetic declination for anyplace in the U.S.

National Geographic Topo!
National Geographic Maps
P.O. Box 4337
Evergreen, CO 80437-3457
(800) 962-1643
http://maps.nationalgeographic.com/topo
Detailed CD map sets that cover most of the U.S. back roads available for some states; also, portages and campsites for the

Boundary Waters Canoe Area of Minnesota. You choose the map scale, orientation, and coordinate system. Order maps or print your own.

National Oceanic and Atmospheric Administration
NOAA's National Ocean Service
Communications and Education Division
SSMC4, Room 13317
1305 East-West Highway
Silver Spring, MD 20910
(301) 713-3060
www.nos.noaa.gov (for maps and charts)
For charts and tide tables of U.S. coasts, the Great Lakes, sections of major rivers, and contoured fishing maps.

U.S. Geological Survey
Box 25286, Federal Center
Denver, CO 80225
(888) ASK USGS; fax (303) 202-4693
www.usgs.gov or http://earthexplorer.usgs.gov
Your complete source of U.S. topographic maps and aerial photos. Ask for a free index and the UTM (Universal Trans Mercator) Fact Sheet. The USGS accepts checks, money orders, and popular credit cards.

www.mapcard.com
Map Card membership allows you to customize, print, and download unlimited topo maps and aerial photographs on your computer.

www.mytopo.com
Build your own custom topo map or aerial photograph of any area in the U.S. Choose the scale, orientation, and coordinate system. Printed on tough, waterproof paper and shipped direct to you.

MISCELLANEOUS ADDRESSES

Canoe Arctic, Inc.
Alex Hall
P.O. Box 130
Fort Smith, NT X0E 0P0
E-mail: alex@canoearctic.com
Alex Hall operates the oldest canoe guide service in the Northwest Territories. He has paddled more miles in "The Territories" than any man. Alex often canoes more miles during the summer than he drives all year!

Chinook Medical Gear, Inc.
P.O. Box 1736
Edwards, CO 81632
www.chinookmed.com
A complete source of medical equipment for the long trip.

IASCO (Industrial Arts Supply Co.)
5724 West 36th Street
Minneapolis, MN 55416-2594
(888) 919-0899 or (9522) 920-7393
www.iasco-tesco.com
Fiberglass cloth, resin, tools for fiberglassing and more. Giant catalog.

Mike Yee Outfitting
23 Norton Drive
Uxbridge, ON L9P1R4
(905) 649-1999; fax (905) 649-1894
www.mikeyeeoutfitting.com
Everything you need to outfit your new whitewater solo or tandem canoe. Mike Yee is a 17-time Ontario Whitewater Open Boat Slalom Champion and a 14-time winner of the U.S. Open Canoe Nationals. He outfits many of the world's hottest whitewater canoes.

Wild and Woolly
Dick Person
P.O. Box 92
Teslin, YT Y0A 1B0
E-mail: dickperson@hotmail.com
Dick Person, who lives in a log cabin in Teslin, Yukon, lives largely off the land and makes his living by teaching Wilderness Survival-Thrival courses. He also lectures, teaches workshops, and guides canoe trips.

SOURCES OF EQUIPMENT MENTIONED IN THIS BOOK

Activon Products
900 Green Valley Road
Beaver Dam, WI 53916
(800) 841-0410
www.activon.com
Effersan dry chlorine tablets; great for sterilizing camp dishes.

Allegro Medical
1733 East McKellips Road
Suite 110
Tempe, AZ 85281
www.allegromedical.com/n_r_laboratories.html
No-rinse body bath and shampoo.

Aloksak waterproof bags
Watchful Eye Designs, LLC
P.O. Box 980007
Park City, UT 84098
(435) 649-9009; fax (435) 940-0956
www.watchfuleyedesigns.com
These inexpensive bags look and function like ziplock bags
but they're stronger and much more reliable. Used by the
military and adventure-racing teams to protect maps, GPS
units, and satellite phones.

Atwater Carey products
Wisconsin Pharmacal Co.
1 Pharmacal Way
P.O. Box 198
Jackson, WI 53037
(800) 359-1646
www.Pharmacalway.com
Atwater Carey expedition-quality first-aid kits and accessories for extended trips.

Bending Branches
812 Prospect Court
Osceola, WI 54020
(715) 755-3405
www.bendingbranches.com
Fine laminated canoe and kayak paddles. BB pioneered tough
resin tips.

Campmor
P.O. Box 700P
Saddle River, NJ 07458-0700
(800) CAMPMOR
www.campmor.com
Hundreds of camping items, plus personal-size bug nets.

Cascade Designs, Inc.
4000 First Avenue South
Seattle, WA 98134

(206) 505-9500; fax (206) 682-4184
www.cascadedesigns.com
Waterproof bags and packs. Makers of the Therm-a-Rest
sleeping pad.

Cell-Safe
23 Newbury Neck Road
Newbury, MA 01951
(978) 948-6670
www.cellsafe.com
Lightweight, crushproof, waterproof protection for your GPS
and cell phone.

Chicagoland Canoe Base
4019 Narragansett
Chicago, IL 60634
(773) 777-1489
www.chicagolandcanoebase.com
One of the most interesting canoe shops in the world. It's
here where canoeing guru Ralph Freese hand-builds the huge
Voyageur canoes. Lots of different solo canoes plus the most
complete canoeing library in the world.

Chosen Valley Canoe Accessories
P.O. Box 474
Chatfield, MN 55923
(507) 867-3961
www.gear4portaging.com
Source of the slick removable pot handles I inspired.

Chota Outdoor Gear
P.O. Box 31137
Knoxville, TN 37930
(423) 690-1814; fax (423) 690-5605
www.chotaoutdoorgear.com
Awesome neoprene boots, portage shoes, and gloves designed
especially for canoeists and kayakers.

CLG Enterprises/Superior Packs
3838 Dight Avenue South
Minneapolis, MN 55406
(800) 328-5215
www.superiorpacks.com
Superior tripping packs and rodeo accessories. Also manufactures Grade VI gear and the insulated pot cozies I designed
(see chapter 11).

Cooke Custom Sewing
Dan Cooke
7290 Stagecoach Trail
Lino Lakes, MN 55014-1988
(651) 784-8777; fax (651) 784-4158
www.cookecustomsewing.com
Cooke manufactures some of the best packs, tarps, canoe covers, seat pads, map cases, and paddling accessories around. I'm proud to say I've had a hand in some of the designs. Cooke gear emphasizes practicality, utility, and killer strength for the long haul.

Counter Assault
120 Industrial Court
Kalispell, MT 59901
(800) 695-3394
www.counterassault.com
Source of Counter Assault bear repellent (pepper spray).

Duluth Pack
365 Canal Park Drive
Duluth, MN 55802
(800) 777-4439
www.duluthpack.com
Duluth Pack has so many wonderful things, you'll just have to get a catalog. Source of Ullfrotté long underwear, Grohmann knives, and Gränsfors Bruks axes.

Empire Canvas Works
P.O. Box 17
Solon Springs, WI 54873
(715) 378-4216
www.empirecanvasworks.com
Serious gear for serious outdoorspeople—modern canvas summer and winter tents, mushing clothes, warm wool long johns, and the best "universal fit" hard-working portage pads around. The "super-size" pads I inspired are wonderful.

Fast Bucksaw, Inc.
Paul Swanstrom
505 McNamara
Hastings, MN 55033
(651) 437-2566
www.fastbucksaw.com
Best (and by far the most beautiful) folding camp saw I've found. Made by hand in small batches. Expect to wait weeks or months for delivery.

FoodSaver
Tilia Consumer Services
50 Commerce Drive
Trumbull, CT 06611-5403
(888) 777-8841
www.foodsaver.com or www.tilia.com
An excellent vacuum-sealing machine.

Forestry Suppliers, Inc.
P. O. Box 8397
Jackson, MS 39284-8397
www.forestry-suppliers.com
(800) 647-5368
All sorts of tools and navigational aids for the professional forester.

Fox 40 International Inc.
Worldwide Head Office
20 Warrington Street
Hamilton, ON L8E 3V1
(800) 66-FOX40

Fox 40 U.S.A. Inc.
4600 Witmer Industrial Estate
Niagara Falls, NY 14305
(888) 66-FOX40
www.fox40world.com
The world's loudest, most reliable, and most popular "river whistle."

Frost River
5555 U.S. Highway 2
Duluth, MN 55810
(800) 375-9394
www.frostriver.com
Steve Emerson, who was Duluth Pack's chief designer for more than twenty years, now runs his own company, Frost River. Products range from tough-as-nails packs (the tiny Nessmuk is my favorite), to tents, garment bags, and gun cases. The signature fabric is McAlister Waxed Canvas.

Grade VI / A Division of CLG Enterprises/Superior Packs
3838 Dight Avenue South
Minneapolis, MN 55406
(800) 328-5215
www.superiorpacks.com

Grade VI was purchased by CLG Enterprises/Superior Packs in 2003. Their paddling luggage deserves a hard look if you want great stuff that lasts almost forever.

Gränsfors Bruks, Inc.
P.O. Box 818
Summerville, SC 29483
(800) 433-2863; fax (803) 821-2285
www.gransfors.com
Absolutely the best axes on the planet. Hand-forged, superbly balanced, and razor sharp.

Granite Gear
P.O. Box 278
Two Harbors, MN 55616
(218) 834-6157
www.granitegear.com
Impeccable packs and paddling accessories that will stand up to the hardest use. Proven in Minnesota's BWCA and beyond.

Grohmann Knives
P.O. Box 40
Pictou, NS B0K 1H0
(888) 7-KNIVES or (902) 485-4224
Fax (902) 485-5872
www.grohmannknives.com
Source of the wonderful Russell/Grohmann knives, which have won numerous international awards. I prefer the carbon steel "camper" model.

Harvest Foodworks
RR 1
Toledo, ON K0E 1V0
(800) 268-4268 or (613) 275-2218
www.harvestfoodworks.com
Source of the wonderful Big Bill's Multigrain Cereal and other unique dried foods.

Idaho Knife Works
Mike Mann
P.O. Box 144
Spirit Lake, ID 83869
 (509) 994-9394
www.idahoknifeworks.com
Source of the Cliff Knife I designed and other terrific outdoor knives. Carbon steel blades only; no stainless steel.

J.L. Darling Corporation
2614 Pacific Avenue Highway East
Tacoma, WA 98124-1017
(253) 922-5000
www.RiteintheRain.com
Waterproof pens, paper, journals, and sketchbooks.

Joynes Department Store
Grand Marais, MN
(218) 387-2233
www.northshorevisitor.com/joynes
Malkin's Canadian jam, Red Rose tea, Woolrich and Pendleton wool shirts, Johnson Guide pants, and much more. An old-time general store that has it all.

Kokotat Water Sportswear
5350 Ericson Way
Arcata, CA 95521
(800) 225-9749
www.kokatat.com
Manufacturer of quality life vests.

Kolpin Outdoors
P.O. Box 107
Fox Lake, WI 53933-0107
(877) 956-5746 or (920) 928-3118
Fax (920) 928-3687
www.kolpin.com
Kolpin Outdoors makes a variety of excellent watertight gun cases.

Littlbug Enterprises, Inc.
P.O. Box 293
Buffalo, MN 55313-0293
(763) 684-0141
www.littlbug.com
The Littlbug wood-burning stove is lightweight, compact, and powerful.

L.L. Bean, Inc.
Freeport, ME 04033
(800) 221-4221
www.llbean.com
Is there anyone who hasn't heard of L.L. Bean?

Lotus Designs
106 Old Mars Hill Highway
Weaverville, NC 28787
www.lotusdesigns.com
Manufacturer of quality life vests.

McMaster-Carr Supply Co.
P.O. Box 4355
Chicago, IL 60680-4355
(630) 834-9600
www.mcmaster.com
Possibly the largest hardware supply company in the world.
Their catalog has more than 3,000 pages! Every bolt and fit-
ting on the planet, natural sponges, epoxies, Kevlar, and
Nomex.

N/R Laboratories, Inc.
900 East Franklin Street
Centerville, OH 45459
(800) 223-9348; fax (513) 433-0779
No-rinse body bath and shampoo; great for personal cleanup
when you can't bathe.

Original Bug Shirt Company
908 Niagara Falls Boulevard, No. 467
North Tonawanda, NY 14120
P.O. Box 127
Trout Creek, ON P0H 2L0
(800) 998-9096 or (705) 729-5620
www.gorp.com/bugshirt
This is just what you need if bugs drive you batty.

Orion Safety Products
(800) 851-5260 or (765) 472-4375
Fax (765) 473-3254
www.orionsignals.com
Colored smoke, flares, whistles, and other signaling gear.

Ostrom Outdoors
RR 1
Nolalu, ON P0T 2K0
(877) 678-7661 or (807) 473-4499
www.ostrompacks.com
Superbly designed high-tech packs and paddling accessories
for those who demand the best. I especially like their barrel
harness and yellow waterproof pack liner.

Outdoor Research, Inc.
2203 1st Avenue South
Seattle, WA 98134-1424
(888) 4-ORGEAR
www.orgear.com
Superb Gore-Tex and fleece hats, gloves, footgear, and more.
The Gore-Tex Seattle Sombrero and black headnet are personal favorites.

Outdoor Solutions
c/o Thomas Benian
P.O. Box 132
Elliot Lake, ON P5A 2J6
(705) 461-9668
www.outdoorsolutions.ca/
Source of the Bob Fisher–designed Kitchen Hooks Rope and
Paddle Pole Pockets. They also make tarps, tents, nylon
splash covers, and other specialty items for canoeing and bik-
ing.

Pelican Products
A Division of the Rocky Mountain Tool Co.
50 East 200 North
Hyrum, UT 84319
(800) 281-4433 or (435) 245-5021
www.pelicanproducts.us
Pelican waterproof boxes are extremely reliable.

Piragis Northwoods Company
105 North Central
Ely, MN 55731
(800) 223-6565
www.Piragis.com
New and used canoes, hard-to-find high-tech gear. Guided
canoe trips. Great Web site (I write a monthly article for it)
and catalog.

PREVENTx
Phoenix, AZ
(877) 2-PREVENT
www.infectioncontrol.on.ca/prevent.html
An alcohol-free hand sanitizer and antiseptic skin protectant,
with aloe vera. Doesn't dry out hands. Great for camp cooks.

Quik-N-Easy Products Inc.
P.O. Box 878
Monrovia, CA 91016
Traditional carriers that clamp on rain gutters.

Sporty's Pilot Shop
Clermont County Airport
Batavia, OH 45103-9747
(800) LIFTOFF
www.sportys.com
All sorts of navigational aids for pilots. I carry the JD-200 transceiver, which is used by Japan Airlines for ground support crews.

Stormy Bay
P.O. Box 345
Grand Rapids, MN 55744
(218) 326-5104
Manufactures the excellent Stormy Bay Wanigan; formerly E.M. Wanigan.

Sturdiwheat
(800) 201-9650
www.sturdiwheat.com
Best pancake mix I've found. Just add water.

Sure Fire
18300 Mount Baldy Circle
Fountain Valley, CA 92708
(800) 828–8809
www.surefire.com
Ultrahigh-powered tactical flashlights—many times more powerful than traditional lights. They are widely used by law enforcement personnel and are so bright they can disable an attacker—or a determined wild animal. Gun mounts are available.

Thrifty Outfitters
c/o Midwest Mountaineering
309 Cedar Avenue South
Minneapolis, MN
(612) 339-6290
www.thriftyoutfitters.com
Everything you need to build a canoe splash cover, make a tent, or repair your stove or Gore-Tex rain gear.

Thule Division
42 Silvermine Road
Seymour, CT 06483
www.thule.com
High-tech carriers that fit airplane-style doors

Trail Blazer Outdoor Quality Products
2736 Robie Street
Halifax, NS B3K 4P2
(800) 565-6564
www.trailblazerproducts.com
Manufactures the Sawvivor and Trail Blazer aluminum saws.

Ullfrotté Original
www.ullfrotte.com
In my view, the warmest, most comfortable, long underwear (merino wool) on the planet. A variety of weights for every season; the choice of Swedish and Norwegian military survival experts. I wore Ullfrotté Original when I camped out in –32°F temperatures at Spitzbergen, Norway. Expensive, and worth it!

Voyageur
3761 Old Glenola Road
Trinity, NC 27370
(800) 843-8985
www.voyageur-gear.com
Waterproof Voyageur bags and paddling accessories.

WITZ Products
502 Giuseppe Court, Suite 5
Roseville, CA 95678
(800) 499-1568 or (916) 773-1433
www.witzprod.com
Waterproof plastic cases for eyeglasses and valuables.

Woody's Outdoor Cookware
134 South Virginia Street
Hobart, IN 46342
(800) 247-6068
If you do all your baking on a fire, you'll love the Woody cast-aluminum Dutch oven.

Yakima, Inc.
P.O. Box 4899
Arcata, CA 95518
www.yakima.com
These high-tech carriers fit airplane-style doors.

Zaveral Racing Equipment, Inc.
242 Lockwood Hill Road
Mount Upton, NY 13809
(607) 563-2487
www.zre.com
In my opinion, the best graphite canoe paddles—and cross-country ski poles—on the planet. Zaveral paddles are also available from We-no-nah Canoe Co.

RECOMMENDED EPOXIES FOR CANOE AND PADDLE REPAIR

Adtech Marine Systems
815 Shepherd Street
P.O. Box F
Charlotte, MI 48813
(800) 255-9934
E-mail: adtech@casspolymers.com
An easy-flowing epoxy that's ideal for canoe and paddle repairs.

System Three Resins, Inc.
P.O. Box 70436
Seattle, WA 98107
(206) 782-7976
www.systemthree.com
A very popular resin for laminating wood and fiberglass.

West System Epoxy
Gougeon Brothers, Inc.
P.O. Box 908
Bay City, MI 48707
(517) 684-1374
www.westsystem.com
West System epoxy, fiberglass, and other boat-repair materials. Ask for their *Building, Restoration & Repair* manual.

CANOE MAKERS WHOSE NAMES APPEAR IN THIS BOOK

Bell Canoe Works
25355 Highway 169
Zimmerman, MN 55398
(612) 631-2231 (factory)
www.bellcanoe.com

Exquisite Kevlar and Kevlar/graphite composite solo and tandem canoes. Designs by David Yost. The Bell Wildfire is my favorite solo canoe for wilderness trips.

Bourquin Boats
Jeannie Bourquin
1568 McMahan Boulevard
Ely, MN 55731
(218) 365-5499
www.wcha.org/builders/bourquin
Jeannie Bourquin builds spectacular wood-canvas canoes. The only woman builder of these canoes, she was a member of the first all-women's team to canoe the South Nahanni River. See her story in chapter 19.

Kruger Canoes
Verlen Kruger
2906 Meister Lane
Lansing, MI 48906
(517) 323-2139
www.krugercanoes.com
Verlen Kruger builds fast, seaworthy, expedition canoes: The partially decked 18'6" Kruger Expedition Cruiser and Kruger Open Cruiser are fast, seaworthy boats for long trips and big loads. The 17'2" solo Sea Breeze and 17'2" Sea Wind are for serious solo trips. Economy and strength Kevlar layups available.

Mad River Canoe Co.
P.O. Box 610
Waitsfield, VT 05673-0610
(802) 496-3127; fax (802) 496-4724
www.madrivercanoe.com
Strong, beautiful Kevlar composite and Royalex canoes for discriminating paddlers.

Marathon Canoes (Grumman Canoes)
One Grumman Way
P.O. Box 549
Marathon, NY 13803
(607) 849-3211; fax (607) 849-3077
www.marathonboat.com
Grumman canoes are now manufactured under the Marathon name but have the same high-quality aluminum and original designs.

Northwest Canoe Co.
308 Prince Street
St. Paul, MN 55101
(651) 229-0192
www.northwestcanoe.com
Here's where to go if you want to build your own fiberglass-covered wood-strip canoe. Building plans, precut wood strips and trim, Adtech epoxy resin, and accessories—all shipped to your door. The company will repair any non-aluminum canoe or kayak.

Old Town Canoe Co.
58 Middle Street
Old Town, ME 04468
(207) 827-5514
www.otocanoe.com
Who hasn't heard of Old Town Canoes? The Royalex Old Town Tripper and polyethylene Discovery series are among the most popular expedition canoes.

Pakboats/ScanSport, Inc.
P.O. Box 700
Enfield, NH 03748
(888) 863-9500 or fax (603) 632-5611
www.pakboats.com
America's source of expedition-ready folding open canoes. These craft are amazing!

SOAR Inflatables, Inc.
20 Healdsburg Avenue
Healdsburg, CA 95448
(800) 280-SOAR or (707) 433-5599
Fax: (707) 433-4499
www.soar1.com
These superb-quality, self-bailing inflatable canoes gracefully go through huge rapids where rigid and folding canoes fear to tread. My wife, Susie, and I were mightily impressed with a 16-foot SOAR boat we paddled through the Gates-of-Ladore section on Utah's Green River.

Stewart River Boatworks
Route 1, Box 203
Two Harbors, MN 55616
(218) 834-5037
www.stewartriver.com
Exquisite wood-canvas canoes, each one lovingly built by hand.

We-no-nah Canoe Co.
P.O. Box 247
Winona, MN 55987
(507) 454-5430; fax (507) 454-5448
www.wenonah.com
Excellent Kevlar composite and Royalex canoes, and the most informative canoe catalog on the planet. Check out their canoe repair video.

BOOKS AND PUBLICATIONS

Journals of voyageurs who've canoed the rivers of your interest may be available for a small fee from the tourism office of the Canadian province in which you plan to canoe. Here are some other useful publications and sources of publications.

Basic River Canoeing by McNair and Landry
American Camping Association, 1985
One of the first really great books on whitewater technique.

Basic Essentials: Cooking in the Outdoors, 2nd Edition
by Cliff Jacobson
The Globe Pequot Press, 1999
www.globepequot.com
Cooking tricks and recipes for serious campers.

Bear Attacks, The Deadly Truth by James Gary Shelton
Published by James Gary Shelton, 1998
This book examines the lives of people who have survived bear attacks. Emphasis is on "What went wrong?"

Bear Attacks, Their Causes and Avoidance, Revised Edition by Stephen Herrero
Lyons Press, 2002
www.globepequot.com
Most authoritative guide available. All the research is here!

Bear Encounter Survival Guide by James Gary Shelton
Published by James Gary Shelton, 1994
A look at bear behavior from a British Columbia woodsman who has spent the better part of his life around bears.

Bear Aware by Bill Schneider
The Globe Pequot Press, 2004
www.globepequot.com
Solid advice, mostly for those who camp in Western national parks like Yellowstone.

Canoeing North Into The Unknown—A Record of River Travel: 1874 to 1974
by Bruce W. Hodgins & Gwyneth Hoyle
Natural Heritage/History, Inc., 1994
Toronto, Ontario
An encyclopedia of information about who canoed what Canadian river and when. Each account includes geographical description, historical significance, chronological records, maps, photos, indexes, and bibliography.

Canoeing Safety and Rescue by Doug McKown
Rocky Mountain Books, 1992
www.rmbooks.com
Includes 117 photographs and 50 diagrams. See Doug McKown's MacFarlane River story in chapter 19.

Canoe & Kayak
(800) 829-3340
www.canoekayak.com
North America's premier canoeing and kayaking magazine, of which I am a contributing editor.

Che-Mun, The Journal of Canadian Wilderness Canoeing
Toronto, Ontario
www.canoe.ca/che-mun
This wonderful quarterly publication was founded in 1973 by Nick Nickels, one of Canada's most prolific canoe writers. Since 1984 it has been edited by Michael Peake (see his comments and story elsewhere in this book), a renowned Canadian explorer and journalist for the *Toronto Sun.*

Chicagoland Canoe Base
Chicago, IL
(312) 777-1489
www.chicagolandcanoebase.com
Your most complete source of new and old canoeing books.

Drill Time and Solo Playboating—The Workbook
by Kent Ford
Performance Video & Instruction
Durango, CO
www.performancevideo.com
Kent Ford is a world-champion paddler and coach for the U.S. whitewater team. His instructional materials are outstanding. *Drill Time* is awesome!

The Forgotten Skills by Cliff Jacobson (2002)
Available from Piragis Northwoods Co. (www.piragis.com). A 90-minute video about how to stormproof your tent, rig single and twin rain tarps, tie essential knots, sleep well on bad sites, choose and use edged tools, make fires.

GPS Land Navigation by Michael Ferguson
Glassford Publishing, 1997
Boise, ID
By far, the best book on GPS navigation. Ferguson demystifies the most complex variables.

Basic Essentials: Hypothermia, 2nd Edition by William W. Forgey, M.D.
The Globe Pequot Press, 1999
www.globepequot.com

Narrative Of A Journey To The Shores Of The Polar Sea In The Years 1819, 20, 21 by Sir John Franklin
Charles E. Tuttle Co.
Rutland, VT and Tokyo, Japan

Northern Books
Toronto, ON
(416) 531-8873
Your best source of used, rare, and select new books on historical and modern Canadian canoeing. Northern Books is the brainchild of George Luste (featured in chapters 5 and 22), one of Canada's most respected wilderness canoeists.

Medicine for the Backcountry, 3rd Edition
by Buck Tilton and Frank Hubbell
The Globe Pequot Press, 1999
www.globepequot.com
Emphasizes assessment, packaging, transport and reassessment issues—a useful companion piece to Dr. Forgey's *Wilderness Medicine.* Buck Tilton's sage medical advice appears regularly in *Backpacker* and other outdoor magazines. See Buck's tips in chapter 22.

The Milepost
Anchorage, AK 99501
(800) 726-4707; fax (907) 258-5360
www.themilepost.com
Everything you could possibly want to know about Alaska. The giant 800-page book weighs three pounds!

Nunavut Handbook
Nortext Multimedia Inc.
Iqaluit, Northwest Territories
(800) 263-1452 or (613) 727-5466
Fax: (800) 461-4179 or (613) 727-6910
www.arctic-travel.com
Essential reading for everyone who plans to travel in the new province of Nunavut. The 454-page 1999 Commemorative Edition includes maps, color photos, directories, important regulations, radio and communications information, periodicals, books and Internet resources, canoeing and kayaking specifics, and much more. This monster "dream book" is well worth its U.S. $21.50 price.

Paddler
Steamboat Springs, CO
www.paddlermagazine.com
Official publication of the American Canoe Association.

Paddling.net
http://paddling.net/
The web resource for canoeing and kayaking information.

Paddling Your Own Canoe by Gary and Joanie McGuffin
Boston Mills Press, 1999
The most useful and beautiful paddling text on the planet.

Path of the Paddle by Bill Mason
Van Nostrand Reinhold Ltd., Toronto, 1980
Beautifully illustrated, classic paddling text. Is there anyone who hasn't heard of Bill Mason?

River Rescue by Less Bechdel and Slim Ray
Appalachian Mountain Club, 1985
An excellent book on river rescue.

Wilderness Medicine, 5th Edition by William W. Forgey, M.D.
The Globe Pequot Press (1999)
www.globepequot.com
Extremely useful and complete. Addresses every imaginable problem you're likely to encounter on a wilderness canoe trip. Details how to build your own medical kit.

CANOEING ASSOCIATIONS

American Canoe Association
7432 Alban Station Boulevard, Suite B-226
Springfield, VA 22150
(703) 451-0141
www.acanet.org
The ACA has been around since 1880. Emphasis is largely on training, racing, freestyle and poling, but there's stuff for everyone. Members get *Paddler* magazine.

Canadian Recreational Canoeing Association
P.O. Box 398, 446 Main Street West
Merrickville, ON K0G 1N0
(613) 269-2910; fax (613) 269-2908
www.crca.ca/
CRCA offers trips, canoeing instruction, and a huge inventory of canoeing books and trip guides. Canadian and American members receive the bimonthly magazine, *Kanawa,* which alone is worth the price of admission. The CRCA paddling center in Merrickville, Ontario is a knockout. If you love wilderness canoeing, you'll love the CRCA.

Minnesota Canoe Association
P.O. Box 13567 Dinkeytown Station
Minneapolis, MN 55414
www.canoe-kayak.org
The MCA is the largest canoe club in America. Emphasis is on building your own strip canoe. MCA has great canoe building plans (solo and tandem) and the best canoe-building book around. *Hut!* magazine—loaded with tips and trips—comes to members each month. Members in fifty states and Canada.

Wilderness Canoe Association
P.O. Box 48022 Davisville Postal Outlet
1881 Yonge Street
Toronto, ON M4S 3C6
www.wildernesscanoe.org
Members receive *Nastawgan,* a quarterly journal filled with wilderness canoeing lore.

Wooden Canoe Heritage Association
P.O. Box 226
Blue Mountain Lake, NY 12812
www.wcha.org/

A nonprofit membership association devoted to preserving, studying, building, restoring, and using wood, wood-canvas, cedar strip, and birch bark canoes, as well as to disseminating information about canoeing heritage in North America.

PROVINCIAL TOURIST INFORMATION

For free travel information contact the tourism bureaus below. Or search the Web site www.travelcanada.ca.

Travel Alberta
Box 2500
Edmonton, AB T5J 2Z4
(800) 661-8888
www.explorealberta.com

Tourism British Columbia
1117 Wharf Street
Victoria, BC V8W 2Z2
www.gov.bc.ca/tourism

Travel Manitoba
7-155 Carlton Street, Department AB9
Winnipeg, MB R3C 3H8
(800) 665-0040, ext. AB9 or (204) 945-3777
www.travelmanitoba.com

Tourism New Brunswick
P.O. Box 12345
Woodstock, NB E7M 5C3
(800) 561-0123
www.gov.nb.ca/tourism

Newfoundland and Labrador
Department of Tourism, Culture and Recreation
P.O. Box 8700
St. John's, NF A1B 4J6
(800) 563-6353
www.gov.nf.ca/tourism/

Northwest Territories
Arctic Tourism, Box 610
Yellowknife, NT X1A 2N5
(800) 661-0788
www.nwttravel.nt.ca

Tourism Nova Scotia
P.O. Box 519
Halifax, NS B3J 2R7
(800) 565-0000
http://explore.gov.ns.ca

Nunavut Tourism
P.O. Box 1450
Iqaluit, NT X0A 0H
(800) 491-7910 or (867) 979-6551
www.nunatour.nt.ca

Ontario Ministry of Tourism and Recreation
900 Bay Street, 9th floor
Toronto, ON M7A 2R9
(416) 326-9326
www.tourism.gov.on.ca/

Prince Edward Island Tourism
P.O. Box 940
Charlottetown, PEI C1A 7M5
(888) PEI-PLAY
www.gov.pe.ca/

Tourism Quebec
C.P. 979
Montreal, QC H3C 2W3
(800) 363-7777
www.quebecweb.com/tourismeintroang.html

Saskatchewan Environment and Resource Management
3211 Albert Street
Regina, SK S4S 5W6
(877) 2ESCAPE
www.sasktourism.com

Yukon Department of Tourism
P.O. Box 2745
Whitehorse, YK Y1A 5B9
www.touryukon.com

OTHER USEFUL CANADIAN GOVERNMENT ADDRESSES

Canadian Firearms Centre
(800) 731-4000; fax (613) 941-1991
www.cfc-ccaf.gc.ca
Check with this office if you plan to bring guns into Canada.
A new law (effective 2001) requires that all guns be registered
at the border.

Canadian Wildlife Service
Environment Canada
4999 98th Avenue, Room 200
Edmonton, AB T6B 2X3
(780) 951-8700
www.cws-scf.ec.gc.ca/index_e.cfm
If you want to canoe through the national parks, contact this
agency. Permits are required if you canoe the Anderson and
Ellice Rivers, which pass through bird sanctuaries.

**Department of Resources, Wildlife and Economic
Development**
Government of the Northwest Territories
Box 1320
Yellowknife, NT X1A 2L9
(867) 873-7411
www.gov.nt.ca/
Contact this office if you canoe through game sanctuaries and
wildlife preserves, where firearms restrictions apply.

Parks Canada, National Office
25 Eddy Street
Gatineau, QC K1A 0M5
http://parkscanada.pch.gc.ca
(888) 773-8888, operator 999 (toll-free in North America
only)
Everything you want to know about Parks Canada.

Prince of Wales Heritage Centre
Government of the Northwest Territories
Yellowknife, NT X1A 2L9
(867) 873-7551
http://pwnhc.learnnet.nt.ca/
Contact this office if you plan to investigate an archaeological
site.

ALASKA AGENCIES

Alaska Department of Fish and Game
P.O. Box 25526
Juneau, AK 99802-5526
(907) 465-4100
www.alaskan.com/akfishgm.html

Alaska Department of Natural Resources
400 Willoughby Avenue, 5th Floor
Juneau, AK 99801
(907) 465-2400
www.dnr.state.ak.us/
Use this Web site if you need information about state parks
and permits.

**Alaska Department of Transportation and Public
Facilities**
(907) 465-3900
www.dot.state.ak.us/
If you plan to drive the Alaska highway, contact this department.

Alaska Division of Tourism
P.O. Box 110801
Juneau, AK 99811-0801
(907) 465-2012; fax (907) 465-3767
www.commerce.state.ak.us/tourism

Alaska Marine Highway System, Alaska State Ferries
P.O. Box 703
Kodiak, AK 99615
(800) 526-6731
www.akferry.com/
Information about Alaska ferries.

**U.S. Bureau of Land Management
Alaska State Office**
222 West 7th Avenue, No. 13
Anchorage, AK 99513-7599
(907) 271-5960
www.ndo.ak.blm.gov/

APPENDIX C
EQUIPMENT LIST

Every experienced tripper has his or her own idea of what's important. Here's my list:

Note: It's wise to double up on important items like cook kits, stoves, first-aid supplies, and canoe repair materials if you're canoeing in remote areas where help is unavailable.

COMMUNITY GEAR

_____Canoe rigged with yoke, shock cords, tracking lines, and splash cover

_____Seat pads for canoe

_____Thwart bags for canoe

_____Running (thwart) compass, GPS, and GPS mount

_____Extra map set, sealed in plastic

_____2 bailing sponges per canoe

_____2-quart plastic pitcher with cover (for bailing and mixing powdered drinks)

_____One four-person tent for every two people

_____Plastic groundcloth for inside tent (important!)

_____Waterproof nylon tarp(s); a fully netted tundra tarp is important for buggy rivers

_____Cook kit

_____2 stainless-steel Sierra cups (for ladles and use as emergency spare cups)

_____Biodegradable soap and cleaning gear for cook kit

_____Stove (expeditions above the timberline may want to bring 2 or 3)

_____Compact wood-burning stove (for trips above the tree line, to burn garbage)

_____Stove fuel (allow at least a half gallon per week for a party of 4)

_____Hand ax, sheath, sharpening stone, file

_____Folding saw (rectangular, full frame)

_____Small jackknife saw with extra metal-cutting blade

_____200 feet of parachute cord, cut into 20-foot lengths

_____Two 50-foot coils of 3/16-inch-diameter nylon rope (carry in separate canoes)

_____Rescue (throwing) rope (optional)

_____Nylon cords or rubber ropes or straps (for securing gear into the canoe)

_____Canoe repair kit (see chapter 20 for suggested items)

_____Duluth packs; waterproof liners and abrasion liners for packs

_____Hard pack(s) or pack basket, wanigan, barrel pack

_____Medical kit (see appendix D for contents)

_____Compact first-aid kit (pack separate from medical kit and carry in another canoe)

_____Candles, fire starters, matches, butane lighters

_____Aluminum tube shovel for burying waste

_____Plastic or nylon folding water jug

_____Weather forecasting instruments: thermometer, barometer, tables (optional)

_____High-powered tactical flashlight (signal a boat or plane, discourage a bear, travel at night, etc.)

PERSONAL EQUIPMENT

The emphasis in this list is on trips in northern Canada.

_____Life jacket (1 extra vest per crew is recommended for remote trips; save space by bringing a Type V inflatable PFD)

_____2 paddles: bent-shaft for flat water, straight paddle for rapids

_____1 wool shirt, 1 long-sleeved nylon or cotton-polyester shirt

_____1 pair medium-weight wool pants

_____1 pair lightweight nylon river pants or cotton-polyester pants (army fatigues)

_____Webbed military-style belt (dries fast)

_____Suspenders (less constricting and better support for weight of sheath knife and multitool)

_____Nylon shorts (for swimming and hot days)

_____5 pair medium-weight wool socks

_____5 pair lightweight wool liner socks

_____4 pair lightweight undershorts

_____Polyethylene urine bottle

_____Sanifem device for women

_____2 pairs gloves

_____3 hats (rain, sun, cold)

_____Wool or fleece balaclava, fleece neck warmer

_____Extra glasses (if you wear them) in hard case

_____Polarized sunglasses

_____Spray solution for cleaning glasses (pack in thwart bag with a clean dry handkerchief)

_____Waterproof knee-high boots with insoles

_____Lightweight ankle-high boots for camp and general hiking

_____Wet shoes (neoprene booties, tennies, reef-runners etc.)

_____Extra set of leather, sheepskin, closed-cell foam or wool felt insoles for boots

_____Nylon day pack or fanny pack (for day hiking)

_____Flashlight

_____Sheath knife, or pocketknife on lanyard

_____Leatherman tool on belt

_____Insulated mug with fitted cover (leash the cover to the cup)

_____Personal supply of matches/butane lighter

_____Fox 40 whistle attached to life jacket

_____2-piece rain suit

_____Nylon wind parka

_____Nylon wind pants (optional)

_____Bug shirt

_____Waterproof paddling shirt, wet suit, or dry suit (optional)

_____Camera in waterproof bag

_____Folding camp stool, secured to personal pack with shock cord

_____Wristwatch

_____2 cotton-polyester or wool T-shirts

_____Hand cream, lip balm, sunscreen, bug dope

_____Towel and toiletries

_____Map set in waterproof case (at least 1 set per canoe)

_____2 head nets, Susie bug net

_____2 brightly colored bandannas

_____Stainless-steel vacuum bottle (optional)

_____Compass (orienteering style)

_____Sleeping bag and foam pad

_____Fishing gear, fillet knife

_____Duluth pack and waterproof liners for personal gear

_____Waterproof binoculars

_____Folding stool (bungee cord to your pack)

EMERGENCY ITEMS

_____Signal kit—orange smoke, flares, heliograph mirror

_____Carabiners and nylon pulleys (for canoe salvage)

_____Firearms and ammunition, waterproof gun case (optional)

_____Cleaning equipment for gun (optional)

_____Cell phone (won't work in most parts of northern Canada and Alaska)

_____EPIRB, CB radio, or VHF marine or aircraft radio (optional)

_____Satellite phone (optional)

APPENDIX D
THE MEDICAL KIT

On the typical canoe trip, where help is less than a day's paddle away, you'll get by fine with a good first-aid kit (you should have more than tape and gauze, even for a day's outing). But if you're going in harm's way, you'll need a full medical kit and the skills to use it.

In his authoritative book *Wilderness Medicine: Beyond First Aid,* fifth edition, Dr. Bill Forgey suggests a sophisticated medical kit that consists of four modules: Topical Bandaging Module, Non-Rx Medication Module, Rx Oral/Topical Medication Module, Rx Injectable Medication Module.

As the minimum the Topical Bandaging Module and Non-Rx Oral Medication Module (components listed below) should be carried. The particulars of the complete kit—and its use—along with other essential medical information are detailed in the new fifth edition of Dr. Forgey's popular book. Every serious wilderness canoeist should read this book and carry a copy in the field.

I carry a very complete medical kit and a small but sophisticated first-aid kit on my canoe trips in northern Canada. My medical kit includes the Topical Bandaging Module, plus sterile water for irrigation. I include a mixture of items from the other three modules suggested in Dr. Forgey's book. I've used Flagyl (for giardiasis) on two occasions. Once I used Lidocain from the Rx Injectable Module. I carry the small first-aid kit on tundra hikes and as a backup for the big medical kit. Each kit rides in a different canoe, just in case.

TOPICAL BANDAGING MODULE

_____ 10 packages Spyroflex 2" x 2" wound dressings (or carry 2 each per person)

_____ 2 packages Spenco 2nd Skin Burn Dressing Kits (or carry 1 for 2 people)

_____ 15 packages Nu-Gauze absorbent, sterile, 2-ply, 3" x 3", 2 per package

_____ 25 Coverlet Bandage Strips, 1" x 3"

_____ 1 Tape, Waterproof, 1" x 15'

_____ 1 Sam Splint, 36"

_____ 1 Elastic bandage, 4"

_____ 1 Max Strength Triple Antibiotic Ointment with pramoxine, 1 oz. tube

_____ 1 Hibiclens surgical scrub, 4 oz. bottle

_____ 1 Tetrahydrozoline Ophthalmic Drops, 0.05%, 15 ml bottle

_____ 1 Hydrocortisone cream 1%, 1 oz. tube

_____ 1 Clotrimazole cream, 2%, ½ oz. tube

_____ 1 Cavit dental filling paste

_____ 2 pair examination gloves

_____ 1 Irrigation syringe

_____ 1 Sawyer Extractor

_____ 1 Surgical kit consisting of 1 needle holder, 2 each 3-0 ethicon sutures, 1 each 5-0 ethicon suture, and 2 each 3-0 sutures

_____ 1 Over-pack container for above

NON-RX ORAL MEDICATION MODULE

_____ 24 Percogesic tablets (pain, fever, muscle spasm, sleep aid, anxiety, congestion)

_____ 24 Ibuprofen 200 mg tablets (pain, fever, bursitis, tendonitis, menstrual cramps)

_____ 24 Diphenhydramine 25 mg capsules (antihistamine, anti-anxiety, cough, muscle cramps, nausea, and motion sickness prevention)

_____ 10 Bisacodyl 5 mg tablets (constipation)

_____ 12 Loperamide 2 mg tablets (diarrhea)

_____ 24 Cimetidine 200 mg tablets (heartburn, certain allergic reactions)

_____ 1 Over-pack container for above

APPENDIX E

RAPIDS RATINGS AND SAFETY SIGNALS

Ratings of rapids as given in guidebooks and trip guides usually reflect a river's *normal* flow. Be aware that flood conditions can turn a bubbly Class II rapid into a formidable run that even experts won't attempt. Conversely, a prolonged dry spell may tame the most violent drop. Water levels *are* important!

It's common practice to increase the difficulty rating substantially (about half a grade) for rapids that are extremely remote and/or whose water temperatures are below 45 degrees.

The universal ratings described below have come under considerable scrutiny in recent years, largely because canoeists are paddling tougher and tougher drops. Rapids that were rated Class V a decade or more ago are now regularly paddled by hair-boaters. Regrettably, the death rate on mean rivers is going up as more technically good paddlers attempt rapids they should be portaging around. The result is that there has been a big push to revise the river rating scale to keep pace with the difficult white water that is being paddled today. Most likely the new system will add plus and minus ratings to the five categories. At this writing the American Whitewater Affiliation has benchmarked for difficulty more than 100 popular rapids.

Class V may be the most radically changed group: The new ratings would increase by tenths of a point, beginning with 5.1 and ending with 5.9. Each 0.1 increase would equal a full jump in class under the old system. For example, going from a 5.1 to 5.2 , would be like going from a Class II to a Class III rapid.

It is likely that Class VI will be dubbed "Exploratory." Once a Class VI rapids is successfully paddled, it will be downgraded to 5-point-something. Look for big changes in the rapids rating system by the time you read this.

Will the new system affect how northern canoe routes are classified? Probably not, because the current ratings are useful to wilderness canoeists in open canoes (albeit with splash covers) who seldom attempt rapids above high Class III.

Class I: Easy

Waves are small (a foot or so) and the route is recognizable from above without scouting. Some artificial difficulties like piers and bridge pilings.

Class II: Medium

Fairly frequent but unobstructed rapids with waves up to 3 feet. Course generally easy to recognize, passages clear. River speeds may exceed hard back-paddling speed. Occasional low ledges.

Class III: Difficult

High, irregular, numerous waves. Course may be difficult to recognize; rapids require careful advance scouting. Frequently require complex maneuvering. This is about the limit for an open canoe. Loaded wilderness canoes should stay out of Class III water unless they are manned by competent paddlers and have full splash covers.

Class IV: Very Difficult

Long, powerful rapids and boiling eddies. Requires powerful and precise maneuvering. This is no place for a wilderness canoe, regardless of cover or expertise.

Class V: Extraordinarily Difficult

Long, violent rapids with big drops, souse holes, and boiling eddies. Class V rapids should be attempted only by expert paddlers in slalom canoes and kayaks.

Class VI: Limit of Navigability

Extremely powerful and dangerous rapids that should be attempted only by the very best canoeists under carefully controlled conditions. Paddling Class VI rapids is a life-threatening experience!

Stop! Danger ahead!

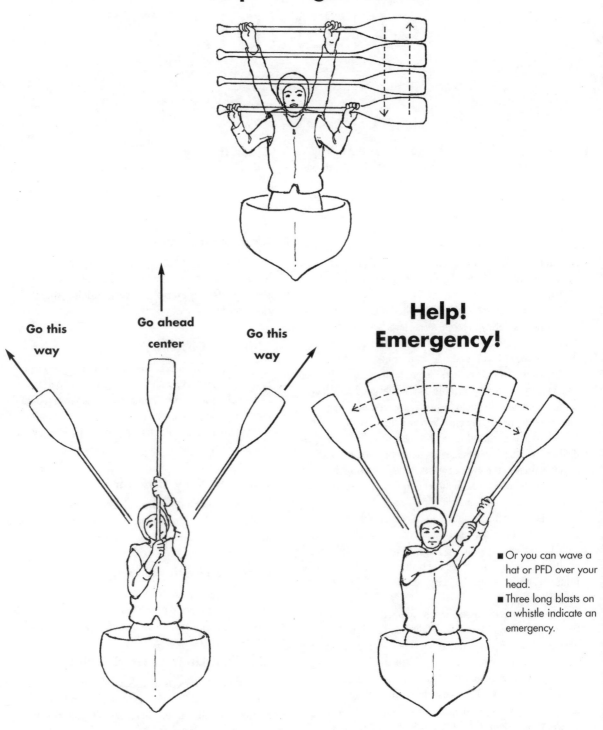

Go this way

Go ahead center

Go this way

Help! Emergency!

- Or you can wave a hat or PFD over your head.
- Three long blasts on a whistle indicate an emergency.

APPENDIX F

TEMPERATURE CHART

Average daily maximum temperatures at selected points across Canada, in degrees Fahrenheit.[1]

	May		June		July		August		September		October	
	low	high	low	high	low	high	low	high	low	high	low	high
British Columbia												
Kamloops	45	72	52	79	55	84	54	83	46	73	39	57
Penticton	43	70	50	77	54	84	52	81	45	72	37	57
Prince Rupert	43	57	46	59	50	63	52	63	48	59	43	52
Vancouver	48	64	54	70	57	75	55	73	52	68	45	59
Victoria	46	64	50	70	52	75	52	73	50	68	46	59
Alberta												
Banff	34	57	39	64	45	72	43	70	36	61	30	50
Calgary	37	61	45	66	50	75	46	72	39	63	30	54
Edmonton	41	63	48	68	54	73	50	72	41	63	32	52
Jasper	34	61	41	68	46	73	45	72	37	63	30	52
Lethbridge	39	64	48	70	52	79	50	77	43	68	34	57
Yukon												
Whitehorse	34	59	43	68	46	70	45	66	37	57	27	41
Northwest Territories												
Frohbisher	19	32	32	45	39	54	39	50	32	41	18	28
Inuvik	28	39	39	61	45	66	41	61	30	45	12	45
Yellowknife	30	48	45	63	52	70	50	66	39	52	25	36
Saskatchewan												
Prince Albert	36	63	45	70	52	77	48	73	39	63	25	50
Regina	37	64	48	72	54	79	50	77	39	66	28	54
Saskatoon	39	64	48	72	54	79	52	77	41	64	32	54

[1] From Canada Travel Information 1982–83. Courtesy of the Canadian Government Office of Tourism.

	May		June		July		August		September		October	
	low	high	low	high	low	high	low	high	low	high	low	high
Manitoba												
Churchill	21	34	36	52	45	63	46	61	37	48	27	36
Winnipeg	39	63	50	73	57	79	54	77	45	64	34	54
Ontario												
Hamilton	46	66	57	77	63	82	61	81	52	72	43	61
Kitchener	45	64	54	77	57	81	57	79	50	70	41	59
London	45	54	54	75	59	79	57	79	50	70	41	59
Ottawa	45	66	55	75	59	81	57	79	50	68	39	57
Sault Ste. Marie	39	57	48	70	54	7	54	73	48	64	39	55
Sudbury	43	63	52	73	57	77	55	75	48	66	39	54
ThunderBay	36	59	45	68	54	75	52	73	45	63	36	54
Toronto	45	64	55	77	63	81	61	79	54	72	45	59
Windsor	46	68	57	79	63	82	61	81	54	73	43	63
Quebec												
Gaspé	37	54	46	64	55	73	52	72	43	64	36	54
Montreal	48	64	59	75	63	79	61	77	54	68	43	47
Quebec City	43	63	54	72	59	77	57	75	48	66	39	54
New Brunswick												
Fredericton	39	63	48	73	55	79	54	75	46	68	36	55
Moncton	39	61	48	72	55	77	54	75	46	68	37	57
Saint John	41	59	48	66	54	73	55	73	50	66	41	57
Novia Scotia												
Halifax/Dartmouth	41	57	50	68	57	73	57	73	52	66	45	55
Yarmouth	41	55	48	63	54	0	54	70	50	64	43	57
Prince Edward Island												
Charlottetown	39	57	50	68	57	75	57	73	50	66	41	55
Newfoundland/Labrador												
Corner Brook	37	52	45	63	54	72	54	70	46	63	39	52
Halifax/Dartmouth	32	50	43	63	52	70	50	66	41	57	32	48
Charlottetown	36	52	43	61	52	70	54	68	46	63	39	54

INDEX

Cliff Jacobson is one of North America's most respected outdoors writers and wilderness canoe guides. He is an outdoors skills instructor and a professional outfitter and guide, a canoeing and camping consultant, and the author of more than a dozen top-selling books on canoeing and camping. Cliff recently retired from teaching middle school environmental science and now splits his time between canoeing and camping, and sharing his love for the sport by writing and teaching about it. In 2003 the American Canoe Association presented Cliff with the Legends of Paddling Award and inducted him into the ACA Hall of Fame.